# FLORA

# FLORA

*An Appreciation of the Life and Work
of Dame Flora Robson*

## Kenneth Barrow

Heinemann : London

William Heinemann Ltd
10 Upper Grosvenor Street, London W1X 9PA
LONDON MELBOURNE TORONTO
JOHANNESBURG AUCKLAND

First published 1981

© Kenneth Barrow 1981

ISBN 434 04775 9

Printed in Great Britain by
Mackays of Chatham Ltd

*for FLORA,
of course, and
my grandmother,
MABEL IRELAND,
now in her
ninety-ninth year.*

# Contents

| | | |
|---|---|---|
| Author's Note | | ix |
| PROLOGUE | AN OVERNIGHT SUCCESS | 1 |
| ONE | 1902–1924<br>YOU ARE GOING TO BE AN ACTRESS | 4 |
| TWO | 1924–1932<br>OUT IN THE COLD AND INTO THE FURNACE | 36 |
| THREE | 1932–1938<br>THE DAMASCENE SWORD | 67 |
| FOUR | 1939–1943<br>NEW WORLDS | 117 |
| FIVE | 1943–1959<br>THE YEARS BETWEEN | 150 |
| SIX | 1959–1970<br>MOST BEAUTIFUL EVENINGS | 193 |
| SEVEN | 1970–1981<br>LADY IN RETIREMENT | 218 |
| Appendix (Awards and Honours) | | 232 |
| Index | | 233 |

# Author's Note

FROM MY CHILDHOOD, Flora Robson's was a household name. My mother, on a rare trip to London, had seen *The Innocents* and had brought back an autographed programme as a present for me. I was raised in a small market town on the fringe of the Lake District. Stan Laurel was born only five minutes' walk from the place where I made my first appearance. Although later a plaque would be unveiled, there was no indication that my fellow townsmen knew even of the existence of one of the world's greatest clowns. We had two cinemas, but it was a journey to the nearest theatre. Apart from the annual week when my entire family was involved in the musical production of the local amateur operatic society, I lived my early life in a cultural desert. The programme with Flora Robson's name inscribed on it brought this stage-struck seven-year-old a whiff of the world of real theatre which I longed to make my own.

My grandmother and I would go to the cinema three or four times a week in those days. Twenty years after it was made, we saw a reissue of *Wuthering Heights*. I wrote the first fan letter it had occurred to me to write and received a charming reply and a photograph from the film's Ellen Dean.

The time came for me to decide what I was going to do with my future. I wanted nothing else but to act. My parents, however, were anxious for me to 'have something behind me' and insisted I train as a teacher. Unbeknown to them I had approached a repertory theatre and there was the possibility of a lowly student assistant stage manager's job. I decided to write to Flora Robson for her advice. A reply arrived within the week urging me to train as a teacher, teach

## AUTHOR'S NOTE

for a few years and then go to RADA. I accepted the advice and followed it through to the letter.

During my time at RADA, she was appearing in *The Old Ladies* and I arranged to meet her between a matinée and evening performance. All I recall is that she was rather tired and I was rather tongue-tied. She gave me some sound advice and I went on my way. My first job was a tour of a Shakespeare programme for schools. I was intrigued to learn later that Flora made her professional début in Clemence Dane's *Will Shakespeare*, for mine was playing William Shakespeare himself! When my tour took me near to Brighton, where she lives, I invited Flora to see a performance. Not only did she come but she invited me to spend the night at her home. We talked into the early hours. Suddenly she reached over to me and said, 'You and I have *so* much in common!'

That was the beginning of one of the most valuable friendships of my life. I have become a sort of honorary member of the family. Flora's younger sister, Shela, suffered a severe memory loss some years ago. She could remember nothing of her past, little of her present, and no one she met. Some days after she met me for the first time, Shela turned to Flora and asked, "Where is he?" Flora said, "Where is who?" "You know," Shela said, "The man." "Which man?" Flora asked. "You know," Shela repeated, "The Giant." As I stand six feet six inches tall, it was obviously me she had remembered. For Shela's benefit I have been known as the Giant ever since.

This is an authorized biography which means that it is written with the full consent and approval of my subject. I have attempted to write a serious study of a great actress and her approach to her work. I am first of all indebted to Flora for her faith in me, and for sharing her memories. As anyone who knows her will agree, Flora loves to talk! And I love to listen. On holiday in the Isles of Scilly, walking by the sea, and more nights than I care to count, talking into the small hours over a glass of wine, I first heard these stories of Tyrone Guthrie, of Errol Flynn, of Ben Greet and of Robert Donat, all part of the fabric which has made up her life. One day she asked me to look out a letter for her, received many years before from Henry Ainley. "It's either in that box, or in that trunk, or at the back of that shelf, or on top of the wardrobe." I asked if I could sort out all the letters. Spread in front of me was a social history of our times. I would like to thank Sue Bradbury, a fellow trainee-teacher who has gone on to other things, for pointing out that I had a biography at my fingertips. That observation crystallized an idea already at the back of my mind. Secondly, I must thank Roger Smith of Heinemann, whose faith in an, as yet,

# AUTHOR'S NOTE

unpublished author gave me the confidence to carry out the project. I have written to many actors, actresses, directors and others for their memories and their opinions of Flora's work. I would like to thank the following, either for writing to me or talking to me and, in the case of many of the latter, for offering me such generous hospitality:

John Abbott, Jack Allen, Dennis Arundell, Dame Peggy Ashcroft, Trevor Bannister, Timothy Bateson, Keith Baxter, Robert Beatty, Hamish Bell, Elizabeth Bergner, Peter Brook, Jane Bryan, Audrey Cameron, Jack Cardiff, Joyce Carey, Sylvia Coleridge, George Coulouris, Elizabeth Counsell, John Counsell, Andrew Cruickshank, Reginald Denham, Richard Digby-Day, Leonard Dixon, Diana Dors, Sir Eric Drake, Ruth Dunning, Robert Eddison, Douglas Fairbanks Jnr., John Fernald, Geraldine Fitzgerald, Leslie French, Lady Gardiner, Graham Gauld, Sir John Gielgud, John Gilpin, R. A. Goodhead, Richard Goolden, Marius Goring, Denys Graham, David Gray, Sir Alec Guinness, Rachel Gurney, Dilys Hamlett, Betty Hardy, Helen Hayes, Julian Herington, Dame Wendy Hiller, Owen Holder, Celeste Holm, John Hunter, Griffith Jones, Jean Kent, Deborah Kerr, Ruth Kettlewell, David Kidd, Esmond Knight, Cleo Laine, Angela Lansbury, David Lawrence, Joseph Losey, Virginia McKenna, Raymond Mander and Joe Mitchenson, Elspeth March, Arthur Marshall, Rodney Millington, Roger Moore, Marie Ney, David Niven, Maureen O'Brien, Lord Olivier, Siân Phillips, J. B. Priestley, Margaret Rawlings, Sir Michael Redgrave, Moira Redmond, Sir Ralph Richardson, Diana Rigg, Alan Rolfe, Rita Room, Oriel Ross, George Rylands, Leonard Schach, Athene Seyler, Dinah Sheridan, Beatrice Straight, Joan Swinstead, Sylvia Syms, Frances Tannehill, Geoffrey Toone, Ella Voysey, Emlyn Williams, Peter Williams, Ernie Wise and Carol Wolveridge. Also to those members of Flora's family for their kind co-operation, especially to Margaret Robson, Hugh Robson, John Robson, Doreen Wade and John Ritter, and to Dorothy Pheysey and others of Flora's friends who have so lovingly maintained her pressbooks.

I would like to express my gratitude to Paul Myers and the staff of the Theatre Collection at the Lincoln Center Library and Museum of the Performing Arts in New York, whose archives were of invaluable assistance. Similarly I would like to thank Alexander Clark and the members of the Players Club, Gramercy Park, New York City, for the use of their library and facilities; the staffs of the libraries of the Academy of Motion Picture Arts and Sciences and of the American Film Institute in Los Angeles, and Wendy Warnken and the staff of the Theatre Collection at the Museum of the City of New York; also Michael Frary, Bruce Kerman, Tony Tucci, Rex Stallings, Walter

# AUTHOR'S NOTE

Wood and Frances Tannehill Clark and the many others for their generous hospitality during the period of my researches in the United States of America.

I am equally grateful to Elaine Burrows of the National Film Archive for all her time and trouble, and the staffs of the General Library and Stills Library of the British Film Institute; the staff of the Newspaper Collection of the British Library; Jacqueline Cavanagh and the staff of the BBC Written Archives, Caversham Park, Reading; Vic Parker and the staff of the BBC Programme Index; Pam Reeve and the staff of the Spotlight Enquiry Service, 42–43 Cranbourn Street, London WC2; Geoff Shields for his talented photography; Ella Hall and John Donat for access to the Robert Donat Collection; Patricia Carthy of the *Radio Times*; Timothy Burrill and Jeannie Stone of Burrill Productions; Charles H. Schneer; Bill Edwards of Metro-Goldwyn-Mayer; Norman Rosemont Productions; I.T.C. Entertainment Ltd. Thanks also are due to Barry Sheppard, Administrator of the Oxford Playhouse, and to Roger Spence, Administrator of the Newcastle Playhouse.

I am indebted to Ronald Mavor for permission to quote from the letters and writings of his father O. H. Mavor (James Bridie); to James Forsyth for extracts from his book *Tyrone Guthrie*; to J. B. Priestley for extracts from his letters and from *Dangerous Corner*; to J. C. Trewin for extracts from his theatrical criticisms and from his book *Robert Donat*; to Grace Wyndham Goldie for an extract from her writings; to John Allen for permission to quote from his father Percy Allen's writing; to The Tyrone Guthrie Centre, Annagh-ma-Kerrig, Monaghan, for permission to quote from Sir Tyrone Guthrie's letters; to the Society of Authors for permission to quote from the letters of George Bernard Shaw and from *Caesar and Cleopatra*; to Dennis Dobson Publishers for a quote from *Paul Robeson* by Marie Seton; to Hamish Hamilton for a quote from *A Life in the Theatre* by Tyrone Guthrie; to Fredrick Muller for a quote from *All the World's a Stage* by Clifford Bax.

I am grateful to the following for free access to their copyright material: The Associated Newspapers Group; British Drama League (*Drama* magazine); *Cambridge Evening News*; *The Cherwell*; the *Christian Science Monitor*; *Daily Express*; *Daily Mirror*; *Daily Telegraph* (for quotes from W. A. Darlington and others); *Financial Times*; *The Guardian*; *Illustrated London News*; *The Lady*; *The Listener*; *Manchester Daily Mail*; *Morning Star*; *Newcastle Journal*; *New Standard*; *New Statesman*; *The Observer*; *Punch*; *Richmond* (Virginia, USA) *News Leader*; *St Louis Post Despatch*; *The Stage*; Taylor and Francis Ltd (*The Cambridge Review*) and *The Times*. I acknowledge permission from *The Sunday Times* to quote from the writings of

# AUTHOR'S NOTE

James Agate and others, and *The New York Times* to make the quotes on pages 107 and 127, © 1937, 1939 respectively by The New York Times Company; reprinted by permission.

In addition I would like to thank the following for permission to reproduce photographic material: Mrs Houston Rogers and the Victoria and Albert Museum for permission to reproduce the work of Houston Rogers; E.M.I.; Enterprise Pictures Limited; Harvard Theatre Collection; London Films; Mary Morris; Metro-Goldwyn-Mayer; P.C. Films Corporation; Pendennis Pictures Corporation Ltd.; Press Association; *Radio Times*; Rank Organisation Ltd.; United Artists Corporation Ltd; Universal Pictorial Press Agency.

The following publications have been helpful in researching this book and may provide additional sources of reference to the reader: *Flora Robson* by Janet Dunbar (Harrap, 1960); *My Drama School* by Flora Robson etc., Margaret McCall (ed.) (Robson Books, 1978); *Dames of the Theatre* by Eric Jones (W. H. Allen, 1974); *A Life In The Theatre* by Tyrone Guthrie (Hamish Hamilton, 1959); *Tyrone Guthrie* by James Forsyth (Hamish Hamilton, 1976); *Robert Donat* by J. C. Trewin (Heinemann, 1968); *One Way of Living* by James Bridie (Constable, 1939); *Mind's Eye* by Basil Dean (Hutchinson, 1973); *Early Stages* by John Gielgud (Heinemann, 1974); *Stars In My Hair* by Reginald Denham (Bodley Head, 1958); *Paul Robeson* by Marie Seton (Dobson Books, 1958); *All The World's A Stage* by Clifford Bax (Frederick Muller, 1947); *Halliwell's Film Guide* by Leslie Halliwell (Granada Books).

Finally I would like to thank Eileen Bell, Carol Snape, Stephen Knight and David Bonitto for all their help, advice and encouragement.

KENNETH BARROW

Summer, 1981

# Prologue

## An Overnight Success

IN RETROSPECT, how special seem the circumstances under which a star is born. Determination, chance and skill and inspiration all conspire to lay an ambush. Both artist and audience make their separate ways to the theatre unaware of the appointment each has made with the other.

On a first night a tension builds before and behind the curtain. Actors busy themselves performing exercises they never need on any other night. They chatter inconsequentially and press gifts on friends whom soon they may never see again. Each prepares himself to make the final compromise upon the reality of the world within the play. In the foyer, the audience keenly senses the opportunity of Caesar, to cheer or to condemn.

On the night of 7 October 1931, the first-night audience, lured by the prospect of Henry Ainley's return to the London stage, came with a greater curiosity. Chauffeurs and cabbies were directed to the Westminster Theatre in Palace Street, an entirely new theatre well away from Shaftesbury Avenue. Mr Ainley was to appear in *The Anatomist* a new play by James Bridie and directed by Tyrone Guthrie, both names quite unfamiliar to West End audiences.

Henry Ainley was, undoubtedly, the draw, and the debut of the theatre a social temptation. There could be no foreknowledge that, listed with the cast of little-known and unknown actors, could be found a name which ever after would shine out from lists of players to identify an artist of importance. Backstage, ready well before her second-act entrance, an actress, unaware of the turning point she was approaching in her life, was trying to keep herself calm and think her way into the play that was before her.

The theatre, itself, was barely dressed and ready to meet its audience. The conversion from the St James's Picture House had taken much longer than anticipated. While Tyrone Guthrie was readying the company, through final rehearsals, to meet its audience, the builders were working day and night to be ready to house them. Final adjustments to the electrical apparatus were still being made when 'Beginners please!' was being called at the dressing-room doors.

The audience was seated and ready. A lady, elegant in a crinoline, appeared before the curtain and began to sing the National Anthem. Surprised, the audience rose to its feet to sing with her.

The houselights dimmed and the curtain lifted to reveal the drawing room of the Misses Dishart in Edinburgh, a gentle picture. Dr Knox was expected. Suddenly there was Ainley in a spectacular entrance, sporting a bizarre black eye-patch over his right eye. The audience greeted him warmly. A sense of the horror of the body-snatchers, who supplied bodies for Dr Knox's dissecting table, gradually pervaded the drawing room. Mary Dishart, appalled that her fiancé should be a party to Dr Knox's 'blasphemy', returned her engagement ring.

The curtain on the second act rose to reveal quite a different prospect – the interior of a gloomy tavern, frequented by the body-snatchers, where the rejected fiancé had come to drown his sorrows. The door opened and in stepped a gaudy woman of the town, 'a glorious looking creature', Mary Paterson. "The door opened and in stepped the most beautiful woman I had ever seen in my life," a member of the audience was to recall forty years later.

Her harsh tone, her gutter talk and her drunken manner made her not a particularly sympathetic character. Late in her short scene she sang a tender lullaby to the disconsolate fiancé, "O can ye sew cushions . . ." The body-snatchers, Burke and Hare, appeared and enticed her to their room. Mary exited to her doom.

This short scene presented to the actress in question the opportunity of which all young actors dream, that moment when inspiration perfumes the air and a spell is cast upon the audience. "Here is an actress," wrote St John Ervine. "If you are not moved by this performance then you are immovable and have no right to be on this earth. Hell is your place." James Agate wrote, "She made the evening memorable by an exquisite piece of acting." *The Times* said, "She brings out with the most delicate skill the tenderness which may be latent in the depths of degradation, and carries off all the honours." James Bridie was to write, "She gave a performance of such appalling beauty that she burst the play in two."

# AN OVERNIGHT SUCCESS

Clifford Bax, fifteen years later, was to write, "What is one so ineloquent as I to say of her Mary Paterson in *The Anatomist*? If in my time there has been a darker, more sombre, more tragic, more fate-loaded performance – well, I cannot remember it or I did not see it. Few people understand how extremely rare is genius. When Flora Robson is on the stage we are a privileged generation."

Flora Robson, several years later, was playing the role of Queen Elizabeth in a film, *Fire over England*. Sewn into her costumes, with a wig and sticky make-up, between takes she was drawn into conversation by a pretty young girl who was an extra on the set. The girl told Flora that she intended becoming a star too. Flora asked her if she had trained for the stage, if she had worked in repertory. The girl replied that she had no time for this. On the contrary, she was quite certain that a producer would spot her on the set one day and her name would be in lights the next.

"After all," she added, as if in confirmation of her plan, "you became a star overnight didn't you?"

There is no getting away from it, *The Anatomist* in one night established Flora as a leading actress. But in October 1931 she was five months short of her thirtieth birthday. There had been more to it than waiting around on a set to be discovered. How many first nights had there been before that one?

# 1

## You are going to be an Actress

### 1902–1924

### 1

SHE WAITED PATIENTLY for the signal to begin. It seemed quite a long time coming. She was, after all, merely five years and eleven months old – almost six, but not quite. It seemed strange to be standing on the stage quite alone. Beyond the curtain were all those people who would soon be looking at her. She knew she looked her best in her new dress. It was white with lots of frills, a pale blue sash, and white satin slippers on her feet. She had seen herself in a mirror and decided she would do. Soon it would all be over and life would return to normal.

She would certainly be very pleased that there would be no need for her to stay behind after school any more. She had nothing against working with Miss Croft on her recitations. It was the dreadful journey home up the dark street with all its strange shadows. She would go the long way round to avoid seeing the cat's-meat man with his terrible cry of "Any ning-a-nings" or the road-sweeper with his wild red eyes. Run from them as she would, in her imagination they followed her home and haunted her dreams. In the light of day, when her sisters were with her, things were not nearly so alarming. After today she would always be able to walk home with them.

She was still waiting. Miss Croft would tell her when to begin. She became aware of her socks. Could she feel them falling down? Because she thought about it so strongly she was sure she could feel them slipping down. Better to check them quickly, she thought. She bent down and pulled them up. Before she had quite finished,

## YOU ARE GOING TO BE AN ACTRESS

someone had swung up the curtain. There was a small flutter of laughter from some of the people. Flora looked out over the audience. Somewhere amongst all those faces looking up at her would be her father. She worshipped her father. He was over six feet tall. When she was very much smaller he would take her on his knee and teach her poems which she would recite back to him. That was how all this had started. She would speak her poem to him now, secretly.

Then Miss Croft whispered to her and she began. It was the tale of 'Little Orphant Annie', who told ghost stories to the children round the fire at night. "And the goblins will get YOU . . . if-you-don't-watch-out!" It was a scary poem full of dark meanings. Of course, it had been in her mind as she made her fearful way home each evening after her private coaching. Some of the creepiness she had felt she put into the poem. When she finished she heard the audience applauding and laughing. But she couldn't quite see her father or her mother. She hoped they would be pleased. The curtain came down and she went backstage to wait until the end of the performance.

She had wrapped up warmly in her coat and muffler and was ready to go home. There was her father talking to Miss Croft. His face was flushed with excitement. Flora knew he was pleased with her. But there was something more. She moved closer. David Robson turned and saw her. "Flora," he cried, "you're going to be an actress. Our next Ellen Terry!" What could he mean? She was pleased because he looked so happy with her. Miss Croft looked happy too. "You are going to be my private pupil," she said.

Flora's heart sank. She would be kept in after school, she knew it. All she could see were the journeys home and the night people who terrified her. She mumbled something polite, but inside she felt wretched.

"Our next Ellen Terry . . ."

She never forgot these words. Seventy years later she would say, *"From that day on I have been a public person."*

Flora was born on 28 March 1902, a Good Friday. Her godmother, Aunt Margaret MacPherson, who would later become a nun, said that because Flora came into the world on a Good Friday, all her sins would be forgiven. Flora's mother was a sea-captain's daughter who had married her father's second engineer. They had moved away from their native Scotland and settled in South Shields where he had a job as a marine surveyor with a firm of Tyneside shipbuilders. Flora was the sixth child born to them in South Shields. Before her were John, Lila, Helen, Margaret and David.

By the time of her recital debut the family had made three moves, first to Yarmouth in Norfolk, then back to Wallsend and then to

# FLORA

Palmers Green, London. David Robson had been appointed Chief Salvage Officer and London Director of the Hungarian shipping line Atlantica. And by the age of five, Flora was no longer the baby of the family. She had a little sister, Shela. David, the brother immediately older than her, was a sickly child. Perhaps he received more than his fair share of attention from his parents and Flora missed out. When Shela was born, everyone's heart went out to the lovable little girl, and Flora was unwittingly overlooked. She longed to be loved. She threw herself, body and soul, into everything she could do to please her parents. Her success at the recital excited her father more than she had ever known. Shortly afterwards, he took her to the theatre to see her first play. It was Herbert Tree's production of *Faust* at His Majesty's Theatre in the Haymarket. Tree himself played Mephistopheles, and cast in the role of Faust was an actor called Henry Ainley. But it was the magical effects, the angels, the acrobats dressed as animals and the sumptuous red and gold of the theatre that caught Flora's imagination. As the tale of the man who sold his soul to the devil unfolded itself on the stage, ambition began to flicker in Flora's mind. If she were to work hard with Miss Croft she could be a part of all this.

So she set to work in earnest. Miss Croft was glad of the extra money. She had ambitions to go on the stage herself, and was taking lessons at Tree's school. Sometimes she would come to the Robson home to give a lesson. "*I shall never forget a warm afternoon when I couldn't go out to play in the hay with the other children. Miss Croft was coming to give me a lesson. I watched them all go and then I waited. I continued to wait. Miss Croft still hadn't arrived when all the others came back. They were all so happy, and laughing. Something had delayed her, I don't remember what, and I was in bed by the time she arrived. I could have had the fun after all. If I could turn back time and have just one thing that I've missed in my life I would choose that afternoon.*"

Flora was not the only one to benefit from her father's ambition. He made sure that all of his daughters pursued some accomplishment. Margaret learned the violin. Nelly played the piano and she and Lila sang. Flora had lessons in singing, ballet and piano as well as elocution. All the girls would perform at a local Eisteddfod and would collect many prizes between them. David Robson taught them the pursuit of excellence and the importance of success. He was never happy if they missed first place and so they seldom did. He impressed upon them the value of money and the necessity to save against rainy days ahead. The Robson children also learned something much deeper, the value of a warm and loving family.

Flora continued to work in recitals and would take leading roles in children's plays in the neighbourhood. Her fame spread and she was called upon to appear in concerts as far afield as the Mansion House and at the Lyceum Ladies' Club in Piccadilly. She enjoyed 'working' there because the butlers would call her 'Madam', which made her feel very grand. The ladies would sit fully dressed in outdoor clothes and large matinee hats complete with feathers and a veil wound together under the chin. One of her earliest successes was a poem called 'Little Gretchen'. It told of a match-girl in the snow who saw a vision of Christmas warmth and cheer in matches she struck for comfort. With this poem, Flora discovered a new talent, that of being able to move an audience. As she took her bow she noticed several of the ladies hastily unveiling so they could wipe away the tears. She found she enjoyed this power more than she enjoyed making an audience laugh.

Miss Croft gave Flora lessons for little more than a year before she enrolled as a full-time student at Tree's Academy of Dramatic Art. She would go on to win the Gold Medal and eventually become one of Tree's leading ladies. She had not been a good voice teacher, in the technical sense, but she had inspired the child's imagination. Now Flora needed help with her breathing and in voice control. Too much exposure on the recital platform had taught her bad habits and she used her instrument badly. Her father had been enthusiastic as any father would, discovering such an ability in his child, but he had pushed her beyond her immature capabilities. Flora worried constantly about her voice. She imagined it being made of precious glass, that, like a boy's voice, would one day break. She feared she would never be able to repair it.

After Miss Croft had left to take up her studies, Flora was sent to study voice production with William Stewart, Professor of Elocution at the Hampstead Conservatoire. Stewart, with Charles Fry, had developed a natural method of verse-speaking. Fry's son, in his biography, recalled his father's examining young Flora for an introductory grade. Fry had come up from the examination room with tears in his eyes. Her pathos had completely unmanned him. Stewart entered her for one of the Royal Academy of Music examinations in verse-speaking. She recited Julia's letter scene from *The Two Gentlemen of Verona* and was awarded a bronze medal. The medal had never been awarded to anyone so young. She was still only ten years old. She was also entered for the British Empire Shakespeare Society's competition and won the second prize at the final at the Theatre Royal, Haymarket. It was a fine achievement but Flora had already caught her father's fierce ambition. Second prize was not good enough for a Robson. The tiny girl stood backstage and thought to herself, "The next time I come here I'll get a standing ovation. They'll all be calling 'Flora Robson! Flora Robson! Flora Robson!' " As she waited for her parents to collect her after the competition a lady, one of the judges, approached her and spoke very warmly of her performance of the letter scene. Flora shyly thanked her and the lady walked away. Someone nearby said, "Do you realise who that was?" It had been Edith Craig, Ellen Terry's daughter. Imagine David Robson's joy on hearing this piece of news! An offer came from Tree for Flora to appear in his production of *A Midsummer Night's Dream* to be staged at His Majesty's. Stewart turned it down without consulting Flora or her father. They were both bitterly disappointed when eventually he told them, but Stewart knew well what might happen to a child actor. Flora was too talented to have her chance of success imperilled by too early an exposure to professional theatre.

As a result of all this success Flora's fame grew. That the success was not accompanied by the preciousness often found in child performers is probably mainly attributable to her father's example in the endeavour for excellence, and to the fact that each success was in direct proportion to the work she put in. Her teachers, her parents and Flora herself felt that all experience in performance was valuable, and by the spring of 1915 she was performing in concerts every evening and sometimes twice a day. Late each night would find a sleepy Flora, her head nestled in the warmth of her mother's shoulder, making a horse-drawn cab journey back home to where the family now lived in Southgate.

It was around this time, when Flora was aged thirteen, that a strange thing happened. She developed a kind of stage-fright and was terrified of appearing in front of an audience. Sometimes a girl in adolescence will feel that all the strange things that are going on inside her must be patently obvious to the rest of the world too, and perhaps this was why Flora felt she could not appear in public. Whatever the reason, she began to do badly in competitions and was sometimes not even placed. Whether as a cause or effect is not certain, but her neck glands became swollen and she lost her voice. It was several months before she could speak properly again and every time she set foot on a stage the symptoms would return.

Shortly after this, Flora and her sisters moved from the school they had been attending and entered the Palmers Green High School. David Robson was naturally disappointed, but Flora seemed content to forget her ambitions. Her early successes and glories were something she left behind a closed door with the rest of her childhood.

## 2

By the time Flora was about to leave school, her father was on the point of retiring. Nelly was married, Margaret was training as a children's nurse, and Lila, who had lost her fiancé in the war, was

## YOU ARE GOING TO BE AN ACTRESS

helping out at home. Flora would have to make her own way in the world without her father's support. Theirs was by no means a wealthy family; David and Eliza had brought up seven children. Flora would have to find herself either a career or a husband. There was little likelihood of the latter. Flora was not a pretty girl. Her sisters had had many beaux, but not she. In immediately post-World War One Britain there were tragically few young men. The youth of Britain had gone away, never to return, and four million 'superfluous women' faced lives alone.

Besides, Flora had an ambitious spirit. Nothing had taken that away. However much failure or disappointment she would meet in her life, and there would be each in large proportion, it would be that spirit which would see her through. The headmistress of the High School had wanted Flora to go to Oxford. But there was little likelihood of her getting a scholarship and, as there were no grants in those days, the idea had been forgotten.

The flame of ambition rekindled itself and a plan began to form in her mind. As soon as she allowed herself the indulgence of this train of thought, it was as though she had unlocked that closed door, and all the happinesses of childhood came spilling out. "Our next Ellen Terry..."

She knew she could do it, if she went about it the proper way. The successes of her childhood had been the successes of a child. To succeed in the theatre, as an adult, she knew she would need a proper training. As Grace Croft had so often told her, the only training that would fit her for a life in the theatre was to be found at Tree's Academy of Dramatic Art. Now to train there, she would need some financial support from her father, support he had already told her he could not afford to give. Flora felt that if she were not able to follow her plan through, then all the money he had spent on her as a child would have been wasted. One day she took a deep breath and told him what she wanted to do.

David Robson was not easily won over. This scheme would still cost him money he could not afford to spend. He could see that Flora had thought it all out. He was not surprised that the idea had not died in her. Flora had always been taught to pursue success and not admit failure, so she fought him with the very weapons he had put in her hands and with the dogged persistence she, unwittingly, had inherited from him. She set out to persuade him that if she were able to win a scholarship, his outlay would be no more than her keep and her fares and she would be doing something she really wanted to do, using the gifts he had always cherished in her. The arguments were appealing. Flora was fortunate in not having to overcome any resistance to her entering what many considered an immoral profession.

# FLORA

In those days an actress was a suspect creature and her calling synonymous with every sort of vice. On the contrary David Robson believed Ellen Terry and her kind to be divine beings. Some time later, when he proudly announced to a stranger that his daughter was going to become an actress, he was bewildered at the man's disgusted response.

In his heart, David Robson had always had enormous pride in Flora's early achievements. Her eagerness at her new plans revived his hopes. With characteristic grit he held out on her long enough to know how deeply rooted her ambitions were. When he saw that she had made a serious decision he relented and sat back to watch for the day when his early prophecy might come true. Flora left the High School at half-term, received special coaching for the entrance examination, and applied for a place.

## 3

Can you picture Flora as she makes her way down Gower Street to begin her first day at the Academy of Dramatic Art? Perhaps the first thing you notice is that, at five feet eight and a half inches, she is unusually tall for a woman. But whereas boldness might seem a natural accompaniment to her stature, there is a kind of nervous, tentative quality about her. Her jaw is set pensively, thrust a little forward, her upper lip is taut. Where a trace of make-up might have softened her uneven features, none has been applied. Her hair is drawn unimaginatively over her head and she wears her clothes almost with an apology for their homeliness. As she sets foot in the lobby of the Academy she feels immediately out of place. All the other girls seem to be turned out as though they are to be presented at court. And could it be that one of the fellows is wearing the rouge that Flora lacks? Should she turn now and run back home? Someone asks her for her name. Her voice will scarcely come at her command, it croaks in much the same way as it did when she faced the audiences of her adolescence. "Am I doing the right thing?" she wonders. A glance around would quickly show her that everyone is quite as nervous as she. The bright, chatty girls who look so calm and relaxed are really talking far too much and far too loudly. From our privileged distance we recognize that the first step is so difficult to take.

When Flora returned home to Southgate that evening she had so much to tell them all. There were twenty students in her class, only three of whom were male. She had been told that when they worked on plays with lots of roles for men, some of the girls would have to don the breeches. She knew she would be chosen as she was one of the taller girls. Most of the girls she had spoken to seemed to think of

## YOU ARE GOING TO BE AN ACTRESS

the Academy as some sort of finishing school and had no thought of an acting career. There were several other schoolgirls, just like her, and a ballet dancer. There would be two acting classes a week, one of which would deal with Shakespeare and Restoration Comedy, and the other with modern plays.

The first person to make an impression on her was Miss Chester. Elsie Chester had been a leading lady in the West End when she had been involved in a dreadful accident which resulted in the amputation of a leg. She would often relate the story in tears. She was now engaged to work on modern drama with the students. One of the first plays in which Flora was rehearsed by her was an American melodrama entitled *Miss Elizabeth's Prisoner*. Flora was cast in the rather dull role of Miss Elizabeth in Act One. Miss Chester was pleased with her because she knew her lines well in advance of the others. A few days before the first performance, one of the three men in the class went down with a severe attack of 'flu and, sadly, died. The plum role of the villainous Redcoat had been his. Because of Miss Chester's faith in Flora as a quick study, she was given the role and learned her lines overnight. At the performance she made a glorious success and was rewarded with the promise of better parts than she might otherwise have expected.

As well as the acting classes there were lessons in voice and diction from Mrs McKern, ballet classes from Louis d'Egville, fencing lessons from Felix Bertrand and a movement class. In this they were taught stage falls as well as period movement and gesture and modern social grace. The voice classes taught Flora a greater range of technique than she had previously covered. Neither the ballet class nor the fencing class were intent on turning out accomplished ballet dancers or fighters. Each taught their own grace, balance and co-ordination, and a facility to learn a sequence of steps. Many of the students in the group were as short-sighted as the generations of students to follow in imagining that there would be little practical application for any of these skills in the theatre. Contrary to this supposition, there was scarcely any area of her training that Flora was not able to draw on in her long career. Actors need to learn a complex vocabulary of skills to meet all unexpected eventualities.

When the first term was over, Flora continued to work at home in Southgate during the holidays. There was a big billiard room where she could move freely and work uninterrupted for most of the day. To begin with, she learned speeches from Shakespeare but found these limiting in their length without someone to act with. She found a copy of *The Trojan Women* and learned one of Hecuba's speeches. The billiard room became the ruins of Troy.

From the commencement of the new term there was a new principal in Kenneth Barnes who had recently returned from the war. His sisters, Irene and Violet Vanbrugh, would come in sometimes to teach the students deportment. There was a prize-giving arranged at which the prizes for the previous term would be distributed. The students spent the morning carrying chairs into the unfinished Malet Street Theatre. Lady Tree was invited to present the prizes and Barnes escorted her into the theatre. The ceremony lasted only a few minutes. Lady Tree then announced, to everyone's consternation, "Oh, I'm not going yet – I want to see some acting." Nothing was prepared! The new term's plays were barely into rehearsal and the last term's all forgotten. The staff looked around in desperation to see who might save the situation. One by one students would stand up and stumble through a half-known soliloquy. Flora sat deep in her seat aware of the embarrassment that had spread through the school. Suddenly one of the staff called out her name and pushed her on the stage. She had never imagined she would be chosen as she was still a junior at the Academy. Automatically she went into the Hecuba speech. Cheers followed her recital, though Flora was sure it was her success at having saved the day rather than her interpretation of the role that won them. The following term she would be awarded Lady Tree's prize, and would be presented with a set of Greek plays in the Gilbert Murray translations.

She was cast as a 'fallen woman' in her next play, Henry Arthur Jones's *The Dancing Girl*. The script called for Flora to smoke a cigarette. Faithfully, whenever the cue came, she would mime taking the cigarette and smoking it. Of course, she had never smoked before. Eventually Miss Chester said she must take a real cigarette to get the timing right. "*I was acting this scene with a tall, handsome ex-Guardsman. He gave me one of his cigarettes. He lit it and I inhaled. Suddenly the room went round. I became giddy, my eyes crossed and I staggered slightly. The cigarette paper split open and my mouth was soon full of tobacco. I was convinced the cigarette was doped! But I puffed away and flirted with the Guardsman as though I was quite used to it all. Miss Chester smiled very kindly and said, 'One day, Robson, you will be a very good actress.'*"

Later in the term Flora was to play Tybalt in *Romeo and Juliet*. This brought her into contact with Moffat Johnson, who had been the one to push her on the stage at the prize-giving. Johnnie, as he liked to be called, was a Scots actor who had been a member of Sir Frank Benson's Shakespearian Company. Flora would learn to recognize the mark of a Bensonian. Actors from that company were always impeccably dressed and had excellent manners – true gentleman actors. Johnnie was a strict disciplinarian and the students found him very demanding. Flora rose to his challenge for she had learned to

# YOU ARE GOING TO BE AN ACTRESS

thrive on hard work. He was an excellent influence on her. She admired the way he could put his finger on exactly what seemed to be troubling her and was grateful for his support.

Johnnie was tired of seeing the girl students, like Flora, struggling with roles written for men and went to Kenneth Barnes to ask him if, instead of tackling a whole Shakespeare play, he could direct the students in scenes that would enable the girls to work at female roles. Because of this, and Barnes' agreement, Flora was able to play the mad Ophelia. Playing men's roles gave her a directness, which was a useful talent to have available, but there were other facets to explore. One day, during rehearsal, Johnnie spoke to the assembled group about their future careers in the theatre. "Some of you may become stars," he said, "others, supporting players. Remember, the supporters are just as important as the stars, who would not shine like diamonds without a perfect 'setting'. If you succeed, do not think you are a special person. You are no better than a good workman plumber. Learn humility." Stardom seemed so far away, but Flora remembered what he said.

Another teacher from whom she learned a great deal was Helen Haye, a woman of great natural dignity, who had also been with Benson. She was a supremely intelligent woman who could be extremely cutting in her criticism. This kept all her students on their toes. "Two hours of hell with Helen" was how they thought of her classes. Flora had learned the whole of Chloe Hornblower's big scene in Galsworthy's *The Skin Game* in case Miss Haye gave her an opportunity to work on it. The opportunity came and Flora performed it with all the stops out. She was distressed when Miss Haye interrupted her. "This is extremely boring," she said. "Would you begin again, and this time hold back your emotion. There can be one climax only." She then proceeded to show Flora how to make an audience cry at a given moment. "The scene should be like a long passage of music, full of nuances of differing colours and shadings," she added. She elaborated on the immense importance of the dramatic pause at an exactly prescribed moment. Colin Clive was cast as Chloe's husband. When Flora delivered the line, "I *am* going to have a child, Charlie", Clive blushed to the roots! At the dress rehearsal Flora wore a cheap little kimono, all she could afford. Miss Haye brought her a long, elegant, rest-gown from her own wardrobe to wear at the performance. Flora felt marvellous and gave the best performance she had ever given. She feels that it was at this point that she became a favourite for the Gold Medal.

There were other marvellous teachers. Although she would not work with either at the Academy, Miles Malleson and Claude Rains were among the strength at the time, and were the idols of many of

# FLORA

the girls. Sir Gerald du Maurier came in to give what now would be described as a master-class, as did Sir Arthur Pinero. Another visitor would have a profound effect on Flora. It was Sybil Thorndike. She came in to direct three rehearsals of *The Trojan Women* in which Flora was cast as Andromache. When she heard the tragic news that her baby would be killed, Flora, forgetting everything Helen Haye had taught her, burst out with a howl, "Oh, God!" Miss Thorndike suggested that she whisper the words. As further ill-tidings were given her, Miss Thorndike still held her back. When the climax of the scene was reached, she told Flora, "Now the audience knows what is going to happen; now you can break your heart!" *"We all worshipped Sybil. She was so kind and generous. When her visit was over, I cried into a towel in the dressing room. One of the girls rushed into the lavatory and kissed the seat where she had been!"*

Eventually the end of the course was in sight. Flora knew she stood a good chance of winning the Gold Medal. Winning this coveted award almost certainly led to a West End job being offered to the recipient. Johnnie cast Flora in the title role of Maeterlinck's *Sister Beatrice*, a verse play based on *The Miracle*. The statue of the Virgin Mary has come to life to take the place, in a convent, of Sister Beatrice who has escaped into the world. When, years later, she returns to the convent, old and diseased, she finds her habit at the feet of the Virgin and dies there in a state of grace. The role proved a trying test but Flora was beginning to find the measure of it when, a few days before the public show, she came down with a severe case of 'flu. She struggled through the performance with scarcely any voice. Joan Swinstead was to receive the Gold Medal, Laura Wallis-Mills took the Silver, and Flora was awarded the Bronze.

She was bitterly disappointed. Ill, and in tears, she bumped into Johnnie in a passage backstage. He took hold of her roughly and dragged her down the passage out of earshot of any of the other students and spoke very sharply to her. "The Gold Medal means nothing!" he said. "No medal means anything in the long run. I believe in you. There might be years of struggle but you've got it in you. You are going to be a very fine actress. I'm going away to America, but if ever you need me, write to me. Even if I'm at the other end of the world I'll do all I can to help."

The medals were presented to the prizewinners in the summer of 1921. The Academy had been granted a royal charter and was now known as the Royal Academy of Dramatic Art. "It was the opening of the theatre in Malet Street," Joan Swinstead wrote to me. "By some miracle, Edward, Prince of Wales came to do the opening and also hand us our medals on a rather bare stage. As he handed me mine, all the lights went out – a complete blackout. Perhaps it was an omen. When Flora received her medal the lights were restored. You see, she was at the beginning of what would be a bright and dazzling career. She has such a great gift for emotional acting and makes it all look so easy – which it is *not!*"

When Johnnie went to America, Flora said 'goodbye' to more than a teacher. *"I have always relied on a father-figure for support, instruction and encouragement. All of them have left me and I have tried to go on alone. Before he left I asked him for a photograph. He sent me a handsome, mounted print which he had autographed to me. On the back he had written, 'To my best pupil. I wish you every success, go on and prosper and God bless you, Johnnie.'"*

## 4

There is very little discernible change in the young woman who now makes her way down the Waterloo Road. Although more than two years have passed since she made her way to the Academy for the first time, she is still poorly dressed, has acquired little social grace and is still shy and nervous. When her fellow students were out socializing and partying, Flora was making a Forest of Arden of the billiard room. She has been doing what actors call 'the rounds' for several weeks with no success at all. Few of the people she has written to have bothered to reply. There have been one or two visits to agents' offices. People seem interested only in seeing what she looks like and she knows she will never win any prizes for her beauty. "Let me act for you," she insists. And when anyone tells her to go ahead she leaps up and delivers her Hecuba at full tilt. "Thank you, we'll let you know": her rejection is spelled out to her before she even gets to the end. All her success at the Academy had given her confidence. Without that, and the things Johnnie had said, she would not be able to cope with the disappointment. At the end of her time at RADA, even with only the Bronze Medal, she had been at the top, at the peak of what she had set out to do. Now she finds herself, with all the out-of-work actors, at the bottom of the more formidable and less easily surmountable Everest of a life in the theatre.

She catches sight of herself in a shop window and adjusts her hat. It makes no appreciable difference. In any other walk of life she might have been able to bear her looks with fortitude. In the theatre, where how she presents herself seems to count for more than anything else, her face is a painful disadvantage. It is something which it is impossible to correct or improve. She remembers that terrible time in early childhood when her brother David, with all the innocent malice of a child, had brought home to her the feeling of inferiority she would feel for the rest of her life. "You're ugly, you're ugly, you're ugly," he cried.

Today, she is a little more optimistic. Miss Thorndike and another teacher have given her letters of introduction to Robert Atkins, Miss Baylis' director at the Old Vic. It is a pleasant interview and he is impressed by Flora's talent. However, he cannot offer her anything without Miss Baylis' say, and she is away on holiday. "Perhaps you will come back later, Miss Robson, when Miss Baylis has returned." There is a small hope and Flora does not write off her chances.

Fortunately there was to be another opportunity for her to show her talents at the Academy. Kenneth Barnes had written a play and arranged a Sunday night performance for which he had gathered an impressive cast. This included Athene Seyler, Ion Swinley and Meggie Albanesi in leading roles. Miss Albanesi was taken ill late in rehearsal and Barnes remembered how quick a study Flora was. He asked her if she would be interested in taking the role of one of the patients who, in the second act, underwent psychoanalytical examination. Flora was none the wiser. She had no idea what a psychiatrist was, but she leapt at the chance.

On the first night of the play, *Undercurrents*, Flora was terribly nervous. On stage Athene Seyler noticed how tense she was and found a moment to slip a comforting arm round her shoulders. The performance was exciting and there were good reviews. "There was some superb acting," reported the correspondent of *The Era*, "and we doubt if the part of Miss Marsh could have been more sincerely played than it was by Miss Flora Robson. It was an exceedingly fine performance, tender and beautiful in its conception." And there were two fan letters. One was from William Armstrong, who ran the Liverpool Repertory Theatre. Unfortunately he had already cast his next season, though he assured her he would bear her in mind for the future. The other was from Miles Malleson. "May I please congratulate you very sincerely on your beautiful performance in *Undercurrents* last night," he wrote. "It is such a real pleasure to watch a sincere piece of acting, so full of insight and sympathy as yours was. Thank you." In addition, there was praise from Kenneth Barnes and his sister, Irene Vanbrugh. In all it was a marvellous tonic after everything had looked so bleak. Naturally Flora hoped that there would be an offer as a result of being seen in the play, but none came. Inevitably the rounds began again – "Nothing today" . . . "What did you say your name was?" . . . "Leave a photograph won't you, dear" . . . "Don't ring us" . . . "We'll let you know" – the dreary litany of the unemployed actor. Occasionally she went into the Academy where there would always be a kind word, a

# YOU ARE GOING TO BE AN ACTRESS

commiseration, a little encouragement. On the grapevine she heard about a production of a new play at the Shaftesbury Theatre in which many actors would be needed for small parts. One day she saw Miss Haye and asked if she would write a letter of introduction to the producer of the play. It was largely due to this letter that Basil Dean, who would re-emerge in Flora's life on several notable occasions, gave her the part in which she made her professional stage debut in Clemence Dane's *Will Shakespeare*.

A letter arrived from Dean offering Flora the part. Never having replied to such a letter before she asked her father's advice. He suggested a format similar to that used in business. 'I note such and such, and such and such in your letter, etc.' Dean was furious when eventually she saw him. He thought she was trying to tie him down without a contract. That was the last time she took her father's advice on a theatre matter! The part was one of the apparitions which appear to Shakespeare before he has written any of his plays. King Lear and Rosalind, Othello and Hamlet and a whole troupe of others, implore Shakespeare to tell their stories. Flora was cast as the apparition of Queen Margaret. She would also understudy Mary Clare as Mary Fitton, and one of Queen Elizabeth's ladies-in-waiting. Shakespeare was played by Philip Merivale, Anne Hathaway by Moyna MacGill, Queen Elizabeth by Haidee Wright and Kit Marlowe by Claude Rains.

Even though she had little to say, Flora was terrified on opening night, 17 November 1921. Her father was in the audience as he always would be, but she found no security in this. It was all rather an ordeal. The family had moved to Peacehaven in Sussex and she was living with several Academy students in lodgings in Gordon Square. It was the first time she had ever had to face London without the security of home within easy reach. The nights were even more frightening than those lonely homeward journeys had been in childhood. Now she was a grown woman, drunks would push into her and proposition her. She would run from them as she had run from the cat's-meat man. When she got to the theatre she would go straight to her dressing-room, but there was no comfort from the two brassy ex-chorus girls with whom she shared. She neither liked, nor really understood their talk. She felt terribly lonely. One weekend she went to visit her family. This made much worse her return to London on the Monday. Caught on a traffic island in the middle of the road, home-sickness overwhelmed her. Her face was a mask of misery. A policeman approached her. "Now then, Miss, what's the matter?" Tears sprang to her eyes. "I've been home for the weekend," she wept, "and I don't like London!" She rushed away from him towards the theatre. The two chorus girls were already there, getting ready for the performance. One of them noticed Flora's distress. "Now then, ducks, what's been happening to you?" she asked. Flora poured out her troubles. She was surprised to find both of them kind and sympathetic. "You've got to get used to all this, you know," the other one said, "if you want to work in the theatre, that is."

The play did not get good notices. Miss Dane had written a very strong play about the women in Shakespeare's life. Shakespeare himself was underwritten and unsympathetic. Audiences found this unacceptable. Attendances were poor, but this was largely due to the 'flu epidemic. The cast were often as severely depleted as the house. "*It was a dreadful time. More people died from that epidemic than had died in the War. I had only two lines to speak as Queen Margaret. Shakespeare was descending a staircase. We were all behind a gauze that went down behind the stairs so we appeared as ghost-like forms walking down the stairs with him. Only my head would appear and I would say, 'My son was taken from me. Tell my story!' Then Ophelia would appear further down and say, 'I died for love. Tell my story!' And so all the characters would appear and say their lines. The week the 'flu epidemic hit the cast, the girls were off one after the other. Only our heads were seen, so I only had to change my head-gear to understudy. One night I had to play three ghosts. Firstly I appeared as Queen Margaret and said my line. Then I rushed down the stairs, changing my head-dress as I went and said, 'I died for love. Tell my story!' and then I rushed down the stairs, again changing my head-gear and said Cleopatra's line. Philip Merivale looked at me out of the corner of his eye, and said, 'Not you again!' Claude Rains was wonderful as Marlowe. I don't think I ever spoke to him at that time, but I had such admiration for him. He was always good. He began life as Sir Herbert Tree's dresser and had a broad Cockney accent. He would walk round Trafalgar Square, late at night, practising his 'aitches!*"

After the epidemic had passed its peak, audiences began to drift back but the play closed after only sixty-two performances. Flora rushed home immediately to enjoy the security of family life. "*That first play nearly finished me. I was so terribly unhappy I wanted to give up theatre altogether. I never wanted to work again.*" In addition, as no letter had arrived to ask her back to the Vic, and Miss Baylis had doubtless returned, Flora had decided to go to see the Lady. Miss Baylis saw her audition and after it said, "I haven't time to be bothered with you. You're far too young and you haven't got nearly enough experience. Go away, young woman, and get some."

From one of her friends, Flora heard that Ben Greet needed someone for his touring Shakespearian company. She used her letters of introduction to get an audition. Sybil Thorndike had been a member of Greet's company and this probably stood Flora in good stead with him. Greet offered her an engagement for six months as

Flora MacKenzie Robson, aged two

Shela, Flora, David and Margaret Robson

David Robson

Eliza Robson

'Johnnie'

Flora, in her twenties

Tony Guthrie, 1930

Anmer Hall

*Iphigenia in Tauris* Cambridge Festival Theatre
(Scott & Wilkinson)

With David Horne in *The Thought* at Cambridge

'An' God hearkened unto Rachel an' she conceived an' bore a son. An' God hearkened unto Abbie! Pray Abbie! Pray fur Him to hearken!' With George Merritt in *Desire Under the Elms*
(Courtesy Mander and Mitchenson Collection)

## YOU ARE GOING TO BE AN ACTRESS

his second leading lady and Flora, with renewed ambition, set off for Bristol where she would join the company.

She arrived in Bristol on Monday 6 March 1922, three weeks short of her twentieth birthday. If London had seemed strange to face alone, Bristol seemed stranger. With difficulty she found her way to the Theatre Royal in the slum area of the city. It was a grim, unwelcoming place. The bills outside proclaimed that Ben Greet and his Pastoral Players were at the theatre all week with seven different plays, opening and closing with *Macbeth*. Flora found a little security in knowing there would be some kind of welcome inside. Her eye moved quickly down the bill and she found the list of players. Oh dear, she was listed as Florence Robson. She felt almost a stranger again.

Inside the stage-door she found there was no one who really wanted to be bothered with her. Everything was being readied for the performance that night. She stood alone and bewildered. Finally she was able to find someone who would conduct her to Ben Greet. B. G. was a huge, strong man with a shock of white hair. "Miss Robson," he said, "Yer not in the play tonight, but yer on tomorrow. Emilia, *Winter's Tale*." Flora's heart missed a beat. On, the next night? She had thought there would be a period of rehearsal before she was put on to play. Emilia? Which was she? When would she rehearse? "Pop in tomorrow and the stage manager will run through it with yer." "But . . ." But he was gone. Flora found digs which were clean. She had the Actors' Church Union list of addresses. The lodgings were twenty-seven shillings and sixpence all in, with a private sitting-room. She would be able to manage it out of her three pounds salary. She settled down and began to learn her lines. How lucky that she was a quick study. At least, normally she was. The prospect of going on stage the following night with a strange company terrified her, and the lines would not go in. "Oh, why did I come here," she thought, "I'm not meant to be an actress!"

The next day came and she went into the theatre and looked for the stage manager. When she found him, he surprised her by revealing that she would also be playing one of the ladies-in-waiting in Act Two Scene One. She wasn't at all prepared for this and tried to learn the lines as he took her through, reading in the lines of Hermione, Mamillius and the other lady-in-waiting. Then he read in Paulina's lines in her other scene. She was hesitant, hadn't developed a proper character, but seemed to pass muster with the stage manager. He disappeared before she was able to ask him what she would wear. She went back to her digs to study the new lines and got into the theatre in plenty of time to find a costume and put on her make-up. "*I went to the wardrobe mistress to ask her what I was going to wear. She* turned round and said, "If B. G. wants to get in extra people to play, he must get extra clothes. I haven't got anything.' I didn't know what to do. Someone said I should ask Madge Whiteman, one of the other actresses in the company. Well, she wasn't in. I put on my make-up. Madge Whiteman came in very late and I knocked on her door. She had the door locked and she said, 'Oh, come back again later.' At the beginning of the tour when the hired costumes arrived, each actor would 'bag' the clothes he wanted and put them in his own trunk. Madge Whiteman had my clothes in her trunk. When I went into the company I took over all the second leads. She was already playing thirds and thought she should have been promoted and was terribly jealous of me. 'Come along later,' she said, 'I can't be bothered with you now.' She went on the stage and I didn't have anything. I couldn't go on! I missed my entrance as the lady-in-waiting because I didn't have anything to wear. Fortunately the other lady-in-waiting covered for me. Eventually I found Ben Greet and told him of my predicament. The wardrobe mistress had nothing for me. 'Nonsense,' he barked, 'Tell her to find something.' A robe was produced, but there were no tapes in the neck-band. A tape was found, then there was no bodkin to thread it through. I tried to force it through with a closed safety pin, then I lost the other end. I had only time to fasten the thing up and it was time for my entrance and I rushed into the wings!"

Flora went out onto the stage and there was the same Madge Whiteman facing her as Paulina. "Dear gentlewoman," Miss Whiteman began. As Flora began her own speech, all her thoughts were racing. She couldn't concentrate on what she was saying. Here she was, in a strange theatre, with a hostile actress, playing a role she hadn't properly rehearsed, wearing a costume into which she had struggled at the last minute with no time to check if it was even properly fastened. She was living through a nightmare! "A boy?" Paulina asked. "A daughter," Flora replied. She could feel her lips moving and she could hear her voice, but she seemed separated by an aching, swimming void. She could tell Madge Whiteman was thinking, 'What kind of an actress has B. G. hired this time?' Now Paulina was speaking and Flora could feel her attention being drawn towards the auditorium. Beyond the scorching haze of the lights she thought she could see people moving about. A baby was crying. Another joined in. A woman laughed a long, loud cackle. Nothing to do with the performance. A crowd of men laughed, amused by the woman. Someone shouted something from the back of the auditorium. Paulina went on, "The silence often of pure innocence / Persuades when speaking fails." The woman shouted something indistinguishable at the men. One of the men shouted something back and a whole section of the audience roared with laughter. 'Why doesn't someone stop them?' thought Flora. As if in answer a huge brute of a man

## YOU ARE GOING TO BE AN ACTRESS

strode down the gangway shouting, "Quiet! Quiet please!" The noise subsided and shortly it was quiet. Too quiet. It was quiet even on stage. 'Persuades when speaking fails – but that's my cue,' she thought, 'What on earth do I say?' "Most worthy madam," Paulina prompted under her breath, a gleam of triumph in her eye. "Most worthy madam," Flora repeated with more than a little gratitude, "Your honour and your goodness is so evident."

Flora was sure she would meet with the full weight of Ben Greet's fury when she left the stage. But the fury was rained down on Madge Whiteman and the wardrobe mistress. It had been the worst ordeal she had ever faced. For the first few weeks the ordeal continued. A blue velvet gown eventually appeared and Flora wore it in virtually every play, with a change of veil or wig. There were twenty plays altogether and Flora was in them all. Every night and every matinee the play changed and at the end of the week the company moved to a new venue. Flora rehearsed all her roles with the stage manager, with the exception of Lady Capulet and Bianca in *Othello*. Her fellow actors in these scenes would be called and B. G. would direct her. He was very helpful on these occasions and an appalling hindrance the rest of the time*.

Flora had to supply her own footwear and jewellery. She would go in search of inexpensive adaptable items from the market stalls when there was time. Someone taught her how to make sandals from cheap Woolworth soles and strips of chamois leather fashioned into crosspieces. When she played Phebe in *As You Like It* for the first time she had not found time to make her sandals and wore a pair of unblocked ballet shoes instead. On she went with Silvius. "Will you sterner be / Than he that dies and lives by bloody drops?" There was a howl of laughter from the audience on the word 'bloody'. "I would not be thy executioner," spoke up Flora, in an attempt to top the noise. "What yer got on yer feet?" someone shouted. 'Who was that?' thought Flora. It didn't sound as though it had come from the auditorium. "I fly for thee and would not injure thee," she went on. "Where did yer get those shoes?" It was Ben Greet, yelling at her from the wings at the top of his voice! "Thou tell'st me there is murder in mine eye." She glanced out of the corner of her eye at Silvius who seemed not a bit surprised by B. G.'s behaviour. " 'Tis pretty sure and very probable." "Will yer look what she's got on her feet," Greet continued.

The leading actress in the company was Esme Biddle, a tall, beautifully elegant woman. She was engaged simply because she knew all the parts, but Flora thinks she was really rather good.

*Before the war, the director of a play was known as the producer. To avoid confusion, I have used the modern form throughout.

# FLORA

Members of the company were forbidden to speak to her outside the theatre and if they were to meet her in the street she cut them. It was still considered a social failing to be an actress and she gave no concession to the theatre when she was away from it. The leading men's roles were taken by several actors. Frank Darch played Romeo, Frederick Sargeant played Macbeth and Frank Denis played Hamlet. Ben Greet played Autolycus and Bottom, Prospero and Shylock. He considered the latter a comic tour de force and played it for all the laughs he could get! Flora played Lady Macduff, which *The Stage* newspaper found "excellent", Nerissa in *The Merchant of Venice*, and in *A Midsummer Night's Dream* she was cast as "dwarfish Hermia"! When I challenged Flora over what seemed bizarre casting in the case of the latter, for an actress tall enough to play Helena, she reminded me that Helena was considered the leading female role and, of course, Miss Biddle played her. As it happened, she was even taller than Flora. An unidentified critic of the time was to write, "The love comedy was brightly and spiritedly handled by Miss Esme Biddle – a too appealing Helena to be so long repulsed . . . and Miss Flora Robson whose Hermia had much of mettlesome grace vivifying its classic beauty and dignity . . . Mr Leslie French was an interestingly commanding Oberon, with an expressively vibrant manner of speech and a rare conceit of fun."

Leslie French and Vera, his sister, were Flora's constant companions. One Friday morning in Liverpool, where the company were playing during Shakespeare's birthday week, they went out to coffee together. When the bill arrived they were all horrified. It came to two shillings! Saturday was payday – it was the end of the week and they hadn't two shillings between them. Flora excused herself and disappeared to the ladies room. When she returned, she had with her a little pile of silver threepenny-pieces which paid the bill, together with a tip. The others were astonished. Where had she found them? It transpired that whenever Flora received a silver threepenny-piece in change or in her pay packet, she would put it to one side. At one town where they played her treasured collection was stolen. After that she made a pocket in her underclothes and carried her savings with her. How opportune for them all that she had!

One day B. G. was rehearsing Flora in a scene from *Romeo and Juliet*. At the point where Lady Capulet left the scene, Flora wandered away, thus forgetting a call Greet had interpolated into the scene of "Nurse, nurse". Greet stopped the rehearsal and called Flora on stage. He proceeded to lecture her on stage discipline in front of everyone. Flora was mortified. Some weeks later she made the same exit during a performance of the play. The company did not tour its own scenery and would make do with whatever the theatre had in its dock. Often this was quite unsuitable – Verona would perhaps be represented by a beautifully painted Windsor Castle and fields of cows. On this occasion there was a door in the set, where at the previous theatre there had simply been a gap between two stage flats. Flora, without thinking, made her exit between two flats. She walked straight into B. G. who stood glowering at her. "What d'yer think yer doing?" he yelled at her. "Why did yer come through there when there's a perfectly good door in the scenery? Why did yer walk through the wall?" Flora listened patiently. "A perfectly good door in the scenery and she walks through the wall. What were yer thinking about?" Flora held up her hand. "Nurse, nurse," she called, exactly on cue and then allowed Greet to continue with his tirade.

At another performance of the same play, in Tybalt's death scene where she had to weep over the corpse, she glanced up and saw the curtain was about to come down on her head. *"I quickly adapted my move and walked upstage crying bitterly. Julian d'Albie, who was playing Tybalt, was not so lucky. He opened one eye and saw the curtain was about to fall on his neck. Not wanting to risk a laugh from the audience in the midst of all that tragedy, he stayed where he was. Then one of the stage hands nipped on at the last moment and dragged him off by the ankles. So the laugh came just the same!"*

It was a complicated tour. No one seemed to know what was playing from night to night. Leslie French told me, "You went in your dressing-room and there was your bundle and you thought, 'Oh, we're doing *Macbeth* tonight!' B. G. came into my dressing-room one night and said, 'Leslie, d'yer know Ariel?' 'No, sir. I don't,' I replied. 'That's a pity,' continued B. G., 'Yer playing it tomorrow night.' I was the first man to play it for two hundred years. When Charles II came to the throne, all the boys were chucked out and the girls came on. So no boy played it from 1649 until 1922. Old Ben Greet was a terrible bully. He bullied Flora really rather more than he bullied any of us. And she didn't like him. I'm sure, though, that he realised she had something which needed bringing out. She worked hard and was tremendously conscientious. She was very vital with a great sense of fun, even then as a youngster. I didn't see Flora again for years, but when you meet her you begin exactly where you left off."

When the company was in Brighton, playing at the Palace Pier Pavilion, Flora was able to live with her family in Peacehaven. Leslie and Vera were invited to lunch and enjoyed the happy atmosphere of the Robson home. "We were playing in *Othello*," Leslie continued, "and she was cast as Bianca. The play was running quite smoothly and Flora came on and suddenly the whole thing was electric, the whole thing lit up. You believed in this fantastic young woman. You understood her background – it was *all* there! And that wonderful, gorgeous voice. There were no microphones and you had to be heard. If you weren't heard, the gallery would let you know. If there was one thing Flora could do, she could project, and not only project her voice, but project her thought. And that was a tremendous thing. I knew she would be a fine actress. It was in *Othello* that I first saw that tremendous depth, first noticed that lovely velvet voice. That's the one thing I remember in *Othello*. I can't even remember who played Othello."

Flora was not re-engaged for the summer tour. Perhaps Greet found her too difficult. Certainly, when she knew all her roles, she proved a conscientious actress but the very seriousness of her pursuit of excellence in her art set her apart from the rest of the company. This is not to say that the rest of the company were slack and haphazard. Most out-of-London companies would attempt to base their house style on what was viable in the current West End. This was carried to the extreme of actors imitating the voices, gestures and mannerisms of contemporary West End favourites. Flora would have none of this. She wanted to develop her own style and made her feelings known to Greet, often quite bluntly. With such idealism it was probably difficult for Greet to accept her physical limitations and he was not sorry to see her go. His companies had been the starting point for many great actors but each of them had to leave him before their careers blossomed.

## 5

The Robsons had made another move. David Robson loved his garden and found the chalky soil of Sussex too unyielding. He had decided on the new town of Welwyn Garden City in Hertfordshire where he was able to buy a small house. It was here that Flora returned to rest after her long tour with the Pastoral Players. Unemployment is seldom pleasant for anyone. Workers in other fields generally long for their holidays. Actors long only for work and would happily forgo a holiday for the opportunity of working. All pleasure, mental stimulation and fulfilment is derived from work, for the actor, and the end of employment means the loss of identity. Though there had been tough times with the Greet company, Flora had again learned to love the theatre. She had enjoyed the comradeship and the challenge and the indefinable quality of magic that comes simply from being a part of it all. Now she felt at a loose end and longed for another job. There was a certain amount for her to do, exploring the new Garden City and meeting the new people there. Many dances and parties were organized for people to meet their neighbours. Flora joined a ladies' choir called the Shrieking Sisterhood and a local theatre society. She played the Meggie Albanesi role in Galsworthy's *The First and the Last* with them. The society had been founded by C. B. Purdom, later critic for *New Britain* magazine, whose son, Edmund, would become a leading actor in Hollywood. With a few people of her own age, Flora formed a group of her own and they called themselves the Barnstormers. Flora had lots of ideas and the society proved a success, with capacity houses at every performance. The local criminal element were quick to recognize the Barnstormers' success. Five houses in a row were burgled while their occupants were at the play.

Flora was out of work for over a year. She made a little money putting on plays with local children. Although she continued to write to agents and managers, she was given no hope of work. One day she went up to London to ask Kenneth Barnes' advice. Flora remembers Barnes with great affection. He had continued to take an interest in her long after she had left the Academy. Considering the number of students who had come and gone in the intervening period she was fortunate to be remembered. He arranged for her to meet J. B. Fagan and Jane Ellis who had formed a partnership and were starting a new repertory theatre at Oxford, based in the Old Red Barn on the Woodstock Road which had been used as a big-game museum. Lila had a smart fur coat which Flora borrowed and she applied a good deal of make-up to her face. She was determined for once in her life to *look* like an actress. She learned speeches of Gwendolen from *The Importance of Being Earnest* and Kaia from *The Master Builder* as Barnes had warned her these were in the programme for the first season. After she had performed these, Fagan asked her to sight-read a passage from Yeats's verse play *The Land of Heart's Desire*. The play was completely new to Flora and her first reading was dull and unimaginative. Fagan then told her something of the play and gave her a second chance. All her early training in poetry came to the fore and she gave a fine second reading. Fagan saw that she was an actress who could take and respond to direction and he decided to engage her.

## 6

"God bless us!" are the first words uttered in Shaw's *Heartbreak House*, spoken by Nurse Guinness. They were also the first words to be spoken in a performance at the Oxford Playhouse, and they were spoken by Flora.

Jane Ellis had persuaded a wealthy gentleman admirer to put up the money to open the Playhouse and it had been she who had persuaded James Fagan to join her in the venture. She was despised by many of the actors for using such means to create work for herself, but without her ambition the theatre might never have existed. Fagan was, himself, an Oxford man, and a Bensonian, and had worked for many years as director of the Royal Court Theatre. The old museum had a cottage which backed on to it. This was converted into a backstage area with dressing-rooms. Fagan had erected a tiny apron stage with side doors leading on to it. The curtain was behind this apron, behind which cloths could be hung or a set erected. Any properties needed on the forestage were carried on, in full view of the audience, by a stage hand in a white coat, before the commencement of each scene. The audience were seated on rows of squeaky cane chairs.

The season had a false start. It had been hoped to open the theatre for the summer term but Dr Farnell, the Vice Chancellor of the University, declared the theatre out-of-bounds to all undergraduates, claiming there were too many distractions in the city as it was. This would have crippled the theatre, which closed before it opened. Flora returned to Welwyn convinced that Fate was against her and did not intend her to be an actress. When the Vice Chancellor's term of office ended that summer, his successor lifted the ban, and the theatre was able to name 22 October 1923 as its projected opening date.

The first day that any group of actors gathers is always exciting in its own way. The commencement of a whole new project like the opening of a theatre is extra special. Everyone is optimistic and ambitious. Fagan had gathered together a very young company, all of them eager and intelligent. It was such a different atmosphere from that of the Greet company. Flora immediately warmed to the director Fagan had chosen. His name was Reginald Denham. Florence Buckton and Dorothy Green, who had both acted at the Old Vic, were the leading ladies. Among the men were Earle Grey and Peter Creswell, and, from the OUDS, Reginald Smith and the diminutive Richard Goolden. Cast in the leading role of Captain Shotover was a striking young man, also from the OUDS, with a square jaw and unbounded Irish vigour. At the first rehearsal he put everything he had into his portrayal of Shotover, which he knew already by heart, flailing his arms about in extravagant gestures, emphasizing everything in a rich and over-projected voice. The company sat astonished at the display. At lunch-time, Fagan found a moment to take the young actor to one side to tell him that perhaps he had made a slight error of judgement in casting him as Shotover. He offered him the alternative of leaving the company, with no hard feelings on either side, or of remaining as the assistant stage manager.

## YOU ARE GOING TO BE AN ACTRESS

Many an actor would have found the second alternative too demeaning and would have graciously withdrawn, but the young man was fiercely ambitious to succeed in the theatre and agreed to Fagan's suggestion. He was not dropped entirely from the cast but exchanged roles with Earle Grey, who had been cast as Hector Hushabye. Along with Flora he was the youngest member of the company and his name was W. T. (known eventually to the world as Tyrone, and to Flora as Tony) Guthrie.

This was to be the first revival of *Heartbreak House*. Lena Ashwell, the Edwardian actress, had been appearing in the West End in a Shaw play. She had told Shaw about her father who was a sea-captain and he had based the character of Captain Shotover on him. The play had been presented at the Royal Court and Fagan suffered heavy financial losses. Before it opened at Oxford, its financial success was assured. Dr Farnell's ban had resulted in widespread publicity for the new theatre and the advance bookings were excellent. Flora's role as the old nurse was quite a small part. She was suffering from a bad cold the night the play opened and felt this helped get age into her voice. Richard Goolden remembered her wearing 'a not very convincing old woman's wig'. At the end of the performance on the opening night Fagan told the audience, "The company are all enthusiasts and love their work. If their work attracts you, we hope you will love them too." The critic of the *Oxford Post* certainly liked Flora's performance. "The Nurse Guinness of Miss Flora Robson was one of the most convincing things in the play," he wrote. "She gave the old servant a dry humour and a way of ubiquity which contributed greatly to the reality of the house itself." In the *Times* review, W. T. Guthrie was highly praised for his performance. Tony wrote home in haste to tell his mother that the reviewer had mixed up the names and that the praise was intended for Richard Goolden! "Poor, pathetic T. G.," he wrote, "was too bad even to be mentioned." Flora was never sure she really understood the play. She felt the same as Richard Goolden, who said, "It's a beautiful play, isn't it? I wish I knew what it meant..."

At the final performance on the following Saturday a very recognizable figure sat slap in the middle of the front row. While it was intimidating for the cast, it was greatly stimulating for the audience to have Bernard Shaw in their midst. In order to please the distinguished visitor, the audience greeted every line with gales of laughter and naturally the actors rose to the occasion. Shaw seemed strangely truculent at the end of the performance when the audience called for 'Author'. He told the audience that he was very pleased to see that Oxford had a 'highbrow' theatre at last, for if Oxford was not 'highbrow' then what on earth was it? He added that he was not speaking in reference to the University alone but rather wanted to stimulate a healthy rivalry between the town and the University. To the great amusement of the undergraduates he said that all the towns now had a greater culture than any of the Universities. Then he began to talk about the play. He said he was very sorry that it was in some parts so amusing. There was much laughter here. He had not, he continued, intended it to be quite so funny. And here the laughter grew. Laughter was a fatiguing thing, and he imagined he had nearly eliminated it from this particular play. Yet that night, *Heartbreak House* had seemed after all to be a very jolly sort of play; the actors had shown no heartbreak whatsoever and had portrayed a very jolly household. Shaw had written a sub-Chekhovian piece which had been interpreted as a comedy. The audience were not entirely to blame, the actors had been working for many of the laughs. Whenever the play is revived, it is played for comedy. Shaw's intention is not clear in the text.

Flora loved Oxford and walked enchanted through the old streets and squares. Everywhere there was an underlying sense of intellectual industry and she liked to identify with this continual striving for excellence. It was one of the most valuable qualities her father had instilled in her. It was not very long before that she had wanted to be a student at Oxford herself. She was thrilled at becoming part of it all. The second play of the season was one which would recur frequently throughout her career, Oscar Wilde's superb comedy of manners, *The Importance of Being Earnest*. This time she was cast as the Hon. Gwendolen Fairfax. An experiment was tried by staging the play in modern dress. Flora felt at a disadvantage as she found it impossible either to feel or to look elegant in modern clothes, and a Gwendolen without elegance is a ship without sails. "Miss Robson tried to enliven Gwendolen Fairfax," reported the correspondent of *The Cherwell*, "and at the same time to bring out the force of her words by assuming the drawl, conventionally ascribed to the 'fashionable'. But Gwendolen Fairfax cannot be enlivened and her epigrams only occasionally succeeded. "Flora felt she had failed with Gwendolen. With one notable exception she would never feel happy with herself in comedy. It is interesting that the exception would occur some forty-five years later in a production of the same play.

She was able to more than make amends in the next play which gave her the finest of all her opportunities at Oxford. She was cast as Violet Jackson in *The Return of the Prodigal* by St John Hankin. Faith Celli, the West End actress well known for her performances in *Dear Brutus* and *The Blue Lagoon*, who was joining the company for the

## YOU ARE GOING TO BE AN ACTRESS

next play, saw Flora in this role and told her that had she played it in the West End she would have made her name in that part alone. Unfortunately no manager would venture as far as Oxford to see an unknown actress. "Miss Flora Robson, who has not hitherto been called on to display any very serious capacity, rose to her part admirably as the stay-at-home daughter, particularly in the protest which she makes in the final act," recorded the *Morning Post*. Reginald Denham was very pleased with her. "*Reggie gave me a curtain call to myself. This was the first time it ever happened to me and I was tremendously thrilled. He gave me my first great boost of confidence with this gesture. Violet Jackson was the first part of the kind that, later on, for a time everyone expected me to play. She was my first 'unwanted woman'. Next we did* The Master Builder *by Ibsen. I was Kaia, the secondary part. Reggie had a gift for helping his cast to get the whole of the author's meaning. He was especially good with Ibsen. He talked quietly, pointing out all the implications of the scene. I can't describe exactly how he helped me in* The Master Builder *except that he made me understand just how that girl felt.*" "Miss Robson's Kaia was splendid," wrote the *Isis* reviewer.

Earle Grey and she made up the Chorus for de Musset's *No Trifling with Love*. This, and the secondary female role of Julia Melville in *The Rivals*, completed Flora's roles for the first term. "The Playhouse is now ending its first season," reported the *Oxford Magazine* in December 1923. "Of the actors, Florence Buckton, Flora Robson, Richard Goolden and Earle Grey have emerged with the chief honours . . . Flora Robson is the most natural of all." It had been a rewarding time. Flora had enjoyed a happy and relaxed social life. Tony Guthrie had introduced her to his dearest friend, Christopher Scaife, who was, at the time, President of the Oxford Union. She and Peter Creswell joined them for tea and Christopher sang for them. She found it difficult to follow their intellectual chatter, it was all rather above her head, but theirs was always stimulating company. She enjoyed being with Tony. Both he and she were rather shy people who pooled their lack of worldliness. He was taller than she and rather handsome in his own individual way. He talked with such vigour about the theatre that, even then, she knew that his was a notable talent. Tony was excited by her work and longed for her to be cast in something which would really test her capabilities. There were few opportunities for her in the second term. The first play was *Captain Brassbound's Conversion*, which had only one female role. The part of Lady Cicely was taken by Fagan's wife, Mary Grey, a large lady with a negligible talent. A member of the OUDS was brought in to play the American Captain Kearney. He was a tall, gaunt Canadian-born actor called Raymond Massey.

Shaw turned up at the first rehearsal and read the entire play through, himself, laughing loudly at all the jokes. Flora was allotted the job of prompt.

Her first acting assignment in the second term was Angelica in *Love for Love*. Jane Ellis, who normally played the ingénues, had opted for the rather more interesting role of Miss Prue and so Flora had the opportunity of showing her mettle in quite a different field. The casting of Valentine afforded Flora her first meeting with twenty-year-old John Gielgud. "Flora Robson, myself, and Reginald Denham are the only members of the Oxford Playhouse Repertory Company of 1924 who are still alive!" Sir John recalled to me in a letter. "Flora was always a brilliant actress and J. B. Fagan, who managed and directed the Playhouse, was very clever in discovering her, though as his wife, Mary Grey, was the leading lady in the company, I think Flora was not given as many opportunities as she otherwise would have had. She is a remarkable and versatile actress, underrated as a comedienne, since her greatest successes have been in emotional and tragic parts. Even in the early twenties her power and accuracy of attack showed originality and a very individual distinction which has pervaded her work ever since. She is as charming a colleague as she is a consummate performer."

"*John Gielgud was very kind to me from the first. Molly MacArthur, who was in charge of the costumes, also played small parts and always paid rather more attention to her own wardrobe than she did to mine. She was cast as Mrs Foresight and came out wearing beautiful clothes which put mine to shame. John took my part. He said, 'I don't understand why, when Flora is supposed to be the rich daughter, she has the poorest clothes of all to wear.' He very kindly showed me how to make the best of what I had been given by adding frills and so forth.*" The production was a success but the reviewer from the Isis felt he had "one trifling criticism to make. It regards Miss Robson's Angelica. Undoubtedly she played her scenes with Valentine charmingly but she did not sufficiently bring out the complexity of the character, losing thereby the full effect of her final revelation. She also lacks speed which is essential for Congreve." But *The Cherwell* felt "Angelica was charmingly played by Miss Robson, who steered her correctly past seduction, defamation, insanity and trickery into Valentine's arms."

There were two further parts in comedies. First of all she was cast as Lady Marden in A. A. Milne's *Mr Pim Passes By*. Richard Goolden scored a notable success in the title role but Flora was very unhappy in hers. Although later in her career she would be called upon to play many characters older than herself, at twenty-two she felt ill-equipped to assume age. Lady Marden was middle aged, and consequently more difficult to realize fully than an older woman might have been. The second comedy was *She Stoops to Conquer*, in which she was cast as Miss Neville. There was no part for her in the next play, Maeterlinck's *Monna Vanna*, and so she found herself in the prompt corner again. She tackled everything in theatre with the same spirit of enthusiasm, and as prompt made every effort to be the best there could be. One night she gave Peter Creswell a prompt. He was slightly deaf from the war and she wondered whether he had heard her. He picked up the cue and continued. Afterwards she asked him if it had been all right. He said, "It was as though the thought had come into my mind."

The last play in which Flora was cast that term was as Mary in the Yeats verse play which had won her the Oxford contract, *The Land of Heart's Desire*. Flora was to fulfil the promise of her audition with an excellent performance. I. L. H. in *The Cherwell* asserted, "An essential characteristic of Mr Yeats' verse is that its words depend for their poetic effect largely upon sound ... Not all the players gave the impression of recognising this sufficiently. Occasionally the lines were slurred and the fairy songs were at times inaudible. But Miss Robson atoned for much by playing as excellently as we have learned to expect her to do. She has a real feeling for the music of Mr Yeats' poetry and an understanding of that curious mysticism, which will hold the most rational and uncomprehending of audiences." Emyln Williams was an undergraduate at the time and wrote to me, "I remember, like a lot of people, the beautiful throb of Flora Robson's voice and her impeccable diction, at the Oxford Playhouse under Fagan."

Flora returned to the prompt corner for the last play of the term. This was *Oedipus Rex* in the Gilbert Murray translation. Tony was cast as Tiresias and had a huge success. One of the critics called it the outstanding performance of the evening and continued, "He alone of the players raised the drama to the real heights of tragedy and passion ... he *was* Tiresias." Flora and Tony were pleased that they were each able to end the term with a success. Flora went home for the vacation expecting to hear what her roles would be for the next term but eventually she heard that her contract was not to be renewed. Neither was Tony's. Fagan felt that, in Flora's case, the undergraduates wanted to see someone who was young and pretty and he had engaged Elissa Landi to take her place. It was a cruel blow. She had been so happy and now it was all over. She was not to know it at the time, but she had made some useful contacts. Tony Guthrie had recognized her true abilities and so had Reginald Denham. In his autobiography, *Stars in my Hair*, Denham would recall of Oxford during this period, "The best performances were given by Flora Robson. She never gave anything but a first rate one.

She seemed to see into the heart of a part – she would always give you a glimpse of truth about a character and when an actress does that she creates magic."

## 7

Some of Flora's friends wondered why she did not give up the theatre altogether as she seemed to get so little out of it. She was in a state of deep depression. Tony Guthrie also faced the fact that he was almost certainly not going to get anywhere as an actor. He answered an advertisement for a post in radio with the BBC, was interviewed by the Controller at Savoy Hill and offered a job. He would be one of the first members of staff of a new station in Belfast, only a few hours' journey from his mother and the family home. The job would not begin until September, which meant that he had the whole summer free and decided to use the time for a last theatrical fling. Christopher Scaife had written a rather sombre verse play called *The Triumph of Death* and Tony decided to present it in a barn theatre in Oxted, Surrey, which he proposed to hire. Christopher's elder sister, Gillian Scaife, already a well-known actress, was excited by the project and agreed to join. Robert Speaight and Cecil Bellamy, who were just leaving Oxford, and actor Guy Bolton were recruited, and Tony wrote to Flora to persuade her to join them.

The play was about a poet (played by Christopher) who was looking for a perfect form of love. Flora played a woman who was raised from a suicide's roadside grave. She was to personify love to him and would retain her immortality so long as the poet abjured the love of women. *"All I can remember of the part is that I longed to get back to the grave. The poet turned to me and said, 'I hate you, I hate you.' I collapsed on the floor with my head down. When he lifted up my head to kiss me, my face had changed to a skull. At a performance a woman in the audience fainted and had to be carried out! Tony played Death dressed all in black. When he came on in the dark I could stick the skull mask over my face. I did it at the dress rehearsal and as it was rather stuffy I crept off the stage to watch the rest of the play. At the performance I was lying there and I suddenly found I couldn't breathe. I had forgotten to make nose-holes in the mask! I lay there wondering what was going to happen. I couldn't move because I was supposed to be dead. I knew that the lights went down when Death went off and I could tell, even in the mask, when this happened. As the lights dimmed I managed surreptitiously to push the mask off my mouth so I could breathe."* The company were lodged in nearby cottages and they all enjoyed the summer weather in each other's company. This happy, carefree time was to help Flora over the rejection she had felt. At the end of it all they found that if the company were each to pay ten shillings and Christopher and Tony a pound, then receipts and expenditure would balance.

The optimism the summer had engendered soon began to drain away as Flora once more began the rounds. Then in August a call came through for her from Reggie Denham, who wanted her for a small part in a play he was directing for the West End, *Fata Morgana* by Ernest Vajda, in an English version by J. L. A. Burrell and Philip Moeller. Jeanne de Casalis, Malcolm Keen and Tom Douglas had the leading roles. Also in the cast were Ion Swinley, who had been in *Undercurrents*, Roger Livesey, and from Oxted in the summer, Guy Bolton. On the day after the reading Flora discovered that the part she had read, which had some comedy in it, had been given to another actress, and she was to play her role, that of an older woman. She was sure that the actress, Audrey Cameron, had engineered this change until Jeanne de Casalis told her that she and Tom Douglas had suggested it. She was to make friends with Audrey, who wrote to me, "My main memory of the play is that we always seemed to be rehearsing cast changes. Many of the cast complained of constant rehearsing but not Flora – she came willingly – to *learn* from the new methods of the new members of the cast. When she wasn't in a scene she sat and *listened*, *avidly*, to every word – she had the dedication of a nun. It is that dedication and the way she steeps herself in every part she plays that is the basis of her exceptional talent." The play, which opened at the tiny Ambassadors Theatre on 15 September 1924, lasted for 243 performances. Denham recalled Flora's playing in his autobiography, "As usual she gave a beautiful, sincere and convincing performance. Nevertheless after that engagement she had a tough time. She wasn't a typical ingénue and *Fata Morgana* hadn't given managers a chance to see her real abilities." He told her one day that he felt her greatest success would not come before she was thirty. "What do I do until then?" she thought.

The rounds began yet again. "Nothing today" . . . "What did you say your name was?" . . . "Oxford what?" . . . "Leave a photograph, won't you, dear?" . . . "Don't ring us" . . . "We'll let you know" . . . And she became more and more aware of other comments . . . "Sorry, dear, we're looking for a pretty girl" . . . "We don't think your face quite fits" . . . "We're looking for juveniles, not characters". As well as enduring all of this, Flora had to face her family each time she returned home to Welwyn. No one ever criticized her but she felt she was letting them all down. Her father wanted so badly for her to be a success. She was so far from proving herself the next Ellen Terry. In a way, all her ambitions at this time were on his behalf. Then one day there was a letter from Tony. He wanted her to go to Belfast to broadcast the title role of *Iphigenia in Tauris*. Excitement and gratitude flooded through her and she wrote her acceptance. Flora had always thought herself truly Scottish, although born in England. She had never seen Scotland until she made this journey to Belfast. She travelled to Stranraer and crossed the border in the crisp, half-light of early morning. There was a romantic mystery about the hillsides as she watched the waking countryside from the train. A white hare leapt through the chill silence. She arrived in Belfast by the ferry. It was her first broadcast, but Tony quietly guided her through it with all his new-found expertise. She responded readily to his ideas on the text. He was an excellent director and hers was a magnificent performance. Tony took her with him to Annagh-ma-Kerrig, the Guthrie family home near Monaghan. It was a greystone house set amidst forests, overlooking its own lake. Flora saw a different Tony here. She had seen the smart intellectual, the shy fellow actor, the accomplished director. Now she saw him, as James Forsyth in his book, *Tyrone Guthrie*, put it, "as the sober young squire-potential of the lands around the lake; and the big house with all its familiar Irishfolk, so friendly to 'Master Tony'. He obviously loved having her there. He rowed her out on the Irish lake, where the wild swans came. There were walks in the tall hushed pinewoods and quiet evenings beside the turf fire. It was a magic and memorable time for them both."

The clamour of London contrasted with all that peace. But she had to get back to the rounds. "Nothing today" . . . "What did you say your name was?" . . . on it ground. She took singing lessons and joined Captain Kelly's fencing club to develop her style. There were occasional visits to the theatre. John Gielgud had kept in touch and, together, they went to see a play starring Haidee Wright, and then Sybil Thorndike in *Saint Joan*. At the Shaw play they both burst into tears at exactly the same moment, when the page called out, "The wind, the wind" and the pennon streamed out eastward. The page was played by a hopeful young actor whose name was Jack Hawkins. It seemed a whole world away, the success of someone like Sybil Thorndike. Flora had attempted to attain that kind of success, but she knew she had failed and there was no future for her in the theatre.

One day a friend of the family, who taught biology in a boy's school, took Flora to the laboratories of London University where he spent his spare time in research. He introduced Flora to a colleague who wrote geography books to make a living and shared the same bench in the evenings. He told her how he wished he could devote his whole life to research. On the way home, Flora told him about her own frustrations. He suggested that perhaps she should reserve her love of theatre for her spare time, working with amateur societies, and

## YOU ARE GOING TO BE AN ACTRESS

find a job. Suddenly she began to see her life in perspective. It was time she stood on her own two feet. She could take a job and show her family she could support herself. She could return to the theatre. One day. Perhaps. She spoke to Captain Kelly about what was in her mind. He suggested she try to find work at the Shredded Wheat Factory in the Garden City. She resolved to write to the manager and ask for a job in personnel. After an interview, Flora Robson, at the age of twenty-three, turned her back on a life in the theatre and began a new career in the Welgar Shredded Wheat Factory, as a welfare officer.

# 2

# Out in the Cold and into the Furnace
## 1924–1932

### 1

ALL HER FRIENDS were very relieved when she took the job at the factory. "At last she's come to her senses. She's got it all out of her system. Now she can settle down to an ordinary life." It is difficult for anyone who has not pursued art as a way of life to understand that it cannot be equated with the day-to-day progress of a routine occupation. Had Flora lived amongst professional artists and actors she would have had her courage bolstered by the success of others. As it was she was gradually worn down by well-intentioned people who simply did not understand the nature of her talent. When, like a phoenix, she would rise from the ashes of her early career, these same people would bathe in reflected glory and claim always to have known that one day she would be a star.

The Home of Shredded Wheat, as the factory was known, was new to Welwyn. Flora did not think she stood a chance of getting a job there as she had no qualifications. Captain Kelly knew from teaching Flora fencing that she would stand her ground but never go into the attack. In his classes he stood her against the wall to make her fight her opponent. He pointed out that all the bosses from the factory were in the front row of the audience on Barnstormer nights. "Ask for a job," he told her, urging her to lunge and attack. "If they haven't a job they might create one for you." That is exactly what happened.

She was given several responsibilities. As receptionist, she met everyone who came into the building and directed them to the right department. She took visitors on guided tours of the factory and was

## OUT IN THE COLD . . .

the person to whom members of staff were advised to bring any problems or complaints. Flora would lend a sympathetic ear, try to understand the problem and take it to the management. One man had a lonely job where he met no one. He was pale and ill-looking. As she passed him on her rounds one day she asked him what was wrong. She was able to have him assigned to a different job on alternate weeks. She fought for the rights of the women on the staff, but with less success. When production was speeded up, the men were given a penny an hour extra and a longer lunch break. They were delighted with this arrangement as there were three million unemployed at the time: not only had they a job, but extra money too. The women were not given the rise. "*The speeding up of the machines meant that the girls had to work very much harder packing the biscuits into boxes. The girl at the end was never able to catch up as she was all the time pushing the unpacked product to one side. Whenever I had an hour to spare I used to go down and help them pack. The management did not like this, nor were they sympathetic when I pleaded the girls' case over the speeding up. I was accused of spoiling them, of taking the heart out of them. I said it wasn't a very good advertisement taking visitors round the factory, seeing sweat pouring down the girls' backs.*"

The workers began at seven and finished at six and had Saturday off. Flora began work at half past eight, finishing at five, but worked Saturday mornings. When she arrived all those people not actually working at that moment would come to the window and wave to her. In the lunch hour she would play dance music on the piano for the girls. Eventually a theatre was built in the factory, where badminton also could be played, and dances held. Flora had left the Barnstormers and formed a drama group amongst the workers. Many of them had never been to a theatre or seen a play. Flora chose ambitious pieces and her actors rose to each occasion. One of the plays she directed was *The Dancers*, in which Gerald du Maurier had scored a hit. Two of the actors needed to be trained in a tango. Flora remembered that her friend Vera Simpson had a sister living away from the Garden City who was trained in ballet. Muriel Baker was asked to come and set the dance. It worked perfectly in the play and Flora sent her a large box of chocolates. Eventually Muriel moved to the Garden City and become involved in the amateur theatre. She and her husband-to-be wrote one-act plays for amateurs to perform. This experience in scripting simple story-lines laid the foundation for a successful career, writing and directing films. Flora would meet them both much later when they were to play a crucial role in her life. As Muriel and Sydney Box they would obtain the means for Flora to bridge her difficult middle years.

There was a tough element among the workmen in the Garden

# FLORA

City. Flora would never walk home alone as she had to pass many other factories on the way. At that time, however, she had a formidable escort. Ernie Broadwood was Flora's boyfriend. His father had been a boxer and had trained all his sons to be champions. He had also trained the McLaglen brothers, one of whom, Victor, was a star in Hollywood. Ernie was very strong, with the quiet assurance of someone who knows his own strength. Flora would be more than a little nervous when he told her, "I'm dying for a fight!" though he would never pick a fight with anyone simply for the sake of it. *"One boy at the factory, really I suppose for fun, used to squeak the trays on the rollers as he fed them into the packing area. It made a disgusting, shrieking sound. It used to drive me mad. I don't think the visitors liked it very much either. One day I mentioned this to Ernie in passing. 'Is he annoying you, Flora?' he asked quietly. I saw the look in his eye and I said quickly, 'Don't you fight him!' He replied, almost casually, 'I don't need to fight him.' He just went up to the boy and said, 'Percy, I hear you've been annoying Flora . . .' 'All right, Ernie, all right,' stammered Percy. There wasn't another sound from him. He didn't even look at me after that!"* Ernie's parents didn't approve of his choice. Flora was older than he and from a different background. Probably she still wore the dubious description – 'actress'. Ernie married and went to work in America. He taught her to appreciate the art of boxing, which she has loved ever since, never missing a championship fight on television. During her time at the factory she saw quite a lot of him. *"He danced so beautifully, you didn't know he was there."*

During the day Flora had no time for introspection; her life was full and busy. But when she came down with a severe bout of influenza, she had a month in bed to brood on the emptiness of her life. She saw a succession of days stretching ahead of her, each as mundane as the day before. The alternative of beginning the rounds again and trying to convince all those smug, fat little men in their offices reeking of cigar smoke, of her worth, was not what she wanted either. These thoughts went round and round her head all day, and at night inspired lethargic nightmares. There was scarcely anyone to whom she could turn. She could tell her best friend, Kathleen Hill. Kathleen told her firmly, "You *will* get back to the theatre." And there was Uncle John. *"Uncle John was my mother's younger brother. I was fond of him since childhood. He was only fourteen when I was born and always made a special fuss of me. He had never been to school. His mother taught him to read. Even so, he became a clerk in one of the shipping firms. Grandmother MacKenzie was an ardent Anglo-Catholic. Uncle Alec was a churchwarden and Uncle John was a server. They had a wonderful man called Canon Osborne. He used to gather all the brilliant young men of the town around him and see that they found an occupation which suited their*

## OUT IN THE COLD . . .

*talents. He discovered that Uncle John could paint. He had been a sickly child and when the other children were bought bicycles he was given a box of paints. Osborne made him go to Art School. Eventually he became interested in entering the Church himself, and it was at this time he was taking steps to go to University. He understood my heartache. He had, himself, worked at a job which didn't fulfil him."*

The days dragged by at the factory even more sluggishly after her illness. All she had to look forward to was a holiday on the Continent. She and Kathleen had decided to go together. They saw Nice and Genoa, Lugano and Monte Carlo. Beginner's luck won Flora two pounds at the tables and she and Kathleen had champagne with their dinner and extended the itinerary to take in Rapallo. Flora looked with a tourist's eye at all the sights along the way and indulged the fancies of a romantic in each new atmosphere she discerned. But the actress, ever watchful inside her, made notes and memorized impressions of the people and the way they behaved. She watched how the Italians talked with their hands and tried to understand the emotions which could not be expressed in words alone. Perhaps she would have to play an Italian or act in an Italian play one day. It struck her that she had as much to learn from the people around her at the factory. A sense of everything she saw should be stored in a vault in her mind, in her everyday life as well as in exotic locations such as this. That was the positive way of looking at her life. The factory was either the end of everything or it gave her the opportunity of preparing for a new beginning. A greater awareness of living and of the quality of life could only enrich her work. Distance can sometimes lend enchantment. For Flora, it lent objectivity and a chance to reappraise the bare bones of her existence.

### 2

Shortly after her return, Flora enrolled for a course in Pelmanism. Her papers did not earn her high marks but it helped her train her mind on a positive goal. She had been given *carte blanche* in equipping the factory theatre. The most up-to-date book on theatre lighting was one written by the lighting director of the Cambridge Festival Theatre, the most ambitious, experimental theatre of the day. Flora had limited technical knowledge and emulated the Cambridge grid, as far as she was able, in her own theatre. The Festival Theatre, with its exciting programme of classical and modern plays, was much more interesting than was Oxford at the time. Fagan's theatre had degenerated into presenting pot-boilers and thrillers. The positive way to think herself back into the theatre was to choose a particular theatre as her goal and she chose Cambridge. She read all she could about it, found out which plays were to be performed there and studied the roles for which she felt herself suitable.

She was asked by the organizers of an amateur drama competition if she could suggest someone to adjudicate for them. She immediately thought of Tyrone Guthrie. It was now four years since *Iphigenia*. Tony had remained with the Belfast station before being asked to direct a touring theatre company, the Scottish National Players. He did occasional work for Radio Scotland and had tried to interest Flora in joining him to tour an hour-long radio programme entitled 'Divertissements' round the transmitters. He had succeeded in persuading her to perform it with him in Belfast in January 1927, and they had been thrilled to see their photographs in the *Radio Times*. The programme consisted of *The Drawback* by Maurice Baring, *Thro' Train*, a monologue which Tony had written himself, *The Tell-Tale Heart* by Edgar Allan Poe, and orchestral interludes. Flora had, however, been unwilling at that stage to give up her secure job at the factory, and there were no more performances. Tony was currently with the BBC in London, where he was employed as a script editor. Two of his own plays had been broadcast. The first of these, *Squirrel's Cage*, was a brilliant piece, years ahead of its time.

Flora and Tony were delighted to see each other again. Tony was vibrant and alive and even more vigorous than she remembered him. It was over two years since she had seen him. She was with him for much of the competition and enjoyed showing him her theatre. "That's the kind of lighting they have at the Festival Theatre, Cambridge," she said. As they watched the plays she would tell him, "That kind of setting would work very well at the Festival Theatre, Cambridge." "*After a while Tony said, 'What's all this talk about Cambridge?' 'Oh,' I replied, 'That's the place I most want to work.' He looked round at me sharply and said, 'Do you want to act again?' Without a moment's hesitation I answered, 'Oh yes!' 'Because,' he continued, 'I've just been appointed director of the Festival Theatre, Cambridge.' I was speechless. 'Would you like to be in the opening play?' he said.*"

Theatrical histories are rife with tales of coincidence and good fortune, but there can scarcely have been a more exciting moment in an actor's life than this. All Flora's hopes were centred on one goal and suddenly it was accessible. If there was one person in the whole of theatre with whom she had hoped to work, it was Tony. Such a remarkable juxtaposition of time, aspiration and opportunity could only mark the beginning of a new era. "*I felt like a champagne bottle ready to burst. I was beside myself with joy.*"

At this stage she did nothing to terminate her job. Tony would obviously have to discuss the matter with someone else. But as well as reading the plays, she began learning the leading roles. She kept

## OUT IN THE COLD . . .

copies of the scripts in her desk drawer so she could study when she was supposed to be working, and shut the drawer when anyone approached. Tony had told her that Peter Creswell, one of their Oxford colleagues, was now working for the BBC at Savoy Hill as a drama producer. Flora wrote to ask him if there might be anything permanent for her in radio drama, and outlined her brief experience. "I have now proved to myself that I can stick any kind of work," she wrote, "but I cannot possibly stick being out-of-work. I have a very well paid job in WGC but it is becoming unspeakably tedious. I have learned a lot about human nature and character which would be useful for acting, and I have produced lots of plays myself . . . If there is no possibility of work with the BBC, please do not hesitate to say *no* quite firmly." Creswell replied, telling her there was no such work, though a repertory company was being considered. Shortly afterwards, he bumped into Tony and told him of Flora's letter. Guthrie was interested as he had wondered if he was doing the right thing in trying to lure her away from the security of her job in Welwyn. As a result of this conversation he went to Anmer Hall, the man who would manage the Festival Theatre in its new regime, and suggested Flora as his leading lady. Hall wrote to her offering her an interview.

'Anmer Hall' was the pseudonym of Alderson Burrell Horne, the son of one of the founders of the Prudential Assurance Company. Ambitious to act in his youth, he had become a manager and was responsible, with Johnson Forbes-Robertson, for opening the Scala Theatre in 1905. His aim was to raise the standard of British drama and he had continued to give the theatre the benefit of his high ideals. Flora was called to interview in his elegant apartment in Albany. She was immediately at ease with the kindly middle-aged gentleman who told her, to her surprise, "I remember your excellent performance in *The Triumph of Death* in the barn at Oxted!" Flora saw there was someone else in the room. It was Gillian Scaife, who was Hall's constant companion. "Yes, wasn't she good?" Gillian said, "Hello, Flora, how lovely to see you." Flora had never felt more confident in her life. The small world of theatre turns in curious spirals. The coincidences surrounding this Festival Theatre season were mounting in an uncanny way.

The letter, offering Flora a season of eight weeks' playing, arrived a week later. The first play would commence in October. It would be the Italian masterpiece, *Six Characters In Search of an Author*, by Luigi Pirandello. She told only Kathleen and Uncle John her news. She knew she must keep on her job until the last minute as she would need the money. "*Everything was changing at the factory. It was being taken over by an American conglomerate. 'Time and motion' experts were visiting all departments. I wasn't popular with the management because, on too many occasions, I had taken the part of the workers. I knew they were wondering how to dispense with my services. I think they were rather miffed when I gave them two weeks' notice."*

Before she left the factory she took part in the annual tennis tournament, and, as always, reached the semi-final. Her Robson pride which would not let her settle for second place, had been swallowed in the past. As welfare officer, it would not have been diplomatic to win. But this year there need be no concession to such scruples. She trained every lunch-time with a good male opponent who plied her with the kind of shots her opposite number was noted for. In the tournament finals Flora won the first set but was beaten in the second. It was a close-matched, tense game. The final set was a battle to the death, but Flora was victorious. Her star was truly in the ascendant.

Naturally, doubts kept coming into her mind. At the end of the eight weeks she might be in exactly the same position as she had found herself four years earlier. There was a chance Anmer Hall might re-engage her, but there had been the same chance with Fagan. She would earn only three pounds ten shillings a week and she had been used to a secure income of six pounds. Uncle John was having doubts, himself, about going to Oxford to take up his studies for the Church. "Do you think I am too old at forty?" he asked. "Am I too old at twenty-seven?" she countered. Had she left it too long? Would there be any chance of making her name? As if in answer to these thoughts she came across a book on the life of Ellen Terry. Flora took courage from reading that Dame Ellen, herself, had left the theatre when she was twenty-one and had remained away for six years. She, too, returned to the stage at the age of twenty-seven and was on the brink of a glorious career "Our next Ellen Terry . . ."

One obstacle remained, *"I put off, time and time again, telling Father. There was only a week to go before my actual departure when I told him. He had often spoken with regret of the money he had lavished on my training but I didn't know how he would react. I had been earning my living and paying my way for several years now. Would he think he would have to support me again? I didn't make a speech. I simply said, 'Father, I've decided to go back to the theatre,' and added quietly, 'I've been offered a job.' Undisguised joy spread over his dear face. After a moment he said, 'You realize, don't you, that you will be on your own this time? I cannot support you.' 'I know, Father,' I said, 'I understand."*

## 3

On 20 September 1929 Flora wrote again to Peter Creswell. "I received your letter when I was preparing to come to Cambridge and

## OUT IN THE COLD...

I had no time to write. You will see from the above address that I am staging a 'comeback'. It is really through you that I got this job, so I owe you my heartfelt thanks. My first part is the Stepdaughter in *Six Characters* which gives me excellent chances for self expression after four years' exile. If I don't make a success, I am no good." The part was marvellous to play. At first, the Pirandello text had seemed incomprehensible, but she had persevered and was beginning to understand it. "*I had felt so much like that girl. It was as though I had been sitting in a writer's desk for years waiting for him to write me a play to act. My most difficult scene was a comedy scene where I had to laugh. I had to scream with laughter and derision. I had never had to laugh on stage before. I had always found it easy to cry but this was a technique I had not been called upon to use. I worked at it, and to some extent the comedy in the scene helped me, but the laughter, right up to performance, always seemed forced and hollow.*"

This was one of the few times in her life that Flora kept a diary. In it she recorded the excitement of meeting all the new people in the company. Tony had arranged for the company to work together for over three weeks before the first play opened, rehearsing completely the first two programmes and reading the following two as well. She was having a wonderful time finding her way round Cambridge and getting down to some acting at last. There was a recurring entry in her diary, "I'm terribly happy!" The actor playing the important role of the manager proved unsuitable and had to be replaced by J. Leslie Frith, and the actors playing the Leading Man and Lady in the fictional theatre company arrived only a week before opening night and had to be rehearsed. The last entry in her diary was dated 9 October – "Flat dress rehearsal, I was miserable about clothes." Along with the other actors Flora had to supply all her own modern clothes. As the Stepdaughter was supposed to work in a smart shop, Flora felt she should dress fairly well but, in the way of smart clothes, had only a rather respectable looking dress which was not right for the character of the girl. She was very unhappy about it and spoke to Tony and Anmer Hall as she had no money to buy anything more suitable. A shiny, black satin gown was waiting for her at the theatre the next day. It was exactly right!

There is an old theatre myth that a poor dress rehearsal generally heralds a successful first night. In this case it certainly proved true. Flora shone brilliantly in the finest performance virtually anyone in the audience had ever seen. Guthrie was to write in his autobiography, "Flora as the Stepdaughter gave an electrifying performance. No one who saw her in that part could doubt that here was the makings of a great actress... I visited Cambridge thirty years later, and a group of Senior Fellows over dinner recalled it with the sentiment which we all reserve for the exciting impressions of our youth. Unanimously they declared that in thirty years of subsequent play-going they had never seen a performance to equal its dazzling originality and force."

There was a schoolboy in the audience who had come to the theatre with his brother then up at Cambridge. They were so impressed by her performance that Flora was invited to tea. The schoolboy's name was Marius Goring. Among undergraduates who formed her audience at this time were James Mason, Alistair Cooke, Arthur Marshall, Robert Eddison, Geoffrey Toone, Patric Dickinson, Jacob Bronowski and Michael Redgrave – who would recall that Flora, as the Stepdaughter, was one of the sexiest things he had ever seen and would never forget her lolling against a stage ladder, taunting her father. Raffaello Piccoli, in the *Cambridge Review*, found her "Very modern, very human, very Italian". The *Cambridge Chronicle* reported, "There was a distinction about Miss Flora Robson as the Stepdaughter and it was a pleasure to hear her speak, for every facet was bright in a highly polished performance. It was plain that Miss Robson has a sense of word values and she aroused keen expectancy."

The two young people who arrived late to play the Leading Lady and Leading Man had both worked with Tony in Glasgow. The reason for their late arrival was that they had been rather busy getting married. Their names were Ella and Robert Donat. Ella Voysey, to give her stage name, or Ella Hall, as she is today married to eminent musician and poet Richard Hall, recalled Flora's extraordinary success in this role. "She was working with Tony whom she'd worked with before. This was the great relationship, in a way, of her life. The synchronicity of doing that particular part at that time at the beginning of the University year, I think hit everybody for six. Six characters! It hit them for six! Her overwhelming success was sudden and *complete in that one play*. She didn't have to do anything else. From then on she had everybody in her lap. She only had to walk on stage! It gave her more confidence than anything could have done. I think it was her strange, not necessarily ugliness, but her feeling that it was so, which gave her a kind of detachment that the undergraduates felt safe with. Hers was a tremendous depth of emotion that wasn't sexual. This, I think, was the core."

David Robson came up for a matinee. He tried to contain his pride in his daughter when Flora introduced him to Anmer Hall. Hall was generous in his praise of her. David Robson said he had known she had it in her since she was a small child. Flora walked with him to the station. "What did you really think of me, Father?" she asked. He looked round at her fiercely and replied, "You make them all look like apprentices, Flora!"

Flora Robson was home again, where she belonged.

## 4

"Several factors combined to make the Anmer Hall seasons at the Festival Theatre most memorably successful," George Rylands wrote to me. "The theatre itself was unique. It had been rehabilitated by Terence Gray, a man of substance and imagination and sometimes eccentric fancy. It was an eighteenth-century theatre, intimate and attractive. Gray installed a curved cyclorama which was quite unusual at the time. The big Victorian Theatre, the New Theatre, presented London tours, D'Oyly Carte and so forth. The Festival programmes were sometimes esoteric . . . contemporary plays . . . experimental . . . even fooling . . . I recollect an *As You Like It* with the hero and heroine as a boy scout and girl guide; could there have been a piece performed on roller-skates? There was a rather special restaurant. The programme had to be held to the light to be deciphered. The whole enterprise was fashionable and fun. But, of course, the Anmer Hall presentations were quite special – a cut above the regular, if varied fare, provided by Gray. These are what are remembered by Old Age Persons today. One's first chance of seeing Ibsen and Pirandello and Chekhov. The acting was admirable. Robert Donat, Flora, Tony Guthrie . . . on the threshold of their distinguished careers." There was somehow a feeling of predestiny in the air. One evening when Flora, Tony and Evan John, the stage manager, were together in their hostel, they each signed their names on a piece of paper and hid it behind a loose brick at the back of the fireplace. One day someone would find it when each of them was famous!

*Six Characters* played for a week and a half. Flora's next role was as The Scornful One in *A Woman's Honour* by Susan Glaspell, which acted as curtain-raiser to Gogol's *Marriage*, The *Observer* reported, "As two women who know all there is to know of feminine 'honour', Miss Margery Phipps-Walker and Miss Flora Robson performed with just that incisiveness that the play lacks." The following week the company toured this programme to the Oxford Playhouse and Fagan reciprocated with a production of C. B. Fernald's *The Mask and the Face*. The *Manchester Guardian*, in reviewing Dryden's *All for Love* the following week at Cambridge, recorded that Flora "brought domestic firmness and a convincing naturalism to Octavia".

The Stepdaughter had been one of the roles which Flora had committed to memory before arriving in Cambridge. The other was the title role in *Iphigenia in Tauris*. She was word perfect at the first rehearsal, which enabled Tony to spend more time on her interpretation than a week's rehearsal might normally have allowed. Apart from the radio broadcast, Flora had not worked on a Greek role since her Academy days. She had been unable to afford tickets to see Sybil Thorndike in any of her great performances in Greek tragedy and needed every minute to try to find the key. Naturally, as in everything she did, she looked for the real woman. Then she looked for the best means of lifting the emotion to match the epic nature of the play. Because the auditorium was so small it would have been inappropriate to use the size normally associated with this kind of drama. Consequently she developed a kind of amplified naturalism which was to form the basis of all her playing in tragedy. Robert Donat matched her with a tender Orestes. "*I have never known any actor work harder. The men had big parts every week; there were never so many for the women, so we might be the star one week and play only a small part the next. I also had jobs as stage manager and prompter. I knew from Robert's face when he needed a prompt; he would open his mouth and I would put the words into it. Invariably he crept round the back of the cyclorama to thank me. I asked him if he always did that, and he said, 'Oh, no! We hated the woman prompter in the Benson company and would rather say other lines than take a prompt from her.' His comedy technique was exact and he had a great sense of humour: almost too much, as he was apt to giggle and start us all off. This was partly because of the high tension we endured, working day and night. He was excellent in character but not so good at emotional parts which came too much from the outside. We worked together as two performers ideally suited, asking each other's help without ever thinking the other was trying to steal the scene. I knew then that he must be a star and that I was viewing his early struggles. But he was not a healthy man. He had a growth in his nose which interfered with his breathing, and he had no money for expert doctors.*"

The *Cambridge Chronicle* gave Flora a headline – 'Miss Robson's Success as Iphigenia'. The *Cambridge Daily News* felt that Flora combined "the dramatic intensity of her performance in *Six Characters in Search of an Author* with a definite beauty of lyrical utterance. The combination is by no means a usual one, even among actors of merit, as too many productions of 'poetic plays' testify. It is this combination alone that can make the sorrow of Iphigenia, torn between bitterness for the Greece that has wronged her and the Greece that is her only home, as real and moving as it is."

Again the company transferred to Oxford for a week. Both Tony and Flora felt a certain pride in returning to that University city with a notable production. Gilbert Murray, whose translation they were using, was appreciative when he came backstage after a performance. The reviewer of the *Isis* wrote, "As Iphigenia, Miss Flora

Robson was very moving. She used her beautiful voice with restraint, and never exaggerated either the tenderness of Orestes' sister or the austere devotion of the priestess. As Orestes Mr Donat was handicapped: bare legs are not easy to manage, and he was a little too self-consciously noble. But there, doubtless heroes often have no sense of humour."

"*As I stood on the high steps, with my back to the audience, the stage lights turned the cyclorama to the deepest blue, and it was as though I could see into the far distance. I had known my own exile and knew exactly how Iphigenia felt as she stretched her hands out to the sea.*"

This was to be the last part she would play in the first term. She prompted the next production, *Dandy Dick*. Although she had hoped for a part in *The Rivals*, the concluding presentation, even Julia was allotted as a reward to a student who had walked on in an earlier production. Evan John directed *The Rivals* and so Flora was asked to be responsible for the stage management. She had one small acting moment when she put on a mob-cap and stuck her head round a door to yell, "Mr Fag – Mr Fag!" She was disappointed not to be acting in every play. Ambition coupled with her successes made her restless. Her one consolation was in seeing Tony play Sir Lucius O'Trigger, a part he had played at Oxford, and in which he was supremely funny. It had been the favourite part of his notable ancestor, his great-grandfather, Tyrone Power. It was under his illustrious forbear's name that he had directed and played in his early Belfast broadcasting days. Perhaps it was fortunate that he did not retain this pseudonym as there might have been more than a little confusion in later years when his cousin Tyrone Power became a star in Hollywood. Ella Hall remembered one night during the run of *The Rivals* that Tony was so affected by Robert's giggling that they both shook with suppressed laughter. The epaulettes on Robert's costume bounced up and down!

How Flora admired Tony! "*He was not only a magnificent teacher but also a director rather like an orchestral conductor. Every instrument under his direction had its own importance and played in tune with all the rest. He taught me everything. He was my Svengali.*" More than admiring him, by now Flora was in love with him. She wanted nothing more than to be with him the rest of her life. She held out little hope for herself as Tony's cousin, Judy Bretherton, was often up from Tunbridge Wells. They made a marvellously witty couple and everyone expected they would marry one day.

Flora was relieved that she would be re-engaged for the following term. However, no retainer was paid during the vacation and she had to throw herself on her father's mercy again. She was happy to join John Robson and his family with all the others at Welwyn for a family Christmas. The first play of the Lent Term was *The Machine Wreckers* by Ernst Toller, in which Tony did notable work in the crowd scenes.

Flora prompted and used her time off from rehearsal to learn her lines for the next production, Shakespeare's *Measure for Measure*, in which she was cast as Isabella. Wrapping her cloak round her she would walk along the banks of the Cam, her book in her hand, always looking out for the rowing crews. "*Those lovely rowing men, so magnificently built! I would always know which crew was which by the sound of their oars as they hit the water. For example, Jesus College would crouch over their oars and jab at the water in short, quick strokes, whereas Pembroke used to have a very long stroke. They would always call to me. It was wonderful to be recognized! It gladdened my heart. Friday night was the rowing crews' night at the theatre. Everyone would say, 'Here comes Flora's audience!'*"

Evan John directed *Measure for Measure* in an experimental modern-dress production. Michael Redgrave wrote in the *Cambridge Review* that "Flora Robson was rather handicapped, as all good Isabellas must be, by having a mind subtle and sophisticated enough to speak the very difficult and subtle verse. It is the same handicap which occasions the platitude about a woman not being able to play Juliet until she is too old to do so. But in spite of, and because of, this, my admiration for her performance is unbounded." Ella Hall remembered, "The scenes between Flora and Robert, as Isabella and Angelo, were so moving that they lifted the roof off the theatre. Flora's was the most passionate, tremendous, electrical performance. But it was not necessarily Flora on her own, but what happened between her and Robert. It was generated between them." She noticed a change in Flora about this time. "Robert and I both felt at the beginning that Flora's self pity was overwhelming, and it seeped through in a way one wished it hadn't. It wasn't really necessary, but it was inevitable. It was part of Flora and part of her development. But she got over that stage very quickly."

The following week in the undergraduate calendar was set aside for the University bumping races. The Festival Theatre presented a burlesque piece to coincide with it which proved one of the company's greatest successes. The evening opened with *Box and Cox* but the main event was *Lady Audley's Secret*, with Flora in the title role. Many of the Press were not amused by this rather irreverent production which did not take the original as seriously as they had hoped. "Everything they did at the Festival was absolutely marvellous," recalled Geoffrey Toone. "People hadn't done pastiche versions of Victorian melodrama before. Their production of *Lady Audley's Secret* was the first of its kind. It was played straight, but

## ...AND INTO THE FURNACE

going right over the top. Marvellous!" Flora played Lady Audley in deadly earnest. It was the only way she ever felt happy playing comedy. She portrayed Lady Audley as a full-blooded tragic character which became funny simply because of the setting, language and plot.

Sir Michael Redgrave wrote to me, "I remember Flora from Cambridge days and one joyful memory is her performance in *Lady Audley's Secret* – and years on as Miss Prism. I don't know why it took so long to discover the exquisite comedienne." Arthur Marshall recalled, "From the moment she first appeared grinning fearsomely on the arm of Sir Michael Audley, the rich and senile husband whom she has ruthlessly ensnared, it was clear that here was a desperate character. In all this fantastic affair Flora was wildly funny. Poor Miss Braddon, on whose popular novel the play was founded, must have been twirling in her grave like a tee-to-tum. The asides, the baleful looks, the lines such as 'And now to resume the mask' followed by a hideously unreal smile. The moment when she pushed her first husband down a well, and put the lid on with a wild shriek. The timing, the economy of effect, the taste, all was perfection. I and my friends went night after night. Gradually, many of us who loved the theatre got to know her and she would come to tea in our rooms and be charming and merry. She had immense charm then, as now, and the entire first rowing eight of Pembroke College was in love with her to a man. I had a lovely evening with her and Robert Donat after the theatre when there was a fair on Midsummer Common and we three went on roundabouts and threw at coconuts. On stage their talents suited each other admirably, and we were in luck indeed!"

After prompting for *A Month in the Country*, she played the Mother in an anonymous fourteenth-century version of *Lancelot of Denmark* translated by Professor Geyl, which Evan John, who was responsible for the production, described as "a peep through an intricately Gothic window in order to see – men and women like ourselves". Robert was Lancelot and Ella was the heroine Sandereen. Completing the evening were Ninette de Valois, Stanley Judson and company in a programme of ballet. The *Cambridge Review* said of the play, "Especially striking was Flora Robson in the difficult part of the Mother . . . [she] might have been dull or wooden, but was instead dignified and almost terrifying; Miss Robson turns all she touches to gold." Prompting for Labiche's *A Pair of Spectacles* was followed by the Sybil Thorndike role of Elise in a Grand Guignol fragment called *The Medium* which Robert Donat directed. This short play accompanied one-act plays performed by Tony's former group, The Scottish National Players. Flora met for the first time several marvellous actors whose work she would always admire – Morland

# FLORA

Graham, Elliot Mason and Moultrie Kelsall among them. In *Le Malade Imaginaire*, the last production of the term, Flora and Margery Phipps-Walker had fun playing Françoise and Jeanne, the two maidservants.

Christopher Saltmarshe who, at that time, edited the theatre programme, instigated a poll in which audiences chose the plays for the Summer Term. It was an attempt to gain greater public support. Anmer Hall had been unable to make the theatre pay. He instituted several economies but, to her surprise, Flora's salary was increased to five pounds a week, only a pound less than her factory wage had been, and free accommodation. This time there was something for her in the vacation. Tony had written a radio play, *The Flowers are Not for You to Pick*, and asked Flora to play the leading female role in a broadcast from Savoy Hill. It was a very different play from her first broadcast, with modern, realistic dialogue. She learned the technique of intimate speech, using very little voice when necessary. The play was innovative in many ways. The leading actor, Harold Scott, used a stammer to distinguish his voice from others in a crowd, and there was extensive use of flashback. The play, written in a stream-of-consciousness style, detailed a man's life, as he became gradually repressed by prohibitions imposed on him, flashing past him as he is drowned. Tony dismissed his radio ventures as 'straws in the wind' and as 'canned drama' but there is no doubt of their influence in the development of radio drama.

After the vacation she returned to the prompt corner for Evan John's production of Ben Johnson's *Volpone*. She also appeared, along with Tony Guthrie and Arthur Terry, as a Magistrate in the court scene, wearing a long grey moustache and spectacles! The second play gave her the opportunity of another leading role in Pirandello, as Ersilia Drei in *Naked*. It was to be one of her greatest successes at Cambridge. *The Granta* called it 'flawless'. As she had done, when playing the Stepdaughter, Flora recalled her time at the factory when she had been longing to act. Ersilia believed that she was "Nothing . . . nobody . . . naked!" a sentiment with which Flora easily identified. The *Cambridge Daily News* declared, "Beyond dispute it is her finest performance since she came to Cambridge . . . She carries the whole weight of the play on her shoulders . . . the remaining characters have no existence except in relation to her . . . The eyes of her Ersilia will haunt us for a long time."

In *The Cherry Orchard* she was cast as Varya, Chekhov's favourite part. It was, like every role in Chekhov, rich with possibilities. The *Cambridge Review* found her "sensitive and intense almost beyond the general pitch of the production". She paired up with Margery Phipps-Walker again in *The Gentleman Dancing Master* by Wycherley,

As Mary Paterson in *The Anatomist*
'She gave a performance of such appalling beauty that she burst the play in two' – James Bridie
With J. O'Rourke and Harry Hutchinson
(Courtesy Mander and Mitchenson Collection)

*Six Characters in Search of an Author*
with Henry Oscar and Morland Graham
(Pollard Crowther)

Her 'little miracle' as Bianca in *Othel*
with Nicholas Hannen (Stage Photo C

At the time of *Dangerous Corner* (1932)

With Ralph Richardson in *For Servic Rendered* (Stage Photo C

Jim Harris and Ella Downey in *All God's Chillun Got Wings*.
With Paul Robeson

Douglas Fairbanks Jnr about to break the ice in *Catherine the Great*
(London Films)

With James Mason in *Measure for Measure* (Sasha)

With Charles Laughton, in his 'bearded lady impersonation' in *Macbeth* (Sasha)

The female strength of the Old Vic Company (1933–4) Elsa Lanchester, Athene Seyler, Flora and Ursula Jeans in *Love for Love* (Sasha)

# ... AND INTO THE FURNACE

as two common women of the town, Mrs Flouncer and Mrs Flirt, and had three roles, as Maria Isabel, Candelas and the Innocent, in the three acts of the Martinez-Sierra *The Kingdom of God*, in the translation by Helen and Harley Granville-Barker, which was directed by Robert Donat.

"Miss Flora Robson can hold her own with any actress on the English stage today," proclaimed *The Nation and Athenaeum* on 14 June 1930. "She is versatile without affectation, emotional without extravagance. We have admired her triumphs in Pirandello, in Shakespeare, in Chekhov and in burlesque. To these is now to be added Ibsen's Rebecca West; and there is no doubt that Miss Robson can inform the strange baldness of the translated Ibsen text with passion and significance, as remarkably as she can speak blank verse. Mr Robert Donat played the part of Rosmer with much feeling and sincerity . . . Anmer Hall's company will be sadly missed by the town and the University next year. Is there no London manager clear-sighted enough to secure the services of Miss Flora Robson?"

Playing the three roles in *The Kingdom of God* and rehearsing the Ibsen play in a week exhausted Flora. In the third and fourth acts of *Rosmersholm* she scarcely left the stage. She would sit up into the early hours of the morning at the back of the theatre where no one could hear her speaking her lines aloud. Evan John would often discover her when he locked up the theatre and order her to bed. He persuaded Tony to postpone opening night by one day to give her a clear day in which to work.

"Rosmersholm *marked one of my most painful moments on stage! I became the victim of Robert's giggling. Some time before, I had told Robert of a girls' school production of* A Midsummer Night's Dream *where the headmistress had changed the name of Bottom to Bothwell. It seemed that in every part I had thereafter the word 'bottom' would come up in different contexts. We would collapse in giggles in rehearsal every time it happened. Tony got very angry. I decided to cut the line in the next play that the word was mentioned. Robert laughed even more because he knew why I had made the cut. Rosmersholm was put on in May week. It was not a very suitable choice; it was boiling weather and the play was very heavy-going, but still, there we were. We got to the last act, where he proposed – I'd been working for it for three acts – and I had to say, 'I'm sorry, I can't. I have a past behind me.' To which he replied, 'Something more?' as if to say, were there five more acts coming! Of course, it brought the house down. Robert's face curled into an almost demoniac mask, but I managed to keep my face straight and went on. When we got to the end where they commit suicide together, I had to say, 'I'm going to the mill-stream. Are you coming with me?' 'Gladly' he* replied, lugubriously. He was all right, he had his back to the audience, I was still facing front! We went off to die shaking with laughter. Poor Margery Phipps-Walker had to continue the scene, looking out of the window, seeing the two lovers kill themselves in the river. All she saw was the two of us killing ourselves giggling!"

The next production was light-hearted fun, a specially written musical called *The Varsity Coach*. Everyone joined in. Tony and Ralph Parker, who now edited the programme, led the chorus of College Boys; Anmer Hall, under his acting pseudonym of Waldo Wright, appeared, as did Evan John, Gillian Scaife and Jean Anderson, who was now a member of the company. They were accompanied by Ella Voysey at the piano. Flora had played a number of fallen women and so the line of one of her songs went down very well – "I'm a woman with a past, pure . . . at last!" "As to the Festival, well, well, well," wrote up the *Granta*, "A year of the reign of Anmer Hall is ended. I don't know if he's coming back . . . I think you will all agree that [the company] entered into the life of Cambridge very effectively. I have seen a man clad only in a towel in the boat-house sweep back his hair with a gesture and, wringing his hands say, 'This is Flora Robson stuff'. Just as we used to tear open our shirts and, pounding our chests, cry, 'This is George Coulouris stuff.' As he passed through and above us I have heard men say, 'That . . . was Guthrie.'"

Robert Donat had chosen Paul Raynel's *The Unknown Warrior* for his farewell to Cambridge before going to London to try his luck. There was no part for Flora. She was truly sorry to see Robert go. Theirs had been an idyllic working relationship. Ella recalled, "With Robert and Flora it was never, 'If only she would do so and so' as it could very well be with anyone else. It was never like that." Robert paid Flora a beautiful compliment, rather devalued by his later problems with asthma, but meant most sincerely at the time. He said to her, "You are as easy to act with as breathing."

Originally, Anmer Hall's tenure at the Festival Theatre should have ended at the close of the Summer Term, but Terence Gray asked him to continue until Christmas. Flora was re-engaged. In order to assist the actors through the Long Vacation, Hall, by way of an experiment, attempted reviving several plays. *Lady Audley's Secret* and *Le Malade Imaginaire* were presented, but attendance at the latter was poor and the scheme was abandoned. During the previous term, Flora had befriended Robert Eddison, who badly wanted to go into the theatre. His mother was unsure of his chances of success. When she visited Cambridge, Robert introduced her to Flora, who spent some time talking to her. Remembering her father's pride in her she told Mrs Eddison that one

## ... AND INTO THE FURNACE

day she would be collecting all Robert's reviews and sticking them in a book. Robert spoke to Anmer Hall and he joined the company at the beginning of the long vacation. Some years later, Mrs Eddison showed Flora the book in which she had kept everything written about Robert.

Tony told Flora to learn to play the guitar during the vacation. When she returned she told him that she had been able to afford neither a guitar nor the lessons. He sent her to a teacher with the instruction that she should know how to accompany herself in the song, 'Sourabaya Johnnie', by the end of the week. The teacher said this was impossible. Guthrie was enraged. He thought a week long enough for anyone to learn anything. Flora did her best and was able to strum chords by the time *Warren Hastings* opened on 10 October, exactly a year to the day since *Six Characters* opened. *The Gownsman* felt that Flora, in the only woman's role, "was less successful than usual in a part that needed more feminine charm and less strength of character than Miss Robson could supply." Undergraduates would ask her eagerly, "What are you playing next week?" "Nothing very much," was the only reply she could give them this term. It was as though Tony had only envisaged Flora in a prescribed set of parts, and she had played them all. He had built her up and was now not interested in her. He had brought Marion Anderson from the Scottish National Players to play the roles Flora might have played. Gillian Scaife co-directed with Tony the English premiere of Jacinto Benavente's *Constanza* the following week. Flora was the Duchess of Berlandia in a false nose and a wig. She felt hers was a dreadful performance as she had no talent for superficial playing. Tony insisted that she play her as a caricature.

Anmer Hall's son, David Horne, had joined the company and designed, directed and played the leading role in Leonid Andreyev's *The Thought*. It was a magnificent vehicle for a strong actor and he played it with great panache. Flora felt inadequate as Tatiana. There was a moment in the play when she and a servant had to stand by and watch a murder committed. Flora could not understand why they would not rush forward to prevent the crime or cry for help. Horne told her that she and the servant should cling together as though hypnotized with horror. Flora was not convinced but she did as she was told. The magic seemed to have gone out of the Festival Theatre. In play after play she was dissatisfied with herself. Maurice Browne, a London manager, came to see *The Thought* and asked David Horne if he would come to London with the play in the new year. Horne insisted that the rest of the company be asked too, his father's son in thinking of the well-being of all the company. Browne was sufficiently impressed by the production as a whole to extend the invitation to the rest of the cast. Flora was relieved to have an opportunity of moving on.

Another melodrama was chosen to try to repeat the success of *Lady Audley's Secret*. Tony chose W. Thompson Townsend's *Temptation, or The Fatal Brand* and Flora was cast as Elise, the villainess. When Tony was staging the curtain-call he asked Flora to snatch a bouquet from the heroine. Flora thought this very cheap business and refused to do it. It blew up into a row between her and Tony. She had been annoyed with him over the question of learning the guitar, and at his insistence on making the Duchess so two-dimensional. This was the final straw in what had suddenly become a difficult and strained relationship. The ill-feeling lasted until the next day. He said, "Let's go for a walk." They walked by the river and aired the whole matter. As they walked on, Tony asked Flora if she would marry him. Flora was surprised, and thrilled too. "We all thought it was to be Judy," she said. It seemed that, on the contrary, it was Flora he loved. Flora told him that she would like a family, lots of children, and she would need to retire from the stage to bring them up. He said he had not envisaged children, that he hoped they would lead a stellar life together in the theatre. Flora said neither 'Yes' nor 'No' but both assumed that they were engaged.

Flora was in the prompt corner for *A Doll's House* and enjoyed watching Gillian Scaife, who was an accomplished Nora. She had only a small role, as Tomkah, in the next play, *Tobias and the Angel*, but it afforded her a meeting with a man who would change the course of her life. His name was James Bridie. He travelled down from Glasgow for the dress rehearsal of his play. Later he wrote, "I sat down beside Tobit who, I was charmed to find, was Anmer Hall himself, masquerading under one of his soubriquets. He had a delightful free-and-easy family-party sort of company. One of them was a tall girl who reminded me of an Irish terrier. She went galloping about with cups of tea for the thirsty in one hand and a needle and thread for the ragged in another. All she had to do in the play was sing a song; but she had constituted herself honorary maid of all work to the company and a general good influence. Guthrie whispered to me, 'You must write a play for Flora Robson some day. Nobody knows it but me, but she is going to be a great actress.'"

The last production at Cambridge was Tony's first attempt at Shakespeare. Flora was cast as Mistress Ford in *The Merry Wives of Windsor*. "The two wives were well played by Miss Gillian Scaife and Miss Flora Robson," reported the *Cambridge Daily News*, "Both were as good as anything they have done. Cambridge will lose them with perhaps more regret than any members of the company." "A small tribute is due to Mr Anmer Hall and Mr Tyrone Guthrie,

# ... AND INTO THE FURNACE

whose fifteen months' work for this theatre is now regrettably at an end," wrote the correspondent of the *Manchester Guardian*. "Mr Guthrie's qualities as a producer await a serious and patient analysis. Mr Anmer Hall's enterprise and geniality have been immediately and continously enjoyed. To both is due the credit for allowing us to watch week by week, the development of Miss Flora Robson, an actress whose control of several techniques is already consummate and should no longer be denied general recognition."

It was all over. Tears of sadness welled up in her. She would leave behind so much that had seemed to have become a part of her. She had made many friends but, as always in the theatre, she would leave them behind or they would move on elsewhere. She packed her bags and took a last look at the river and then returned to the real world.

## 5

The real world, on a dull December day in London, was a cold and cheerless place. Even the familiar faces from Cambridge seemed strange in alien surroundings. Flora had been relaxed and comfortable with them at the Festival Theatre; now she was conscious of her polo jersey and tweed coat, neither of which seemed suitable attire for an actress who had come to play the glamorous Tatiana. Maurice Browne's Little Theatre was in John Street, near the Gray's Inn Road. There were ten of them from Cambridge and only small roles, walk-ons and understudy duties for Browne's resident company. As this company included actors such as Alistair Sim, Margaret Rawlings, Catherine Lacey, John Clements and Reginald Tate, none of them can have been very pleased to be usurped by a provincial theatre company of unknown actors. Flora hadn't enjoyed playing Tatiana before and, as David Horne would once more be responsible for the direction, she knew she was not going to find it any more fulfilling.

The first performance of *Betrayal*, as the Andreyev play was retitled, was an unhappy experience. Flora had been allowed fifteen pounds to purchase the three outfits she needed. Almost all of it went on a fashionable coat. She had a red silk dress she had bought for a Cambridge play and was able to afford a new full-length black taffeta skirt. One evening she went to Mr Henderson, her parents' next door neighbour, to ask his help. His collection of costumes was rather old fashioned, marvellous for dressing-up games with the children, but not particularly suitable for a fashionable, attractive woman. However, he pulled out a short Chinese coat which actually suited her quite well. She felt desperately unhappy about her makeshift wardrobe. At the dress rehearsal Maurice Browne told her he had

# FLORA

arranged for a friend of his to take Flora shopping in Mayfair. They were able to find a glamorous tea-gown, which cost forty pounds. Browne was delighted with it and the gown was returned to the salon for minor alterations. The second dress rehearsal proceeded. Robert Eddison recalled that Browne had working with him an American lady called Ellen Van Valkenberg. At the end of the rehearsal she told them all, "You have none of you any idea of the architectonics of motivation". No one had the slightest idea what she was talking about! The next morning Flora was sent to Elizabeth Arden's, at the management's expense, for a complete beauty treatment. When she arrived at the theatre for the first performance she *felt* beautiful. There were telegrams and flowers from friends at Cambridge. But the tea-gown had not arrived. A messenger was sent to the shop to collect it. The salon was locked and there was no sign of anyone there. So Flora had to go on in the taffeta skirt and Chinese coat. She felt dreadful. There was business lighting a cigarette by a taper from the on-stage stove. The fire-officer had forbidden the use of either a taper or a match only hours before the performance, when Flora was at the beauty salon. It seemed ages before the property match she was given would light from the tiny night-light at the back of the stove. Flora was sure she had ruined the play. The audience was strangely cool and she felt she was a total failure.

David Horne was given a tremendous ovation at the end of the performance. Flora wandered slowly back to her dressing-room. She was invited to a first-night party at a nightclub with David and Maurice Browne. Ordinarily she would have been excited as she had never ventured into London night-life before. But she was heavy with her lack of success. The cheers she had won at the Festival Theatre echoed cruelly in her memory. They seemed to be mocking her now. She slipped out of her despised costume and put on a dressing-gown. Her Elizabeth Arden face looked like a mask in the mirror. There was a tap on her dressing-room door. She really felt she couldn't see anyone, but pulled open the door. A thrill of joy surged all over her body. "*There stood seventeen beautiful men – the Pembroke College Boat Club, all of them wearing white ties, tails and opera hats!*" When Maurice Browne came to collect her he found the tiny dressing-room bursting with happy, laughing undergraduates. Flora painted the town red that night and woke the next morning with her first, and very dreadful, hangover.

James Agate, in *The Sunday Times*, found *Betrayal* "exactly the type of play which should be put on at an experimental theatre . . . Every moment of it was good theatre, it was beautifully produced, and the acting was as good as anything seen in London for a very long time . . . Miss Flora Robson played the difficult part of the wife with

## ...AND INTO THE FURNACE

high perception and tact... As Kerjentzeff Mr David Horne, giving a performance of great imagination and super-abundant power, was recalled many times, and I advise any playgoer who appreciates an extremely interesting and unusual play, brilliantly acted, to visit the Little Theatre. I also advise him to go quickly."

Agate was an influential critic and the audiences responded. The run of the play was extended by a week to five weeks. Nevertheless all Flora's anxieties about the future returned. She dreaded the thought of setting out on the rounds again but she knew it was almost inevitable. Reginald Denham had advised her to write a letter every day to managers. The discipline was good for morale. "You might write fifty letters and get one reply," he had said, "but keep on writing." One manager, to whom she had written, was Peter Godfrey, who ran the Gate, a small club theatre under the arches at Charing Cross. He had written back to inform her that his next play had only one female role and he had already cast Marie Ney. She knew that the Little's resident company would return at the end of *Betrayal* but asked Maurice Browne to consider her for the small secondary part of Giovanna in Clifford Bax's *The Venetian*, which he was putting on for Margaret Rawlings. Browne engaged her, offering the salary of seven pounds per week. Rehearsals had begun when she received a letter from Peter Godfrey. Would she call in to see him? Marie Ney had been offered an engagement at the Old Vic and he had released her. Would Flora like to take over the role? He had called in at the Little Theatre and stood at the back to watch Act One of *Betrayal*. Flora wondered what he could have seen, as she scarcely spoke in the first act. He said he had seen that she could act in a small theatre.

She badly wanted to accept what was an excellent role but the Gate could afford to pay only three pounds which was less than her original Cambridge salary. The performance would end too late to allow her to catch the last train back to Welwyn, and her reduced circumstances precluded finding decent lodgings. Old friends came to the rescue. Robert and Ella Donat had a small flat on the top floor of a house in Seven Dials, only minutes away from the Gate. Robert had played in *Knave and Queen* for a short run at the Ambassadors. There had been a success in an adaptation of Mary Webb's *Precious Bane* at the Embassy Theatre, another of the small experimental theatres, but now Robert was out of work. With a baby on the way, a share of Flora's salary would help them all survive the winter. She would sleep on the sofa and Ella would cook for them all. She asked Maurice Browne for her release and accepted Peter Godfrey's offer.

The play had been banned by the Lord Chamberlain's office and could only be presented by a private club theatre. It was Eugene O'Neill's *Desire Under the Elms*, and Flora was cast as Abbie. Ephraim

# FLORA

Cabot, a hard New England farmer who has fought for survival on his bleak, barren farm-lands, brings home a new wife, Abbie, much younger than himself. He has three sons, two cast in the mould of their father, who up and leave the farm early in the play, and Eben, the youngest, who has inherited the fine qualities of his mother. Abbie is in her thirties, is unattractive and has been left on the shelf. She married Ephraim for the opportunity of having the home she never thought would be hers. She falls in love with Eben and eventually bears his child. The old man thinks it is his. Before the play ends Abbie murders her own child in defiance of the old man and she and Eben go off to face trial and execution together. "*Sometimes one speech will give me the clue to an entire role. Abbie had a long speech about how she had worked all her life in other people's homes and had married the old man to get a home of her own. When I first rehearsed that speech I made it very dramatic. Peter Godfrey showed me I was wrong. He said the people on that New England farm would repress all emotion in their talk. I was terribly slow learning to speak in a slow, monotonous way – but when I finally got it I found that I had the whole woman's character. I knew how she felt.*" Tony Guthrie had had a most disconcerting habit of leaving Robert and Flora to rehearse love scenes alone. He was embarrassed by them and would always invent an excuse such as going to rehearse the students. It prepared Flora for working with Godfrey, who would leave her and Eric Portman, cast as Eben, to work up their scenes together. They would work on the stage, never knowing whether Godfrey was at the back or not. One day a voice came out of the darkness, "That's right," it said. "That's exactly right. Now leave the scene entirely alone. The rest of the play will be quite straightforward now."

"Miss Flora Robson, who has brought high reputation from the Cambridge Festival Theatre," wrote the correspondent of the *Manchester Guardian*, "gave a beautiful performance as the old man's bride. She gave the part the right elemental animal quality, and yet raised it when needed to meet the raptures of a true love which gives great magnanimity in the end." Ivor Brown, in the *Observer*, thought her performance a remarkably fine one. "She composes a most impressive mask for the part, heavy, as befits the stony ground of the Cabot acres, and yet flashing in her moments, since the rock is igneous. Miss Robson keeps a wonderfully firm hold on the part, which shows great judgement, since Mr O'Neill is apt to let his emotions run away with him."

She was a success indeed! She was pleased to welcome Kenneth Barnes and his sisters backstage, Phyllis Neilson-Terry and Sara Allgood. Sally, as she preferred to be called, burst into her dressing-room, her face streaked with tears and mascara. It was the kind of

# ... AND INTO THE FURNACE

part she would have loved to play in her early days at the Abbey Theatre. There were fan letters from Alistair Cooke and Raymond Massey and then a visit which thrilled Flora more than any other. Christopher Casson, who had been enormously impressed by her performance, had persuaded his parents, Lewis Casson and Sybil Thorndike, to see the play. It was impossible to get tickets but chairs were set up for them at the side. Dame Sybil was to recall thirty-five years later, "I remember the show very well. It was the first time I had seen Flora and I was absolutely knocked sideways. The play was very wonderful and when I saw her she looked extraordinary. I thought, my goodness, here's a new sort of face in the theatre. And what a tragedienne. I remember saying to Lewis, 'We've got a tragedienne who's going to be as big as Edith Evans is in comedy.' I went round afterwards and saw her. I was really bowled over by it and she said to me, 'Could I understudy you in *Saint Joan?*' which we were reviving. And I said, 'No! No, you're much too good for that, don't be so silly.' And then I said to her, 'Where did you learn to act?'" Flora smiled at her. "Don't you remember?" she said, "You taught me at the Academy of Dramatic Art and wrote me a letter of introduction." Sybil stared at her. "I cannot remember you at all," she said. She concluded her later recollection by adding, "She didn't learn it. She knew it."

"*Sybil Thorndike was the first actress to welcome me, with her great generosity, to London. She sat in my room and I poured out my troubles to her, saying, 'I can't get anybody to come and see me act and I'm afraid it's all going to end here. She said immediately, 'I'll send someone to see you.' Well, she did.*" A man from Rudolph Meyer's office saw the play and arranged for her to have an interview with Meyer, as a result of Sybil's promise. Meyer was casting for a West End production of *Precious Bane*. Robert Donat had been offered the same part he had played at the Embassy and both of them were extremely excited at the opportunity of working together again. Her hopes sank as she was shown into Meyer's office. As soon as he looked at her she knew he had been expecting someone pretty, though the part was that of Prue Sarn, the girl with a harelip. "Can you look seventeen?" Meyer asked her. "I've never looked seventeen, even when I was seventeen," replied Flora, "but I could act seventeen." Meyer was not prepared to take the risk of presenting the play with two unknown actors and cast Gwen Ffrangcon-Davies, seven years Flora's senior, in the role. It was this play which made Robert Donat a star.

A film producer, Sinclair Hill, saw Flora at the Gate and offered her the part of a middle-aged French woman of the world in *A Gentleman of Paris*. It was strange casting and Flora was not really surprised, when she reported for filming, that the director could not see the quality Hill had seen in her. A letter arrived to inform Flora that a star would be cast in the part. It was ironic that the job went to Sybil Thorndike.

Peter Godfrey asked Flora to remain at the Gate for his next production, which was of Oscar Wilde's banned play *Salomé*. Flora would play Herodias, with her old friend Robert Speaight as Herod, John Clements as Jokanaan, Margaret Rawlings as Salomé and a cast which also included Esmond Knight, Norman Shelley and Rodney Millington. Ninette de Valois was responsible for staging Salomé's dance and for presenting a programme of 'Danses Divertissements' after the play with herself and Hedley Briggs.

Flora had received an invitation from the Pembroke Boat Club to be their guest at the last day of the bumping races. A friend was able to drive her up as she was in the early stages of rehearsal. D. H. Booth, later Archdeacon of Lewes and Chaplain to the Queen, and Eric Drake, now Managing Director of British Petroleum, were in the rowing crew. "My college, Pembroke, had just gone head of the river," Sir Eric recalled. "When we were resting on our oars, having reached the Pike and Eel which is the ferry at the end of the course, someone in the bows of the boat saw Flora standing on the bank and waving to us. He tapped 2, 2 tapped 3, 3 tapped 4, and so on all the way down. I was 7, I think. I got the tap in the end and we all turned round and waved at her." "*I think this really was the greatest and proudest moment of my life – at that moment standing in the crowds at the side, and the whole boat turned and waved to me! I was so happy, I nearly fell in the river!*" Pembroke won the races and burnt their boat that night in celebration.

A few days later, Flora was asked to make a test for British Instructional Films, whose studio was at Welwyn. Lady Oxford had invited Flora to one of her celebrated parties and introduced her to her son Anthony Asquith, the film director. 'Puffin' Asquith had begun his career in 1928 and had recently completed *Tell England* on which Muriel Box had worked as a continuity girl. He was now preparing a film version of Compton Mackenzie's *Carnival* and was interested in Flora for the part of Mrs Raeburn, the mother of the heroine, who was to be played by Ann Casson, the daughter of Sybil and Lewis. The test was a success and Flora prepared to make her first film, after the play had opened.

*Salomé* was not a great success. Flora agreed with the critics who could not see anything in the play to justify its scandalous reputation. "Can it be that, in refusing to countenance this febrile fantasy, the censor was saving us not from ourselves, but merely from a smothered yawn?" asked the *Observer*. "This production seemed to me to stress the poverty of Wilde's dramatic invention and to expose a sterile

### . . . AND INTO THE FURNACE

imagination. . . . Salomé's dance, . . . though undertaken by Miss Margaret Rawlings in no prudish spirit, seemed of a nature to warm a professor of calisthenics rather than to convulse an unholy hedonist. And although Mr Robert Speaight wore the Tetrarch's gilded sackcloth and scarlet wig with notable apprehension, and Miss Flora Robson winked gilded eyelids as his angry queen, this picture of a barbaric court seemed curiously suburban. The piece, in short, seemed a windy curio, hollow at heart and shallow in beauty as a splash of oil that glisters on a puddle."

Anmer Hall occasionally invited Flora to his country house in Sussex for the weekend. He was planning the opening of a new theatre at Victoria and wanted Flora to join a permanent company there to do the kind of work they had done at Cambridge. Flora would have a twelve-months-contract at £8 a week beginning in the autumn. She was in very good spirits when she began work on the film. Each morning she would cycle from her parents' home to the studio, passing the factory on her way. Many old friends would lean out of the windows and wave. They had seen her name in the newspapers after *Desire Under the Elms* and now she was making a film. As far as they were concerned she was already a famous star. The film was called *Dance Pretty Lady*, and was the story of Jenny Pearl, a little Cockney girl, who became a ballet dancer. Flora played the mother with a light Cockney accent, and a gentleness with the camera taught her by Asquith. In this film one is conscious that here is a different kind of actress. Contrasted with the comedy film 'types' in her scenes, her qualities of warmth and earthiness make a great impression. It is a fine film with excellent photography by Jack Parker and clever editing. The atmosphere of turn-of-the-century London is brilliantly evoked and there are some of the first ballet sequences on film, staged by Frederick Ashton, with the Marie Rambert *corps de ballet*. When filming came to an end, Flora set off for the Isles of Scilly with her sisters. It was her first holiday for three years and she returned, relaxed and refreshed, to begin work at Anmer Hall's new Westminster Theatre.

### 6

Tony Guthrie was, of course, engaged to direct the first play. Shortly before rehearsals began he had married Judy. Nothing further had been said about his supposed engagement to Flora. In fact he had asked several others to marry him before he settled on Judy, who had always been his family's choice. She was almost as tall as he and was so much a part of his life that each would end sentences the other had begun. To many they seemed more like brother and sister than a married couple. Flora had not lost her feeling for Tony but accepted the turn in events as philosophically as she could.

Flora's first success in the mainstream of theatre had been her performance in *Desire Under the Elms*. It had been seen by a very limited audience. The Gate was a club theatre where only members and their guests were able to see the play. Her first public success was at the new theatre and the opening night was just forty-one days short of the tenth anniversary of her debut in *Will Shakespeare*. Her emergence in *The Anatomist* was not the overnight success some imagined, but the result of an amalgam of years of dedication and despair, of fierce ambition and recurring failure. In this, the least secure of professions, there can be no finer example for the struggling actor than the ten years that led to Flora's first recognition by the theatre-going public.

Among the many actors who wrote to me there were few who didn't cite this performance as being one of their most enduring theatre memories. Sir Alec Guinness wrote, "I first saw her playing a small part, with Henry Ainley, at the Westminster Theatre in Bridie's body-snatcher play, and I can *still* see her in it." George Coulouris wrote, "I admired Miss Robson from the time I saw her in *The Anatomist*, as she walked across the stage singing to herself in a low voice." Emlyn Williams wrote to me, "I knew she would be a star from her poignant performance." Clifford Bax wrote to her after seeing a performance, "Dear Miss Robson, Another triumph. I honestly believe you are one of the hopes of the theatre and of its playwrights."

It is difficult, reading the play, to understand Flora's astonishing success in the role. *The Anatomist* is a three-act play. Mary Paterson appears only in Act Two Scene One. It is a short scene and, on paper, the character seldom takes the focus. Mary is a harsh-spoken Scots prostitute who shows a moment of tenderness to a drunken young doctor and is then lured away by Burke and Hare. In the next scene the doctor finds a lock of her hair caught in the lid of a crate bearing a new body to Dr Knox's surgery. On the last page of the play, the doctor recalls on the piano a song Mary had sung.

There had been an earlier production of the play in Scotland. There has been one notable revival when it was directed by Alistair Sim with Molly Urquhart in the role, and a television presentation, but in no production other than Tyrone Guthrie's at the Westminster has Mary Paterson shone in any particular way. Flora's success was truly that of inspired genius, for there can be no other explanation. "*As always when approaching a role I went back into my own experience. I try to find some emotion that I have felt in my life that is near the emotion of the character I am playing. Then I can find the right mood. I was*

# ... AND INTO THE FURNACE

*brought up on Scottish songs. I sat on my father's knee and he would sing those old songs to me. Mary had to sing a beautiful Scots song. Because of this I felt she had come from a good home and had gone on the streets because there was nothing else for her. I sang it with all the deep sadness she must have felt at the way her life had changed. At the end of the scene, as I was taken out by the two men to be murdered, one to each side, petting me, I sobbed tragically all the way up the stairs as though I, perhaps, sensed what was going to happen to me."* A critic, reviewing a later play, wrote, "Her great gulping sobs seemed to come from so deep a recess in some wounded heart that one could scarcely endure to listen." Agate would later say that anyone coming out of a Flora Robson play could scarcely endure to look anyone else in the eye. *The Anatomist* was the first opportunity the general public had of seeing Flora's qualities of tragedy. She had a fine singing voice which sounded especially lovely when unaccompanied. With the song she could draw the audience into her until she held them in the palm of her hand. And she had, and has, a kind of sad, tragic beauty. Bridie had not seen the extent of the qualities she blended into the character when he had written the play. Her performance transcended the author's intention and added unexpected depth to the play as a whole. "Her best performances are larger and more complete than I am certain any of her authors contemplated when they wrote their plays," Douglas Fairbanks Jnr. wrote to me. "She bursts the framework which contains the ordinary run-of-the-mill interpreter of characters, of story-telling. She *is* the part she's playing – *plus*! She is a virtuoso of the art of acting. What makes Rubinstein or Horowitz better or different from a multitude of superb musicians? The notes they play are the same – and the time taken to play them the same! *But*, for some magical reason, *they* play them more memorably, more movingly, more nearly perfectly. The phrase 'star quality' has been over-used – but even so, her work has something in it that is beyond 'stardom'. There may have been a few others who have been her equal in timing, characterisation, concentration, appeal to the heart and mind – but damned few!"

She seldom saw Henry Ainley at rehearsals as they never appeared on stage together. Whenever her scene was rehearsed he would go to his room to rest. He had been ill and *The Anatomist* was something of a come-back. *"Dear Henry Ainley was such a generous actor. Just before we opened we were rehearsing on the stage without wings or scenery. Ainley stayed to watch the scene from the side. It came to the point where I was taken out by the two murderers, sobbing as I went. As I walked by him, he said quietly, 'You know how to do it.'"* Praise from Ainley, the first actor she had ever seen, and an acknowledged master of his art, acted on her like champagne. On opening night she was nervous but confident as she climbed the two flights of stairs from her dressing-room to the stage. Somewhere out in the dark would be her father and Uncle John. She would play the scene for her father as she had done since she was five years old. The best judge of her work, it was his standards of excellence that had always inspired her to do the best she possibly could. Joan White, who played Mary's companion Janet, joined her and they went to stand together outside the door of the tavern. The cue came and Flora flung open the door and stepped into history.

The scene was short and soon over. Uncle John noticed David Robson feeling under the seat for his hat. He was ready to go. He had seen all he needed to see. Uncle John persuaded him to stay. He was glad to hear the cheers Flora received at the end, and he cut all the reviews from the newspapers the next day. When Flora went into the theatre the second evening she passed Ainley's dressing-room door. "*He had received over two hundred telegrams the previous night. By the time I got in he had answered a hundred of them in his own handwriting on postcards. As I passed his door he called out to me. He said, 'The papers say if we'd been on the stage together you would have acted me off it!' By making a joke of it, he cleared the air of any difficult atmosphere there might have been. He was a dear, kind man.*"

There were distinguished visitors to the play when the Duke and Duchess of York (later King George VI and Queen Elizabeth) came with a party to the Westminster. Flora and the rest of the cast were invited to the official opening of the Gower Street premises of the Royal Academy of Dramatic Art, and of a new small auditorium which came to be known as the GBS Theatre. The Duchess was performing the opening ceremony. It was 17 November 1931, ten years to the day since Flora's professional debut in *Will Shakespeare*. At tea, she kept herself out of the way, somewhat awed as Kenneth Barnes presented Lady Tree, Bernard Shaw and Owen Nares to the royal couple. Barnes beckoned her over and suddenly she was face to face with the Duke of York. He recognized her from the play and held out his hand. Flora was dumbfounded. She forgot to curtsey and stared at him open-mouthed. Then she began to speak rather too animatedly. Very politely he did not interrupt. Henry Ainley eventually rescued Flora and took her to meet the Duchess. She remembered her curtsey this time, but nerves had got the better of her and she began to babble again. Henry Ainley this time rescued the Duchess from Flora!

Amongst the many letters of appreciation for her performance, she received a charming message from Edith Craig. Flora was astonished to discover that Miss Craig remembered her as the same ten-year-old girl she had seen reciting Julia's letter scene for the British Empire

Shakespeare Society's competition nineteen years earlier! Miss Craig's memory extended to recalling that Flora had worn a blue dress with a pocket of not quite the same blue which had been added to accommodate the letter. One of her most treasured letters came from Moffatt Johnson. Johnnie wrote from America when notices for *The Anatomist* were printed in the New York press. "I knew you would get there," he wrote. Years later when Flora went to America, she looked forward to a reunion with her beloved teacher. To her great sadness he died just before her arrival.

"*The Anatomist* was an enormous success," remembered Betty Hardy, who played Mary Dishart. "The entire play was a success but Flora was at the centre of it. She looked wonderful in a rough red wig, tattered and tousled. At the beginning I don't think she knew what she was going to do with it, nor did anyone anticipate the enormous power she showed. It was absolutely heartbreaking. The secret was in her timing, which, even in those days, was extraordinary." Alan Rolfe had a small walk-on role. "Throughout the run of the play," he wrote to me, "it became the rule for all the cast, not actually in the same scene, to emerge from their dressing-rooms and stand at the side of the stage to watch Flora Robson's dynamic performance as Mary Paterson. She was adored by all the boys in walk-on roles." These boys included John Allen, John Whitehead, Ormerod Greenwood, Robert Flemyng and Geoffrey Toone. Toone had decided to go into the theatre, when he was at Cambridge, rather than go into his father's prep school. Flora had spent a whole day with his father and convinced him that the theatre was a suitable profession for his son. "My father insisted that I went into the theatre 'through the front door'," Toone recalled, "This meant him paying for me to walk on at the Old Vic. I only did two plays that season because Flora helped me by getting me a paid job in *The Anatomist*. I was paid a princely salary – I suppose it was £4!"

Flora had left the Donat flat when Ella's baby became due and was now living in a small back room in a women's club in Victoria. She could live there quite cheaply and walk to the theatre. At the stage-door she would lower her head, ashamed of her shabbiness, in case anyone should recognize her. No one could know she had just achieved an enormous success; she always seemed depressed and pessimistic. Anmer Hall had told her there would be no parts for her in the next two productions. She had risen a little but she was convinced the fall would come and she would be out of work, alone and unhappy again, her success as Mary Paterson forgotten by everyone. After her scene one night she was violently sick in the wings and she was excused the curtain call so she could return to her room to lie down. The next evening Tony, sensing her distress as of old, invited her to spend the night with him and Judy at their Lincoln's Inn flat. She poured out her problems to them. She was £12 in debt to Anmer Hall. She could not learn her parts aloud in her room as the other tenants would bang on the walls, and she hated her room. Geoffrey Toone had told her of an unfurnished bed-sitting room in the building where he lived in St George's Row, Pimlico. It seemed a good idea for her to move in there, but she had no furniture. Tony told her he would speak to Anmer Hall who would surely cancel the debt. Such a sum would scarcely break the Prudential. He offered to lend her £10 to buy a bed and other necessary items. "*It was a kind gesture but I was terrified of taking on another debt. I said, 'What if I can't afford to pay you back?' Tony just laughed, 'We can always take the bed!'*" Flora moved in and, though it was bare, made it her own home.

*The Anatomist* had a run of 127 performances. Anmer Hall continued to invite her to weekend house-parties. It was her first taste of comfortable living and she enjoyed the attention she received. One night he invited her to meet Tamara Karsavina, the Russian ballerina, and her husband, Henry J. Bruce, at the Café Royal. Carleton Hobbs, who played the young doctor in the play, saw Flora home afterwards. He congratulated her on the success she was having. "I know it will all be over soon," she said, "and everyone will forget all about me. There's nothing for me when it's over. Sometimes I think I should give up the theatre." Hobbs suddenly stopped in his tracks and turned on her. "Don't you dare speak another word," he said, "You are wicked not to be happy and grateful when you have found fame at last. If you knew how many people had struggled to find such success as yours." His words only made her more unhappy and she continued to brood about her future. "*One evening I was walking home. It was drizzling with rain. I suddenly realized I was singing to myself. I stopped. Why was I singing? It was at that moment that I realized I was making life miserable for myself. I remembered the positive thinking that had taken me to Cambridge and the happy, glorious time I had there. There was no reason why my entire future should not be the same. What a fool I had been. Here I was, a successful actress in a hit play. Why should it not be the beginning of a brilliant career? I decided I must make the best of what life had brought me and believe in myself a little bit more.*" The burden of worry melted away and she felt clean and renewed. It was a momentous decision. She walked on along the glistening pavements, her whole being singing for joy.

# 3

## The Damascene Sword
### 1932–1938

### 1

WITH HER NEW resolution to live life as it came, from day to day, Flora had turned a corner into a new era of her life. In a few weeks she would be thirty years old. Thirty is, for anyone, a milestone in life where youth seems finally to be left behind. It was certainly, in 1932, a time for most unmarried women to realize that they had lost all hope of a secure and happy future, of the homes, husbands and families they might have had. Flora, on the other hand, held within her the possibility of rich, creative fulfilment. She must stride forward confidently.

Her confidence was slow in asserting itself. The problems she had faced in her middle twenties, when she had despaired of ever finding work in the theatre, had not gone away. She had to hope for a role that would allow her to show the West End what, in *Six Characters in Search of an Author*, she had been able to show Cambridge. *The Anatomist* was due to close on 30 January 1932. The theatre would then remain 'dark' until the next production, *Tobias and the Angel*, opened on 9 March as Henry Ainley needed to rest between productions. Tony persuaded Anmer Hall to let him put on a low-budget revival in the intervening period. As if in answer to Flora's prayer, the play he chose was *Six Characters*. Henry Oscar joined the company to play the important role of the father. Allowing for a run of two weeks there would be only two weeks of rehearsal. Flora would have liked longer to re-explore the possibilities within the role, but when opening night came she had found her old form as the Stepdaughter.

# FLORA

There was little advance booking for the play. It is a difficult piece for audiences and, as there were no stars, the revival aroused little interest. Attendance on the opening night was sparse but not so the response of the audience or the critics. *The Times* reported, "The horror of the tale of real life that characters separated from the mind of their creator are trying to unfold comes home to us no less sharply at the third reading than at the first. This time, indeed, the impression may be sharper, for Miss Flora Robson is an actress who has the art of clothing without concealing all the odious traits of character. In her performance of the Stepdaughter depravation, self-mockery and self-loathing are set forth with crystal clearness, yet quite without offence." W. A. Darlington, in the *Daily Telegraph*, called her "an actress with a genuine emotional gift, whose future should be worth watching".

Robert Eddison, who was in the cast, particularly remembered one of the ways Tony made clear the life of the theatre in which the drama unfolded. Margery Phipps-Walker was left sitting on stage during the interval eating from her lunch-box and "throwing banana skins at the audience". Actors would enter through the auditorium and, at the very end of the play, at the end of her big emotional scene, Flora would leap wildly from the stage and into the auditorium to make her exit.

News spread of the fascinating production at the Westminster Theatre and queues began to form at the box-office. Unfortunately there were few performances left and hundreds of people were turned away. Alan Rolfe, who played a member of the company, wrote to me, "As the theatre was supposed to be empty my partner and I made our entrances by way of the pit door, and on several occasions we nearly came to blows with angry would-be ticket holders who thought we were trying to push past them. I can still remember the hordes of people streaming away from the theatre, bitterly disappointed because of their failure to obtain seats, and it is obvious that the play could have run for months. Every night when Flora Robson took her solo call, the entire audience stood up, cheering and waving programmes, a sight I never saw again during my thirty years in the theatre." Dame Peggy Ashcroft recalled this as the most memorable performance of Flora's early years. "She has an exceptional gift of power of emotion," she added.

Flora hoped that the play might transfer as it was proving such a success, but no theatre was available and Anmer Hall was committed to his next production. So the play closed on schedule. It was a great disappointment, particularly as there would be callers at the box-office for many weeks, asking for tickets for the Pirandello play everyone was talking about. There was a note of hope. The young

# THE DAMASCENE SWORD

novelist J. B. Priestley, who had scored great successes with his novels *The Good Companions* and *Angel Pavement*, had seen her at the Westminster and was interested in her for a role in a play that he had written. He also wanted Tony to direct it. But it was only in the planning stages and she would have to wait before it came to anything.

The fruits of Flora's recent successes were already making themselves manifest. After a short period of not knowing what the future had in store for her, she was faced with a rather dizzying decision. She had to choose between three offers! Two of the parts were as elderly ladies and the other was in Shakespeare. She chose the latter, another return to an earlier success. She was cast, as in Ben Greet days, as Bianca in *Othello*. Ernest Milton was presenting the play, directing it and playing the Moor. Henry Oscar was cast as Iago and Lydia Sherwood as Desdemona. The casting of Emilia afforded Flora a reunion with Athene Seyler.

Flora's image of Bianca was a wild-haired gypsy girl with an earthy temperament and a dark skin. "I shall be the only dark one in this play," was Milton's response. No doubt he was recalling Irving's response to Ellen Terry who had wanted her mad Ophelia to be dressed in black. Flora had to be content with rich clothes, and to achieve the effects she wished to create by the power of her thought. Her work did not go unnoticed. James Agate, the influential and verbose critic, who would become her champion through the thirties, was extremely impressed by her performance in this relatively minor role.

"Miss Athene Seyler makes Emilia a comfortable soubrette to have about the house," he wrote, "and Miss Flora Robson, equally unsuited as Bianca, achieves a little miracle. Since Miss Seyler is a first class comedienne, and since Miss Robson could play all the hags in *Richard III* lumped together, it is obvious that the two should have changed roles. Even so the piece would still have been run away with by Miss Robson and Mr Oscar pounding neck and neck, with Mr McKnight Kauffer's beautiful scenery half a length behind."

Flora was more than a little embarrassed by this review particularly because she admired Athene Seyler's performance. Miss Seyler had chosen to play Emilia's early scenes with an unexpected lightness of touch which made her later scenes infinitely more moving. Her apparently effortless ease was something Flora longed to learn. The production, sadly, lasted for only a week. It was flawed by Milton's over-extravagant Othello and the complete lack of pace he achieved as director.

Anmer Hall wanted Flora to play two of the small parts she had played in *The Kingdom of God* at Cambridge. Gillian Scaife would again play the leading role. However, Priestley had been able to set up production of his play at the Lyric Theatre and Tony took her along to meet him. The novelist and the actress were pleased to see in each other a similar northern straightforwardness and lack of affectation. He certainly wanted her for the role and it was a good part for her. Flora's first loyalty was to Anmer Hall who had shown such faith in her over the last three years. She had benefited both privately and professionally from his generosity. He had been a loyal friend and it was the same friend who now released her from her contractual obligations. He saw it was important for her to spread her wings. With the same unselfish spirit, not only did he continue to pay a retaining salary through her month of rehearsal, but paid her the full amount of £30, her total earnings from the play, even though, under the terms of the contract, he was obliged only to pay her the £8 to which she had originally agreed.

## 2

It was a dinner party like any other, with a group of friends and acquaintances engaged in trivial conversation. One of the guests recognized a musical box which had belonged to someone they had all known before he committed suicide a year earlier. The conversation turned a corner and, one by one, each told what they remembered of Martin before his death. To everyone's surprise each had been involved in his life and death far more deeply than might have been suspected. With everything out in the open, attention centred on the musical box once more. But time had played one of its tricks. The conversation had not yet taken place and the dangerous corner still lay ahead.

*Dangerous Corner* is a difficult play. A seemingly normal situation develops into hysterical unreality. It is up to the director and cast to maintain credibility for the audience who do not know, until the curtain falls, that what they have seen is not all it might have appeared. Flora was cast in the pivotal role of Olwen Peel who, it transpired, had shot Martin as he attempted to rape her. "He began taunting me. He thought of me – or pretended to – as a priggish spinster, full of repressions, who'd never really lived. All rubbish because I'm not that type at all." Flora could have been describing the way people thought of her. There was more to Olwen and more to Flora than may immediately have met the eye, so, in many ways, this was a splendid role with which to launch her West End career. It was a difficult role to come to terms with. Controlled emotion seemed to be the key so she drew on what she could remember of her lessons with Sybil Thorndike and Helen Haye, and made a slow build towards her great dramatic moment at the end of the play.

# THE DAMASCENE SWORD

There would be an out-of-town try-out before the London opening and the company travelled to Glasgow. "*I expected to feel at home in Scotland, but to my surprise I was treated as a Sassenach. It was a great shock to me. I had always thought of myself as truly Scots. All of my ancestors were Scots. I felt like a displaced person with no country to call my own.*"

Whatever strangeness she might have felt was more than compensated for by a reunion with her dear sister Shela who, with her husband Eric Ritter, a doctor, was living in Glasgow. She always felt at home with Shela and it was good to have somewhere friendly to stay as Glasgow, during the Depression, was a frightening place. At night the eerie cries of the Red Biddy drinkers echoed about the streets. Pathetic, hungry down-and-outs roamed the city and raided the dustbins in search of food. Flora and Shela would watch with pity from the safety of Shela's home. Shela would often leave out food specially for them.

The first night went well. The critic from the *Glasgow Evening News* wrote, "A very able company drifts in ghostly fashion through the parts. People like Marie Ney and Richard Bird remind us of what they could display had they more generous material whereon to display it. Flora Robson alone conjures up a picture of real flesh and blood, and having accomplished that feat, goes on to embellish it with the warmth of human emotion. A very material personal success for this actress."

The opening at the Lyric, the following week, was to a very mixed reception. "The world is not a bran tub," wrote the *Times* correspondent, "in which no one does anything but dive for the gifts of truth. So, it seemed, the audience discovered, for they were inclined to titter in the wrong places." Priestley was furious at the audience for laughing. "I could stop that next time," he said, "by writing a comedy." Flora recognized it as the kind of laughter that comes from nervous release. The *Times* review went on to say that "when the curtain fell, [the audience] made the heartiest amends for their irreverence". Flora was praised for her acting by most of the critics. The Sunday papers were more enthusiastic about the play and the production eased itself into a comfortable run.

Priestley wrote to me of Flora's talent. "Most performers," he wrote, "capable of taking over a scene and dominating it, are persons, or at least performers, with very hard edges. But it has always seemed to me that Flora has, from the first, been one of those exceptional actresses who could dominate a scene without these hard edges, maintaining a deeply feminine quality."

Now that she had a good income, Flora was able to repay the money she owed Tony, keep the bed, and move it into her first

London flat. Years before, when she had appeared in *Undercurrents*, she had received a fan letter, her first, from actor-writer Miles Malleson. The address at the top of the letter was 6 Mecklenburgh Square. What an extraordinary coincidence it was that when, as a West End actress in a leading role, she could afford to take a flat of her own, it should be at the very same address. There were two rooms and so she was able to take a lodger to help pay the high weekly rent of £2. 12s. 6d. This made it possible for her to save against the day when she might be out of work again.

During the summer months, while the play was still running, she was able to work on a film. *One Precious Year* was a quota-quickie made for Paramount British. It was the story of a woman who is told she has one year to live. She agrees to try a new cure but forbids her doctors and her best friend to tell her husband of her illness as he might be led to neglect his brilliant career at the Foreign Office. She has an affair with a handsome cad but is later reconciled with her husband and then learns she is cured. Anne Grey played the part of the woman, Owen Nares was the husband, Basil Rathbone was the cad and Flora had the role of the best friend. It was the kind of part which called for her only to pop up at critical moments as a confidante. Rathbone called her 'Snooping Annie' because she always seemed to know the right moment to appear! It was a happy cast and crew. This was the first taste of what would, one day, become a way of life, commuting to the studios early in the morning and back to the West End in the evening in time for the theatre and an exhausting role. The extra money she received, however, helped furnish her flat. It was important to be seen in a medium which could further her career. However, she could not claim to be particularly happy in front of the camera and her lack of ease was somewhat apparent.

One day she called on James Bridie and his wife. During tea she told them she was worried that her career might be only a line of 'tortured spinsters' like Olwen Peel. Bridie recalled that Tony Guthrie had once suggested he write a play for Flora and suddenly heard himself ask her, "Would you like to play Mary Read?" "Who is Mary Read?" asked Flora. "She was a pirate," said Bridie. "Yes," said Flora, "I should very much like to play a pirate!" So a seed was sown in Bridie's mind that would flower brilliantly for them both in years to come.

As well as the film, Flora was able to work on a play with the Sunday Players. Mercia Wayne in *The Storm Fighter* was no 'tortured spinster' but a normal, attractive woman. There were three performers at the St Martin's Theatre. One of the terms of the contract for *Dangerous Corner* was that at the end of the run at the Lyric, the company would go on a four-week tour. With more than two months

# THE DAMASCENE SWORD

of the original run still to play, Barry Jackson approached her with the offer of a role in the new Somerset Maugham play which was due to open at the Globe Theatre before the tour of the Priestley play began. It was another 'tortured spinster' but the part read well and she wanted to play it. She was willing to honour the terms of the contract if Priestley insisted, but he generously released her from any obligation. She was able to take a short break and began rehearsals while *Dangerous Corner* was still playing at the Lyric.

## 3

"We may wonder if the dramatist has not underrated the healing power of time," wrote the critic of *The Times* after the first performance of Maugham's *For Services Rendered*. He was not alone in this view. Many felt that the theme of bitterness which gripped the characters of the play as a result of the Great War, which had ended fourteen years earlier, had been exhausted in previous plays. It was, on the other hand, a theme with which Flora easily identified. Eva is approaching forty and is still unmarried. Like Flora and two of her sisters she is one of four million superfluous women. Flora's sister Lila had been looking forward to marriage after the war. She was engaged to a tall handsome Scotsman called Hugh Rennie. Originally with the London Scottish Regiment, he was commissioned into the Cameron Highlanders in France. One day Lila thought she heard a shot. She told the family she did not think it meant that Hugh was dead. When he was reported missing, believed dead, she persisted in this belief. One morning, three months later, the telephone rang and Lila answered it. Hugh was alive, a prisoner-of-war. He had been shot in the spine and was paralysed. Later he was taken by train to Poland and he died on the journey. Lila remained unmarried and, when she died in 1976, her trousseau, which she had kept lovingly all those years, was found amongst her possessions. The loss was a great personal tragedy for all of the Robsons and on many occasions when Flora needed to find tears on the stage or in films, she would think for a few moments about Lila and her beautiful Scotsman.

Eva, in the play, is in love with a young ex-naval officer now trying to find his feet in civilian life. In a desperate effort to find a future for herself she makes him an ill-timed proposal of marriage. Later she hears of his death and is subject to an attack of hysterical grief which develops into madness. It was exactly what everyone considered a 'Flora Robson part'. Ralph Richardson was cast in the role of the naval officer. It was to be a trying first night for both of them. Flora was directed to play the proposal scene in agonized whispers. Someone in the audience laughed for no apparent reason and broke what atmosphere Flora had been able to achieve. And then someone coughed and the feeling of restlessness spread to other throats that felt a sudden urge to join in. Flora pressed on with her whispering. Then a voice from the gallery cried, loud and clear, "Speak up!" Flora's heart sank and she hardly dared look at Richardson as she left the stage. "I'll show them," she thought.

The hysterical scene in Act Three, when Eva hears of the sailor's suicide, was her chance to show them. She let herself go completely. All the stops were pulled out as every ounce of emotion screamed from her body. Everything Sybil Thorndike had taught her was lost in an exhibition of uncontrolled passion. "Why shouldn't I have a chance of happiness?" she sobbed, "I hate you, I hate you all!" She was carried off-stage screaming, as directed, and set on her feet. She had shown them, all right, for the gallery cheered and cheered. She managed to pull herself together and played the last scene with her usual restraint. There were further cheers for her at the end but Flora was not happy. This was not entirely due to the earlier incidents but to what she felt to be a lack of company spirit in the production as a whole. Working with Guthrie at Cambridge, later with others in the small experimental theatres, had spoiled her. Actors such as Robert Donat were prepared to share moments on stage for the good of the whole, rather than to take, selfishly, all the time. The play had been the thing, not the actor's individual success. With the exception of Cedric Hardwicke, no one would give Flora anything in her hysterical scene. When she suggested something to another actor he said, "Why should I do that to help you?" There was no answer she could give. Yet it was the same selfishness of which Flora, herself, had been guilty, behaving as she had on opening night.

To her great surprise, and somewhat to her relief, none of the critics seemed to have noticed that she had overacted. Indeed, the critics of *The Times* wrote, "Miss Flora Robson plays the neurotic woman with restraint and force, and even contrives to make a fit of hysterics movingly significant." There was a letter to her from Priestley. "Your performance last night was magnificent, easily overtopping everyone else's. The hysteria and madness were both terrific. The audience was calling for you at the end." Perhaps, after all, unwittingly, she had been provided with the key to the role, and she had been right to behave as she had. She began to feel that she had over-reacted to her own judgement, when there came a blow from an unexpected quarter. James Agate, one of the critics who had championed her early success, writing in *The Sunday Times*, rebuked her for overplaying. He said she was "a good enough actress to realise that because a character is at the end of its tether, is no reason why the actress should be at the end of hers". Flora was dismayed.

# THE DAMASCENE SWORD

She admired him for writing the truth but was sad that he did not mention her playing of the last scene. She wrote for a further opinion to St John Ervine, the former *Observer* columnist who had recently retired. Perhaps he would give her a private, objective assessment of what had happened. His reply was soothing. "I found no fault in your performance of the scene with Richardson. It was beautifully done. So was your hysterical scene. The suddenness of it was part of its nature. What else could it be but sudden? I was not expecting the news of the sailor's death but of his arrest and the announcement of it was shocking to me. How else could you have behaved?"

Post-mortems in the theatre are something of a pointless exercise as seldom will the conditions which created the moment recur. The experience of the first night behind her, Flora played with the restraint she had planned for the first night. She always dreaded the hysterical scene but it was never out of proportion again. She enjoyed working with Ralph Richardson and a warm friendship blossomed between them. Almost fifty years later he recalled for me his memories of working on this play. "Flora was wonderful in *For Services Rendered*," he wrote. "She was always gay and happy in rehearsals. She had wonderful *eyes* – expressive. On the stage she had an extraordinary concentration and she had a wealth of emotion to *concentrate*. That's what makes the actress – useless to put the magnifying glass on something that does not exist. She had an unselfish spirit – that makes the actress – useless to show what is small and self." John Gielgud remembered seeing the play and wrote, "I thought her wonderfully fine in the original production of *For Services Rendered* at the Globe Theatre, when she acted so vividly at the end – mad and singing God Save The King in a cracked voice." Maugham would later say he could not imagine what would have happened to the play without Flora.

After the congratulations in his letter Priestley had continued, "Apart from some moments in Act Three I did not like the play, though warmly agreeing with its pacifist sentiments. It was ten years out of date and very unreal, and behind its anti-war attitude is a hatred and fear of life itself, a dreadful negativism. My wife was saying, and I agree, that you would be well advised not to accept another part of this kind. It's easy to fix yourself in the public mind." How well Flora understood the truth in this. Ervine also wanted to press this point home. "Don't for God's sake let anyone make a 'type' of you. The managers will try. Automatically when a neurotic part occurs in a play they'll say, 'Oh, yes, a Flora Robson part!' By the Lord Christ, if you let them 'type' you I'll hound you into your grave. You are not a type, you are an actress." He told her that the remedy lay in her own hands. "Do comedy! . . . Do anything! . . . I don't suppose you'd be very good in artificial parts but you might try one or two. It's part of your job to have a shot at anything. Redden your nose and tousle your hair and play in pantomime! Anything that will add to your experience and knowledge of yourself and your powers and limitations. I don't want you to refuse parts. I want you to refuse to be made a type. If you are compelled by economics to do the Flora Robson part, then move heaven and earth to get an exactly opposite part in any sort of Sunday night show simultaneously so that you can prove to managers and the public that you have variety of style. I'll write a play for you or die in the attempt."

Flora had always needed encouragement, and such interest from so distinguished a critic gave her renewed courage. Ervine thought her talent to be quite exceptional and didn't hesitate to say so. In words that echoed others spoken to her many years before he told her, "I've set my heart on seeing you universally acknowledged as a great actress. I want people to say Bernhardt, Duse, Rachel, Réjane, Terry – and Flora Robson! Don't disappoint me, will you?" He recognized an Achilles' heel too and wrote, "your extraordinary, flexible face fascinates me. I love to see your mind and your emotion flowing down your body so that your toes are expressing something. A woman beside whom I sat at a public dinner said, after I'd raved about you, 'Yes, but she's ugly. All her bones are in the wrong place.' 'Blast you,' I replied, 'She's beautiful! Her face is lovely with intelligent emotion!' And I told her that Duse was ugly. Don't believe them Flora. . . . When I looked at you and then looked at that mannequin Gladys Cooper at Playfair's party I couldn't understand why anyone pays tuppence ha'penny to see her when they can have the honour of paying to see you!"

Essie Robeson, wife of the great Negro singer, had seen Flora in the play and had written to ask if she would consider a script written by a young friend of hers. She had seen a Flora Robson part in it. Flora wisely saw that it would be pointless to plunge into yet another role as a frustrated ageing woman and politely turned the play down. She took tea with Mrs Robeson, however. Paul Robeson was about to appear in an O'Neill play at the little Embassy Theatre at Swiss Cottage and was looking for a suitable actress to play opposite him. It would be a short run as Robeson had to return to the States to make his film debut in *Emperor Jones*. The idea of playing again in O'Neill and the opportunity of acting opposite so great a talent excited Flora. No sooner had she instigated negotiations with the Embassy than H. K. Ayliff, the director of the Maugham play, came to her dressing-room to ask if she would accept a part in a new play by an unknown author which was going into rehearsal later that week. Barry Jackson would be presenting the play and Ralph Richardson and Cedric

# THE DAMASCENE SWORD

Hardwicke had already agreed to take part. Flora asked if she could read the play but there were no copies available. The last act was, in fact, being rewritten at that moment. Flora wondered what to do for the best. Everything was crowding in on her for, as well as having to choose between the two plays, she was rehearsing a revival of Tony's production of *Lady Audley's Secret* for a Sunday-night presentation at the Arts Theatre. She asked Cedric Hardwicke's advice. She told him that the job at the Embassy would mean a cut in salary from £35 to £10. He said that as far as he could see, the matter was settled by that admission. Of course, she should take the better-paid job. He added that if she turned down a West End job in favour of a theatre like the Embassy she might never be offered a part in the West End again. Flora agreed to do the new play, feeling as well that she owed it to Barry Jackson for giving her the opportunity to play Eva.

The new play bewildered the entire cast. Each actor had only his own part typed out, not an uncommon practice, and it was impossible to understand the development of the characters until the whole thing was put together. Even when this was accomplished it was still difficult to understand. The action was set in the hall of the ancestral mansion of the self-confessed half-mad Lord Bretton. Packing cases were strewn around for he had just returned from India. His son had been run over and killed by a drunken motorist. The play opened when, by some highly preposterous means and for highly questionable motives, the motorist was brought to the mansion to confront the father of his victim. He had been conveyed there by a mysterious, fury-like figure called Penelope Otto (Flora). Apparently she hoped to see what drama might occur. Thus the extraordinary plot unwound. And still none of the actors had seen the final act. When the script finally arrived they were all horror-struck. Cedric Hardwicke, who was playing Lord Bretton, had been convinced that his role developed into comedy in the last act. He discovered that, on the contrary, he would have to take poison. Flora felt that her character was headed for a tragic demise. All she had in store for her was a stilted, stereotyped police cross-examination. She asked if she might see Lawrence Miller, the author, so that she might make sense of it but was told he was a cripple who lived far from London in the country, and it would be impossible to arrange. The whole affair was like the classic nightmare that all actors have before an opening night, yet all the actors were wide awake and they had no guarantee that matters would improve before the play opened. The greatest irony was the title of the piece which in itself heralded doom. It was called *Head-On Crash*. And that is exactly what it proved to be.

Opening night of the Maugham play had been straightforward by comparison. It was little wonder that the audience could not understand what was going on, as few of the actors knew either. There was booing at the curtain call. Flora had to admire Barry Jackson who bravely went out and took all the jeers and the cat-calls on their behalf. He made a speech in which he said he was proud to introduce a new, young playwright to the West End. The West End did not seem to want to reciprocate his enthusiasm. Most of the critics refrained from naming the actors in their reviews. No one would have been surprised had the play closed by the weekend but it lasted for three weeks. It was not a happy time. Morale was low as now all the cast knew they were playing in nonsense. An actor's loyalty to his playwright normally takes many weeks to lose its intensity as the actor is so subjectively involved, but each of the actors in this piece had been set up to ridicule. Some of them behaved rather badly. Hardwicke, and even Richardson, would do their best to make the oh-so-serious Miss Otto laugh. Flora was very relieved when it was all over.

The short foray back into the past with *Lady Audley's Secret* had been great fun. Tony had gathered together a happy company. Dennis Arundell was Sir Michael, Jessica Tandy was Alicia and Robert Eddison was Robert Audley. Robert remembered Flora's performance, "She was wonderful. She looked superb. I can see her now storming round the conservatory, snorting rage and the roses wilting. Tony had them on rubber stalks, and they all fell before her as she stormed around." The critic of *The Times* declared that the evening would be memorable "for the intensity and judgement that Miss Robson brings to her nonsense. She plays the absurd part as though it were a masterpiece and so, in her light, makes it one."

The only happy result of the *Head-On Crash* débâcle was that its early closing meant she could do the O'Neill part with Robeson after all as it had not yet been cast. This was to be a return for Robeson to the most controversial role of his career, as Jim Harris in *All God's Chillun Got Wings*. It was the first play to be written since *Othello* about intermarriage between black and white. Flora would play Ella Downey. Jim and Ella are first seen as children when, in their innocence, both swear love for one another. Nine years elapse and the poison of colour prejudice has turned Ella away from Jim, and bred hatred for him in her. Five years later, the white prize-fighter with whom she has been living deserts her after the death of their child. Ella agrees to marry Jim, her only alternative to going on the streets. They live abroad for two years before returning to live with his mother and sister. Ella's prejudice is as strong as ever and drives her towards insanity. Jim is about to sit his bar examinations and she wants to see him fail. She wants to punish him for being black. Eventually she loses her mind and reverts to childhood. Jim abandons all his ambitions to stay at home and care for her.

Production of the play in America had been bitterly opposed, particularly by the Hearst Press. The producers had to censor mail sent to Mary Blair, who was cast as Ella, because there were so many obscene letters from the Ku Klux Klan. The Klan had threatened that the producers would be responsible for the deaths of two hundred people by their hand if the play opened in New York. The Hearst-Press-sponsored mayor of New York withdrew permission for the children to appear in the first scene, only hours before the play was to open and ordered the normally south-bound traffic past the theatre to be reversed to keep audiences away. The director, himself, read the opening scene. Few of the critics even mentioned that Mary Blair had been in the cast.

Flora was overawed by Robeson. When she first tried to put down her book, and speak her lines from memory, everything went clean out of her head as soon as she looked at him. She was afraid that he might be offended and told him, "I'm afraid I'm rather shy of you." He smiled, and said, "Yes, I know. I'm shy of you." There were no problems in their relationship from that moment. He helped her towards a deeper understanding of her role by explaining the background of race-relations from his own experience. He had studied for the bar, himself, but had not been beaten down as so many had. He was able to speak objectively of the problems, but she could see how deeply affected he was by them. She learned her accent from him as this was new to her. The character was a great challenge. In one scene she was to wave a knife at a primitive Negro mask, muttering savagely, "I hate you, I hate you," and suddenly change her mood, flinging away the knife and becoming quieter. "*I remembered a crazy old man we children used to see. He would walk past us talking to himself, but he would talk so fast that we couldn't hear a word he said. I made Ella talk like that. Suddenly she was to forget what she was saying and drop the knife. I wondered how I could make the change so quickly. Then I remembered a monkey I had seen at the zoo. He played with a stick. Suddenly he lost interest in it, threw it away and was interested in something else. So that key scene of Ella's was derived from my memories of a crazy old man and a monkey.*"

There was a worrying time immediately before the play opened, when O'Neill's representatives tried to withdraw the rights. O'Neill had wanted Robeson to do a major West End production of the play. They demanded a thousand-dollar advance. The theatre was able to find part and Robeson, himself, put up the rest. He believed in supporting a theatre like this one. Ronald Adam and André van Gyseghem tackled only challenging subjects with a strong political or social bias. Few theatres would have taken a risk with a play like this one and Robeson was only too happy to back them up.

The first night was an intoxicating experience. The stars were named as a major new team. "Mr Robeson [has] the simplicity that gives pathos its depth and the dignity that saves it from historical declamation," claimed *The Times*. "Miss Flora Robson's Ella is, as it must be, a more elaborate portrait. It exhibits with uncommon subtlety the many planes on which the girl's mind travels . . . and it produces the effect of madness, through which recollections of sanity arise, by exhibiting these planes, not in turn but simultaneously. Miss Robson has power to turn this wretched woman's mind into glass so that the whole truth of her is visible and to stain the glass with the changing colours of her longing, her suffering and her insane escape." André van Gyseghem is quoted by Marie Seton in her book about Robeson as remembering this play as his one unforgettable experience in theatre. "Time and again at rehearsals, directing Flora Robson and Paul Robeson, I had the feeling of being on the edge of a violent explosion; I had touched it off but the violent conflagration was terrifying in its blazing intensity. I have seldom known two performances fuse so perfectly; Miss Robson's emotional power and the uncanny skill with which she stripped bare the meagre soul of the wretched Ella was almost more than one could bear at such close range. Such a technically superb performance found a perfect foil in Robeson's utter sincerity." The play proved so successful that the run at the Embassy was extended from two to three weeks and then transferred to the Piccadilly Theatre for a further four weeks before Robeson was forced to withdraw to honour his film commitments.

Flora would remain friends with the Robesons for many years. Paul visited the Robson family at their home in Hove. How the neighbours talked, wondering at the black man with so similar a name! All her life Flora has had to put up with the mispronunciation of her name. So many still pronounce it as though it were spelled the same as Paul's, and not, as it should be pronounced, to rhyme with 'Hobson'. Indeed, Flora once blacked up at a charity show and sang 'Ol' Man River' so that no one would ever be confused again! Many years later she was to see the dress rehearsal for Paul's famous *Othello*, in Boston. In the scene where Brabantio speaks of Desdemona's running "from her guardage to the sooty bosom/Of such a thing as thou" she noticed that Paul hung his head and bit his lip. Paul had often maintained to Flora that black actors should always show humility. She was unable to see him after the rehearsal but managed to speak to Essie. She told her she felt he shouldn't give in like that. "So he should be defiant," said Essie. Flora replied, "No. He is a general. He should be dignified. You cannot hurt people

# THE DAMASCENE SWORD

who have dignity." Paul told Flora later that her suggestion had not only changed his playing of that scene, but it had changed his whole performance.

Flora was to return to the Embassy Theatre for her next engagement. The play was *Vessels Departing*, a reworking of his earlier play *Port Said*, by Emlyn Williams. Flora played Narouli Karth, the half-caste proprietress of a disreputable café in Port Said. It was not a good play and there was little opportunity for Flora to extend herself. In the story, she had had an affair with an Englishman who had deserted her while she was in prison for stealing for him. He has taken their son to England and his wife has accepted them both. Narouli swears vengeance and the English wife comes to plead with her. By accident, Narouli meets the son and sees that only harm will come to him if she persists in her vendetta. The story is set against the life of the café, and the flotsam and jetsam of its *habitués*. "There is a pathetic and emotional quality in her voice which is quite heart-breaking," wrote Rodney Millington, who played Sulieman Ali. "Very near the end of the play, Narouli, who has wanted very much to visit the Englishman's home in Cumberland, says something like the following: 'Cumberland – I can feel the rain on my face. . . .' The pathos she gave that line is still with me as I write this letter, forty-seven years later."

## 4

"I need a holiday," she thought. It was the summer of 1933 and she chose to spend some of it in the sun in Majorca. It was a rare luxury. Actors can seldom afford to go on holiday. When they are out of work and have all the time in the world there is seldom the money to pay for one. Only when there is a long run of an established success can the management afford to let an actor leave the cast for more than a few days. There had been no spare money for Flora and this would be her first real holiday since her days at the factory. She was out of work, but she had a splendid new job to look forward to in the autumn.

She had often thought that one way of breaking her run of tortured spinsters might be a return to repertory and a variety of roles – a large part one week, a smaller one the next, mixing comedy with tragedy. A doctor had written to warn her that she could go mad is she continued to play mad women, though this amused Flora as such roles gave her the greatest release. The problem had been finding an opportunity to play in repertory near enough to the West End that managers and the public would not forget her. It had seemed an impossibility. But Tony again came to the rescue. He told her that he

# FLORA

had agreed to become the resident director at the Old Vic, Lilian Baylis's 'People's Theatre', south of the river at Waterloo. He badly wanted Flora and Robert Donat to join him so that they could together rekindle the spirit of the Cambridge Festival Theatre in a new home. Robert had, by now, embarked on a profitable film career. He had a young family to support and the money at the Vic was much less than was paid even in the West End. Flora, however, was prepared to take a cut in earnings to enjoy the great artistic opportunity and the lively Old Vic audiences. One evening she held a dinner party and discovered that one of her guests felt exactly as she did. Charles Laughton had recently arrived from America where he had made a lot of money. The Academy Award that he had received for his portrayal of Henry VIII had made him much sought after. He longed for experience in classical theatre, especially in Shakespeare and in verse-speaking. He and his wife, Elsa Lanchester, had made friends with Flora earlier in the year and she had invited them to dinner to meet Tony and Judy. Tony suggested to Laughton the kind of parts he and Elsa might expect to play at the Vic. Flora later enthused to the Laughtons over Tony's great skills as a director and the challenge such a season would offer them all. They were inspired with the same enthusiasm and pledged themselves to the venture.

Happy with these new prospects, Flora set off on holiday. She liked being an actress. What was more, she enjoyed being a successful actress. Now people knew who Flora Robson was, they would recognize her and point her out. There would be fans waiting at the stage-door for her to autograph their programmes, and there were kind letters for her to answer. It was a wonderful tonic after all those years when no one knew her name. She arrived at the hotel and waited, with a secret delight, to be recognized. It really would be the loveliest treat to be made a fuss of by the other guests. Well, everyone was very friendly but no one seemed to recognize her at all. "Flora Robson" she would pronounce, with deep significance, when asked her name. There was still no response. She leafed through all the magazines she could find in the hotel. In one of them there might just be a portrait of her or a shot of her dining with someone. She would leave it casually open where someone would be sure to see it. Not one of the beastly magazines made any mention of her at all. Then there was the incident on the beach with the young man who looked like the film star Harold Lloyd. He seemed to be a movie producer and offered a couple of the prettier girls a screen test. Flora realized that here was an opportunity of showing them who she was and dropped a little of her knowledge of the film industry into the conversation. "You seem to know rather a lot about it," the young man said. "I should do," said Flora, "I recently made a film at

*Mary Read*, the play Bridie wrote for her

With Robert Donat in the scene Guthrie would not direct
(Stage Photo Co)

As Queen Elizabeth in *Fire Over England* with Laurence Olivier and Vivien Leigh (Pendennis Pictures Corporation)

*Mary Tudor* with Marius Goring as Philip of Spain (J. W. Debenham)

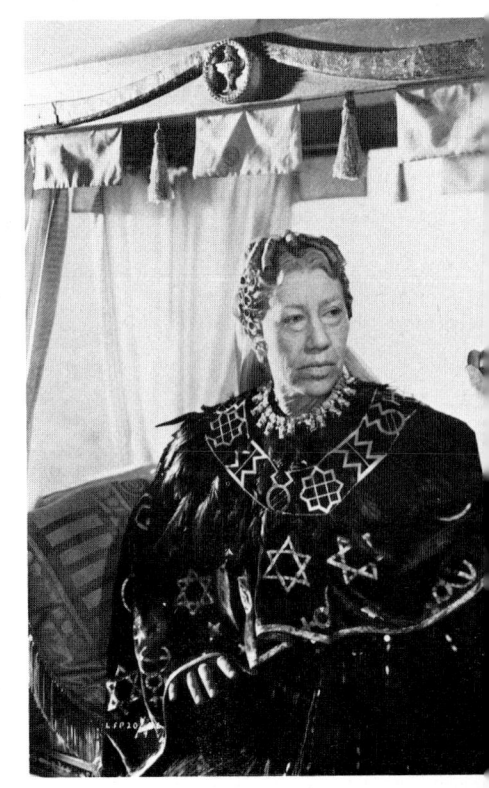

The Empress that never was. As Livia in *I Claudius* (London Films

Her greatest success. As Lady Catherine Brooke in *Autumn*
(Peter Clark)

Ellen Dean and Cathy. With Merle Oberon in *Wuthering Heights*.
(Samuel Goldwyn: Courtesy Enterprise Pictures)

The scene from *We Are Not Alone* which drew applause from the entire crew. With Paul Muni. (United Artists)

Elstree." Everyone laughed. It had been a game and the joke was on Flora. To hide her mortification, she made an excuse and plunged into the sea. What a fool she had been! She had spoiled her holiday thus far with all these foolish thoughts. What was it Johnnie had said? "If you succeed, do not think you are a special person. You are no better than a good workman plumber. Learn humility." She had believed him then; why had she forgotten it now? She emerged from the sea with a new philosophy and quietly enjoyed the rest of her holiday.

There was quite a bit of humility on her return to London. She had spent rather more on her holiday than she had intended and was in debt. She released her charwoman and did all her own chores. One such task was to clean down her part of the communal stairs. One day she was down on her knees on the steps when the telephone rang. At the other end was Alexander Korda. He wondered whether she would consider playing the Empress Elizabeth of Russia in his new film about Catherine the Great. Flora had to laugh. It was the archetypal Cinderella story, from drudge to empress in a few seconds!

*The Rise of Catherine the Great* was the film with which Korda hoped to repeat the earlier success of *The Private Life of Henry VIII*. Throughout the thirties he was obsessed with bringing to the screen the private lives of historical notables, but none would have the originality and flair of the first. Elizabeth Bergner, the Viennese actress, and her Hungarian film-maker husband, Paul Czinner, had recently arrived in England and were under contract to Korda's London Films company. Under a tie-up with United Artists, Korda was able to call on the services of Douglas Fairbanks Jnr., who would play Prince Peter to Bergner's Catherine. Czinner would direct the film.

Flora was four years younger than Miss Bergner and had to be made to appear much older. Layers of yellow make-up were applied to her face and she wore court wigs that were a pale shade of blue. She was assured that these would photograph quite naturally. There were busy days of costume fittings for the Empress who boasted a wardrobe of five thousand dresses. There was no finished script for her to see and Flora found herself reporting for stills photography before she understood anything about the character. It was a huge production with vast sets and hundred of extras and Flora felt quite lost. She had no experience of a large-scale production; her other films had been rather cosy in comparison. She felt hideous in her yellow make-up, blue wig and heavy farthingale. Someone introduced her to Douglas Fairbanks Jnr. She had admired him so often on the screen and here was the man, in person, standing a few feet from her. She was completely tongue-tied and able only to force a weak smile and a mumbled 'hello'. He stared at her for a moment, looking her up and down, and then smiled. "Do you know," he said. "I keep thinking that if I were to lift you up by the neck, I'd find a telephone underneath!" Flora laughed. He had broken the ice between them. She would remember to do the same for young actors meeting her on the set for the first time.

Shooting began and Flora was surprised that Korda took charge of all her scenes. Czinner was noted for his naturalistic directing, for the soft, low-key quality which so well suited his wife's talents. Perhaps Korda felt that the Empress's scenes needed a more full-blooded approach. Unfortunately, his technical expertise did not stretch to capturing Flora at *her* most full-blooded and he did her a disservice. She appears to be overacting, her voice devoid of its resonance. In one scene with Fairbanks, her eyeline is so badly misdirected that she appears to be looking over his head. One often learns the best lessons from one's errors, but making mistakes so publicly can be painful. The experience showed Flora how much she had to learn to be able to master the medium. C. A. Lejeune, in her *Observer* review of the film, commented: "Flora Robson falls short of the Empress Elizabeth by about thirty years of experience. Her voice is the voice of a young woman, and her acting has intellectual authority, but no amplitude."

The film overran its schedule and Flora had to commute between final shooting at Elstree and rehearsals at the Old Vic. There was a certain piquancy in being invited to play at the Vic. Flora hadn't forgotten how Lilian Baylis had dismissed her all those years before with her "Go away young woman and get some experience." Now Flora, as a star in her own right, was to head the company with Charles Laughton. Miss Baylis wasn't fond of stars. Perhaps this was because they so seldom came into the category she much preferred and prayed for ("Dear God, send me good actors – cheap . . .") She had great faith in "our people" as she called the Vic's regular audience who packed the theatre whoever might be playing, and she certainly had no reason to want to attract the "lah-di-dah people" from across the bridge. Was this Laughton, a film star who had never played in Shakespeare, "a nice man, Mr Guthrie? Does he go to church, dear?" she wanted to know. What would be the point of having him in the company? Well, he would bring with him costumes for some of the plays and he had been able to arrange funding from the Pilgrim Trust for any Shakespeare plays in which he and Flora Robson appeared together. "Did you say the Pilgrim Trust, dear?" She had tried on many occasions, in vain, to secure funds from the Pilgrim Trust to help with "the work". Well, perhaps she would give Mr Laughton a chance. When challenged by the Press about never having played in Shakespeare, Laughton countered, "I sleep with Shakespeare under my pillow." It became something of a catchphrase. At their first encounter Miss Baylis looked him straight in the eye and said, "I'm very glad to hear you sleep with Shakespeare under your pillow, Mr Laughton, but what I want to know is, can you speak his beautiful verse?"

Neither Charles nor Flora were in the first play of the season. Tony had chosen *Twelfth Night*, which was a fairly safe proposition for what would be only his third venture into Shakespeare. Apart from *The Merry Wives of Windsor* at Cambridge he had recently done *Love's Labours Lost* at the Westminster. Flora was at the opening night at the Old Vic and was astonished to be cheered by the gallery as she made her way into the auditorium. Miss Baylis brushed past her at the end of the performance. "Lovely reception, dear," she said, and added, "Before you did anything to deserve it. . . . "

Flora's first appearance at the Old Vic was as Varya in *The Cherry Orchard*. Guthrie's production brought Chekhov into the major repertoire of the English theatre for the first time. Previously his plays had been presented only at special Sunday-night performances. The company included, as well as the Laughtons, "lovely Athene Seyler", Roger Livesey, Ursula Jeans, Leon Quartermaine, Morland Graham, James Mason, Dennis Arundell, and, as Epihodov, the young man who, as a schoolboy, had invited Flora to tea at Cambridge, Marius Goring.

Varya was a good part with which to ease herself into the company and get the measure of the theatre. But it was not the most auspicious of beginnings. W. A. Darlington wrote in the *Daily Telegraph*, "It seemed to me that I have seen actresses of less quality than Flora Robson do better than she did with the part of Varya. Perhaps this is merely because one expects much of Miss Robson and Varya gives her only limited scope." During the first week, she had the kind of experience all actors dread. She rushed on stage, giving chase to Epihodov, tripped over a rug and fell. She felt terribly embarrassed but quickly stood up and continued with her speech. There was no particular reaction from the audience, but she was glad to get off the stage where she and Goring could laugh about it together. Director James Whale, recently returned from Hollywood where he had filmed his successful stage production of *Journey's End*, was in the audience that night. When he visited her dressing-room after the play, Flora asked him why no one had laughed when she fell. "But why should they?" he asked. "We all thought 'How very Russian!'"

The following Sunday, Flora leafed through *The Sunday Times* to read what Agate had written about the play. He was complimentary to Laughton and to Miss Seyler; but of Flora he wrote, "Miss Flora

Robson's Varya was somehow less moving than I expected; you cannot enlarge the self-effacing, and in a smaller theatre I can imagine that it might have been the best performance." The latter assertion at first puzzled Flora and then worried her. It worried her even more when Tony suddenly told her she could not be heard. "You don't know how to use your voice," he said. It was true that the Vic presented a problem to her. Its strange acoustics have foiled many actors over the years. There are blind spots each actor must learn to avoid. But hers was a greater problem. She had become accustomed to playing in small, intimate theatres. Her ability to project to the gallery when she had toured with Ben Greet seemed to have left her. To compensate she tried lifting her voice but this merely lightened it and she lost weight and resonance as she had in *Catherine the Great*.

Tony sensed how concerned she was and brought Bertie Scott over from Belfast to help her. Flora became his pupil in her spare time and he proved to be a master of vocal technique. "You must not be self-conscious about your voice," he advised her, "That is death to the actor," but added, "You must be conscious of self. That is quite another matter." Scott's lessons laid the foundation to Flora's mastery of the vocal arts. It was the voice of which Agate would write – "distilled from all beauty, all mystery, with a dollop of low comedy thrown in!" When I recently spoke to Helen Hayes, the first lady of the American theatre, I asked her what quality it was that had made Flora exceptional. Without a second's hesitation she said, "Voice. Flora Robson has the most romantic voice in the theatre," and added, "It was the voice that Garbo lacked." In answer to the same question, Sir Alec Guinness wrote to me, "The quality above all she possesses is a beautiful warm voice. I have always maintained it is the most beautiful voice of a woman in the theatre in our time."

It seemed fitting that Laughton's Shakespearian debut should be in the role with which he was most closely identified, that of Henry VIII. After playing what one critic described as 'background parts' in the Chekhov, both he and Flora would come to the fore as Henry and Katherine of Aragon. The part of Katherine suited Flora much better than the role of Henry suited Laughton. Shakespeare's Henry is by no means as rich a character as the Henry he had played on the screen. Indeed the part of Wolsey (played in this production by Robert Farquharson) is the superior role, though Laughton was, perhaps, better off playing a character which allowed him to concentrate more on presence than on marvellous speeches. Wearing the clothes he had worn on the screen, he strutted about in the manner of the film Henry and seems to have hoped to get by on that alone. Flora certainly walked away with the play and all the notices were in her favour. Harold Conway wrote in the *Daily Mail*, 'Miss

# THE DAMASCENE SWORD

Robson is an artist of whom it is difficult to write other than in superlatives; her Katherine is a profoundly moving performance, indignation and supreme graciousness being mingled with an artistry which is as rare as it is delightful. Hers is truly great acting." Percy Allen in *Drama* magazine alone pointed out that he thought neither Flora nor Laughton "to be fully equipped vocally and otherwise, to meet the exacting requirements of Elizabethan drama".

Flora felt Tony had let her down in the trial scene where she and Laughton and Farquharson were all bunched together on a small platform which, although it gave a better overall stage picture, allowed them no opportunity of bringing size to the confrontation. She felt, too, that Tony favoured Charles in any decision that involved the two of them. Perhaps this was because he recognized Laughton's lack of experience in classical drama. He had once before told her that he had nothing more to teach her and perhaps he expected her to stand on her own. Whatever it was, she felt that he had created a distance between them that would mar the whole of the season at the Old Vic. Added to this Charles was a difficult fellow player. He was a self-obsessed actor who would only be related *to*. Flora was exasperated at the way he would always look slightly downstage of her when the sense of the moment called upon them to be looking fully at each other. With her background of giving and receiving and relating, Flora would frequently find herself in a bad position, simply because she was feeling the scene and not feeling the audience. She was amused by Robert Farquharson, who was a genuine eccentric. He had dyed hair and wore canary-yellow socks. There was a mysterious quality about him. He was said to have been Oscar Wilde's inspiration for the character of Dorian Grey.

Tony wrote home to Anaghmakerig, "Oh – a nice thing. I slipped into the back of the gallery at yesterday's matinee in Flora's death scene just to see if it was properly audible. Up there I found a great policeman who had looked in to see that all was well – hadn't been able to tear himself away and was standing weeping – great pear drops – at the poor, dear dying Queen. Rather a tribute! . . . the dresses are very suitable to her – red velvet with enormous ermine sleeves. Her big exit from the trial scene was applauded – and cheered – to the echo – completely held the play up – very disconcerting for poor Charles who had to play the rest of the scene with a slight feeling of anti-climax."

Laughton found greater success in *Measure for Measure*. Angelo is a testing role and he rose to the challenge. He created the physical being of a man perplexed by his own sensuality. Perhaps he wooed Isabella as a man who was accustomed to overthrowing virtue, but it was generally conceded to be a fine performance. Flora rather took second place. Bringing a naturalistic approach to the verse she tried to make Isabella a real human being. One critic wrote of Laughton's monotonous delivery, that he used only one of the notes in his voice. Flora's experience of verse went back to early days. She had a natural feeling for rhythm and metre and colour. Tony accused her of singing her lines as Queen Katherine. In trying to employ a different approach to Isabella, she appeared to many to have misread the role. C. B. Purdom wrote in *New Britain*, ". . . Miss Robson should have played Isabella as a tragic character that has a happy fate. Instead . . . we got a rather hysterical good-natured girl, who slapped Angelo's face for insulting her. She could have played the part, I have no doubt, had she been rightly rehearsed; for she has gifts of tragedy; but she made the part sentimentally appealing and kept it well on earth." Instead of meeting the difficulty of the lines head-on, ways were found round the difficulty. For example, the lines which prove a stumbling block to many an Isabella: "Then Isabel live chaste, and brother die/More than our brother is our chastity" were spoken quickly, almost drowned by Claudio's lamentations. It would seem to have been well within Flora's capabilities to have played the line with her usual sincerity, rather than to have taken a short-cut like this.

Marius Goring recalled Lilian Baylis's being impressed by Laughton's interpretation, if not by his speech. "I don't always like him dear, but he's a genius," she conceded. "Flora was perhaps the finest Isabella I ever saw," Goring told me. "She brought such sincerity to it and such innocence. Her Isabella was continuously making discoveries in the play. The last act was a masterpiece in Guthrie's hands. It went at break-neck speed and was truly thrilling."

In *The Tempest*, which followed after Christmas, Laughton was able to stand alone, and at some moments his Prospero found a music of its own. Flora was literally singing her lines in this production, with Tony's blessing. She was cast as Ceres, one of the goddesses. The correspondent of *The Lady* wrote, "The real delight of the production is the masque of the three goddesses, sung to very attractive music, and the discovery that Flora Robson possesses a clear and lovely singing voice. With the field of opera as well as of the tragic drama open to her this young woman will long continue to astonish us." James Agate quipped that Iris, Ceres and Juno "look like goddesses from the forest of Elizabeth Arden".

It was with a greater sense of inadequacy that Flora approached the next production – a comedy – a return to *The Importance of Being Earnest*. "I have no sense of humour," Flora says to this day, "I never understand jokes." On the first occasion she had played Gwendolen Fairfax she felt she had failed. The whole excitement of repertory was being able to attempt roles that, in the natural course of things, might not have come her way. A success in a comedy would perhaps convince managers of her greater range. At Oxford she felt she had failed largely because it had been played in modern dress. At the Vic she was given a lovely green taffeta gown and a remarkable hat and she felt much better. She decided to forget that this was a comedy and approach the role as seriously as she would any other. She stepped very nervously onto the stage on opening night. She was not helped by hearing that Irene Vanbrugh and Alyn Aynesworth were in the audience. They had been Gwendolen and Algy in the original production. Athene Seyler recalled the first scene with Flora, in a letter to me. "Flora was playing Gwendolen and I was playing Lady Bracknell. She was unaccustomed to playing comedy – and when her first line got a laugh from the audience, she turned to me with a delighted smile of astonishment, though strictly she should have remained quite serious. It was a most endearing lapse of the actress into the woman. And, of course, never repeated."

She knew she had been completely successful when she read in *The Sunday Times*, "I don't think I shall ever again get so much delight out of Gwendolen as Miss Robson gave. She delivered that young lady's conscious inanities with that throaty intonation she normally uses for approaches to pathos, only emptied of its pathetic significance. This was lovely, and in the mirror of such playing Gwendolen appeared to quiver within the wave's intenser day! She looked delightful, too, uttering cool paradoxes with an air wittily at variance with a hat resembling a bird sanctuary."

A success in comedy! She wrote to everyone she could, hoping that managers would see new potential in her. Another comedy, Sheridan's *The Rivals*, was to have followed. Miss Baylis was perplexed at the choice of this play because there were fewer parts for women than there were women in the company. She resented paying wages to people who weren't playing. Flora suggested Congreve's *Love for Love* to her as a happy substitute and Miss Baylis agreed. The production proved to be a joyous romp for company and audience alike. In a less showy part, Flora strengthened her new reputation. "Miss Flora Robson's dashing and humorous Mrs Foresight," wrote the correspondent of the *Yorkshire Post*, "will be a revelation for those who have regarded her hitherto only as an actress with an essential flair for the sinister and tragic. She proves, too, that she can sing a Purcell air very prettily." Marius Goring recalled, "Flora was very funny as Mrs Foresight. Immensely sexy too, a true voluptuousness. She adored it; loved making risqué remarks. She did it with incredible charm and immense suggestion."

The final production of her season at the Old Vic gave Flora her most eagerly awaited role. Lady Macbeth offered her the greatest challenge of her career. An indication of the ripeness of the moment was pronounced by Harold Hobson. "She should be the most memorable Lady Macbeth of her generation," he wrote. "Not, perhaps, since the earliest days of Ellen Terry has a young actress appeared on the London stage who has given such promise and foretaste of achievement." ("Our next Ellen Terry . . .")

Tony asked the cast to read A. C. Bradley's lectures on *Macbeth*. Flora found that here was the Scottish queen for her. She would not be as Mrs Siddons had represented her, a murderess on the grand scale. "*Lady Macbeth is an unimaginative woman. She pushes her husband on to fulfil his ambitions, not her own. They are very much in love with one another. In my interpretation the whole play led up to the sleep-walking scene. She has pushed Macbeth to the limit and doesn't want it to go any further. Unimaginative people are horrified by what can happen as a result of their actions. You know what she feels from 'Yet who would have thought the old man to have had so much blood in him?' She is horrified by what she has done. When she is left alone on the stage she says, 'Tis safer to be that which we destroy/Than by destruction dwell in doubtful joy'. She doesn't want any more. At the same moment he is plotting another murder. He is the imaginative one and Shakespeare gives him all the poetry. He has already plotted the murder of Banquo when he tells her she should show friendship to him. The murder comes between them. Gwen Ffrangcon-Davies said to me of the sleep-walking scene, 'Don't forget that she's asleep,' and that's how I played the scene, in deep sleep. So many Lady Macbeths are patently awake and rub furiously at their hands when they say, 'Out damned spot.' I made scarcely any movement. My 'Oh, oh, oh' was the sound of sleep. A nurse, who saw the performance, told me that it was the sound of someone coming out of an anaesthetic. The line 'Hell is murky', which is usually Lady Macbeth's great dramatic cry, I threw away as though turning over in my sleep. Tony asked me if I wanted the Doctor and the Gentlewoman cutting from the scene, but I felt that if Shakespeare had wanted it to be a soliloquy he would have written it as such. I found ways of using them by coming in very close to them, though obviously not aware of their presence. When they backed out of my way and I did not notice, it strengthened the illusion of sleep. There was a moment with Laughton which happened by accident as such moments do. It was in the 'retire we to our chamber' part. I was holding his hands, drawing him up the steps. We both had blood on our hands and they slipped apart. It was a terrible moment. When, in the sleep-walking scene I said, 'Give me your hand,' I recalled the horror of that moment with my hand, but not with my face as I was still fast asleep.*"

Darlington put Flora's name in headlines '**FLORA ROBSON'S LADY MACBETH** – A Magnificent Performance'. "If there has been a finer Lady Macbeth in our time I have not seen her. She had all the baleful horror of a Medusa, and yet managed to show a pitiful humanity." He was virtually alone in praising her. Flora, the production, and particularly Laughton came in for a hammering from the critics. "What the audience made of it all I do not know," wrote the correspondent of the *Saturday Review*, "but I myself do not believe that Shakespeare intended Macbeth to be a petulant and sulky schoolboy who went in perpetual fear of being sent to bed by his wife, his thanes or one of his lackeys. Nor do I believe that he would have mouthed and ranted and stamped his foot like a child of ten: he need not, I suggest, have always soliloquised on A flat and allegro vivace at that. I can find no textual evidence to support the idea that he looked in person like the bearded lady at Mitcham Fair." Ivor Brown wrote that Flora "brings her own strong, yet sensitive intelligence and her emotional resources to Lady Macbeth; her diction is excellent and she has not, like her husband, left her music at home. But she too suffers from the self-conscious intellectualism of the whole business; the dread of being melodramatic seems to inhibit her power as it inhibits all around."

Bridie wrote a letter to Flora, voicing his disappointment at her performance. "I thought your Lady Macbeth wrong, wrong, wrong; lifeless, inept, even stupid... You acted Lady M like a schoolgirl in a Dalcroze school in love with her headmistress. Do read the lines before you go on again and get the horror of them into your soul. Do you know that when you said the raven itself was hoarse, I expected you to follow up by saying when you had got the spare bedroom ready for Duncan you'd go up and rub the bird with Sloan's liniment. And your delivery of the death's picture line was unpardonable. Everyone was terribly bad except Laughton who was only bad. But you had no RIGHT to be bad." Betty Hardy recalled, "I think there were many things about that production that weren't right. Bridie was very cross with her, but he was very cross with the whole production. We walked out. He couldn't take it. I don't know particularly what was driving him mad but I know it got worse and worse and we just stalked out of the theatre." Later Bridie wrote again to Flora, "You are to stop being psychological – you know nothing about it and it is a very technical job – and to become an Old Pro which is the best thing for an actress to be. Pretend as much as you like – that is your job, but when you are acting develop a reflex system that flashes out the effect without the process of thought coming into the business at all.... You are an artist of the theatre and a clumsy amateur of philosophy. So is Tony. He is not so clumsy as you but he has it all wrong. He is one of the 'planning' 'hard thinking' brigade... Your job is to flick Lady M through your soul

FASTER THAN THOUGHT and explain why you did what you did afterwards, if you can be bothered." Betty Hardy continued, "Some time later she performed 'They met us in the day of success' at Drury Lane. She had the most wonderful red wig with long plaits and a magnificent dress and she looked glorious. I was sitting half way back and I clapped my hands together, 'Flora, Flora,' I cried, 'You've done it, you've done it.' I went on and on. I was with Ivor Brown's wife and I think she thought I'd gone off my nut. But you see it was the sudden fulfilment of what she hadn't done that time at the Vic. It cut very deep that she hadn't done it."

Flora was indeed deeply distressed by her lack of success in the role. She believed her interpretation to be correct and when she again tackled the role, in America, fourteen years later she would base her performance on the same premise. She was saddened, too, that what she had hoped would be the crowning success of her season at the Vic was her greatest failure there. Agate said he was not convinced that she was entitled to be called a tragedienne. "If she is, then I submit that the tragedy is of Dryden's colour and not Shakespeare's." But she was certainly not written off to the extent that Laughton was. All his faults were amplified in this role and he had nothing to bring to his performance to redeem himself. A few years later his wife, Elsa Lanchester, would claim that he got the murderer and the husband, but not the soldier. She added that he certainly could not speak the verse, with the sense thrust far in advance of the rhythm. At that accidental moment when Flora was drawing him up the stairs and their hands, covered in blood, slipped apart, on the first night Flora retched involuntarily. At the second performance Laughton retched at an earlier point, thus stealing what he considered a good piece of business. It was another unhappy indication of the kind of actor he was.

At the end of the season Miss Baylis suddenly presented Laughton with a bill for more than a thousand pounds, being the balance of expenditure over and above the money he had voluntarily raised from the Pilgrim Trust! He was furious with her as, apart from anything else, they had played to full houses all season. He was not wholly convinced that the deficit was largely due to her having to pay 'star' salaries to himself and the other five stars. Each had received twenty pounds a week rather than the usual wage of fifteen. Laughton demanded to see the books and discovered that she had re-costumed the entire Sadler's Wells Opera and Ballet from the Old Vic profits! He understandably refused to meet her demands. After the first-night performance of *Macbeth*, as he sat alone and exhausted in his dressing-room, depressed at what he knew had been a far from successful performance, Miss Baylis appeared at his door dressed in

# THE DAMASCENE SWORD

her usual first-night apparel, her academic robes. "Never mind, dear," she said, "I'm sure you did your best. And I am sure that one day you might be quite a good Macbeth." And out she walked.

On the last night there was always a special celebration at the Vic. Laughton made a speech and there were calls from the gallery. "Good old Nero!" they shouted, recalling his performance in *The Sign of the Cross*. Then they shouted for Elsa Lanchester, who was in the stalls. "Bring her up!" someone shouted. Charles replied in glee, "Many people have tried to do that, my friend, but none have succeeded." Flora was distressed and embarrassed when it came time for presents to be handed up by the audience of regular patrons to the actors. There was no present for Charles. Dislike his work as she often had, she liked him very much as a person and was sorry to see him rejected in this way.

It was all over. Flora had mixed feelings about her time at the Old Vic. Her successes were somewhat tarnished by her failure in *Macbeth*. There had not been quite the variety of roles for which she had hoped; rather, Athene Seyler was allotted the good comedy parts, Ursula Jeans the romantic roles, and so forth. She also felt that she had lost her special relationship with Tony. In the early days he had worked to build her up. Now, when she had some stature in the profession, he seemed to want to pull her down. It was all rather disturbing and Flora had no idea how to cope with it. Yet she knew what a gifted director he was and had she to choose she would never choose anyone other than Tony. It is interesting to note that she would act only once more in Shakespeare on the London stage and that, not for more than seventeen years.

## 5

Flora was in a very good position. Korda had put her under contract to London Films. His obsession with making films of the private lives of great historical characters had led him to search for a property about Queen Elizabeth, believing her to be history's greatest 'star' beside Henry VIII. He intended that Flora should play Elizabeth. This meant that she would have a regular income whether she was in or out of work and enabled her eventually to take a smart house in Downshire Hill in Hampstead, buy a car and engage a chauffeur. This spared her the embarrassment of taking taxis to the theatre with an old felt hat pulled down over her eyes in case anyone should recognize her.

As well as this material well-being she had the promise of a splendid part in the theatre. Bridie had been true to his word and, with Claud Gurney, had written a play for her about Mary Read, the woman pirate. Flora had followed the progress of the play through its development. Bridie had kept her informed by letter of any change and she was able to read through each new draft as it was completed. The play called for a large cast and it would be expensive to mount, so managements were less than eager to take it on. Bridie sent the play to Basil Dean for his consideration. It was still not in its final form but Bridie assured him that it would be completed by the autumn. Around this time Dean was about to produce a comedy at the Theatre Royal, Haymarket, and asked Flora to appear in it. Flora told his business manager that she needed to keep herself free for another part later in the year. He suggested that she might go into the comedy for three months and give notice when she knew the other play to be ready. While talking to him she managed to negotiate a salary of £40 a week, £5 more than her last West End wage. She felt very pleased with herself. Because of her contract she had to notify Korda before finally accepting the offer. He was furious that she had tried to settle the salary herself and warned her never to do it again. She was chastened when she learned he had been able to secure twice what she had been offered. Thereafter, she left all her business arrangements to an agent.

The play at the Haymarket was Dodie Smith's *Touch Wood*. Flora's part was not really a star role. Elizabeth Enticknap was, as Ivor Brown put it, "needle woman and general consultant on the sexual aspects of vacational life", an observer rather than a participant in the main plot. This concerned three children staying in a hotel in Scotland. The eldest, a romantic, attractive girl, falls in love with a stranger and tries to break up his marriage. Ian Hunter and Marie Ney were the married couple and Dorothy Hyson the girl. A splendid cast also included Dennis Arundell, Elliot Mason and Frank Pettingell. Flora was to make firm friends with Oriel Ross, the beautiful actress from musical comedy who had once stopped an entire show by walking across the stage with a borzoi. Oriel was the sister of Joan Swinstead. Flora admired her approach to the play. She would always stand in the wings when not involved in the action. "I like to keep in the mood of the play," she told Flora.

"*Mr Dean came to see me in* For Services Rendered *and he looked at his programme and kept asking, 'Who* is *that girl? I've never seen her before.' When he came round backstage after the performance he asked me what other work I had done. I reminded him that I had played in* Will Shakespeare *under his direction, and that we had had a jolly good row. He thoroughly appreciated the joke! I enjoyed working with him enormously. Many hated the way he would give an inflexion to an actor but I always welcomed it. He showed me how many ways it was possible to interpret a line. What I learned from Tony Guthrie was pace. He worked in big strokes and saw the play as a whole. He knew when the action must be rapid and when it should be slow and impressive. Basil Dean, on the other hand, was particularly fine at details. He took pains with them and taught me to do the same."*

The play was a great success and Flora received glowing reviews. Agate wrote, "I am not sure that when all is said and done the palm must not be given to Miss Flora Robson." It was a welcome variant of the part she dreaded – the 'tortured spinster' in a lighter key, the woman left over from the Great War who had learned a sense of humour. The most treasured tribute came from Noël Coward, who visited her in her dressing-room. "I waited and waited, expecting you to suffer," he said, "and I was so happy to find you were funny!"

It seemed that Basil Dean was not interested in *Mary Read* and so Flora went to see Korda. To her great joy he decided to back the play himself, his first venture into theatre. From the beginning, there seemed to be only one director appropriate to work with Flora and Bridie. Bridie had already decided on Tony, and Flora agreed. No one would be able to handle the huge crowd scenes as well as he. There were two characters in the play whom Bridie insisted should be carefully chosen to complement Flora – Mary's lover, Edward Earle, and the other woman pirate, Ann Bonny. Barry Jones, Herbert Marshall and Laurence Olivier were all considered for the role of Earle. But Bridie was able to interest the man who had been his original choice. Earle would be played by Robert Donat, and Ann Bonny by Betty Hardy. Flora was in seventh heaven! She stayed with *Touch Wood* for the first few months and then joined her family for a summer holiday in the Isles of Scilly.

John Robson had married a girl from the Scillies and the family visited her home as often as they could. They would all cram into the little fisherman's cottage which had been his wife's home. The people of the Scillies are warm and friendly, treating everyone as their equal. It was relaxing for Flora to become an ordinary person again. John Robson's youngest son, Hugh, recalled, "Flora had one of the first hand-held cine-cameras I'd ever seen. She wrote the scenario of a pirate film, hired a boat and we had the pirates rowing ashore and coming up the beach. I was a sort of Jim Hawkins character. There was a scene where she directed the camera to 'Pan up to John's hand'. My father had the half of one finger missing and so the camera moved up and caught the hand on the edge of the boat. It was a silent film, but from what I can remember it was well made. She used her experience of acting in films and constructed it as though it was being made for the cinema, not just shown as a home movie."

While in the Scillies she took many trips by boat and sat in the

# FLORA

prow so she could feel the salt spray on her face. It was all training for *Mary Read*. She watched how her brother John walked and copied his movements. For much of the time she would be dressed as a man, and Mary Read convinced soldiers that she was one of them. She was able to relax, to swim and to sunbathe and breathe the wonderful fresh air, but being in that sea-bound environment she could not help but draw what she could for her part. In the evenings, the family would recall for the children the exploits of Grandfather MacKenzie, who had been the master of a sailing ship long before they were born.

*"When steam came in, my grandmother said, 'Why go into dirty coal ships?' because he had to go in as second-in-command while he learned the job of sailing them. Later on he went to Japan. The Japanese lured English and American sailors to go over and train their Navy. (They had Germans to train their Army.) Even today they keep their logs in English. He became senior commodore for the Nippon-Yusen-Kaisha line. His last voyage was on their best ship, the tenth biggest in the world. He was just entering the Mediterranean in 1904, making for the straits, when Russia and Japan declared war. The entire Russian fleet in the Mediterranean went after him. The ship was very fast and he got away and got into Malta where the docks are very deep. The ships blockaded Malta and he couldn't get out. The British fleet advised him of their position. He stayed in dock and painted the ship another colour. Then he went out through the blockade, skilfully manoeuvring through the Russian ships, playing on an old gramophone all the time, 'Waltz Me Around Again Willie.' He went back through Gibraltar and round the Cape. He was later decorated by the Emperor of Japan with the Order of the Rising Sun."*

The sea was certainly in her blood and Flora was soon putting her history to good use. Her fencing lessons from M. Bertrand at RADA and with Captain Kelly were also useful for playing in *Mary Read*. All actors must learn to be prepared for the unexpected to occur. She can never have realized she would be called upon to use this skill on stage. It was wonderful to work with Robert Donat again. She trusted him implicitly. She noticed that filming had taken away all the external mannerisms which had sometimes negated what his characters should feel. She was able to tell him, "Your emotional acting has improved. You now speak from inside."

"She and Donat were so good together," Betty Hardy remembered. "Tony had a devastating way of retreating to the very back of the building when they were doing their love scene. This upset Flora terribly because she could not find the key to the scene. Tony left it to Flora and Don [Donat] to work it out for themselves. One night Don gave her a lift home in his car. He held her hand all the way and they talked about the scene. After that it was all right. It's very important to her, you know, touching. He was such a beautiful, loving, glorious person. He understood through blank walls. Oh he was a dear man, a rich gift. That scene between the two of them was fascinating."

The company travelled to Manchester to break the play in. Opening night was postponed because the city was covered by a blanket of thick fog. Flora developed a bad cold. Though she managed fairly well for the first few performances her voice began to suffer. Tony called rehearsals between the matinee and evening performances and expected it to be delivered at full power. Flora's voice disappeared. Bridie took her to a specialist who diagnosed a nodule on her vocal chords. Flora was ordered to rest and not to speak until the nodule was gone. She was sent home to London and Shela came to nurse her. The nodule vanished while the company were rehearsing for the London opening and Bertie Scott was summoned to bring back her voice to performance pitch. Scott stood in the wings at His Majesty's Theatre on opening night, 21 November 1934. It was a difficult performance. Flora had to shout orders above the roar of cannon and she barely managed to get to the end. By the end of the week she felt her voice to be strengthening and continued, faithfully, to practise the exercises Scott had taught her.

Her performance was an unqualified success. The critic of the *Morning Post* wrote that the play "gives us the finest piece of all-out acting that the year has seen in the performance of the title-part by Miss Flora Robson. Her dash and zest and dare-devilry, and faith and courage, and ringing voice and – at the right time – feminine tenderness and sacrifice, roused the audience to such a pitch of enthusiasm at the finish that the rest of the company forgot all about themselves and just joined in – one of the rarest of all tributes." "Flora Robson lives Mary Read," claimed the *Daily Express*, "It is the performance of a great actress." Darlington called it "the part of her life-time, in the sense that no other actress could play it. It calls for a combination of qualities that she alone possesses." Agate declared, "If I must see another Hamlet before the year is out I would sooner see Miss Robson's than anybody's. In fact I *have* seen it, and in this play." The play lasted for little more than a hundred performances but Flora regained confidence in her abilities after the demoralizing experience of *Macbeth*.

Towards the end of *Mary Read*, Earle asked Mary to kill him rather than let him be tortured as a spy. Flora had to kiss him, pull out a gun and fire it straight at his heart, with a realistic flash of gunpowder from the gun. His shirt was covered with a chemical which gave the illusion of wetness, for Earle had been in the sea. One night the shirt caught fire from the gun. Robert crushed the flames out with his fingers as he fell. Flora rushed to him as soon as the curtain was down. Robert sat up and pronounced, "Flora has singed my navel!" On another occasion, the gun failed to go off at all and she drew a dagger she carried for just such an eventuality and stabbed him to death! In an earlier scene there was a line Robert felt should get a laugh and the laugh would not come. He asked Flora what she was doing at that moment. She replied that she was punching holes in her belt. He asked if she would delay her business until after the line and she did so. The laugh always came at subsequent performances. Flora remembers this incident with affection. This was the joy of working with a sympathetic fellow player. Donat had not won the laugh at her expense. They had created it together by sensitivity and timing. This was the kind of acting they had looked for in vain when, inspired with ideals, they had both come to the West End from Cambridge. Later in life Donat was to gain the reputation of being a difficult actor, but in *Mary Read* he was quite the reverse. Flora was overjoyed that he should be by her side in this great success on the stage of the theatre where, as a child, she had dreamed of becoming an actress.

## 6

She strained her eyes as she looked across the desert. A lone horseman grew from a tiny dot on the horizon. Moments later she could see he was dressed in the white robes of a sheikh which billowed out behind him as his horse thundered closer. The two Englishwomen looked at one another in apprehension. They knew their camels would not be swift enough to save them. The dragoman looked unconcerned. Perhaps he had lured them to this secluded spot so that they might be captured. The white stallion was almost upon them but, British to the last, they stood their ground, their hearts beating faster. The sheikh was now only feet from them. He reined in his stallion. They could see his dark eyes burning. "Hello there!" he cried.

No, this was not a scene from one of Flora's films, though Korda and London Films had backed the whole adventure. Noticing how pale and tired she had looked after the exhausting *Mary Read* episode, Korda decided to send her on holiday. "If I were to ask you where in the world you would most like to go," he said, "where would you choose?" Without a second's hesitation, Flora replied, "Egypt!" "Then you shall go," he told her. Flora invited Margery Phipps-Walker, her old friend from Cambridge, to be her travelling companion, and the two of them set out together at the end of February 1935.

# THE DAMASCENE SWORD

This explains why the two found themselves in a situation redolent of a Valentino romance. The sheikh turned out to be the dragoman's cousin. There was no danger at all. But the actress in both of them revelled in the heady situation and dramatized it out of all proportion! Flora and Margery were both inspired by the romance of Egypt – the Sphinx and the Pyramids, Karnak by moonlight, Cleopatra's Palace at Memphis. Three weeks in the sun and the dry desert air cured Flora of all her throat troubles and she returned to England tanned and healthy, with all the excitement of the holiday, captured on film, to share with her nephews.

Flora expected her film to be ready to begin on her return but the script had not even been written. London Films were quite prepared for Flora to continue to draw salary for as long as it took them to get production under way. But Flora was not happy to remain idle. She had worked for her success and was not prepared to let the public forget her while she marked time waiting for the film to be readied. Ronald Adam of the Embassy Theatre had sent her the script of a two-handed play he hoped to present. Flora asked Korda if she could do the play. He was reluctant to agree because he wanted Flora available for the film. She was able to persuade him that she would leave the play as soon as she was required. It was fortunate for her that she was able to do so, for it would be another year before she began work on the film.

*Close Quarters* was Gilbert Lennox's adaptation of a play by Swiss author W. O. Somin. It related the story of Gustav and Liesa Bergmann. He was a Socialist agitator who has denounced a man murdered a few hours later. Suspicion falls on him as he had passed through the wood where the crime was committed. A missing glove appears to form a clue which might convict him. Eventually his wife confesses that she was having an affair with her husband's political enemy and it was she who murdered him. At the end of the play he shoots his wife and then himself, and a wireless announcement informs the audience that the glove found belonged to a woman. It was an intensely difficult play as it involved only the two actors on the stage for the whole time. An essential ingredient for success in such a production is to have a pair of actors of great sensitivity and mutual respect.

Ronald Adam had engaged the Viennese-born actor Oscar Homolka to play Gustav. Homolka had worked for several years with the Max Reinhardt company before coming to London to appear in a play which was subsequently cancelled. He spoke little English but he had an unusual quality which Adam felt would be an asset to the play. He was very polite to Flora and she did her best to put him at his ease although the language barrier was a problem. She realized that she had to drive past his hotel on the way to rehearsal and offered to give him a lift in her car. As time went by she would have to wait for him longer and longer each day. One morning she had waited for twenty minutes before deciding to go on without him. For all she knew he might have set out earlier, and she would herself be late. When he eventually arrived at rehearsal he was angry that Flora had not waited. From that day onwards a frigid wall grew between them. He played his part in isolation. He would flinch from Flora whenever she touched him, as though repelled by her. There was no sharing, no giving and receiving. With Homolka she found that everything she gave met with the wall of his indifference. Perhaps she was more conscious of his shortcomings, having so recently played with the sensitive and sympathetic Robert Donat. Betty Hardy was her understudy for a time and saw how desperately unhappy Flora was. She would come off stage sobbing with frustration, and the tension often made her sick in the wings.

Whatever might have been their personal relationship, this tension did not reach the audience and the play was enough of a success to transfer first to the Haymarket and then to the Savoy. London was undergoing a heatwave and at first the audiences were slow to come. Agate, in his usual rhetorical style, launched an attack on the theatre snobs, in a piece headed 'J'ACCUSE!' "I accuse the intellectuals, fashionables and merely wealthy of London of taking no interest in true theatre, in a good play, and in what I hold to be the finest acting in London since Bernhardt's visit," he wrote. He was mostly impressed by Homolka and the range of his acting at the Embassy but had this to say when the play transferred, "The acting, in my opinion, is truly grand. At Swiss Cottage Miss Robson was a little over-partnered; she has now brought more guns into action, and returns salvo for salvo. There is no courtesy question of the English or the Austrian troops firing first, they blaze away together and at point-blank range." Flora wrote to Rita Room, "This part is mostly 'giving' and not many people realise that I deliberately keep myself in the background so that Homolka may keep the focus. We both of us get very worked up by the third act and always stream with tears, but it is a relief for me to let things go after the tension of the other acts." She received a great deal of praise for the confession scene, which was her moment to shine. *The Times* proposed that hers was the more difficult role because she had to maintain a condition of nervous anxiety and the woman was on the point of becoming a bore by the time she collapsed into her confession. Ivor Brown wrote that "during the first two acts she plays a waiting hand finely; in the last she can show all her strength and we know the

# THE DAMASCENE SWORD

dominion she can exercise," and added, "We have watched a rare partnership."

Flora's health was under such strain that her doctor advised her to leave the cast. She asked for Korda's help and he formally asked for her withdrawal so she could be available for filming. Gwen Ffrangcon-Davies replaced Flora as Liesa but, shortly afterwards, Homolka himself became ill and the play finally closed.

The imminence of the film had simply been an excuse to get Flora out of the play. There was still no sign of a production date. There always seemed to be just a few more weeks to wait. Flora was dejected. She went away again to the Scillies but found it difficult to be as light-hearted as she had felt the previous year. She wrote to St John Ervine, utterly depressed, blaming her inferiority complex for the way she felt. His reply, as always, was wonderfully encouraging.

"You are now at the stage in your career when critics watch you with coldly judicious eyes. This is a sort of tempering time for you. You've been out in the cold and you've been in the furnace. Now you're being skilfully hammered into shape. I don't suppose steel likes being hammered into damascene swords, but will the hammering matter, or be remembered when the sword is finished and flourished? . . . Tush to your inferiority complex! You ain't got one. Or you didn't ought to 'ave! . . . Buck up, my dear. You must never let your sails flap in the doldrums. Make them swell out like proud banners!"

She was busily researching Elizabeth. She read Professor Neale's *Queen Elizabeth*, and Korda told her to read Strachey's *Elizabeth and Essex* and Gobineau's *Renaissance*. She spoke to Hal Rosson, the American cinematographer who was working in England, and learned a lot from him about acting in front of the camera. She played Elizabeth in *The Golden Hind*, by Arthur Bryant and Peter Creswell, on the radio. Godfrey Tearle was cast as Drake. Also in the cast were George Sanders, Carleton Hobbs and Richard Goolden and the incidental music was written by Dennis Arundell. This was followed by a radio production of *Macbeth* in which she played once more opposite Tearle, with James Mason, Carleton Hobbs and Jack Allen in the cast, and directed by Peter Creswell. Somewhat against her interpretation of the role, *The Times* found her "more imaginative than her husband" but Grace Wyndham Goldie was more sympathetic to her point of view. She wrote in *The Listener* that Flora had given "a careful, sensitive and moving performance which I found the most interesting thing in the production and which filled me with pity, but never with horror or awe." Flora performed the letter scene from *Macbeth* at the Shakespeare Matinee in aid of the National

# FLORA

Theatre which was given before the Duke and Duchess of York and Princess Elizabeth at the Theatre Royal, Drury Lane. This was the occasion previously recalled by Betty Hardy.

An offer came which interested Flora. She was asked to play the title role in a new play by Wilfrid Grantham, *Mary Tudor*, an interesting and sympathetic approach to Elizabeth's elder sister, which dealt with her longing for love and the child she would never have. Korda consented to her doing the play with the usual proviso that she be available to do the film when it was ready. Peter Creswell was engaged to direct and Marius Goring was cast opposite Flora as Philip of Spain. The play, which was presented at the Playhouse, was not well received although some of the critics enjoyed Flora's sure touch. Ivor Brown wrote in the *Sketch*, "the play is well worth the attention of those interested in Tudor times; for those who are not, there is the presence of Flora Robson, in some lovely Tudor dresses, to offer as fine a piece of acting as she has ever given us. There are no high points in her part; it is a sustained journey on the lower slopes of dramatic emotion, but it is sure footed travel, achieving abundant pathos as Mary acquires and loses both her husband and her hope of a child."

"My own sorrows get mixed up with the play," she wrote to Rita Room, "especially the longing for a son. I can always identify with that. Sometimes I feel the part intensely, usually the performances after matinees. The more tired one is, the more one's emotions rise to the surface. But my technique is improving so much that I can act sorrows well enough to convince myself, and that brings up the real feeling again. There is hardly a single night when I have not cried in the last scene."

A small girl was taken by her parents to see Flora in this play as Flora, herself, had been taken to see *Faust* by her father. She was so enthralled by what she saw that she decided there and then to go on the stage. Later she became a child broadcaster and actress and eventually an international singing star. Her name was Petula Clark. The play had a short run. It suffered at the box-office, as so many other plays did, after the death of King George V, and it came off. Flora was freed only weeks before she would have had to leave the play anyway. At last, in the Spring of 1936, Flora was called to begin work on her film – *Fire Over England*.

## 7

It was a relief finally to get to work on the film, but Flora was disappointed at the size and scope of her part. She had imagined that the focus would be as much on Elizabeth as it had been on Henry in the Laughton film. On the contrary, the Queen was only a minor role in the script. Based on the A. E. W. Mason novel, the screenplay had been written by Clemence Dane. The original novel was the story of a lady-in-waiting at the court, Lady Cynthia. Cast in the role was a bright-eyed English rose whom Korda was grooming for stardom. It was Vivien Leigh. Opposite her, as the hero, was Laurence Olivier. All the action seemed to be devoted to this love affair and the exploits of the young man in Spain.

Flora was immediately caught up in costume fittings and make-up tests. Her make-up would be very elaborate. An American make-up expert, Guy Pearce, was brought over to transform Flora into an acceptable image of the Queen. To be on the set by nine o'clock, Flora had to be up at a quarter to six and in the make-up department an hour later. Pearce worked from a death-mask of Elizabeth. The Queen had no eyebrows so Flora had to lose hers, and thin brows were painted in above her natural line. The hooked nose was made of putty which was glued to her own nose, covered with layers of cotton lint and finally coated in latex to match her skin. *"Physically I was all wrong for the part. I am not in any way like Elizabeth. The nose was quite a masterpiece of cosmetic art. James Wong Howe, the cameraman, described it as a 'photographically eloquent nose'!"* Flora begged all interviewers not to make her laugh as it might bring the nose off.

The costumes were extremely heavy and she would be sewn in to hoist up the collar. This meant that she had to remain in her costume and make-up the entire day. One of the dresses, worn in the Tapestry Room scene, was covered in jewels and weighed more than a hundred pounds. The wig, too, was decorated with heavy jewels. Because of the width of her dresses, there was nowhere she could sit other than bolt upright on a stool placed underneath her petticoats. With no support, it was only a short time before her back would be aching under the weight of her head-dress and before her shoulders were raw and sore as the bones in her costume rubbed against her skin. Yet she would have to remain like this for up to eight hours at a stretch. People who did not know her found her quite disagreeable until they realized that perhaps she had every right to be. When she did get on the set, she had often to make long, sweeping exits in take after take and found herself wheezing for breath under the strain of carrying the weight. She felt quite wretched, as well she might, and wondered what had induced her to imagine that this would be a great opportunity. The American director William K. Howard didn't seem at all interested in her, and her researches seemed to have gone for naught. He seemed interested only in making the film comprehensible to farmers in the Middle West of America who had never heard of

# FLORA

Elizabeth, rather than to anyone who might expect an intelligent character study.

She seemed to have been waiting for hours. The entire day had been lavished on Vivien Leigh, who had little acting experience. Flora resented the fact that Vivien should be paid so much more than she with all her years of work and training. Resentment burrowed through her mind as she sat in desperate discomfort, hour after hour, feeling the sweat coursing its subtly torturous way down the inside of her putty nose. She tried to think positively but found it difficult. She was dressed to do the first big scene in the film in which Elizabeth gave audience to the Spanish Ambassador. Henry Oscar, who was cast as the Ambassador, wandered over to talk to her and they chatted for a while about old times. Flora suggested that they might go over their lines. It was a nine-page scene and she was worried about drying in the middle. They were able to rehearse the scene several times and knew it perfectly when, an hour before the crew would wrap up for the day, Flora and Henry Oscar were called to the set. Bill Howard, the director, apologized for keeping them waiting and told them he wanted to use the hour for running the scene through without the cameras. Flora had known this would happen. The extras were positioned and Howard settled down to watch the run-through. Flora put all she had into that performance. The hours of waiting had sharpened her ambition. She would show them what experience meant. Both she and Henry Oscar were word perfect and gave magnificent performances. At the end of the audience Flora swept past the Spanish Ambassador, "Must? . . . Little man, little man," she said, looking down at him, "Must is not a word to use to princes. Our council shall confer with you. Meanwhile go home and keep quiet," and, taking Leicester's arm, she majestically left the chamber.

Great excitement broke loose. Howard wanted to shoot it straight away! "But, aren't you going to direct us?" Henry Oscar asked. "We shoot, we shoot," yelled Howard. One whole week had been scheduled for shooting this scene. All the work was completed by late morning the following day, saving the company thousands of pounds. The only people to be unhappy about it were the disgruntled extras who lost a whole week's money.

Suddenly everyone began to treat Flora rather differently! But she still felt sorry that the role was not more fully conceived in the script and that even well-played scenes would be lost amidst Olivier's swashbuckling scenes which were being built up daily. One day Raymond Massey, whom she remembered from Oxford Playhouse days, came to sit beside her for a chat. "Do you think anyone will notice you and me in this film?" Flora asked him. "You can't make small parts of Elizabeth and Philip of Spain," was his reply. There were other old friends. James Mason had a small uncredited role and Henry Ainley was cast as Olivier's father. Drink would destroy his distinguished career and it was already beginning to take its toll. He filmed only one scene before Korda discharged him and the character's remaining scenes were played by another actor. Leslie Banks was cast as Leicester and there was the fine old actor Morton Selten, who had acted with Irving and Ellen Terry, as Lord Burleigh. Selten was believed to be an illegitimate son of Edward VII. In make-up tests, the original beard with which he was fitted was vetoed in favour of a longer one. The original proved him to be the image of his royal 'parent'. Laurence Olivier made a splendid, dashing hero and, in the best tradition, insisted on doing all his own stunts, to the consternation of Erich Pommer who was in charge of production. Flora defended Olivier saying, "Larry would feel a fraud for being praised for a scene he did not do himself." "All film acting is fraud," replied Pommer.

The previous year, Flora had turned out to watch the Silver Jubilee procession. She had wanted to see how a real queen behaved. Queen Mary had been so overcome by the loyalty of the crowd that she had been in tears. Flora was to have a similar experience when she played a scene in which she had to walk in procession through cheering crowds. She was overcome by the expression of so much love and, quite unwittingly, she cried herself. Bill Howard called to her, "Miss Robson, will you please remember you are not at a film premiere!"

In her researches, Flora had come across the original speech Elizabeth had made at Tilbury. It was a wonderful speech which fired the troops with the patriotic fervour that would sink the Armada. "I know I have the body of a weak and feeble woman, but I have the heart and stomach of a king, and of a king of England too . . ." It was not a speech that was widely known in those days, but it had such power and majesty that it leapt from the page. Charles Laughton was filming *Rembrandt* on another sound stage and she asked his advice. Clemence Dane had written a four-line speech which had nothing of the ring of the original. Laughton suggested she shorten Elizabeth's speech as it was rather long. Flora rewrote it and because audiences of the day might have thought the word 'stomach' humorous in that context, replaced it with the word 'valour'. Laughton suggested she ask the director if he would mind filming two versions of the speech, the one that was in the script and the one she had discovered. This way no one would take umbrage at her wanting to rewrite the script.

During the procession to Tilbury, Flora had been mounted on a fine handsome Grand National runner who was used to cheering crowds. On the day of the shooting of the Tilbury speech the horse

## FLORA

was found to be lame. The substitute was a rather poor beast by comparison and so Elizabeth arrived at Tilbury in somewhat reduced circumstances.

The horse was nervous of the crowds and the cameras, and experienced horsemen had always to be at hand in case it bolted. Flora felt uncertain enough as she had never ridden side-saddle and was wearing another large gown and a steel breastplate as well. She had still not mentioned the speech when the moment came to shoot the scene. "*I was just about to get on my horse when I spotted Pommer out of the corner of my eye. I told him about the speech and recited it to him. He called the director over and they both agreed to shooting it. There were terrible problems with the horse. It was terrified of all the technical equipment and just wouldn't stand still. Everything would be ready and then at the last moment the horse would be frightened by something and would shy away. They tried holding it from the front, and holding it by the tail. Some of the technicians sat on the ground and stroked its legs but still it shied away at the vital moment. Eventually someone had the bright idea of boxing it in as though it were at home in its stall and it was a lot happier about this. I asked the director which speech I should do first. 'Why, the one you wrote,' was his reply!*" Flora launched into the speech. The horse was frightened by the sound of her voice and wheeled about a bit but eventually satisfactory takes were made and Elizabeth's wonderful speech passed into common knowledge. So successful were all of Flora's scenes that the production team decided there should be more pomp and pageantry and a scene was added to the end of the film in which Elizabeth leads her people in a prayer of thanksgiving for a safe deliverance from the Armada. The camera holds her face in full close-up and we see the lovers behind her, to each side of her, looking at each other. The film was wrapped up.

Flora had no regrets at leaving behind all the wigs and costumes and trappings of the part. Raymond Mander, the theatre historian, who played a small part in the film, recalled that at the end of the last day of filming, Flora tore off her putty nose and, flinging it to the ground, declared, "That's the end of old Liz!" Mander treasured the putty relic for many years. Her only regrets were still to do with her inability to make the role a definitive interpretation that would enhance her career. As it was, she felt it would be merely a cameo. One day she went with some friends to see a film at the Odeon, Leicester Square. The programme included a trailer for *Fire Over England*. "*First of all there was Vivien Leigh sitting at the spinet, singing, and her name in big letters across the screen, and then there was Larry Olivier battling away in a sword fight. I thought to myself, 'Aren't I even in this picture?' And then that wonderful Richard Addinsell score suddenly swelled up and there I was on my horse on the way to Tilbury*

# THE DAMASCENE SWORD

*and it said, 'And Starring FLORA ROBSON as Queen Elizabeth'. I couldn't believe it. Until that moment I didn't realize I was the star of the film!"*

Raymond Massey had been right. It was impossible to make small parts of such great historical characters. Both of them stole all the notices and it is the best remembered and best loved of all of Flora's films. "Flora Robson is Gloriana to the life," proclaimed the *New Statesman. The New York Times* observed that she steered "a shrewd middle course between caricature and glorification . . . presenting her as she must have been: torn between her dignity as a queen, her frailty as a woman; tender yet ruthless, ambitious yet weary, vain yet honest. It is a sincere and eloquent performance, one of the best this year." The film itself was not as successful. It is too episodic. A better film could have been made by concentration on fewer of the themes. The photography is seldom inspired. With the exception of the sumptuously lit closet scene when Olivier takes his leave of his lady and his Queen, it is flat and dull. The Armada is made up of obvious models. There is no through-line to Flora's performance. This is perhaps not surprising when Flora was never aware of her character's status in the film. Graham Greene, in his *Spectator* review, likened this Queen Elizabeth to the headmistress of a girl's school. Perhaps he was going too far, and he admitted he was in a minority, but on the director's own admission, the film was made with the farmers of the Middle West of America in mind. If it was also being exhibited to a sophisticated theatre-going public there was bound to be a dilemma of taste. The one quality which stands out above any other in Flora's performance is her warmth, a rare commodity in the cinema of the thirties. It was for this reason that *Fire Over England* won her a place in the hearts of audiences everywhere.

It seemed as though Flora was certain of a successful career in films. Projects for her to go to Hollywood to play Elizabeth again, with Katharine Hepburn in John Ford's *Mary of Scotland*, and to appear as a Chinese peasant with Paul Muni in *The Good Earth* for MGM, came to nothing. But Flora believed there might be more prestigious projects at home. She hoped to persuade Korda to film *Mary Read*, which was certainly a filmic subject, and because of her striking physical resemblance to Amy Johnson, the aviatrix, she hoped for a film to be based on her exploits. For the present she had to content herself with a character role as the octogenarian Empress Livia in the film version of Robert Graves' novels of ancient Rome at its most decadent, *I Claudius*, which Josef von Sternberg was filming for Korda at Denham. Charles Laughton was cast as Claudius, Emlyn Williams as Caligula and Merle Oberon as Messalina. Von

# FLORA

Sternberg, the director who brought Marlene Dietrich to prominence, was the last of the old-time directors. He still wore the director's uniform of riding boots and breeches. An expert at lighting, he created wonderful effects in the huge sets at his disposal. This was Korda's most ambitious project to date. Flora needed an even more complex make-up than she had worn as Elizabeth, with a latex mask which covered most of her face and neck and uncomfortable padding round her mouth. Charles Laughton was quite as difficult to act with in a film as he had been on stage. He would angle his head round to the camera as he had done to the audience at the Old Vic. When they were on camera together he would draw attention to himself all the time. Raymond Massey had been cast as Justus but demanded to be released when he learned he would be working with Laughton. There was a frigid atmosphere between Charles and the director. Laughton would play a gramophone record of Edward VIII's abdication speech before every scene because in it he found, so he claimed, the key to his character. Production went way over schedule while von Sternberg waited for Laughton to develop his characterization. Merle Oberon was involved in a dreadful car crash and was rushed to hospital. She had worked only briefly on her scenes and Korda decided to cut his losses by abandoning work on the film. The existing footage which is stored in the National Film Archive in London, which it has been my privilege to see, and some of which was linked together in the television programme, 'The Epic that Never Was', indicates what a fine piece of cinema was lost. Laughton was every inch Claudius and it showed promise of being his finest performance. Flora almost completed work and though the footage of her death scene has vanished, what remains shows she gave a performance of depth and imagination in the scenes at her disposal. Her ageing was excellently achieved and there were flashes of wry humour. Had the film been released she would probably have been offered a whole line of ancients to play which might not have been to her advantage but perhaps the film would have shown the public more of her range.

None of the projects she really wanted to pursue seemed to be materializing so Flora asked for a part in Pommer's production *Troopship*, which would be released in Britain as *Farewell Again*. It was the story of a troopship bringing the 3rd Royal Lancers, a cavalry regiment, home to England after a five-year tour of duty in India. Hours short of their destination, the orders are changed and the company are told that they will dock at Southampton for six hours before returning to the near East. The film detailed the effect of this news upon a number of the men aboard. Leslie Banks was cast as the Commanding Officer and Flora was interested in the part of the wife who knows she is dying from an incurable disease. She leaves the ship at Southampton without telling her husband that she will never see him again. Korda was not keen for her to play the part. *"He agreed that it was rich in dramatic and emotional opportunity but there was nothing 'grand' about it. Mr Korda rather fancied me as a 'grande dame' on the screen."* She managed to persuade him that there were qualities of grandness in the way the woman concealed her illness from her husband. It was a smallish part in an excellent film which was directed by another American, Tim Whelan. James Wong Howe was again the cinematographer and he was to say of Flora that she was the most interesting actress he had ever had to photograph. She looks lovely in this film, her hair-line broken by soft, flattering curls. Some of her scenes are quite moving and it is good to see Flora as she really was and not hidden behind the mask of an extravagant character. "Flora Robson adds one more laurel to her crown," remarked the *Sunday Chronicle*. The *News Chronicle* added that she gave "a sweetly sensitive and touching performance".

## 8

"When I was five or six," Hugh Robson recalled, "Flora would send a limousine down with her chauffeur to our little house in Hinckley and whisk us up Watling Street to London. We were taken to Flora's house in Downshire Hill which, although it was only a small London house, to me, living as we did in tiny rooms, was the grandest house I had ever seen. At Christmas she would take us to a pantomime and to Gamages. There was no parking problem – the chauffeur just deposited us. There was always a really big family party. She was a family person. We weren't ever aware of the actress side. She adored the family side. We told stories around the fire. She didn't mind that we weren't fashionable or that we were country bumpkins. She had the gift of being the same to all members of the family. She was a *real* aunt!"

There was no doubt that Flora loved to be surrounded by family. Few of her memories of childhood are of herself alone, but of her as a member of the Robson clan. The loneliness of her private self was the area she was least able to cope with. She longed for a family of her own, a large house in the country with lots of her own children, and dogs! The home life of childhood had set an enormous emotional precedent. *"My parents' marriage was such a happy one. They were so much in love. I remember how they would romp about. Father would chase mother around the room. She would be pretending to get away and both of them, and all we children, laughing with such joy!"* There were men friends in Flora's life but the question of marriage was avoided.

# FLORA

Whenever it came to the point of having to choose between marriage and her career, her acting always came first. However much she longed for a husband, the druglike ambition overwhelmed any other emotion.

After her year in films Flora wanted to ease herself back into theatre. An opportunity came when Anmer Hall asked her to come back to the Westminster in a play of her choice. She had made two brief stage appearances in the interim. The first of these had been for the RADA Players. Margaret Webster had directed her in a new adaptation of *The Lady from the Sea*, the only Ibsen play Flora really cared for. There were professional actors in leading roles and students in the smaller ones. It would be an excellent showcase for them. The production had not been a happy one as Flora and Peggy Webster had disagreed on fundamental aspects of the character of Ellida. Flora tried to find the real woman as she did with all her roles and so her Ellida was more firmly rooted to the earth than others might have made her. "Neither Miss Flora Robson as the nereid wife, nor Mr Torin Thatcher as the Stranger who is the centre of her fantasy, attempts to leave the solid ground. Miss Robson may talk of her strange affinity with the life of the deep seas, but always, as she conveys its meaning, it is the talk of a woman wrestling with an obsession," reported *The Times*. B. W. Downs, the Ibsen scholar, wrote to her from Cambridge of her "splendid interpretation of the title part, where again you hit off just the right mean between intellectual explanation and emotional revivification." Wangel was played by Nicholas Hannen and among the students were Patricia Hayes as Hilde, and, as Lyngstrand, Charles Carter, who had been with the company at Cambridge. There had been only one performance of this play, as there had been of *Shall We Join the Ladies?*, the Barrie play, which was given in aid of the Brighton Society of Symphonic Players at the Brighton Hippodrome on Sunday 7 March 1937. Tony Guthrie had gathered a very distinguished company together which included Gwen Ffrangcon-Davies, Margaret Rawlings, Margaretta Scott, Marie Ney, Jessica Tandy, Jill Esmond, Jean Cadell, Ernest Milton, Francis Sullivan, Nicholas Hannen, Jack Hawkins, George Howe, Frank Allenby and Leo Genn. Flora was cast as Miss Isit.

The play Flora chose for her return to the Westminster was her third venture into Eugene O'Neill territory. She was given *carte blanche* by Anmer Hall, and Flora selected *Anna Christie*, the role in which Garbo had made her first talking picture. It was not an ideal part for her because of the intelligence she brought to every part she played. Some found it difficult to imagine that her Anna had made so little of her life. "Miss Pauline Lord who created the part in

# THE DAMASCENE SWORD

America and was presumably the author's ideal," wrote Agate, "was a pathetic little rose, oddly innocent and, I see, by my old notice, full of queer fun. Now comes Miss Flora Robson magnificently aware of life and masterful as a hollyhock." He had presumed wrongly. Had he read O'Neill's description of Anna he would have found it more nearly described Flora than Miss Lord. "... all this play asks Anna to do is wilt," he continued. "Now there is wilting and wilting. There is wilting against a Greek column à la Phèdre. There is wilting against a door jamb à la Varya in *The Cherry Orchard*. And there is wilting of this play's order, wilting à la Lilian Gish. Miss Robson who is perfectly up to the first two sorts cannot do much with the third. If anyone asked me to cast Medea, Hecuba and all the Greek lot, the whole of the heroines of Racine and Corneille, which means all of Rachel's parts, Lady Macbeth, Queen Katherine and Queen Constance and those notable viragoes Boadicea, Catherine de Medici and our own Queen Elizabeth, I should unhesitatingly name Miss Robson and hold that here was cut and come again. But I am defeated that this fine actress attempts an Anna Christie, not because this is outside Miss Robson's scope, but because her scope is outside it!"

Flora had, for a long time, wanted to express her gratitude to Anmer Hall for all the kindness he had shown her and to her delight the play was a huge success at the box-office. After the London run the company took the play to Cambridge. Immediately after the Saturday-night performance at the end of the run, Flora had to rush from the theatre to catch an overnight train to Edinburgh where she was to join rehearsals for her next play on the Sunday morning. This was a rather strange piece by the American playwright Paul Leslie. Something of a reworking of *Ghosts*, it was called *Satyr* and concerned a young man who had had a horn removed from his head at birth. He has a passion for music, and homicidal tendencies of which he is unaware. His mother firmly refuses to give her consent for his marriage, refusing to give any reason for her decision. After the deaths of several children by his hand, she brings herself to end his life. Flora had the role of the mother and Marius Goring was the haunted boy. After playing at the King's Theatre, Edinburgh, it opened at the Shaftesbury Theatre. A. E. Matthews, who was cast as the family doctor, was to say later that Flora was among the three best actresses he had worked with. When asked what special quality it was that she possessed, he thought for a moment and then said, "If I take her hand I know she can withdraw it without embarrassing me."

*Satyr* was not a success and lasted for less than a month in the West End but Flora was soon at work on the play which she would later claim was the greatest success of her theatrical career. The play, *Autumn Violins*, by Ilya Surguchev, had been first produced by the Moscow Arts Theatre in its 1914–15 season. Gregory Ratoff, a friend of the author, who was to become a film actor in Hollywood, had acquired the English-speaking rights for his wife Eugenie Leontovich. While Jascha Haifetz was on one of his concert tours and appearing in London, he suggested to Basil Dean that it might be a play he would care to present in the West End. There would be finance from the Twentieth Century Fox Film Corporation. It would need an English adaptation made of it and Dean decided to contact Margaret Kennedy.

The new version, which was entitled *Autumn*, updated the action from nineteenth-century provincial Russia to contemporary London. The leading role of Lady Catherine Brooke was first of all offered to Diana Wynyard and then to Fay Compton. Neither was interested because of a poor third act. Basil Dean sent the play to Flora and she was immediately interested. It was the kind of part normally offered only to actresses like Wynyard or Compton and Flora longed for a chance to further extend her range. The part was that of the wife of a barrister who has fallen in love with a younger man. She sees him gradually being won away from her by her stepdaughter. One critic was to suggest that Flora was not seductive enough to have captivated the man in the first place, but this kind of romance does not only come to seductive women. In fact the critic was succumbing to one of the oldest and shallowest clichés of the theatre. The tragedy that an actress of Flora's calibre could find in a role like this was of a rarer quality than a beauty might find. Unfortunately managers tended to think audiences were far too naïve to appreciate this. Flora was fortunate in having Basil Dean as an ally. There was a good first act, a wonderful second act, but the third act was certainly without accomplishment. Margaret Kennedy came to the first rehearsal and told Flora and Wyndham Goldie, who was cast as the husband, that she would rewrite the third act when the two of them had decided what the most suitable development would be, a happy or a tragic conclusion. When she returned they told her that a quiet ending with the husband and wife reunited was how they felt the play should end. Margaret Kennedy rewrote the act accordingly.

The play opened in Manchester to an ecstatic audience. "Flora Robson swept Manchester off its feet last night," announced R. J. Finnemore in the *Manchester Despatch*. "When the curtain fell on *Autumn* . . . there was a storm of applause. The producer Basil Dean made an appreciative speech. So did author Margaret Kennedy. Then someone pushed Miss Robson forward. This was the moment for which the audience, taut with excitement, had been waiting and

# THE DAMASCENE SWORD

she was acclaimed with rousing cheers. Without hesitation I hail Flora Robson's performance last night as the greatest acting I have ever seen. Miss Robson plays the wife with a glowing fire, an intensity of passion that I have never seen equalled on any stage. Her face with its attractive rugged contours is so marvellously expressive. Darkly sullen when she is brooding, it lights with a sudden radiance into strange beauty when she smiles," "Manchester gave her eighteen curtain calls," declared the *Glasgow News*, "and the town has gone wild about her." "Miss Robson is stunningly successful as Lady Brooke," added the *Newcastle Journal* when the tour went there, "Praise for such a performance as this is superfluous."

The play opened at the St Martin's Theatre on 12 October 1937, a week later than scheduled. Wyndham Goldie had gone through the dress rehearsal with a temperature of one hundred and two, and collapsed at the end. Flora was in her dressing-room on opening night, as always, well in advance of the performance. She is often asked how she approaches a first night. "*I once found a quotation in a diary – 'Ask God's blessing on your work, but don't ask him to do it for you.' I work and work during rehearsal, I work at night and lie awake half the night thinking about it. It isn't until I am going on for the first night that I go to a secret place, usually the lavatory, and say my prayers to God. I'm very direct with God, like a Negro, the Scots in me, I think. 'Now God,' I say, 'I've done everything I can do. Please give me inspiration. . . .*"

"The memory of her playing in the last act," wrote her great admirer, W. A. Darlington, "has kept me sniffing all the way back to Fleet Street. I realise this is a shameful confession for a seasoned and presumably hard-boiled critic to make, but it would not be fair to the actress if I did not make it." Stephen Williams, in the *Evening Standard* wrote that it was "a performance of shattering emotional power and one possible only to a rich and deeply sensitive nature." "Our best tragic actress," proclaimed the *Daily Mirror*. "Her great gulping sobs seemed to come from so deep a recess in some wounded heart that one could scarcely endure to listen," noted the *Evening News*. "She plumbs the depths of bitterness and despair," observed A. E. Wilson in *The Star*, "She communicates the sufferings of a woman moved by ardent passion, and the effect is lacerating." "I have never seen a woman do more with less promising material," suggested the *Daily Express* and Ivor Brown added, " . . . the unlikeliness of it all can be burned away by the candle of first-rate acting, and Miss Robson can always light a candle with the power of a furnace which will fill a play's darkness with luminous magic and shrivel up our unwillingness to believe." Not to be outdone, Agate gave Flora his headline, 'ROBSONSHOLM – A Feast Of Acting'.

# FLORA

Once more, in Douglas Fairbanks Jnr.'s words, Flora had "burst the framework of the play". The depth and quality of playing achieved in every role she attempted due to her training, experience and individual insight, succeeded in her making Lady Catherine Brooke a character of tragic stature. This was not tragedy of the Bernhardt school, or of Duse, which she more nearly matched, but on a new, humanly accessible level which was uniquely her own. Flora found in the writings of Tolstoy a philosophy which matches hers. He believed that it was not enough to give the meaning of words, one must give the *feeling* of words. The literal meaning of the word 'home' is 'one's dwelling with one's family'. But the word 'home' means so much more. In different contexts, and with different emphases, the word can be used to convey different feelings. Tolstoy believed that the actor should attempt to understand how the author felt as well as what he meant. If the actor's attempt to convey this feeling *moved* an audience, then Tolstoy believed that this was art.

The feeling which Flora conveyed in this role affected everyone who saw *Autumn*. Elspeth March, who was in the play, recalled that she, and other members of the cast, would remain in the wings, night after night, to watch Flora's wonderfully moving scene at the end of Act Two. Uncle John MacKenzie had been in the first-night audience with Flora's father as usual. In the interval he noticed that many of the male members of the audience hurried out into the air at the end of Act Two, attempting to conceal how deeply moved they were. One man tried to light a cigarette for another. His hand was shaking so much with emotion that he lit the poor man's beard! Queen Mary came to see the play and asked for Flora to come to her box in the second interval. She congratulated Flora on her performance in *Fire Over England*. When asked if she was enjoying the play, the Queen replied, "It's very touching, very touching. Tell me, Miss Robson, has it got a happy ending?" Flora was pleased to be able to tell her that it had.

One night during the run, Victoria Hopper, who was playing the stepdaughter, suddenly fainted. The curtain was dropped and Betty Marsden, the understudy, took her place. It came to the point in the play where Lady Catherine should have fainted. At the very last moment Flora realized that another fainting would confuse the audience and so that night Lady Catherine had a sudden fit of hysterics instead! For much of the run Flora was in great pain from a boil in her ear. For several weeks she went to a Harley Street doctor for an anaesthetic which lasted only until the middle of the last act, when she would be in agony. Basil Dean pleaded with her to remain in the show as he was in great financial difficulties due to his having lost on a play which he had presented with Philip Merivale and Gladys

The last scene of *The Sea Hawk*. With Brenda Marshall, Errol Flynn and Donald Crisp. (United Artists)

The director claimed no one would notice Flora in *Saratoga Trunk*. How wrong could anyone be? With Gary Cooper and Ingrid Bergman. (United Artists)

The Marlboroughs at home. As Viceroy Sarah in the extravagant flop *Anne of England*. With Frederick Worlock.
(Vandamm Studio)

By this point the *Ladies in Retirement* audience would be calling out to warn Isobel Elsom of Flora's approach.
(Vandamm Studio)

The play John van Druten wrote for Flora. With Celeste Holm and Myron McCormick in *The Damask Cheek*
(Mary Morris: Courtesy Celeste Holm)

Ftatateeta in *Caesar and Cleopatra*
(Rank Organisation)

As Thérèse Raquin in *Guilty*
(John Vick)

Ftatateeta meets Gabriel Pascal and George Bernard Shaw on the set of *Caesar and Cleopatra*.
(Rank Organisation)

# THE DAMASCENE SWORD

Cooper. The run of *Autumn* and its subsequent tour, which Flora was to do with a ten per cent cut in salary, saved Dean from bankruptcy. Wyndham Goldie had another commitment and was not able to do the tour. Jack Hawkins, who had played the lover in the original cast, switched roles. His role was taken over by Stewart Granger.

It was to be the first of Flora's great tours and she enjoyed every minute of it. Every night there were crowds of admirers at the stage-door. This was her first intimation of how much she was loved by her public. Many had seen her in *Fire over England* by this time. She enjoyed working with Jack Hawkins, who taught her the secret of playing in long runs. He would check the timings of their scenes each evening and if they had overrun he would say, "Flora, we are beginning to enjoy playing that scene, we need to tighten it up." Thus discipline, and consequently morale, was maintained in their playing. One day someone took Flora out to tea between the shows and there was a glorious salad of spring onions. She could not resist them, and when she arrived back at the theatre she apologized to Jack. He was furious with her because he had been offered onions too and had declined them because of his intimate scenes with Flora. Both he and Stewart Granger ganged up on her and teased her mercilessly through the show. Everytime she came near either of them they would overtly turn their heads away!

*"We played Blackpool on a Bank Holiday. During the first act the audience was very restless, coughing and shuffling about. I said to Jack Hawkins in the interval, 'Are we getting the bird?' But when that wonderful second act unfolded we could feel the audience leaning towards us. There were always people crying in the audience, they were so moved. One night I remember a woman wailed along with me as I was crying on the stage. Over forty years afterwards I had a letter from a member of that audience asking me if I remembered the Bank Holiday performance in Blackpool when we had taken no less than twenty-seven curtain calls...."*

Basil Dean had another play for Flora to follow up her wonderful success in *Autumn*. *Last Train South*, by R. C. Hutchinson, was again a play with a Russian background. It is set in a Russian railway station during the revolution. A former White Russian general is lured there with his wife and daughter while attempting to leave the country. They are detained by the stationmaster's Red son, Fyodor, to avenge the sufferings of a young man who was made a mental and physical wreck through being flogged, while wounded, for desertion in the last war. Flora's role was the wife of the wrecked man. For the majority of the play she was a background figure. Indeed, her first entrance was furtively made, hidden by others, to avoid the star's being greeted by inappropriate applause. She had no great scene until the end of the play when, in moving language, she told how her child had been stillborn through her witnessing the horror of her husband's punishment. "Those who like Miss Robson's emotional tempests will enjoy those scenes where she is given the chance to open the floodgates," claimed the *Sunday Pictorial*. Flora felt the only really fine performance was given by John Abbott as Fyodor.

*Fire Over England* had played to great success all over the country. Flora was asked to attend a luncheon given by *Film Weekly* where their annual awards would be presented. It was a foregone conclusion that Anna Neagle would win the Best Actress Award for her portrayal of another British monarch in *Victoria the Great*. No one was more surprised than Flora when it was her name that was read out for the award. Anna Neagle very sweetly congratulated her. As the award was made by popular vote Flora felt that her successful tour had contributed to it. Some time later another paper sponsored a popular poll for the Best Actress in International Films. Garbo came top for her portrayal of Marie Walewska in *Conquest*, Luise Rainer second for *The Good Earth* and Flora third for *Farewell Again*. It was shortly after this that Flora's four-year contract came up for renewal. Korda chose to drop the option on her contract. Flora was devastated. She had been hoping he would let her do a film similar to *Autumn*, but Korda was firm that she was not a lucrative proposition. She could not understand his attitude. It was true that she would never win fame for her glamour but there was a whole range of other roles open to her. It was infuriating that when a plain woman was called for in a script, a pretty girl would be chosen and made up to look like her. It took very little prompting for feelings of inferiority to return. "On my tombstone they will write, 'SHE WAS A PLAIN WOMAN'," she thought to herself bitterly. In her stage career she was at the peak of her artistic fulfilment. She had served her apprenticeship. The damascene sword was in her hand. But in the cinema, which had given her access to an international career, as well as national recognition in Britain, and in which she had proved her abilities, she had been rejected. This chastening blow led her to believe that awards of any kind heralded a period of uncertainty when no one would want her.

# 4

## New Worlds
### 1939–1943

### 1

KORDA HAD MADE it clear that there was no money to be made from Flora. If this important company were to show such little faith in her she wondered how she could convince other film-makers that there was a future for her in cinema. What her career needed was a boost of confidence. It was at this moment that Hollywood, providentially, beckoned. She was invited by Samuel Goldwyn to play Nelly Dean, the housekeeper, in *Wuthering Heights*.

The part was very definitely a supporting-character role. With *Farewell Again* she had finally achieved star status and top billing. But appearing in a quality Hollywood film would add prestige to her career whatever her billing might be. There had been the prospect of a film for Associated British but this was cancelled due to the Munich crisis. The play in which she was appearing, *Last Train South*, was destined for a short run and so Flora accepted the Hollywood role.

She was told to report to the United Artists studios in Hollywood as soon as possible and set sail, with her niece Helen as a companion, on the *Queen Mary*. The crossing was like a holiday. During a brief stop-over in New York, a city which fascinated and excited her, she broke a tooth and had to have it fixed. This held her up a few days after which she raced to Hollywood on board The Chief. There was a man to meet her from the Selznick agency who greeted her with the news that the film had been postponed for two weeks. There was nothing in her contract to allow for her to be paid anything before the commencement of the film. Because of the poor rate of exchange she had taken only fifty pounds and had spent a good deal of this on her dental treatment. She and Helen were booked into the Grand Hotel. Flora took a small apartment at about three pounds a week. She was asked for two months' rent in advance. Landlords were wary of the kind of people who arrived in Hollywood. "Go West, young man" had driven all the riff-raff of America to the West Coast. The modesty of her apartment intrigued the Press, who declared she was stingy. She made two visits to the studio with her agent and met various people to do with the production and then there was a call for her to go in for tests with the hairdressing department. Because of the heat in California every effort was made to avoid wigs and use the artist's own hair. She decided to go in alone.

"*Because I had very little money I went in by bus. I walked down to United Artists and went in the car gate where we had gone in before. I was met by an enormous policeman, with a gun, who had seen me alighting from the bus. He said, 'What are you doing in here?' He was very tough. I said, 'I've come to have a hair test.' 'Are you in a film here?' he asked. I replied that it hadn't begun yet. He said he knew it hadn't begun yet because there were no films in production. 'Get out,' he barked. It was bad enough being the furthest from home I had ever been, not only across the Atlantic, but right across America. I'd never felt so lonely in my life. The tears poured down my face. What I should have done was go straight back and ring up and ask for them to send me a car. But I never think of those things at the time. I went from door to door and eventually found the gate where the extras went in. There was a girl behind the grille. I told her, with tears running down my cheeks, 'I've come for a hair test and they won't let me in.' She recognized me, I think, and told me which way to go. When I walked through the passage and out to the back I met one of Goldwyn's assistants. He had terribly nice assistants. Goldwyn never spoke to us but his assistants were always polite and cheerful. He saw I was in distress and walked along by the side of me. I kept blowing my nose, and he said, 'You seem to have hay-fever.' 'Yes . . . I have,' I sobbed. We arrived at the hairdresser's and I sat for an hour while they tried first one thing and then another. I never spoke, I just sat and cried. Eventually I pulled myself together and they asked me if I would go back a few days later for film tests. I said I would. The assistant looked at me and asked if there was anything I would like. I thought I had recovered enough to speak and asked him if he would give me a card which I could show whenever I came into the studio. A knowing look came into his eyes. 'Why?' he asked, 'Did you have any trouble getting in today?' 'Yes,' I moaned, 'They threw me out on my ear!' The tears welled forth again!*"

Flora caught another bus home. She paid her money and asked the driver to let her know when the bus had reached her destination. The driver failed to tell her and eventually she was deposited miles beyond her stop, though he did refund enough money to get her home again. When she got back to Helen she collapsed in tears. She had never felt so lonely in her life. A few days later a friend helped her to get money from home by introducing her to his bank and so the economic strictures were lifted. Laurence Olivier, who was to play Heathcliff, arrived in Hollywood two weeks after Flora. He got her telephone number from the studios and rang her from where he was staying at the Beverley Wilshire Hotel. "Flora!" he said, "Come and see me quickly!" "Larry, what's the matter?" she asked, quite concerned at his agitated voice. "I was at the studios today to have some tests done," he replied. "I was in the commissary and suddenly I found I was crying into my coffee!" "So was I, Larry, so was I!" she exclaimed. "Yes," Olivier said, "but you're a woman . . .!"

Eventually production got under way. Though she admired all the technical expertise she found in the Hollywood studios, she was less happy about the artistic side. To begin with, several scenes had been cut from what had, in the original Ben Hecht and Charles MacArthur script, never been more than a small, though interesting, role. Furthermore, there seemed to be some alarm about her style of acting. William Wyler, the director, accused her of underplaying her scenes. This puzzled Flora for she had always understood this to be the secret of screen acting – to do ten times less than one would on the stage and feel ten times more. It transpired, however, that current Hollywood trends preferred supporting actors and actresses to busy themselves round the star in order to fix the spotlight firmly on the leading player, who was permitted as little movement as he or she liked. It is to Flora's great credit that she managed to commute this imposition by creating a character strong enough to achieve its own stillnesses and, at the same time, create the kind of contrast that gave the screen to Merle Oberon at just the right moments.

One day Wyler said something which made Flora make an involuntary face of dismay. He later took her aside and said that if ever there were anything she wished to say about the way the film was being approached she should tell him. "This is an English classic," he said, "and I very much want it to be liked in England."

Because of Merle Oberon's delicate health the shooting schedule was seldom strictly adhered to. Geraldine Fitzgerald, who was cast as Isabella, would find that when Merle was absent it would be her scenes that were rushed in to fill the gap, usually when she was least prepared for them. This fiery young Irishwoman made her feelings known and it was often up to Flora to pacify her and give her a word of encouragement. Miss Fitzgerald was also relatively new to Hollywood and Flora could see what a marvellous performance she was giving. Miss Fitzgerald recalled, in a letter to me, "Flora was, to me, the calm eye in the seemingly daily emotional hurricanes that took place on that set. Knowing the power and passion I have seen her express on the stage I wonder now, looking back, what it must have cost her to keep us all from flying apart." Another newcomer, David Niven, recalled, "When I was a total beginner in *Wuthering Heights* she was charming to me when she could have been horrid and ever since then in the many pictures we have shared together she has always been a joy to be with."

One of the most difficult scenes to shoot proved to be the one that is most crucial to book and to film, the scene where, unwittingly, Cathy rejects Heathcliff and thus instigates the misunderstanding from which all the later tragic circumstances arise. There is a short scene between Ellen and Heathcliff which is interrupted by Cathy's coming into the room. She has just made her farewells to her young suitor, Edgar Linton, played by David Niven in the film. Cathy is not aware that Heathcliff is in the room, but we and Ellen know that he is hiding in the shadows. She compares the love she has for Linton with the passion she feels for Heathcliff and declares, "It would degrade me to marry Heathcliff now!" At this point the candle burning on the table in front of Ellen flickers and we, and she, know that Heathcliff has opened the door and gone out into the yard. Cathy, oblivious to any change, continues. Her love for Heathcliff is basic to her own being. And she sums up all her feelings with, "Ellen, I *am* Heathcliff!"

It was this key line that proved to be the stumbling block. For the greater part of one day Wyler tried it first one way and then another. Merle Oberon exhausted all the permutations she thought possible on the line and begged Flora to help her find new ones. By the end of the day no satisfactory take had been made. When, next morning, the crew reassembled, Merle Oberon asked Wyler where they were to start. "Scene forty three, Ellen, I *am* Heathcliff!" was his reply. Merle Oberon was almost in despair and asked him what he expected her to do when she had already tried everything. Wyler suggested that she ask Flora. "*This was highly flattering. I had to think of something fairly quickly and so I said. 'You know the love of Cathy for Heathcliff is like the wild weather of the moors. It is almost a wicked love. They would do anything to have each other.'*" At this point the audience should see Cathy at one with the earth and the elements, she suggested, as though she and Heathcliff and the barren Yorkshire moors are all part of some primeval order. "*If you could do this out in the open with the rain and the wind behind you it would help the scene enormously.*" So they took this suggestion to Wyler. However, this interfered with the construction of the scene where Cathy would rush out into the rain as Heathcliff galloped away on horseback. Wyler suggested that, as an alternative, Merle could be seen against the window and the beating rain as the storm sweeps over the moors.

The next morning he took Flora along to the rushes and she was able to see that her idea had worked. However, Wyler was still not convinced. He though it all too melodramatic. "All right, but now it's 'Ellen, I *am* Heathcliff' . . . Cue thunder . . . Thunder crash!" Flora replied, "But that's what it is! It *is* melodrama! It's *Way Down East* and everything! You're doing *Wuthering Heights*!" Eventually Wyler agreed with her interpretation and the moment still works marvellously in the film. Merle Oberon was very relieved and grateful for Flora's help. *"Merle was a darling. She was lovely to act with, a really lovely lady."*

Flora had now earned greater respect. She was consulted on many more decisions. Goldwyn had been worried that too much time elapsed before Merle Oberon's first appearance. She was, after all, the star and the audience would be waiting to see her. An earlier appearance would necessitate cutting the prologue and the arrival of Mr Lockwood at the beginning of the film. This evocative scene which introduces the eerie house and its grim, aged inhabitants, is nearer to the real, stark atmosphere of the novel than any other part of the film. It would have been a great loss. Geraldine Fitzgerald, Olivier, Leo G. Carroll and Flora all turn to look at the unwelcome guests, Mr Lockwood and ourselves, as we make an intrusion into their bleak world. It is a chilling moment. Flora opposed the decision to cut the scene. She was backed up by a young writer, John Huston, who was two years away from his directorial début *The Maltese Falcon*, and was employed to rework scenes and provided additional dialogue. He and Flora were often called to conferences and they were able to have the scene retained. A preview of a rough-cut of the film was given at a cinema in Pomona. The audience was composed mainly of school children. When there was a laugh in the wrong place the executives ordered that moment to be cut. Flora asked why this was. "Because the children laughed," she was told. "But," Flora argued, "if you're doing a classic, you're not doing it for children." She was told, "The average age of cinema audiences in America is sixteen." Flora, again, opposed these cuts. As a result of her involvement extra scenes were incorporated into the earlier part of the film involving the children and Ellen as a younger woman. Merle Oberon was now seen much later but she was given a gradual build. Eventually the last scene was rewritten and given to Flora, whose character, in the original script, had faded out long before. Finally, Wyler decided to include Flora's voice on the soundtrack as story-teller. In the novel Nelly tells most of the story to Mr Lockwood and it seemed natural that she should do the same in the film. The convention of a story-teller's voice being added to a film is now commonplace but, in this film, it was an innovation. By the time this decision had been made there were no writers left on the lot, even John Huston had moved on to other things. Flora volunteered to write her own dialogue and took the novel home with her. She was careful to construct the text as simply as possible so as not to confuse the audience. This added to the continuity of the film and to the overall presence of Flora's performance.

*Wuthering Heights* won the New York Film Critics' Award for the Best Motion Picture of 1939, beating its contemporary *Gone With the Wind*. The film has been frequently revived in commercial cinema and in art houses and is regarded as one of the few perennial screen classics. Every time it is shown on television it attracts a huge audience, many seeing the film for a second or third time. There is seldom a selection of screen classics made that does not include it. There is a story that George Bernard Shaw had been the first to suggest to Goldwyn the subject of the film, a derisive suggestion which Goldwyn took seriously. It became Goldwyn's favourite film and immediately after its completion he was reported to play it through three or four times a day. Although the film seldom reflects the strengths of Emily Brontë's novel it has somehow caught a kind of turbulence from the original which supports all the romantic Hollywood tricks to the point where one accepts them as necessary contributory factors to the story. It becomes a masterpiece in its own right. The passion of the lovers lacks some of the extremes of anger and tenderness of the lovers in the novel, but what restraint there might be between them is more than adequately compensated for by Gregg Toland's superb Oscar-winning photography which concentrates essences of all the elements into the images we see.

Flora's performance has not dated in any respect. Perhaps this is because she chose to be simple, direct and honest. These qualities do not date. Only bravado, the grander passions and stylized humour seem to be affected by the passing of time. Her Stanislavsky-learned rule of 'giving and receiving' was the ideal basis for such a role as this. She listens marvellously. To be seen to be listening is an art. When we see someone listening properly and not simply confronting their fellow players with eyes, or pulling every conceivable kind of 'listening' face, then we listen comfortably ourselves. This talent would be exploited in most of Flora's subsequent films.

Archie de Bear, in reviewing *Wuthering Heights*, commented: "Among the principals Flora Robson's performance stands out. It is she who tells the story, in retrospect, after the opening scene in which a stranger takes refuge in the farm during a snow storm and hears the spirit voice of the girl, Cathy, outside. And so when the film presents a background of spoken narrative to the empty foreground of magnificent moorland desolation, the voice of Flora Robson lends an added enchantment to the lovely view."

There is a stability in her performance which always supports the narrative, adding quality to a film which might, at any moment, otherwise ignite of its own volition and burn itself out. It is only because of her reassuringly human voice when, with fond emotion at the end of the film, she bids farewell to the now dead lovers, "Goodbye, Heathcliff... Goodbye, my wild, sweet Cathy...", it is only because of this that we so readily accept the Hollywood climax which reunites ghostly images of Laurence Olivier and Merle Oberon to the celestial accompaniment of the Goldwyn chorale.

## 2

England in the Spring of 1939, seemed many miles further from Hollywood than the thousands of miles Flora had travelled. The country was trying to ignore the inevitability of what lay ahead, yet there was caution and economy in the theatre world. There were no parts for Flora. The Press, however, were glad to see her back. She was radiant with Californian sunshine. 'WILL THERE BE FAME AT LAST FOR FLORA?' the fan magazines screamed. "Did you like Hollywood, Miss Robson?" "Like Hollywood?" she replied, with a grin. "You can't help liking it. It's all so crazy!"

Fortunately there was work for her in a film. The Associated British property was once more on the stocks. Flora's new stature in Hollywood had given her career the necessary boost and *Poison Pen* was put into production. The film was based on Richard Llewellyn's play about the tragic consequences the writer of anonymous letters accomplishes in a small country town. Flora had the starring role of Mary Rider, the sister of the rector who was ostensibly an observer in the drama, but ultimately revealed as the perpetrator of the poison. Robert Newton was cast as a simple farmer inflamed to murder by the slander levelled at his pretty wife and the local publican. Catherine Lacey played Connie Fateley, a local seamstress, who hangs herself in the church belfry after the finger of suspicion has been pointed at her by the mob of enraged townspeople. Geoffrey Toone, Flora's friend from Cambridge now under contract to Associated British and playing juvenile leads, made up the love interest with Ann Todd.

*Poison Pen* was directed by Austrian director Paul Stein whom Geoffrey Toone remembers as 'rather solemn'. His solemnity seems to have had a dampening effect on a story which otherwise had great potential. Fritz Lang, three years earlier, in *Fury*, had shown the terrifying power of the mob in anger. Even allowing for the difference in temperament of the American and English communities, this is very lukewarm stuff. In the circumstances Flora's performance is remarkably good. Her character is established as "Miss Rider . . . not the marrying type," the archetypal role that Flora would be called upon to fulfil in most of her more routine films. We see her as the kind friend of the small boy whose lollipop was trodden on; the concerned aunt; the polite hostess; the outraged Christian confronted with bigotry. Mary Rider is obviously the anonymous letter writer as there could be no other justification for allotting to the star such an uninteresting role. Until the last reel she is no more than a background figure. One moment we see her sitting knitting, as we have for much of the film, then suddenly she is dark and demoniac, babbling madness and throwing herself to death in a gorge. This startling development is rather difficult to assimilate, however excellently it is acted, and the fault lies equally with the scenarist and the director. When Mary Rider is relaxed and happy, Flora glows with all the good health she has brought back from Hollywood, and when she is allowed to reveal the manic side she acts with conviction, panache and control.

Flora was staying with her family in Hove. Her mother had been ill and Flora had hurried down to see if she could help. An offer for her to return to Hollywood arrived from David Selznick, who was producing the first American film to be directed by the brilliant English director, Alfred Hitchcock. It was for the role of a housekeeper and Flora turned it down. Hollywood producers tried to find a niche for every actor and it was difficult to break away from typecasting. Flora was still anxious to find a film in the mould of *Autumn* which might establish her as a leading lady in films, rather than as a character actress. It was, consequently, of the utmost importance that she avoid being typecast, and she felt that two films in a row as a housekeeper in Hollywood would be against her best interests. Her friends thought she was foolish to turn down well-paid work in America when so many people wanted to get out of Europe. Someone said, "How marvellous for you to be typecast as a housekeeper. In a few years you will have made enough money to retire." Flora replied, "I don't want to retire. I want to act!" She cabled back that she didn't want the part. The following week a cable arrived from Hitchcock himself which she again refused by return. Perhaps she was right to turn down the role for these reasons at that time. But, in retrospect, what a loss it seems that she spurned the role of Mrs Danvers in *Rebecca* simply because she was another housekeeper.

The BBC offered her the role of Vanessa in *Words Upon the Window Pane*, a television dramatization of Jonathan Swift's love affair, but the arrival of three cables from Hollywood led her to defer a decision. Two of the cables were from Warner Brothers offering parts in films. The third was another communication from Hitchcock. "*He asked whether I had turned down Mrs Danvers because it was an unsympathetic role. 'No,' I cabled back, 'Because she's a housekeeper.' To my regret, Mr Hitchcock never asked for me again.*"

Warner Brothers offered a two-picture deal comprising *We Are Not Alone* and *The Sea Hawk*. The first was an adaptation of the novel by James Hilton, whose previously filmed work included *Lost Horizon* and *Goodbye Mr Chips*. The film would have as its stars Paul Muni and Dolly Haas. Paul Muni was an actor's actor who deeply immersed himself in the roles he played. In each of his great roles, his expertise at disguising his face, his painstaking interpretation and differing physical characterization offered him seemingly limitless casting. He is less well remembered today because we more readily recall actors who established an easily recognizable image. The 1979 publication *The Warner Bros. Story* carried on its cover a display of the portraits of eighty-one stars, some of whom had only a negligible connection with Warners. Muni, who had, at one time, been Warners' top star, was not included. His achievement on film is a legacy of individually memorable performances – roles such as the Capone-like figure in *Scarface*, the Chinese peasant farmer in Thalberg's *The Good Earth*, made for MGM, the title roles in *I Am a Fugitive from a Chain Gang*, *Juarez*, *The Life of Emile Zola* and *The Story of Louis Pasteur*, which won him the Best Actor Oscar in 1936. Unlike many Hollywood stars he had graduated from an immensely successful career as a Broadway actor. Flora was excited at the prospect of working with an artist she greatly respected.

The second film, *The Sea Hawk*, would be a Technicolor re-make of the 1924 Milton Sills adventure from the novel by Sabatini. Errol Flynn would play the title role and Flora would recreate her Queen Elizabeth. The role was a mere cipher compared with the opportunities afforded in *Fire Over England* but Flora would have a wonderful speech at the film's climax in which the plight of England under the threat of the Armada would be likened to the contemporary situation of Britain under the threat of Hitler's Germany. Flora accepted both roles and left for Hollywood, hoping to return home soon. She had no idea that it was to be four years before she would see her family and friends again.

## 3

The setting for *We Are Not Alone* was vividly familiar – immediately pre-First World War England. The story concerned a charismatic, small-town doctor married to a harsh wife. Their union has produced

# FLORA

an unusually imaginative and attractive small boy. A young Austrian dancer, who met the child when she was being treated by the doctor, is engaged as his governess. The doctor is inspired with an unspoken love for the dancer and when the wife is accidentally poisoned they are both accused of her murder, convicted and then executed. It is only in the witness box, when the doctor is accused of being in love with the dancer that he realizes his feelings. The title is his reassurance to her that they will be sharing their deaths with unnumbered masses of innocents who would die in the ensuing struggle. Muni was cast as David, the doctor, Flora as Jessica, the wife, and seven-year-old Raymond Severn as the child, Gerald. Englishman Edmund Goulding would direct. In tests with Raymond Severn, Dolly Haas had proved unsuitable for the role of the dancer. The child would simply not respond to her. Bette Davis' protégée Jane Bryan was tested with him. The boy's face lit up. She was given the marvellous role of Leni.

The admiration Flora felt for Muni was certainly reciprocated. There was always a chair on the set of a Muni film specifically reserved for Bella, his wife and most constructive critic. After their first scene together Flora saw Muni look towards his wife. "She's all right," Bella signalled back. Subsequently Muni would trust Flora's opinion and suggestions on their scenes together.

Flora's character, Jessica Newcome, was a cold, strait-laced and neurotic woman who found motherhood an unacceptable irritation. Her remedy for her son's fear of darkness was to force him to sleep in the dark, to face and conquer his fear. She would even remove the light bulb to ensure this discipline was adhered to. Jessica's narrow attitude is perfectly summed up in a line she addresses to her husband: "You, as a doctor, should know that a child can't digest icecream." Jessica is the darkness in the film and it is Leni who brings light into the child's life. The contrast between Flora and Jane Bryan is perfect. Flora's face, so much belying her own warmth of nature, easily took on the disguise of cold repression, whilst Jane Bryan had all the sweet vulnerability of youth.

Miss Bryan wrote to me, "You brought back in a flood many rare and strong memories and a stunning revelation of the privilege it was for me to be associated with two giant talents – Miss Robson and Mr Muni . . . unique! Miss Robson was all professional – all kindness – all patience. Her sureness became an anchor of confidence for me and the boy who played her son."

Flora doesn't play a cold woman. She becomes one. Her performance is cleverly understated. She allows each of her fellow players to dominate her scenes with them, using her exceptional talent of standing back and listening. In only one scene, the major confrontation with her husband, when each tells the other of all the bitterness they feel, does she move in and match Muni. "*Muni wanted to copy my English accent so he never left my side. We became very close. We had a wonderful director in Edmund Goulding. He had a pattern all his own. He always used to do one long scene in the morning. The front office used to grumble at this. They said, 'You're not showing us enough to look at.' He spent a lot of time on the one scene which might run for six or seven minutes. Instead of breaking it up into bits he would do it in one so we could get the whole feeling and the timing. We were both stage actors so we had some control over it ourselves. In the quarrel scene Muni shouted at me, went out and banged the door and I was left on my own, sobbing. They shouted 'Cut!' and where, normally, the technical people would fuss round us adjusting our hair or make-up, the entire crew, technicians and actors applauded us. That never happens in films. I loved working with Muni. Robert Donat was my favourite fellow actor on stage and Muni was my favourite in films.*"

When the film was shown in preview the audience was asked for its comments. Flora was awarded ninety per cent of the popularity vote. On the strength of this Jack L. Warner, the head of production, offered her a standard seven-year contract with the studio. To the incredulity of Hollywood society Flora turned the contract down. It was important for her to return home as soon as the two-picture deal was completed. A long-term contract would almost certainly preclude this and make a return to the stage more difficult. It was an important decision not lightly taken, as a contract might have afforded her the pick of character roles at Warners. But the news from Europe filled her with grave anxiety. The theme of the film had accentuated the situation at home.

The film had very little success at the box-office. When Muni had heard news of one particular crisis in Europe he told the assembled cast on the studio floor, "We might as well abandon the film now." The warnings against war were inopportune in such sensitive times. However, along with such luminaries as Garbo, Bette Davis and James Cagney, Flora was voted into the Top Ten of the National Board of Review's Best Acting Category for 1939, and the Press was favourable. Frank S. Nugent wrote in *The New York Times*: "Paul Muni's performance of the little doctor, Jane Bryan's as Leni, Flora Robson's as the wife are of a piece in their perfection."

Flora was to renew her friendship with the Munis on several occasions. Some months after the completion of *We Are Not Alone*, Muni literally tore up his contract with Warner Brothers, thus relinquishing to Humphrey Bogart the role of Roy Earle in *High Sierra*. Muni disappeared to New York. At Madison Square Gardens late in 1941, Flora appeared at a rally in aid of Russian war refugees.

# FLORA

Flora read a verse and shortly afterwards the British ambassador rose to make a speech. Communist factions in the audience began to chant, "Open up the second front" over and over. When, after five minutes or so of chanting, they calmed down, the ambassador made his speech. Muni, who was also on the platform, followed him by reading a letter to the rally. Flora went up to him afterwards. He was delighted to see her and invited her to his home on Long Island for a weekend. They spent a lot of time tramping round the countryside together. Flora asked him why he wasn't working. "I've had Hollywood," was his reply. "But what about the theatre, with all your following?" she asked. "How English," he riposted. "In England your public remains faithful, but not here." Then Flora reminded him that he had received the greatest ovation the evening of the rally. "*I became aware of Bella out of the corner of my eye. She was urging me on. She had noticed how Muni's ears had pricked up. I talked to him about Shakespeare, about current trends in plays, in fact I talked nothing but theatre the whole weekend. I remember how his heavy brow lifted. A month later he returned to the stage and a new career as a Broadway actor.*"

Production of Flora's scheduled second film was cancelled due to the outbreak of war. Large-scale film productions recouped their costs with release in America but relied on exhibition abroad to realize a profit. Under the terms of her deal with Warners she would be offered another role in the event of such cancellation. Anxious to fulfil the contract and attempt to return to England at the earliest opportunity, Flora was obliged to accept a rather poor part in a routine programmer, with an option that, should production of *The Sea Hawk* be resumed, she should have first refusal of the part of Elizabeth.

*Invisible Stripes* was a gangster picture served up under the thin disguise of social significance in dealing with the sociological and psychological scars worn by ex-convicts. Flora was cast as Ma Taylor, mother of the film's star, George Raft, and co-star, William Holden. Jane Bryan was again acting with Flora, also playing a character of little depth, as Holden's girl. It was the convention for film mothers always to be grey-haired old ladies, so Flora donned a grey wig and an ill-fitting American persona. Perhaps the aged make-up was necessary as George Raft was seven years her senior! At one point the two of them executed a jitterbug to the strains of 'Sweet Georgia Brown'. It was not one of Flora's more memorable roles, nor is it a memorable film.

By the time she was free from the film it would have been unwise to attempt to return to England. So Flora contented herself with the problem of finding a career in America. She had no contacts in the theatre and would have to wait for further film work. Life in America was no great hardship, in fact, quite the reverse. She was able to buy a small car and now had a circle of friends. On the Warner lot she befriended the boxer 'Slapsie' Maxie Rosenbloom who had his own sparring ring set up there. Watching him in training reminded her of Ernie Broadwood twenty years before in Welwyn Garden City. "*I have always liked tough guys. I played tennis with the people who played a little bit, and eventually became quite a good player again.*" She was living, at this time, at the legendary Garden of Allah, a member of the English community there. David Kidd, a talented young Scots costume designer, was one of her best friends. He recalled that 'halcyon summer' when they stayed at Alla Nazimova's old Hollywood home, converted into a hotel. Among the other guests were Charles Laughton and Elsa, Louis Bromfield, Forrest Tucker, Edna Best, the John Steinbecks, Robert Benchley, the John Loders and Marc Connelly. There was a heatwave and no air-conditioning. In the middle of the night David would hear a 'plop' as someone dived into the pool to keep cool. Then someone else would get the idea and in they would go, then another and another. By four in the morning the whole of the little colony would be out by the pool having a party by moonlight.

It was about this time that Reginald Denham, Flora's old friend from Oxford, came to Hollywood. Reggie had had a great success with a play he had written in collaboration with Edward Percy. The reluctance of managements to back straight plays at the beginning of the war had meant that there was no West End management interested in taking up the play, an atmospheric thriller. However they had managed to interest the management of the Richmond Theatre and the play was tried out there. Seeing that a well-written thriller would still play to packed houses in such perilous times, persuaded a West End management to present it. Subsequently Gilbert Miller called Reggie to America to produce the play at the Henry Miller Theatre. He was anxious to have Flora star in the play. Flora was thrilled to be asked and, on the strength of Agate's having said in the London Press that the part was suitable for her, agreed to play the leading role without even reading the script.

While all this was happening, Warner Brothers had decided to mount their production of *The Sea Hawk* after all, in a black-and-white version, and Flora was called to test for Queen Elizabeth. She was laced into the costumes worn by Bette Davis in *The Private Lives of Elizabeth and Essex* and the tests were made. Now she was presented with a dilemma, whether to turn down the film role in favour of the play or do the film and risk losing her chance of returning to the stage. It was an appallingly difficult decision to have to make. Because she delayed making up her mind two Warner executives came to her bungalow to persuade her to do the film. She realized she was in a marvellous bargaining position. She said she would agree to play the part if there was a guarantee that the schedule would be arranged to suit her and not interfere with her plans to rehearse the play in New York. After a moment's hesitation she added that she would rather like to have new costumes for Elizabeth made especially for her and not refurbished from Bette Davis's cast-offs. To her amazement the film executives conceded every point. All of her scenes would be shot 'end to end' and she would be dressed in a brand-new wardrobe!

## 4

Flora has seldom looked happier than she does in *The Sea Hawk*. She is relaxed and confident and consequently gives what may be her finest performance as a screen actress. There are several reasons why she should have been so contented. As we have seen, she was looking forward to a return to the theatre. It was now over eighteen months since she had left the stage in *Last Train South*. Any actor will feel his feet itching to tread the boards after such a time. Now Flora had the prospect of her first Broadway opening, in a proven success. Secondly, Warners' agreement to her terms had given an enormous boost to her confidence. The costumes were marvellous. At Denham, in *Fire Over England*, she would often have to be cut out of her costumes because the authentic lacing was too intricate. Here they used zip fasteners and other easy methods without damaging the line of the gowns. Whereas in England the lace ruffs were constructed to original patterns and consequently fell limp under the hot studio lights, Hollywood had adapted ruffs to suit the medium and made them from horsehair padded shapes finished with a decorative lace façade. The make-up was simplified and less tiresome. All in all she knew she looked superb in the part with very much less effort. Thirdly, the part of Elizabeth was one she knew. The piece was even more historically inaccurate than her first Elizabeth but she had the wealth of her earlier research on which to base her interpretation. Finally, there was Errol Flynn.

Biographers researching Flynn's life are always surprised by Flora's memories of him. Where others seem only too eager to jump on the bandwagon and dish the dirt about him, Flora remembers him fondly, as charming and gentlemanly. She suspects that, because she was from the theatre, Flynn had a greater respect for her than he had for film people. They had many friends in common in England. "How is Geoffrey Toone?" he asked. Flynn had been Toone's understudy in earlier days. "*Errol Flynn was very nice to me. One day when we had a break in filming he said, 'Would you prefer to talk, or would you prefer to be quiet?' How considerate of him. I replied that I would prefer to talk. He was notorious for not knowing his lines so I had a word with him. 'If you don't know your lines,' I said, 'Then we will be delayed and I won't get away to New York in time for my play.' On* The Sea Hawk *he always knew his lines. We would finish filming sometimes as early as four o'clock. No one would believe it was an Errol Flynn picture!"*

The court of Elizabeth at the Burbank studios was almost an institution. Michael Curtiz, the brilliant Hungarian director, was the power behind the throne as he had been in *Elizabeth and Essex* days. In different guises Flynn, Donald Crisp, Alan Hale and Henry Daniell could all be found in attendance. Brenda Marshall, not Olivia de Havilland, was lady-in-waiting and the Spanish ambassador was played by one of Warners' most distinguished character players, Claude Rains. Rains had, of course, appeared with Flora when she made her professional stage début in *Will Shakespeare* almost twenty years earlier.

Flora had been a little apprehensive about working with Curtiz. He was well known as an action director who disliked doing dialogue scenes. She had seen work done on the scenes at the Spanish court, marvellously lit as in all Curtiz's films, but stiff and formal. She decided to tackle him on this and suggested that the mood of Elizabeth's court should show a marked contrast. The Hawks brought into her presence should argue and answer her back and give her something to fight against. Curtiz welcomed ideas which would make the filming of the scene easier and he summoned writers to provide new dialogue. The actors who played the Hawks were delighted as it meant they would be better paid, and Flora had a good basis for her interpretation. Mike Curtiz had been given a fresh insight into shooting dialogue scenes and would make many subsequent films with no action content with great success. Indeed *Casablanca* would win him an Academy Award. He acknowledged Flora's influence and said he wanted her in every film he made. Unfortunately they were not to work together again.

*The Sea Hawk* of the title is Geoffrey Thorpe, a gallant sea captain in the time of Elizabeth I, dedicated to oppose Spain as she builds her Armada to set sail against the English fleet. One of the delights of the film is the warm and flirtatious relationship between the rascally Thorpe, played by Flynn, and the Queen, especially in the long and charming scene between them, shared with a monkey he brings her as a present.

Curtiz was often the butt of practical jokes played on him by Flynn and his cronies. One morning their ribbing was relentless and joke

# FLORA

after joke was played on him. Flora was called, just before lunch, to do the scene in which she discovers Flynn and Henry Daniell, the villain, engaged in a desperate sword battle in her palace. Flynn had a quiet word with Flora before she went on the set. The script called for Flora simply to stride into shot, hold up her hand and stop the fight. 'Action!' was called and Flora walked in. She held up her hand, paused a moment, and added, "Break it up, boys!" The entire crew collapsed in hysterics. Curtiz was furious and called for his lady secretary. A door flew open and an old man in a long white beard and a shock of white hair appeared. Curtiz yelled again for his secretary. The old man spoke and said 'he' was the secretary. It *was* her, of course, another of Flynn's conspirators! Curtiz burst into tears and rushed from the set.

After lunch Curtiz took Flora aside and asked her why she had changed the dialogue. "I'm sorry, I thought it would be funny," she apologized, anxious not to implicate Flynn. Several months later Flora was to help Flynn out of a scrape when both of them were working in a radio broadcast of *The Lady Vanishes*. Flynn was cast as the hero and Flora as Miss Froy, in the 'Philip Morris Playhouse' production. In the story Flora had to teach Flynn the tune of Percy Grainger's 'Country Garden', which was supposed to contain the code Miss Froy wished conveyed to the Foreign Office in London. In a run-through, before the broadcast, Flynn had a blackout when it came to whistling the tune to the Foreign Office officials and substituted the Wedding March! He confided to Flora that he was certain he would never remember the tune when it came to broadcast which was being transmitted live and in front of a vast studio audience. "I will be standing behind you," Flora reassured him, "and I will prompt you if you forget." When the moment came Flynn looked round to her in desperation and she 'dubbed' his whistle.

The main reason Flora had been interested in the role in *The Sea Hawk* was the long speech Elizabeth made to the fleet at the end of the film about "the obligation of all free men to affirm that the earth belongs not to any one man, but to all men, and that freedom is the deed and title to the soil on which we exist". Although the speech was included in prints sent to England it was decided by executives at Warners to delete it in its entirety from domestic prints. Perhaps they decided it was too inflammatory and propagandist for American audiences in those sensitive times. Flora was disappointed as it had seemed such a perfect opportunity for her to help the war effort. *The New York Times* got wind of the deletion and tried to obtain a transcript from Warners. The script copy was withheld but they eventually published the speech after it appeared in a London newspaper. Korda had seen the possibility of making a similar kind of statement through the medium of Elizabeth. He incorporated much of the Tilbury footage from *Fire Over England* in a semi-documentary feature entitled *The Lion Has Wings*. Flora was billed with Merle Oberon and Ralph Richardson, who were seen in the fictional segments, but received no remuneration.

Flora's performance in *The Sea Hawk* was deservedly acclaimed. "Miss Robson proved long ago that no one else should ever be allowed to play Elizabeth on the screen," wrote Colvin McPherson in the *St Louis Despatch*. Elizabeth Copeland in the *Richmond* (Va.) *News Leader* added, "Flora Robson plays the role of Queen Elizabeth with such finesse and such respect for her art that she alone stands above the fairly mediocre conception of the story. She handles the Queen entirely from the scholarly standpoint rather than from the bumptious one and endows her with the mentality of a stateswoman rather than making sport of her shortcomings as is usually the case when this unique monarch is depicted dramatically."

Flora was reluctant to leave Hollywood. The atmosphere was compellingly seductive, "but I was afraid of losing my ambition," she recalled. After she had left for New York, Flynn wrote to her, "Darling we did miss you when you left, and Queen E still reigns. I shall never forget your 'Break it up boys' entrance. It was as regal a one as I have ever seen."

## 5

Gilbert Miller was well known for presenting the best of British talent on Broadway. He had been responsible for introducing Leslie Howard, Herbert Marshall, Charles Laughton, Basil Rathbone, Cedric Hardwicke, Wilfred Lawson and many others to American audiences. In addition he produced many plays in the West End of London. The 1939–40 season there had been depressingly unsuccessful. Because of public uncertainty in coping with the blackout regulations he had been forced to keep his English activities to a minimum. Business in New York had been no more encouraging. There had been two flops and a very short run of Shaw's *Geneva*. Brooding on the situation Miller had leafed through a month-old edition of the London *Sunday Times* and read James Agate's review of *Ladies in Retirement*. The production had met with Agate's approval with the exception of the playing of Mary Clare in the leading role. He had found her self-possessed where she should have been possessed. "In other words," he had concluded, "a pathological case of the kind which Miss Flora Robson knows so well how to portray."

This was the play for which Miller had engaged Flora to make her

Broadway début. It was a fine, strong role. Ellen Creed takes a job as housekeeper to Miss Fiske (Isobel Elsom) a retired music-hall performer. For a while Miss Fiske allows Ellen to have her rather dotty sisters (Estelle Winwood and Jessamine Newcombe) to stay with her. Growing tired of their waywardness Miss Fiske says she wants them to leave. To keep her family together Ellen murders her employer, walls her up in the house and continues to live with her two sisters as though Miss Fiske has gone away.

Flora was delighted to be directed by Reggie Denham again. She had always admired the way he looked into character, into the several layers of personality, so she would know the innermost feelings of the character. She was always mindful that this would be the first time Broadway audiences had seen her and was keen that they might see all that she, as an actress, had to offer. "Flora was very anxious to find a moment in the play where she could cry," Denham told me. "She believed that audiences responded to her emotional abilities as she had no beauty to offer them. Well, we found a moment and she cried, real tears. She had a talent for it. And then Gilbert Miller came to a run-through and afterwards he took me aside. 'You must tell Flora not to cry,' he said, 'American audiences don't like it. They will find it false.' Flora accepted this and the crying was cut. It was good advice which I never forgot. In fact, it provided the basis for me for directing in the American theatre – realizing the difference between audiences in America and audiences in England."

The try-out in Canada made them all rather apprehensive. The reception was as cool as the chill wintry weather. The train bringing the company back into New York was snowbound. The snow lay in deep drifts against the windows of the carriages and the rations gave out long before the snow ploughs arrived. The company warmed themselves in whatever coats and blankets they could muster. They were back in New York just in time for the dress rehearsal, which was being given as a public preview. The company were despondent at what again was an unenthusiastic reception. Reggie was almost in despair but Gilbert Miller was philosophical. "No play that I put on is as bad as that," he said.

"Go to see it and get the hell scared out of you," advised Walter Winchell in the *Daily Mirror*, while Richard Watts Jnr. in *The New York Herald Tribune* enthused, "Just the sort of good, sound murder play that the dramatic season has been so insistently demanding. It is a tense, taut and properly literate melodrama. Miss Robson in nothing short of brilliant."

Flora was "in a daze of delight". She now felt so very much more confident and optimistic. However long she was forced to stay in

America she could now make the best of it and look forward to a career in the theatre.

For the murder scene Reggie Denham had Isobel Elsom sitting at the piano accompanying herself in a song. Out of the shadows Ellen Creed crept up behind her and strangled her. Reggie plotted it so that Miss Elsom would slump over the keyboard, crashing against the keys so that the sound would tell the audience what had happened as the curtain fell. But as soon as Flora began her approach, the rope in her hands and murderous intent in her eyes, the audience yelled out to warn the hapless Miss Fiske! By the time the deed was done the clamour from the audience was so intense that no one even heard the piano noise. Then the exclamation swelled into tumultuous applause.

Audiences came to applaud and cheer for a run of five months. After this the company set out on a seven-month tour across America. Gradually Flora became aware of the real America. She began to appreciate the fact that although New York and Los Angeles were important business centres which dictated the terms by which Americans were known, they represented only a minor part of the life of America. Her journey took her over a vast country of differing peoples and traditions. The logical way of American life and the bright warmth of the people appealed to her wherever she went. She went out of her way to learn everything she could and was met with the kind of hospitality that Americans alone offer their visitors. As the star of a successful play Flora was called upon to attend many functions. She had always been reluctant to commit herself as a private person in public, shy of venturing into any area where she might not have control of the situation. Somehow in America the general spirit of optimism and faith in one's capabilities, which inspires so many visitors, carried her into a new and rewarding attitude to her life. She began to enjoy her public self, as Flora Robson and not as a character she had learned and studied. She discovered that she found people as fascinating as they found her. This love affair with her public is one of her more enduring attributes, for she has never lost the capacity to be genuinely fascinated by everyone she meets.

During the tour, Evelyn Ankers, who played the maid, left the cast to take up a Hollywood contract that her success in the play had won her. She had been one of Flora's ladies-in-waiting in *Fire Over England* and through the forties would find her own special place in the cinema as the 'Queen of the B's'. A young actress of Scots descent was rushed out to join the company. Frances Tannehill arrived at the theatre for rehearsal loaded down with a huge bag of groceries she had been unable to deposit at her hotel. Immediately inside the stage-door she encountered Flora, who warmly introduced herself. To Frances' amazement she then relieved her of her groceries and hauled them round with her as she introduced the rest of the company. "What kind of star is this?" Frances thought. It was the beginning of a long friendship.

The one city which all tours dreaded was Los Angeles. All the moguls and stars would assemble, but few would pay any real attention to the performances. Each would be weighing up the potential of the play as a film property. The audience at the opening of the *Ladies in Retirement* was characteristically polite but unresponsive.

The following morning Flora had a call from Humphrey Bogart's press secretary. Mr Bogart had seen the play and was anxious to meet Flora. She had actually already met him briefly on the lot at Warners but arranged to go up to the Bogart house later that day. Bogart met her and they walked by his pool as he told her how excited he had been by the play and her performance in particular. He was interested to hear about her career in England. "I understand you've done one or two movies as well," he said. "I never go to the movies myself so I haven't seen any of them." Flora asked him if he never saw any of the ones he made himself. "I never do," he replied. "Why?" Flora explained that, even though they had not been in the same scenes, they had, in fact, made a movie together. In *Invisible Stripes* Flora's name had been billed directly beneath his!

Perhaps, in the back of her mind, Flora wondered whether she would be offered the role of Ellen Creed in a film of *Ladies in Retirement*. It was not to be. When the film was eventually made, the much younger Ida Lupino was given her role. Flora felt this made nonsense of the play and the title which implied that the ladies were old. Had Ellen been a younger woman she need not have been driven to such extremes. With youth on her side the motive was removed. She could have gone out and got another job.

When the tour was over, Flora returned to Hollywood as there was an offer from Paramount. She was to play a character role in *Bahama Passage*, a tropical romance to star Madeleine Carroll and Sterling Hayden, which would be her first film in Technicolor. Her role was that of Hayden's mother, a bitter, neurotic woman. It was another rather sinister part, which worried Flora. One day, when she was on tour, a man had come up to her in a restaurant and asked, "Haven't I seen you haunting a house somewhere?" It was meant lightly but it indicated to her that perhaps she was becoming type-cast in the public eye. On another occasion she was waiting in a queue outside a cinema when she noticed one or two small boys pointing at her excitedly, recognizing a star. She smiled at them, but they turned, in terror, and ran away. When she thought it over she realized they knew her only as a sinister character.

There again, she had to go where the work was and it was essential to keep herself in the public eye. The part of Mrs Ainsworth was a difficult role to judge. There was scope for plenty of histrionics and the atmosphere of the setting had dramatic potential. But the whole film seemed to be shot around Sterling Hayden's beauty and little attempt made to develop any of the situations or characters fully.

Flora has experienced few real flops in her long career. This one was a disaster. The first-night audience, when the film was premiered in New York, laughed uproariously all through her death scene. Howard Barnes, in *The New York Herald Tribune*, suggested that such laughter was "either bad manners or good criticism". Some time later Flora saw a performance of the film when a large party of marines was present. They were out to have a good time at the cinema and when she appeared on the screen they began to titter like a crowd of children. But they, too, were laughing uncontrollably by the time of the death scene. Flora decided their laughter was completely understandable. Key scenes, which explained the character's behaviour, were removed at the insistence of one of the actors who was exercising a contract option. It was the kind of decision that destroyed everyone's work.

She was able to put this unfortunate episode easily behind her as there was a splendid project on the horizon. Maurice Evans was planning a major new production of *Macbeth* on the Broadway stage with himself in the title role. He wanted Flora to be his queen. Flora knew that she had a Lady Macbeth in her and had longed for an opportunity to make a better attempt at the part than she had managed at the Old Vic eight years previously. She remembered all the good ideas Tony Guthrie had given her and had developed her own theories of the areas where there had been disagreement between her and Tony. She was very excited that Evans should think of her and wrote and told him so immediately.

A complication arose over the choice of director. Evans wanted Margaret Webster to do the production. In fact they had planned it together. It seems, however, that Miss Webster was unhappy about the choice of Flora. She had worked briefly with Flora on the production of *The Lady from the Sea* six years earlier and there had been certain differences of opinion over Flora's interpretation of Ellida. Miss Webster was not prepared to invest the work she had already done on the play with Flora in the role and Evans had to decide whether to choose between Peggy Webster and a different Lady Macbeth or Flora and a new director.

# FLORA

Flora's agent had to do some skilful juggling. Gilbert Miller was keen for Flora to appear in his next production and there were film scripts to consider. Eventually, with much regret, Evans opted to cast the role elsewhere, and Flora's agent was able, at the eleventh hour, to secure for her the Miller play. She was terribly disappointed as it would have been an opportunity to show Broadway her true mettle. Shortly afterwards Evans announced his cast. Together with Mrs Danvers in *Rebecca*, Lady Macbeth afforded Judith Anderson another major role which might have been Flora's. It would be the Evans/Anderson *Macbeth* against which, for more than a decade, all productions would be evaluated, including the one which was to bring Flora to Broadway six years later.

So Flora returned to New York to begin rehearsals for *Anne of England*. This was an adaptation by Mary Cass Canfield and Ethel Borden of Norman Ginsbury's hit play *Viceroy Sarah* which had, in 1934 at the Arts Theatre, been a huge success for Edith Evans and, after a transfer to the Whitehall Theatre, for Irene Vanburgh. Tony Guthrie had directed the play which detailed the relationship between Queen Anne and Sarah Churchill, Duchess of Marlborough. A definitive interpretation of Queen Anne had been given by Barbara Everest and Gilbert Miller had arranged for her to come to New York to recreate her role. Also in the cast were Jessica Tandy with whom Flora had worked in England and Leo G. Carroll with whom she had played in Hollywood in both *Wuthering Heights* and *Bahama Passage*.

The role of Sarah was a superb opportunity for Flora. The Duchess of Marlborough was a powerful and beautiful woman who was the power behind the throne. The story told of the usurpation of her influence by an ambitious and ruthless cousin, Abigail Hill, played by Miss Tandy. Miller, who staged the play himself, mounted it with great flair. It was the most sumptuous production Broadway had seen for many seasons. Mstislav Dobujinsky was engaged to design the settings and the costumes. No expense was spared in creating the loveliest gowns that Flora had ever worn. The extravagance and wealth of detail extended to every member of the cast. Frances Tannehill, who played one of Flora's daughters, remembered wearing a pair of very costly buttoned boots, made especially for her, which were completely hidden by her gown. She and Dobujinsky alone knew how authentically she was dressed!

At Flora's insistence, Barbara Everest was given equal billing to her. This was, after all, a recreation of a great performance and, in this production, the title role. Miss Everest came with terrible news of the Blitz. Flora listened with a growing apprehension for all her family at home. In their letters they had told her only what they

## NEW WORLDS

felt she would want to know. A smiling photograph of her mother and father had arrived with the inscription, 'To our lassie, so far away'. Miss Everest had been through the worst of the bombing herself and made the dangerous Atlantic crossing by boat. One day in the middle of rehearsal she faltered in the middle of a sentence and broke down. Frances remembered that everyone was rather embarrassed. Not so Flora, who took her quietly to one side and comforted her.

The adaptors of the play had taken only as much of Norman Ginsbury's original as they had wished and added freely to it dialogue that pointed the similarity between the situation that existed between eighteenth-century England and France and the contemporary confrontation between Britain and Nazi Germany. Unfortunately these alterations upset the balance of a finely constructed original. Norman Ginsbury did what he could and wrote to Flora to ask her to use her influence to have some of the original elements restored. But little was achieved and the play opened to scant enthusiasm. "Ponderous, lavish and boring," was the way the *Newark Evening News* summed it up. George Freedley, in the *New York Morning Telegraph*, wrote, however, "It is pleasant to welcome back Flora Robson from Hollywood in a role which becomes her and allows her a few moments of comedy. Looking very handsome and regal, her tempestuousness is an excellent foil. Her playing of the touching scene in which she tries to win back the queen by recalling to her their past friendship was moving in the extreme. In this, and, in fact, throughout the play, she was aided by the perfect team work of a fine English actress, Barbara Everest, unknown to these shores." Walter Winchell, in his influential *Daily Mirror* column, was more down-to-earth. "The Mirror's Oracle sees a dim future for it," he wrote. The play lasted for only seven performances. Apart from the adaptation, it seems there was little sense of pace in Miller's production. In addition, it was presented at the barnlike St James's Theatre, which was much more suited to spectacular musicals than the intimate qualities necessary to focus the subtleties in such a play.

### 6

Flora found herself, suddenly, out of work with nothing whatsoever to look forward to. Because of an Equity ruling she was able only to take parts on Broadway which could more suitably be played by an English actress. Nothing presented itself for her in Hollywood after the disastrous *Bahama Passage*. There had been other projects. She had tested for the role of Ma Baxter, the wife, in the film of Marjorie Kinnan Rawlings' novel, *The Yearling*. She had studied the difficult southern American accent for over a month and eventually made the test with Spencer Tracy, who was to play Pa Baxter. Tracy was impressed by her test and told her the part was virtually in the bag for her. The producer of the film agreed but the director took a dislike to Flora and opposed her casting. Anne Revere was given the role, but a week later the whole production folded. When, eventually, the film was made, Gregory Peck had Tracy's role and Jane Wyman the part Flora had so badly wanted to play. She had hoped for a part in a Bette Davis film at Warners and there had been talk of her playing in *The White Cliffs of Dover* and *Jane Eyre*, but all these projects had come to nought.

So Flora spent several worrying months wondering what would happen to her. She was more than anxious to return home to England, but it was impossible to get passage on a convoy without a priority for return. She wrote to Tony Guthrie to ask if there was anything he could do. And she knitted. Flora was always knitting. She has never stopped. Whenever there is a moment, and her hands are free, the needles and huge bales of wool come out and she clicks her way round a pair of socks. How many thousands of pairs she has made and miles of wool she has woven into them is beyond estimate. In those days she was knitting for Britain. Over the years a whole host of nephews, fellow actors, film technicians, backstage staffs, neighbours and casual acquaintances have joined the army of soldiers and sailors who have enjoyed the fruits of Flora's labours.

There was occasional radio work and early in 1942 she discovered a new world which, in later years, she was to make very much her own. She made her début in television drama as Mrs Smith in *Suspect*, an early play by Reginald Denham and Edward Percy. It was the first full-length play to be screened on American television. The play was certainly not as good as *Ladies in Retirement* but it offered a part Flora could play well. The role had, in fact, been specially written for Flora, but she had been unavailable for the original London production in 1937 and the play did not reach Broadway until *Ladies in Retirement* was into its successful run.

Mrs Smith was suspected of a Lizzie-Borden-style axe murder thirty years earlier, had stood trial and been acquitted, 'Case non-proven'. The facts are reviewed when her son is about to marry and his fiancée's father learns of her past. In a chilling climax Mrs Smith admits her guilt. The live studio presentation was no problem for Flora as she was used to performing both in the theatre and films. Her reputation as 'one-take Flora' stood her in good stead for a medium where one take only was possible.

She had the opportunity of playing Mrs Smith twice more that year in summer theatres. At the Pittsburgh Playhouse she was supported by a totally non-professional cast. Because of Equity rulings every single member of the theatre staff was amateur. Unlike many professional actors, Flora was excited to go back to this kind of theatre. She was full of happy memories of the comradeship of putting on plays at Welwyn. At Pittsburgh she was delighted to be able to enter into that spirit again. The local Press were surprised that she should not want preferential treatment, content with her tiny dressing-room. She would never rush back home after the show but would sit in the bar with all her new friends and chat about art and the theatre. It was a renewing, restoring time.

She also played in *Suspect* at the Cambridge Summer Theatre and did a short tour in Maxwell Anderson's *Elizabeth the Queen*. Anderson's Queen Elizabeth was a part which might have been written for her. It is a strong, literate script, written in blank verse relating the story of Elizabeth's relationship with the Earl of Essex. It had originally been performed by the Lunts and was the basis for the dull Bette Davis – Errol Flynn film, *The Private Lives of Elizabeth and Essex*, three years earlier. Flora's talent for verse, her technique of slowly building towards a magnificent last scene and her deep knowledge of the character of Elizabeth, made it a task to which she was ideally suited. It is unfortunate that she was never able to play the role in a major production.

One of the venues for this play was in Philadelphia and it was presented in the Bellevue Stratford Ballroom. The manager of the Bucks County Playhouse had a free week and had brought in this play merely for its prestige value, fully believing that it would have no real success at all. At the end of the play, after the masterly last scene in which Elizabeth is forced to choose between Essex (played by Staats Cotsworth) and her throne, and rejects love for duty, the curtain fell to absolute silence. Flora was devastated as the silence continued. She had not anticipated that the play would flop so badly. And then the spell was broken. The audience began to applaud with a fervour the like of which no one could remember. The production proved the high spot of the entire season. Next morning, Arthur Bronson wrote in the *Philadelphia Record* that Flora was "by turn warm and stern, yielding and imperious, in every inch the Queen. She dominated each scene easily, with an electric force that carried beyond the footlights".

All this was merely an interlude. John van Druten and Lloyd Morris had written a play especially for her and she returned to New York. *The Damask Cheek* was a light romantic comedy, the kind of play Flora was so seldom given the chance to do. Her role was that of Rhoda Meldrum, a shy, quiet, English girl in her thirties who visits her aunt in the New York of 1909. Everyone hopes she will find a husband. She has secretly loved her cousin, Jimmy, for years. "She never told her love/But let concealment, like a worm i' the bud/Feed on her damask cheek . . ." (*Twelfth Night*). Jimmy is involved with a pretty actress, Calla, and treats his cousin as a sister. It is not until Rhoda takes a scandalous cab-ride in Central Park alone with a handsome roué, that he recognizes his true feelings, escapes his actress, and gives the play, and Rhoda, a happy ending. The play was to be directed by van Druten, himself, owing to the tragic death of his colleague Auriol Lee in a motor accident. He had no experience as a director and told the company that he would depend on them to help see him through. There was an exceptionally strong cast with the marvellous character actress Margaret Douglass as the aunt, Myron McCormick as Jimmy, Joan Tetzel as his sister, Zachary Scott, who was to give Flora her first, much publicized, Broadway kiss, and in the role of Calla, a pretty young ingénue named Celeste Holm.

"The first time I met Flora Robson," Miss Holm recalled, "was at the Playhouse on 48th Street. It was the first day of rehearsal. I arrived at the theatre full of joy. I was delighted and enchanted to be in the play and I was going to be working with a wonderful star. You can imagine my surprise when I came out onto the stage and found Flora Robson galloping around the stage chasing a large boxer dog. 'Is this our star?' I thought."

Flora had quite often been called upon to sing on stage but in this play she was required to accompany herself at the piano as well. Somehow with all the work necessary in rehearsing Rhoda in New York she found little chance to rehearse her playing, although she was quite an accomplished pianist. She was naturally a little apprehensive as to what might happen in Boston. To her great delight the audience applauded and called for an encore. "I stopped the show," she recalled.

"I was quite in awe of Flora," Miss Holm remembers, "By awe I don't mean afraid but I loved and respected her. I loved the wonderful quality Flora has of never holding anything back. When she talks to you she talks with her whole self. She had a wretched time with the make-up man. It's awful when people say, 'Well now we must do something about your make-up' because you know you must look awful. But then Flora said something so terribly appealing, she said, 'Oh I know I'm homely, but you see, I don't have to look.' I found that quite heart-stopping."

The climax of the play involved a no-holds-barred fight between Flora and Miss Holm. Miss Holm had a fight "left over from another play" and staged it.

# NEW WORLDS

The play opened to the kind of notices that at least one play gets every season, that it was 'the most literate play of the season'. Flora's notices were generally favourable but reflected largely what she felt to be unsatisfactory about her role. Van Druten had written the play with Flora too much in mind. To a great extent he had written a play about Flora and there was nothing in it for Flora to act. He had caught her warmth, her intelligence, her gentle sense of humour and, when it was necessary, her fiery spirit. Throughout much of the action Rhoda would sit in the background and sew and watch what happened. This is all very well if there is a dramatic climax to follow, but whenever Flora took centre stage it was to be a further extension of herself. "She scrupulously clinches the point that beauty is in the eye of the beholder, and so honestly carries out the intent of the authors," wrote John Anderson in the *New York Journal*, "But the surface contrast that ought to enhance the laughter is lacking, suggesting that she is too true to be good for the play." Indeed, as the run progressed, she knew she was unpopular in the cast, although everyone was kind and friendly. She simply could not get the laughs which they felt should have been hers. Perhaps this was partly due to Flora's unease in comedy, but she didn't possess that brilliant brashness with which an American actor can turn a line from a straightforward sentiment into a delicious bit of fun. She told the other actors to exploit all her moments of comedy for themselves.

But audiences were enchanted with the play and there was always applause for Flora. During the performance there was a short period when Flora and Miss Holm were off-stage together waiting for their next entrance. Each evening they would chat about how they had spent their day. One evening, quite out of the blue, Flora said, "You know you're going to be a star, don't you?" Miss Holm was taken completely by surprise. "You have what makes people watch you," Flora continued, "I've had rather a time keeping the audience's eye." "Oh, I'm sorry," Miss Holm interposed. "No, no, it's exactly right. You're playing the part just as you should. One day you will be in a play that is so good and you will be so good in it that you will rise like cream. And then no one will play with you unless you are the star. I only hope it doesn't happen to you too soon, Celeste." "Why, what do you mean?" Miss Holm asked. "Because," said Flora, "that's when your troubles start."

During the run arrangements were made for the company to visit an army camp to give a special Sunday performance for the troops. Flora described the adventure in a letter to John van Druten. "I have been trying to find a moment all week to tell you about our visit to Fort Meade. It was the most wonderful experience. We left at 8.30

# FLORA

and were not back till after midnight – eight hours' travelling but all well worth it. The stage hands went down at night so they had the hardest time of any – that is why I always include the crew backstage in any of my festivities. The soldiers were standing outside the theatre an hour before we started, stamping their feet in the snow, and as we dressed we heard a painful orchestra rehearsing musical interludes. Much dash and no tune, with a French horn which moaned like a cow in pain. Luckily the last was not included in the dance music off-stage otherwise I would never have been able to continue. There was a huge roar on Zac's line 'It won't take more than half an hour, no one will notice' [the ride around the park]. That line came too near the kiss for comfort! And the fight! Can you imagine how we felt carrying on with a thousand men *roaring* their delight. Then Celeste got left outside the curtain and had to run for it. They yelled and roared until the curtain went up again and cheered solidly at the end because they didn't want us to go. We had to face the audience while the Anthem was played by the terrible little orchestra, the horn again gallantly playing the bass all out tune, and our stomachs shaking with repressed laughter! Did you know that Warners are dickering for *Damask Cheek* and *Garbo* wants to play my part and wants MGM to buy it for her. She has been several times. Everyone in the company sends their love to you. We are most united, playing together beautifully and all *very* happy and grateful to be in such a lovely play. Thank you dear John for giving it to us."

Although it would seem Flora had only happy memories of her visit to Fort Meade, a rather unpleasant incident might well have marred her day. All the visitors were invited to dine in the officers' mess. All, that is, except for Flora's coloured maid. Flora was deeply upset. The back-stage people had worked harder than anyone else to make the day a success. Her maid was anxious to point out that she would, indeed, be happier dining alone in the ladies' room. The officers were adamant in their prejudice and so Flora, with characteristic humanity, declined their invitation and joined her maid for dinner in the ladies' room.

She was forced out of the cast shortly after Christmas with a streptococcus throat infection. The doctors advised her to enter hospital. The infection spread to her eyes. She was to suffer for many months from streaming eyes. Whilst in hospital she often listened to the radio and was delighted one day to hear a reassuring English voice. As she listened she became quite alarmed at the unpatriotic things he was saying. It was later she discovered she had been listening to 'Lord Haw-Haw'. She was distressed to learn that the play had quickly closed. Business had not been good enough for it to play on without its star. She made the best of her rest and was well treated by the doctors and nurses.

Van Druten badly wanted Flora to play Rhoda when it was possible to set up a production in England. She politely turned him down. "You know how I love playing quiet parts, biding my time," she wrote to him, "but it seems to irritate London audiences who keep waiting for an explosion. I have an idea I would just spoil the play there. I feel badly about this, and maybe I'm wrong. I hate letting Rhoda go. Over Christmas when I heard carols I burst into tears and became very homesick. If I go back next year I shall go to the Old Vic. I want to act in all the little villages. I haven't much longing for the West End." *The Damask Cheek* eventually was put on in England and Flora was interested to see that the actress playing her role opted to perform in a similar key. In concluding her letter to van Druten she quoted from a letter written to her by a Private McKee, one of the Fort Meade audience, who summed up what audiences had felt throughout the run. At Flora's instigation it had been quoted amongst the critics in newspaper advertisements for the play. Private McKee, who was to become a life-long friend, wrote, "You brought two hours of utter charm into our lives."

Hollywood was calling again and so Flora prepared once more to cross America. Some time earlier, she had welcomed to New York, after a perilous Atlantic crossing, the notable Greek tragedienne Katina Paxinou. She had been instrumental in arranging Paxinou's New York début in the title role of *Hedda Gabler*. Paxinou never forgot Flora's kindness at this time. *Hedda* had led to her being cast in her Academy Award winning role in the film *For Whom the Bell Tolls* with Gary Cooper and Ingrid Bergman. One of the friends she made in Hollywood was working in the art department at Warners. In those days art directors would design the look of a film well in advance of shooting. Individual frames would be drawn up and the faces of the stars would be sketched in. Paxinou heard of a role which she felt would be a marvellous opportunity for Flora and her friend drew Flora's face throughout the 1,320 sketches, wherever the character appeared. Consequently, when it came time for Sam Wood, the director, to cast *Saratoga Trunk*, he could see no one else in the role but Flora!

At first she was not interested. *The Damask Cheek* was still running and she was happier to stay on Broadway and await a possible return to England. It was somewhat strange casting. Angelique was a dusty-faced mulatto serving-woman. It was also the kind of sinister role she had wanted to avoid. Sam Wood, however, was so eager to get her under contract that he personally flew to New York to persuade her. He was most attentive and persuasive and, because Flora realized the advantages of getting away from the New York winter and into the Californian sunshine, she gave way, and agreed to play the role.

## 7

Her old friend John Abbott, who had been so good in her last London play, *Last Train South*, lived in one of two tiny Alpine-style wooden cottages perched on the side of Mannix Drive in the Hollywood hills. He was able to arrange for Flora to rent the other cottage and she was happy to be so near an old friend. She told John that there was a part in the film which would be ideal for him. She made every effort to have the casting department consider him, but they showed little interest. John had made one or two films, but at this time was working in a showcase theatre production. One evening Hal Wallis, the Warner Brothers executive, saw his play and immediately offered him the role of Roscoe Bean in *Saratoga Trunk*, the part Flora had tried to get for him. Shortly afterwards John moved to another house and Flora was able to move some other old friends into his cottage.

Moyna MacGill had been in the cast of Flora's first professional play, *Will Shakespeare*, as Anne Hathaway. At that time she had been married to Reggie Denham. Now she was in America with the three children of her second marriage, twins Edgar and Bruce and daughter Bidsie. They had all seen Flora in *The Damask Cheek* and had looked her up in Hollywood. The tiny cottage was bursting at the seams with its new occupants. Flora was pleased to be in such close proximity to the family and enjoyed having them call in on her at any time.

Work began on *Saratoga Trunk*. Bette Davis made a special point of welcoming her back to the Warner lot. Flora was very unhappy in her role. She had to wear a thick ugly grey-black make-up. The story of the film was yet another spin-off from the *Gone with the Wind* formula, this time from a novel by Edna Ferber, with Flora in the equivalent of the Hattie MacDaniel role. She discovered that Sam Wood hated black people and this was one of the reasons for casting a white woman. Strangely, when Flora was made-up, he treated her as though she really were black. Gone were all the niceties he had used to charm her into accepting the role. For some of the scenes Flora had to drive to different locations and was shocked to find exactly how black people were treated. Policemen ordered her about and a crowd of soldiers shouted obscenities at her. She longed to pull back the collar of her blouse and show she was white underneath but, instead, opted for the less attractive alternative of remaining black.

Sydney makes Flora drink her poison *Man About the House* (Alexander Bender)

Margaret, the mistress, and Margaret, the wife. With Barbara Couper in *Message for Margaret* (Alexander Bender)

Countess von Platen plots to ambush Count Koenigsmark. With Anthony Quayle, extreme right in *Saraband for Dead Lovers*. (E.M.I.)

Lady Cicely Wayneflete
(Angus McBean Photograph:
Harvard Theatre Collection)

Lady Macbeth in her dressing room

With Carol Wolveridge in *The Innocents*
(Angus McBean Photograph:
Harvard Theatre Collection)

With Anthony Ireland in *Black Chi*
(Houston Ro
Victoria and Albert Muse

Paulina in Peter Brook's production of *The Winter's Tale*
(Norman Parkinson: Courtesy of *Vogue*)

Outside Buckingham Palace with Uncle John and Maud Bell *after* Flora's C.B.E. Investiture
  (Universal Pictorial Press Agency)

Flora gave over seven hundred consecutive performances of *The House by the Lake*. With Sylvia Coleridge
  (Houston Rogers: Victoria and Albert Museum)

## NEW WORLDS

Angelique was the serving-maid of Clio Dulaine, the half-Creole illegitimate daughter of a New Orleans aristocrat come to New Orleans from Paris, after the death of her mother, to revenge herself on her father's family. Ingrid Bergman was cast as Clio, and Gary Cooper as Clint Maroon, a gambler who became entangled in her life. Also in Clio's retinue was Cupidon, a dwarf, played by Jerry Austin. Sam Wood was no help to Flora in what was a difficult characterization. When she asked for direction he simply said, "Look at Miss Bergman, honey, look at Miss Bergman." There was a scene in which Clio and her two servants had to take a ride in an elevator. Flora suggested that she and Jerry Austin might exchange a look as it was extremely unlikely that either Cupidon or Angelique had ever been in an elevator before. Sam Wood said there was no point as no one would be looking at them, everyone would be looking at Miss Bergman. At this stage in her career Ingrid Bergman was in a position of great power in Hollywood. Everyone bowed to her opinion. Naturally she was ambitious to retain her standing and fought at all times for the focus in the film. The director was bound to support her. In this instance the balance of the film was badly disturbed by too much exposure for Miss Bergman and too little development of the other characters.

Gary Cooper was an altogether different actor. He had been around Hollywood a long time and looked on, amused, as the film deteriorated around him. He knew that one flop would not hurt his career. Flora was very much taken with this shy actor and enjoyed his company as often as she could. Coop was accorded the privilege of his own pair of socks. "*He was very quiet and introspective. When he was on camera he seemed to do nothing at all. I was amazed when I saw the rushes at just how much the camera had picked up. I had collected autographed photographs of all the stars with whom I worked to send home to England to help boost morale. Paul Muni had signed a photograph 'To Flora Robson, who is something of a swell'! I asked Gary for a photograph. He told me he never gave them. I told him that anything, even a snap shot would do. He said he would think about it.*"

When she finished work Flora would go straight home and jump into the shower and wash off all the little bits of make-up she hadn't been able to remove at the studio. Sometimes Bidsie would come in for a chat when she had finished work at the department store where she was a salesgirl in the perfumery. One day she came in, quite excited, to ask for Flora's help. She had the opportunity of a screen test for MGM who were looking for an English girl to play a cockney maid. Bidsie was seventeen and had a bright attractive face that would be eminently suitable for films. "I do believe that Flora recognized the fact that, as a youngster, I did have the potential, so she helped me with that reading and with the test. Not as a coach or a teacher but just as a very warm friend. And as someone who knew, so I was certainly listening. Of course, I also had Moyna, my mother. But Moyna was Irish. This was a cockney girl and so I thought it was more up Flora's street," she told me recently.

There was great rejoicing when Bidsie got the part which led to a long-term MGM contract for her. George Cukor and John van Druten were responsible for the test for their forthcoming picture *Gaslight*. Bidsie was the nickname of Angela Lansbury. "Flora was a vitally attractive woman, in a very extraordinary way," she continued, "I realized that as quite a young girl. I recognized that she had a mystique about her. As an actress she was alone in her ability. She always had the ability to humanize, by dint of her own understanding and intelligence, everything she did. I will always remember her diction which seemed so effortless but was absolutely there. I picked up on it and it stayed with me. Flora is a very rare and unique actress."

She was certainly not sorry to wind up work on *Saratoga Trunk*. Release was delayed until late in 1945 because it was thought unsuitable for a wartime audience, although it was shown in selected army camps. When it did emerge Flora received great praise for her performance which she had managed to imbue with a richness of characterization. Howard Barnes, in the *New York Herald Tribune*, wrote of "the florid and exuberant mood of the motion picture with Flora Robson contributing a brilliant bit as Clio's domineering maid". The greatest accolade she was to receive, however, was her nomination for an Academy Award as Best Actress in a Supporting Role. She was narrowly beaten to the coveted award by Anne Baxter who took the Oscar for her performance in *The Razor's Edge*. Others nominated for the same award that year were Ethel Barrymore, Lillian Gish and Gale Sondergaard, so Flora was in distinguished company. She, herself, was philosophical about it as the last time she had won awards heralded the period when the British film industry turned its back on her.

In Hollywood, out-of-work actors would often get together and form little theatre groups. Such a group enlisted Flora's support for a programme they were presenting of four one-act plays of the Grand Guignol school at the unfashionable Belasco Theatre in Los Angeles. Flora had a part in the final play of the evening, *The Thirsty Death*, a psychological study of terror in an African settlement, with George Coulouris and Lester Matthews as her co-stars. Also appearing in the programme, which was called 'Horror Tonight' were Henry Hull, June Havoc, Moyna MacGill and Barbara Everest. Bidsie Lansbury was recruited to assist in the proceedings. The director thought it would be a novel gimmick to have a nurse walking up and down the aisle with smelling salts to revive anyone who was too horrified by the action on stage! This was Bidsie's role.

"To be perfectly frank I can't remember much about the production or the performances," Miss Lansbury recalled. "All I remember was lots of blood which I didn't like very much. I always had to turn my head away. *I* was the one who needed the smelling salts! And here have I just got through a year on Broadway in *Sweeney Todd*. I've got used to blood I can tell you!"

The play ran for only two weeks but Flora was grateful for this when news arrived that Tony Guthrie had obtained the priority for her to return to England for a C.E.M.A. tour. She was enormously relieved and happily began to pack. It was now easy to turn down a long term MGM contract which was offered and would have commenced with the role of the mother in *National Velvet*. Moyna was delighted to be able to spread her family into the other cottage and Flora left her all her bed-linen and crockery. She was to regret this when she learned how difficult it was to come by such items in England. Before leaving Hollywood she saw Gary Cooper's stand-in one day and asked him to remind Coop that he had promised her a snap-shot.

Flora hurried back to New York, which was in the grip of a heatwave. There was no sailing date and she had to remain at the ready. She hardly dared go out in case the telephone rang. However, she ventured out to see the show which had made Celeste Holm a star. Like Flora, Miss Holm was no overnight success. Ado Annie in Rodgers and Hammerstein's *Oklahoma!* was the fifty-fourth role of her career. It would lead to many other brilliant successes and an Academy Award in Hollywood.

At last the call came. Just as Flora was about to set off for the quays, a special messenger arrived from Hollywood with a package for her. Inside was a huge photograph of Gary Cooper in the outfit he wore in *Saratoga Trunk*. On it he had written, 'I promised you a snap-shot and here it is.' Preparatory to boarding the ship, all her luggage had to be opened and inspected. As she walked by the officials, Flora proudly held up her treasured snap-shot, beaming with excitement. Soon she was under way. As the ship steamed out of New York Harbour, Flora looked back at the Manhattan skyline with a sudden sense of loss for all the friends she had made in the land beyond. She had found more than one new world to the west of the Atlantic. One day, when there was peace again, she would return.

# 5

## The Years Between
### 1943–1959

### 1

"ONE... TWO... THREE..." They all waited in silence, scarcely daring to breathe. "Four... five!" No one moved. A possibility hung in the air. Six bells meant 'Abandon ship'. But it had been five bells. Suddenly everyone was on their feet, hurrying to their cabins. Eve finished off what she was doing. Flora said, "We had better get on deck. It was five bells." She looked at her fur coat hanging in the closet. That coat represented four years' savings. It was all the tax-man had left her to show for the fortune she had earned in America. She looked at it for only a moment before grabbing it and wrapping it round herself. She struggled to fasten her life-jacket over it as she hurried towards the deck. "You're never going to keep that fur coat on, are you?" one of the sailors asked as she passed. "I certainly am!" she replied. "But madam, if we go down, you'll drown in it, the fur will absorb water," he warned. "I've worked for years for this coat," Flora declared fiercely. "If it goes down, I go too. But no damned Nazis are going to separate us!" Despite her protests an officer ordered the coat removed and she watched in grieved silence as it was taken below. A heavy vibration shook the ship and a boom of sound plummeted through the water. Flora caught her breath in a little cry of shock and fear, her face turning first white, then green. "Don't worry," someone said: "only a depth-charge." "*I thought the depth-charges were torpedoes. They made a watery waddle-waddle-waddle sound as they went down in the shallow water. Our little ship heaved and shook and I thought our last moment had come.*" "Where are we?" Flora asked. "Somewhere off Newfoundland," came the reply. The ship continued its zigzag course, depth-charges shaking the firmament, and all the time the thought that, somewhere below, an enemy submarine might be lurking. The fog lay thick all about them. "Look!" someone said. They all strained their eyes to look in the direction he was pointing. Through the fog Flora could see a dull orange glow. "What is it?" she asked. There was a silence. She looked at the grave faces about her and realized it was one of the other ships in the convoy, less lucky than theirs, burning in the night.

The suffused light from the ship turned the fog a grim and menacing red. Hours had gone by and still they sat on the deck playing games to pass the time. The sailors told them jokes in the dark. No one laughed until the punch-lines were explained and then the laughter was never more than half-hearted. Eve had made an excuse to go back to the cabin. Mlle Curie was working on the proofs of the French edition of *Journey Among the Warriors*, her story of the battle fronts, east and west, which had recently been published in its English edition. Flora also shared her cabin with two girls of the Free French movement. She had been horrified when she saw the ship for the first time. It was painted white. She was assured that a white-painted ship more easily merged with the horizon than one of any other colour and was difficult to spot through a periscope. It was a banana boat bringing food and about forty passengers to England.

On the deck they talked in hushed tones. No one dared speak very loudly; there was no point in tempting providence. The silence was ominous. Without warning it all began again. Flora looked towards heaven. Would she see the end of this? At that moment a torpedo went clean across the bows of one of the ships in front of them.

Lila stared at the stranger who stood in the doorway. "Is it Flora?" she ventured. There had been no way of letting them know. The terrible journey had been extended by several more hours as the convoy sat in the Bristol Channel, ten minutes late for the tide. She had been past sleep, too tired to relax, as the train carried her to London. Then she had travelled through the night to Hove, near Brighton, where her parents were now living. She looked dreadful. An ashen pallor drew all the warmth from her suntan. No wonder Lila had difficulty recognizing her. She stumbled into the front room, embraced her mother and collapsed into a chair. It was Sunday morning and her father was at church. Lila hurried along to meet him. She realized how great would be the shock of finding Flora so suddenly returned in such a poor state of health.

Flora stayed in bed for two weeks with severe bronchitis, surprised that her health had so quickly deteriorated. Her family had been denied all the good things she had enjoyed and yet they were strong and fit. The human body adapts to privation after a time and Flora was only at the beginning of her period of adjustment.

Rehearsals for the tour which had occasioned Flora's return priority would not begin until December. The Gainsborough film company came up with an offer for her to play in a film called *2,000 Women*, about a women's internment camp. The internees turn the tables on their Nazi captors by smuggling RAF pilots, who have parachuted into the area, out of occupied territory. Frank Launder and Sidney Gilliatt were responsible for the script and direction and with Flora was a roster of Gainsborough's female stars – Phyllis Calvert, Patricia Roc, Renee Houston, Anne Crawford and Jean Kent among them. *Time and Tide*'s reviewer wrote, "It is . . . not my sort of film. One of the spinsters is played by Flora Robson; she didn't look as if it was hers either." Indeed, Flora thought it a dull part. Later, in 1947, when the film was due for release in Hungary, it was banned by the Minister of the Interior. The Democratic Women's Association had claimed that the production portrayed concentration camps as "pleasant hotels and SS men as ideal representatives of human kindness and politeness".

Flora had broadcast many radio plays since *The Flowers are Not for You to Pick*. Tony Guthrie had written another part for her to play in a surrealistic piece called *Matrimonial News* which he directed on radio shortly after she finished work on the film. It provided Flora with one of the few opportunities she had of working with her dearly loved teacher and old friend, Sybil Thorndike. "Its chief character", reported the *Manchester Guardian*, "was a woman played by Flora Robson, and the play revealed the currents of thought in her mind as she was about to meet a man in answer to a matrimonial advertisement. Miss Robson played this part most skilfully, and with a dramatic intensity keyed down to the requirements of radio. The part of her mother, a nightmare voice recurring in her consciousness, was played in the most colourful way by Sybil Thorndike, who introduced a grim and macabre note."

"I am now on a tour of munition towns with *Guilty*, in which I play Zola's Thérèse Raquin," Flora wrote to John van Druten. "I keep getting ill – luckily just during rehearsals – 'flu and quinsey, and am finding it very hard to acclimatise myself and most of the time I am *freezing*. The Lancashire audiences are amazing. They have built up this theatre themselves at Oldham, with private subscriptions of ten shillings each. They have a night's duty either in the box office, selling programmes or serving coffee and Oxo, and they are really enthusiastic, more so since it is their own efforts that have made it a success. We are sold out for the week. Most encouraging. I am doing mostly small theatres in munition towns, a hard tour but our hosts usually find us rooms. I am staying with the schoolmaster and his wife and am looked after like a queen. Travelling is hard and we wait in queues for taxis with a three-guinea fine if you try to sneak in. It is an excellent thriller with good comedy though I find some of the melodrama a bit embarrassing. But we are under-rehearsed and I think those bits will get better as we go on. The audiences in Lancashire are so attentive and well-mannered with never a laugh in the wrong place."

The tour of *Guilty*, adapted from Zola by Kathleen Bouttall, who had been in the cast of the Gainsborough film, was sponsored by the Council for the Encouragement of Music and the Arts. It opened in Liverpool, where Tony Guthrie had established a regional Old Vic Company. Flora was unhappy at the way Tony handled the production. Violet Farebrother, who was playing the paralysed Madame Raquin, was bathed in bright light, holding the audience's attention, whilst Flora and Michael Golden as Thérèse and Laurent tried to play their key scene in the shadows. When the production arrived in London to play at the Lyric, Hammersmith, many of the rather poor touring costumes were refurbished. Kay Bannerman, who was playing Suzanne, was given an entirely new gown but Flora was expected to make do with the shabby costume she had worn on tour. As she was playing the leading role she went to Tony to ask that necessary alterations should be made to her costume. He turned on her angrily. "Don't you know there's a war on?" he spat at her. Flora was shocked and hurt. Perhaps she had just returned from a glamorous life in America, where she had been a star who had earned a fur coat, but she thought he had realized from her letters how much she had always wished to return and help the war effort. Tony was under great strain. His energy level was low after a long run of strenuous work and a disastrous season at the Playhouse. He had developed a bad case of shingles. Flora was not to know this and the unpleasant disagreement resulted in a rift between them. In the days of the flowering of their individual talents they had been devoted to one another. *Guilty* was the end of their long association. Apart from a short collaboration for a reading for a festival in Belfast, late in both their lives, they would never work together again.

"Was Miss Flora Robson's Thérèse an Emma Bovary of the gutter," asked James Agate, "without heart, conscience or soul? Nonsense. Miss Robson had lots of all three, as worn in Kensington." The play ran for six weeks at the Lyric. After the run ended she immediately began work on *Great Day*, a film for RKO British. The film was dedicated to members of the Women's Institutes for their invaluable work in rural areas during the war. Flora played Mrs Ellis, who has been elected by the members of her local W.I. to greet

Mrs Roosevelt, who is to visit their village. Mrs Ellis's husband had been commissioned in the Great War and still clings to his rank of captain though ill-health has precluded him from service in the second war. He has no money and is refused credit at the local pub. In order to buy a drink to return a soldier's hospitality he steals from a girl's purse. He is caught and arrested. Stripped of his bluff and false pride he goes home to his wife. Although she stands by him he cannot face the future and the gossip of the villagers and runs out into the night intent on ending his life. His daughter finds him and persuades him to face his life with the same courage that won his medals in the last war. Father and daughter proudly watch as Mrs Ellis receives the wife of the President of the United States.

Captain Ellis was played by Eric Portman. It was the first time he and Flora had worked together since *Desire Under the Elms*. The circumstances of rehearsing that play had meant the development of a warm and sympathetic working relationship which was easily revived fourteen years later. Their major scene together is beautifully developed. Flora's best work on film is in roles which call either for great bravura or subtlety. Her playing in *The Sea Hawk* is, to my mind, the best example of the former. Her playing in *Great Day* is warm, calm and understated and is the finest example of her low-key playing. "In the scene which Mr Eric Portman . . . and Miss Flora Robson share," reported *The Times*, "the film shows an understanding of character and motives more sensitive and subtle than the cinema normally achieves."

## 2

Flora smiled into George Bernard Shaw's rugged Irish face. Gabriel Pascal, the Hungarian producer-director introduced them. "This is Miss Robson who has just been a success in a play in London," he said. Shaw replied, "Miss Robson is always a success in her plays in London." Certainly they had met before, but perhaps Shaw would not recall her as the untried girl who had played Nurse Guinness more than twenty years earlier. The actress whom Shaw saw on this particular occasion was wearing a long, dark-brown wig and her skin was stained olive for her role as Ftatateeta in the film version of Shaw's play *Caesar and Cleopatra*. "*He smiled benignly at me. I was overwhelmed. He asked me if I had any worries and I told him I was afraid of comedy lines because I have a sad voice. He just said it didn't matter at all as long as it was musical. 'You have a musical voice,' he said.*" Of course he knew who Flora was. He had modified the role so it was suitable to the actress. Ftatateeta was described in the play as being "a huge, grim woman, her face covered with a network of tiny wrinkles, her eyes old, large and wise; sinewy handed, very tall, very strong; with the mouth of a bloodhound and the jaws of a bulldog." It was more the description of a Marie Dressler than it was of Flora. However, in the notes in the screenplay preceding the newly written scene set in Cleopatra's bedchamber, Shaw had described her thus: "Ftatateeta enters. She presents a figure different from that of the night before. She has not put on her official robe; and her powerful and handsome body is seen apparently naked except for a rich sash or sumptuous belt which serves also as an apron. (Her hair must not be woolly; she is an Egyptian slave, not an Ethiopian one: dark red brown but not black.)"

Ftatateeta was Cleopatra's slave – a case of role-reversal for Flora and Vivien Leigh, who had been Flora's lady-in-waiting in *Fire Over England*. Miss Leigh had made several successful films, not least of which was her Academy Award winning Scarlett O'Hara in *Gone With the Wind*. Flora still found it difficult to warm to her. She was not alone. Claude Rains, who was cast as Caesar, came over to her on the set one day. "May I sit with you, Flora?" he asked, adding, "That lady has such cold hands." "*Dear Claude Rains was one of the best actors I worked with. As a leading man he was difficult to cast. No sooner had film studios put him on a long-term contract than they would try to dispense with his services, trying to break him down, casting him opposite very tall actresses. He was very short and would be made to stand on a pile of books. In the forties he found a niche playing supporting character roles. He became very worried when he made a success in a film with Bette Davis. Success meant that he was likely to lose his job!*"

It was the autumn of 1944. Coal was rationed and there was not enough fuel to heat water for baths at home. The studio showers were set at such low pressure that Flora was never able to remove all her body make-up successfully. She grew darker by the day! Her dressing-gown was stolen and she was refused extra clothing coupons to buy a new one. She had to make do with a coat, even though she pleaded a dressing-gown was essential to her work. The filming was an unhappy experience for most of the actors involved. Pascal was the only person trusted by Shaw to film his plays, yet it seemed to many of the actors who worked for him that he understood little of Shaw's quality and was unable to draw more than barely adequate performances from his actors. Claude Rains and Vivien Leigh rehearsed their scenes privately and any success they had was due entirely to their own instincts. Several years later when Flora was visiting Shaw at Ayot St Lawrence, he asked her whether she thought Pascal was the right man to film his plays. "*I was tempted to tell him exactly what I thought of Pascal but instead I said, 'Your work should only be directed by people who understand English very thoroughly. Your plays lose their lightness of touch when directed by foreigners.' He thought this over for a moment and then he said, 'Perhaps you are right.' I grew a little bolder and said, 'It's a pity Leslie Howard died, he understood your work and knew how to adapt it for the screen.' I knew I had said the wrong thing immediately. I should have remembered that Howard had changed the ending of* Pygmalion *by bringing Eliza and Higgins together without altering a line of the original text. Shaw went bright red, stamped over to the door, and thundered, 'The pity of Leslie Howard is he thought he was Romeo!' That was the last thing Shaw ever said to me."*

She was cast as governess to the household of a rich, city magnate in the London of the 1860's, in Patrick Hamilton's play *Ethel Fry*. Fry abducts the baby of the family and exercises an evil influence over another child as well as seducing her employer. All is revealed in a dénouement in which the child, in a sleep-walking scene, convicts the governess. "Flora Robson is cast in the title part," reported the *Stage* after the opening in Southsea at the King's Theatre. "To it she brings the highest dramatic art. At first she appears something of an enigma but she develops the part like the great actress she is." The play toured from February to April but there was no available London theatre.

The house at Downshire Hill had been sold whilst she was in America and her furniture stored. She had been looking for a permanent home, preferably out in the country within easy reach of the film studios. A short journey in the morning and a late return from the theatre were infinitely preferable to a long journey in the early hours. A house came up for sale at Chalfont St Peter, near Gerrard's Cross. Two nieces living in London where the flying-bomb terror had begun, were expecting babies within a fortnight of one another. Anxious to get them to the safety of the country, Flora took the house. Mount Fort was not as old as she might have wished but it was spacious and comfortable with a large, though overgrown, garden and an uninterrupted view of woods and the Buckinghamshire countryside. She had not lived there very long before she invited her eldest brother, John, and his wife to stay with her. Both were seriously ill, John from a wasting paralysis and his wife from tuberculosis. Hugh, their youngest son, came with them. It was at the same time a joy and a heavy burden to Flora. She had always cherished her family and longed to make Mount Fort an ever-welcome home-from-home for every member of the family, but the responsibility of caring for two invalids and a teenage boy as well as continuing a strenuous time-consuming profession at times made demands on her she was scarcely able to meet.

The Rank Organisation came along with a film called *The Years*

*Between*. It was based on a Daphne du Maurier play and the screenplay was written by Muriel and Sydney Box. It was the first time their paths had crossed since Welwyn days. The story was of a prisoner-of-war, believed dead, who returns to find that his wife has re-married. Michael Redgrave and Valerie Hobson were the stars and Flora was cast as Nanny. "Only twice does she play an important role in the story," wrote Helen Fletcher in the *Graphic*. "She interposes her own bitter experiences during the 1914–18 war of twenty years ago when she lost the man she loved, and contributes this confidence in order to appeal to the Wentworths not to break up their own marriage. . . . Flora Robson speaks as if she were thinking about every word and weighing each carefully: the result is our complete belief in what she is saying and the character she is portraying. It must have been hard to find a worse part for this magnificent actress than the one she played in *Caesar and Cleopatra*. Still they have found it." Repeating the role he played as the son of the family in the stage production was John Gilpin, who would later become Britain's premier male ballet star. "You can imagine how exciting it was to work with her," he recalled for me recently. "I was only fourteen years old at the time and very star-struck. She was a big, big name and a tremendous actress, yet she never behaved like a star. As I recall her she was always shy, self-effacing even."

Flora was by now forty-three. She had been home two years and although she had been extremely busy, the quality of the roles she had played was far below the standard she had set herself in the thirties. The years between forty and fifty are difficult for any actress to bridge. Few authors write for middle-aged women. The best roles are for actresses in their thirties and Flora had been fortunate to play her fair share of these. Her unexpected exile in America could not have come at a more inopportune time. It had covered the years when she might have been consolidating her success in both theatre and films. Only the most ardent of theatre-goers remembered her great acting in the theatre and she was relegated to character roles in British films because Hollywood had never seen her as a leading actress. To a certain extent she had to prove herself all over again in the theatre. There was a new generation of playgoers and she had not been seen in the West End for seven years.

She was asked to play Agnes Isit in John Perry's adaptation of the Francis Brett Young novel, *A Man About the House*. It was to be directed by William Armstrong who, so many years earlier, had written an appreciation of her performance in *Undercurrents*. This was the first opportunity they had had of working together. Two spinster sisters move into the Italian villa inherited by Agnes, the elder of the two, on the death of their uncle. They have lived a narrow, fruitless existence under the domination of their stern father. Eventually Agnes marries the Italian butler who, himself, has been hoping to inherit the estate. He subjects his wife to a slow process of arsenical poisoning. A visit by an English doctor unmasks the plot, and the butler shoots himself. Basil Sydney was cast as Salvatore, the butler, and Wyndham Goldie as the doctor. The last time Flora had worked with Sydney he had slit her throat. He was Rufio in the Shaw film. Flora was thrilled to have one of her dearest friends working with her in the play. He was just nine years old. His name was Bart and he was her wire-haired terrier! The play called for a mongrel but Flora had persuaded the management to employ Bart and the lines had been re-written accordingly. *"He would be kept on a lead when he was on the stage otherwise he would have wandered off in search of mice. He was an excellent actor. There was a moment at the beginning of the second act where Basil Sydney would come on stage. Bart would prick up his ears knowing his cue was coming. 'Take that dog out of here.' Basil yelled, and Bart would shoot off into the wings. He sometimes got a laugh, sometimes an exit round, and always a biscuit from my dresser!"*

One of the great challenges of the part was representing effectively the symptoms of the poisoning. Francis Brett Young had been a doctor and had described in the book the slow paralysis of the hands and feet and the kind of high-stepping walk. *"One day a crowd of us had been riding in a small sports car. Someone had been sitting on my knee and when I got out my legs had gone to sleep. They wobbled and I almost fell. I remembered the feeling exactly and used it in my performance. Poor brother John, who was staying with me at the time, had a form of paralysis. I remember how he would look at his hands with a puzzled expression on his face, slowly flexing his fingers, trying to make them behave as they formerly had done. He was losing his sense of touch and would wander into the garden and rub his hands on the bark of a tree to restore the sensation. I found moments in the play where I could look at my own hands and try to flex them, unaware of what was happening to me."*

There was a ten-week tour before the play opened at the Piccadilly, with just a week between the end of tour and the London opening. During that week Flora suffered the greatest loss of her life. David Robson, at the age of eighty-three, died at his home in Hove. Flora was able to spend a few days with her family. Her mother broke down and cried to Uncle John, "What am I going to do without him?" Flora faced the most difficult first night she had ever had to cope with. There would be no wise and trusted friend out there in the audience to whom she could secretly play. She had to clear her mind completely of her sorrow. There was one line it hurt her very much to say. Agnes Isit had hated her father and had to scream defiantly, "Father's dead! Dead and buried!"

There was acclaim for Flora's performance in the Press. Ivor Brown, an old champion, wrote in the *Observer*, "Miss Flora Robson is there to play that expanding blossom of an autumn crocus, the elder Miss Isit. She brings to it her unique, tremendous power to express a dumb, baffled suffering. Her little ecstasies and her large pains vibrate in the memory." The critic of the *Evening Standard* noted, "Miss Flora Robson's portrayal of a woman being poisoned by arsenic is almost unbearably convincing, even if one's knowledge of arsenical poisoning is somewhat limited. Her grotesque, quivering limbs that make her walk like a mechanical contrivance create a sense of horror which lingers grimly in the memory." The play did not run long. Flora felt the short run was due to the fact that the play had neither hero nor heroine. She did not like Miss Isit and had not played her for sympathy, although audiences had sympathized with the courage Agnes showed.

## 3

One of Flora's most memorable film roles came in the summer of 1946. *Black Narcissus* was based on the novel by Rumer Godden and was the story of Anglican working nuns in India. A contingent of them are sent to found a mission eight thousand feet up in the Himalayas in the former Palace of Mopu, which had been a 'house of women'. "There's something in the atmosphere makes everything exaggerated," says one of the characters. The atmosphere affects each of them in different ways and eventually the party are forced to leave the mountain. Flora was cast as Sister Philippa, who tends the garden. The Sister Superior, Sister Clodagh, was played with delicacy and feeling by Deborah Kerr.

The film is mainly successful for its superb evocation of India. Quite incredibly, with the exception of short passages of second unit photography of the mountain ranges, the entire film was shot in England. The exteriors of the Palace of Mopu were built on the back lot at Pinewood. Over one hundred and twenty thousand feet of tubular steel formed the framework of this monumental piece of landscaping. Timber was fixed to the scaffolding and covered with pre-fabricated plaster or cement sheets, painted to resemble the natural rock. Thirty tons of gravel and soil were hauled by rope and pulley to the top of the 'mountain' in order to make paths and terraces that were strong enough to take the weight of horses. Trees and plants were tubbed into the mountainside. Locations were used for the tropical forests on the slopes of the mountain. These 'exotic' scenes were filmed on Sir Giles Loder's estate near Horsham in Sussex! The production design was the responsibility of Alfred Junge, who had scored a notable success with *A Matter of Life and Death*, which had been selected for the first Royal Film Performance. His beautifully conceived palace was photographed with genius by Jack Cardiff, who broke a good many rules in achieving effects which had previously been thought impossible in Technicolor. His use of low-key lighting with little or no 'fill' lighting was regarded, at the time, as unique and innovative. Both he and Junge would receive Academy Awards for their work on this film.

Flora's best scenes are shared with Deborah Kerr. Sister Philippa is supposed to grow vegetables in the garden. The atmosphere of the place leads her to plant flowers everywhere. Looking out to the mountains, she says, "I think we can see too far. I look out there and I can't see the potato I'm planting and after a bit it doesn't seem to matter whether I plant it or not." Sister Clodagh instructs her to work until she is too tired to think of anything else. Slowly Sister Philippa lifts her hands, and looks at them, then shows them to Sister Clodagh. We see they are covered with calluses. Flora is superb in this underplayed scene. She has a warm, bemused earthiness. It is a small part but she brings to it qualities no other actress possessed. Miss Kerr wrote to me, "You are right in assuming that the short period of filming really does not give one any *real* insight into the personality or character of an artist, but of course, as a life-long admirer of Dame Flora's work, it was exciting and fascinating to watch her *way* of working." She was interested in hearing everything Flora could tell her of Hollywood, where shortly afterwards she would carve for herself a unique career.

Double summer time was in force and Flora was able to find two hours of daylight at the end of a working day to spend in her own garden at Mount Fort. She didn't have to worry about her garden-soiled fingernails at the studios – they were exactly right for the part! David Lawrence, a technician on the film, recalled, "While many of the stars, extras and even directors were the butt of sarcastic, sometimes lewd, and rude remarks by some of the crew and by other actors and actresses, never, never were such remarks made about Miss Robson. She was given the greatest respect by everybody and was regarded as a genuine and lovely lady. During the filming of *Black Narcissus* young Jean Simmons had to eat a slice of watermelon. Well, as you can imagine, so soon after the war, melon was a long-forgotten luxury. Dear Miss Robson, without any fuss or ballyhoo, somehow managed to find some for the technicians which, of course, was greatly appreciated." The film was a great success on its release and there was praise for Flora's performance.

At a charity performance at the Palace Theatre, Flora played

Queen Elizabeth I in Reginald Arkell's *1066 And All That*. In an all-star cast Leslie Henson was the Common Man, Robert Morley was Henry VIII and Michael Redgrave was Henry V, with more than eighty other famous names from the theatre.

She had already accepted roles in two films, *Frieda* and *Holiday Camp*, when Henry Sherek offered her the leading role in a new James Parish play, *Message for Margaret*. Naturally it was important for her to find a good role in the West End and she was able to arrange her contracts so that she could fulfil all three commitments. This meant a severe schedule beginning at daybreak when she rose and made her way to the studios to be on the set for nine to play in *Frieda*, followed by an afternoon dash to the theatre, and a railway journey before returning to Mount Fort little short of midnight. *Holiday Camp* took the last call when she was free from the other film.

*Message for Margaret* opened at the Westminster Theatre on 28 August 1946. A man killed in a road accident left a message for Margaret before he died. His wife assumes the message was for her until she learns he had a mistress also known as Margaret, who is about to bear his child. She plans to murder the mistress but succeeds only in sending a harmless young poet to his death. Flora played the wife, Barbara Couper the mistress, Edgar Norfolk was a friend of the family and Jack Allen was the poet. In the days when Flora worked at the factory she had attended a conference at Balliol College, Oxford. Also attending was Jack Allen who held a similar post at I.C.I. but they were not to meet properly until their paths crossed on the radio production of *Macbeth*. "In *Message for Margaret*," he recalled, "Flora had to scream. It came at the moment where I fell to my death from the balcony intended for Barbara Couper. She wouldn't do the scream until a few days before we opened. We were all sent to the pub while she tried it out and we didn't hear it until the dress rehearsal. I remember saying to her that I didn't think she was properly relaxed when she did the scream. She insisted she was. When she did it she was standing half inside the door to the balcony. I said, 'Can I come and take your hand off-stage when you're not expecting it?' She agreed to this. I left it a few days and at one performance took her hand as I had said, just at the moment she screamed. She was completely relaxed. It was fantastic! To be able to scream with all that emotion and be completely relaxed at the same time. That was part of her greatness, that and her charisma." Allen's wife, actress Ruth Dunning, recalled that back-stage wherever one looked there were clean white handkerchiefs, all neatly pressed. Flora spent so much time crying on stage that her handkerchief would soon be wringing wet and she would need a new one. Darlington wrote, "I do not think this fine actress has done anything more moving than her scene of agonised remorse when one of the men falls into the trap into which she has failed to lure Miss Couper." After two months the play transferred to the Duchess, where it continued for a further four months.

*Frieda* was a controversial film. A wounded English officer brought his German-born wife home to England during the last few months of the war. Although she was anti-Nazi and had saved her husband's life at risk of her own, it took time for his family and the community to accept her. David Farrar was cast as Bob, Flora was Nell his M.P. aunt, and Mai Zetterling was Frieda, the German wife. Nell was forced to denounce Frieda at a public meeting, voicing a lot of the resentment prevalent in England at the time. In the last scene, when Frieda has been prevented from suicide, Nell acknowledges her former bigotry and speaks the message of the film – "You can't treat human beings as though they are less than human without becoming less than human yourself." Joe Pihodna, the American critic, wrote, "As usual Flora Robson walks off with the acting honours. She is the bitter aunt of the piece who hates the Germans and makes no bones about it. She has been chosen to represent the attitudes of the nation. Michael Balcon chose wisely."

*Holiday Camp* was quite a different proposition. The *Grand Hotel* formula was brought down to earth at a 'Good morning campers' type resort, the likes of which flourished in Britain after the war. A psychopathic killer, a spinster who has nursed her dying mother, a cheerful cockney family, two runaway lovers and a couple of con-men descend with several hundred bathing beauties and pleasure-bent factory workers on a holiday camp. Their several stories are played out against a background of fun for all the family. The film's most notable accomplishment was that it introduced to the public the Huggett family, who would delight British audiences for more than a decade on radio and on the cinema screen. Jack Warner and Kathleen Harrison were Mr and Mrs Huggett, Dennis Price was the murderer, and Flora topped the bill in the role of Esther Harman, the spinster. It was a thankless part. "The impression of noise, press, blatancy, hurry, organized jollity, heartiness and unclothed, roasting flesh is strong enough to purge the soul of the ungregarious with pity and terror," commented C. A. Lejeune in the *Sketch*. "There is an incident when Miss Flora Robson, playing a lonely and genteel spinster, registers a strong shudder at the sound of the blast from the loudspeaker. For a moment I hoped she was going straight back to her chalet to pack her bags, and give the superintendent a few cogent words on the importunity of radio. But alas! it seems that all that is up with Miss Robson is that she recognized the announcer's voice as that of a sweetheart of long ago. She goes back to her chalet, yes, but only to yearn over a faded photograph. Hope dies." Flora's best scene comes when she visits the control tower and meets her former suitor, played by Esmond Knight, now a blinded amnesiac who has found a new life for himself. It is the end of Esther's dreams of a husband, a familiar theme for Flora, and she plays it with deep feeling.

Jimmy Hanley, who was in the cast, volunteered Jeremy, his one-year-old son, to play Hazel Court's baby in the film. Dinah Sheridan, the baby's real mother, acted as chaperone. During the filming she discovered she was again pregnant. Jack Warner, Hazel Court and Flora asked if they could become godparents to the newcomer. It was a little girl who grew into the actress and presenter of children's television programmes, Jenny Hanley. "Jenny was much blessed as Flora has been the most excellent and caring of Godparents," Miss Sheridan wrote to me. "Never a birthday or Christmas has passed without loving recognition from Flora, culminating in Jenny's great delight in Flora's supreme effort to get to her wedding. She is a lady of exceptional qualities, mostly selflessness."

During the run of the play Flora was also asked to play the Governess in a radio adaptation of Henry James' novella *The Turn of the Screw*. It was not an easy piece. Hugh Robson recalled that in attempting to understand the psychology of the children Flora misread his own adolescent behaviour. By this time both of his parents had died and were buried at Chalfont. Flora was now *in loco parentis* for him. She had sent him to art school in London where he behaved as all art students do. His own particular rebellion was to grow his hair long in emulation of his hero Aubrey Beardsley. Flora made the mistake any parent might and harsh words were spoken. Hugh left Mount Fort to live with his brother. The rift was not long in healing. Hugh is now a successful artist and Flora the proud great-aunt of his four daughters.

Early in 1947 Sydney Box arranged for Flora to be offered a ten-year contract with the Rank Organisation. Flora was reluctant at first to accept the contract, remembering the years she had wasted with Korda before he had given her *Fire Over England*. Box assured her that she would be given a starring role during her first year and that she would be free to take what theatre work she wanted. Flora's agent Haddon Mason negotiated a contract which assured Flora a substantial sum of money to be paid regularly throughout the period of the contract. It was a modest settlement by film-star standards but high in theatre terms and it would see Flora through her difficult 'years between'.

There had been a long tour of *Message for Margaret* after the West End run and Flora was exhausted. Towards the end of the tour she was given her first assignment under the new contract, a part in *Good*

*Time Girl*. It was a small role but Flora had a lot of dialogue in the scenes in which she appeared. The story was of Gwen Rawlings, a teenage girl who finds herself in the juvenile courts before going from bad to worse. Jean Kent played Gwen. Flora was the magistrate in the juvenile court which sends her to an approved school. She learned the whole role during the last week of the tour and discovered that Dennis Price, who was with her in the court scene, was word perfect too. Reminiscent of that memorable occasion with Henry Oscar in *Fire Over England* their scenes together were filmed in a day and a half instead of the scheduled week.

The story was told in flashback as a cautionary tale to another delinquent, played by a lovely young girl with long, fair hair. "I was overawed to work with Flora Robson on *Good Time Girl*," recalled Diana Dors. "At the time I was only fifteen, but I had seen her in films over the years and considered her to be our finest character actress. I only did a day's work on the film, but she put me completely at ease, and chattered away all the time between 'takes', even joking that *she* was one of Mr Rank's young ladies too! The only difference being that I was an unheard of starlet, and she was an international star. She is a British institution and I am honoured to think I worked with her, even only briefly." Jean Kent recalled working on this film too. "Flora played the magistrate who sent me to Borstal, or whatever, and paid me the most wonderful compliment on the set that day. It was the most difficult scene for me as I had to have hysterics and be dragged from the court sobbing and screaming. When I had done the scene and came back on the set, there was Flora with tears in her eyes and she said to me, 'You know, I feel such a beast, I'm quite upset.' I was as proud as anything as you can imagine." To help her get under the skin of the character, Flora had attended magistrates courts and read all she could find on juvenile delinquency. This, to some extent, equipped her to be able to answer the letters she received from worried mothers who had seen her in this role and wanted advice on their wayward daughters.

In July 1947 Flora was, for the first time, reunited with a former class-mate from the Palmers Green High School. This was the poet Stevie Smith. Flora recorded a broadcast of Stevie's poem 'Syler's Green'. Many years later she was enormously impressed by Glenda Jackson's portrayal of Stevie. "*I understood only too well the dried-up wasted lives of the women of my age.*"

Flora was to make her first radio appeal for charity in 1947. Someone had seen her as the nun in *Black Narcissus* and told her of the ordeal of the Skolt Lapps in Northern Lapland who were starving because war had scattered their reindeer herds and they had no money to buy new beasts. The tribe was reduced to little more than two hundred. The Skolt Lapps spoke an ancient form of Tibetan and had probably the oldest unmixed ancestry in Europe. Flora was fascinated to hear of their strange gifts of second sight. Telepathy amongst them enabled one to make an appointment with another miles apart simply by dreaming a place and a time. She asked for money to buy reindeer and fishing tackle to give them a new start. The appeal raised an unprecedented five thousand pounds which as well as enabling the Skolt Lapps to purchase what they needed, allowed them to build new homes against the cold Arctic winters. Flora was overwhelmed at the response. It helped her to realize not only the extent of her popularity but the power it could wield in helping others. She dedicated herself to helping whoever she could in the years that followed. As a result of the appeal on behalf of the Skolt Lapps, Flora was awarded the Finnish Order of the White Lion and the White Rose for Services to Humanity, one of Finland's highest honours. When he presented her with the order the Finnish minister told her, "In Finland you are regarded as second only to God."

## 4

"No one willingly makes an enemy of me. When I came to this court I had nothing. No friends – no money. Just my wits. Some women have only to show their faces to make their way in the world. I wasn't created such a woman. I know that. But I've succeeded in spite of them, even at the games others play."

The role of Countess von Platen in *Saraband for Dead Lovers* could have been written for Flora. As it was, there was some opposition to her casting. It was felt that the role should be played by an actress who had been a noted beauty. Marlene Dietrich was offered the part but is reputed to have misunderstood the offer. "Don't you think I am a little too old to play Sophie Dorothea?" it appears she inquired, believing she had been asked to play the child-bride heroine. Flora was tested and everyone agreed that the part of the Countess was hers.

Countess von Platen had really existed. She had lived to a great age and had been instrumental in the imprisonment for life of Sophie Dorothea, the wife of the future George I of England, and in the murder of her own former lover, Count Koenigsmark, who had been in love with Sophie Dorothea. She had kept the secret of this until, on her death-bed, she confessed that her passionate love and jealousy had been responsible for Koenigsmark's betrayal and death. Opposite Flora, as Koenigsmark, was Stewart Granger. Joan Greenwood played Sophie Dorothea and Françoise Rosay was the Electress of Hanover. The period was one which suited Flora. She had seldom looked lovelier on the stage than she had as Viceroy Sarah on Broadway, in elaborate brocade gowns, her hair in clusters of curls high over her forehead and falling in ringlets over her shoulder. She was similarly attired in this film and looked as though she could have held her own with any of the great beauties of the age with striking looks and dazzling intellect. It was the kind of role which should have led on to better parts for Flora in films. It revealed a malevolence in a classical tradition and there was no other actress her equal in taking hold of such a role and playing it to the full. As it was, it would be four years before she would again play in a film, by which time this performance was history.

"*In one scene I was called upon to ride a horse. Of course I had to ride side-saddle. Neither the horse nor I were trained for it but I managed to look perfectly at ease as I trotted the horse into shot at the beginning of the hunting scene. I discovered to my horror that the director was sufficiently impressed to want me to ride in the hunt myself, not the 'double' as I had expected. When 'Action' was called we had to gallop down a hill but my horse, unused to the weight on its side, swerved round and made for a clump of trees. I managed to duck under the lower branches without leaving my hat or my head behind, lifted myself off the saddle like a jockey and, to my amazement, was able to guide the horse to the right place and end up on camera, retaining my reputation as 'One take Flora'. I was furious when I saw the film to find that the scene had been cut!*"

Resting at home after a minor operation, Flora received a telephone call from Michael Redgrave. Ever since Cambridge he had looked forward to a time when he and Flora might work together. Working with her briefly in *The Years Between* had renewed his ambition. He had been playing Macbeth in the West End and was to repeat his performance in America. Michael wanted Flora to go with him, first to Canada and then to Broadway, as his Lady Macbeth. Geoffrey Toone would be with them as Banquo, Hector MacGregor as Ross and Gillian Webb as the First Witch. Flora agreed immediately and within a week she was flying the Atlantic for the first time. To her amusement the pilot sent back a note which read, "We are travelling at no petty pace towards tomorrow."

In New York they met the American actors who would make up the rest of the cast. Beatrice Straight, who would eventually win an Academy Award for her performance in the film *Network*, was cast as Lady Macduff. Way down the cast as a murderer was listed the name Martin Balsam, and as the second witch, at the beginning of her eminent career on Broadway, was Julie Harris. The company left for Canada and a successful tour before returning to New York. As always, on the other side of the Atlantic, the hospitality was wonderful. Flora made up for the rationing at home. One evening she was tempted to order steak. "*It had just a breath of garlic on it. I was a little worried as Macbeth and Lady Macbeth speak into each other's mouths and I recalled how Jack Hawkins and Stewart Granger had bullied me over my tea of spring onions. I sent a little note to Michael Redgrave saying, 'Miss Robson's compliments but she had a steak with a little breath of garlic on it.' Michael wrote a little note back, 'Mr Redgrave's compliments. He had the same.'*"

Flora was not very happy with her costume. The designer had built excellent sets but seemed to have used the same criteria for the clothes. David Kidd was in New York and was able to obtain permission to redesign and make Flora's costume. As a result she looked very beautiful as Lady Macbeth. David had spent quite a lot of time with Flora at Mount Fort and had one day asked her to marry him. Once again she allowed her career to take precedence but she and David remained firm friends. At his apartment near Central Park in New York he recalled for me his "extraordinary love for Flora".

"*In the Old Vic production of Macbeth Tony had all the nobles clustered round the table in the banqueting scene. I was placed centre back of them and they were sitting with their backs to me. It was impossible for me to take command of the scene when I said, 'Sit worthy friends.' In the New York production the table was long enough for me to be at an impressive enough distance from the lords to give the scene some impact. When they are all gone that is the moment Lady Macbeth collapses and in New York this made sense. He goes on talking, where was Macduff and so on. All she says is 'Did you send to him, sir?' He's plotting more and more and she's horrified. At the end of that scene Michael Redgrave went up to his throne, sat on it and beckoned me to follow. Instead of joining him I went down the stairs and off. They never meet again. The sleep-walking scene stopped the show. The audience wouldn't stop applauding. The entrance for that scene was very impressive but terribly difficult for me to do. I came down a long staircase and I was lit from below so that the lights blinded me. I couldn't look down to see if I was placing my feet properly because it would have destroyed the illusion of sleep.*"

Sir Michael Redgrave, recalling the production, wrote to me, "To my way of thinking the most important quality that a player should have is a compelling *voice* – an organ which has besides the usual qualities of strength and flexibility – an individual colouring that rivets the ear. I remember the first night of *Macbeth* in New York. The opening scenes did not catch fire and actors always know when this has been the case. As I waited for my third entrance Flora started to read the letter. Instantly I knew she had the audience by the throat, as it were. I said to myself. 'That is a STAR!' After this long time I am sure Flora will forgive me if I say she was badly cast as

Lady Macbeth. There is a note of tiredness and sweetness in her voice which strangely enough makes it possible for her to permit the audience to listen to her even when she is wrongly cast." Geoffrey Toone suggested. "I don't think Lady Macbeth is Flora's part. She is wonderful when she is suffering and 'feeling'. Although the voice is rich and wonderful and strong, it's a warm voice. On paper you would say, 'Oh yes, Flora Robson, powerful actress, Lady Macbeth.' Neither she nor Michael were really right. They were both fighting against their particular temperaments."

One critic claimed she was "baleful without being moving". Howard Barnes, in the *New York Herald Tribune*, was more enthusiastic. "Miss Robson rarely fails the Bard," he wrote. "Her characterization of Lady Macbeth combines to a remarkable degree the impulses of overweening ambition, maniacal courage and fright which prompted her to drive her weak-willed Thane to murder his King, only to find that he did not have the iron core of the true tyrant. In passages which should have been truly dominated by Redgrave, she gives Macbeth some of the subtle, psychological probing which Shakespeare wrote into the play. From her cleaning of the bloody daggers, to her realization of her doom when Banquo's ghost appears before her husband, she is assured, eloquent and tragically regal." Beatrice Straight wrote to me, "Flora brings her enormous warmth and strength to whatever she touches, classic or modern, so that every part comes alive as a human being. One always cares for her. She can play every kind of character, good or bad, but never makes them black or white. There is always that human touch. No one is completely evil."

Flora would treasure a letter she received from Shakespearian scholar and historian Garrett Mattingley, who claimed he had seen every production of *Macbeth* in the thirty years he had been old enough to get past the door unaccompanied. "I have never seen," he wrote, "and indeed never hoped to see – a performance as perfect and as illuminating as yours, intelligently analysed, deeply felt, completely integrated, and therefore profoundly moving. To watch it developing was a major artistic experience – and like any such experience, a revelation."

The production as a whole was not favourably reviewed, failing in comparison with the Maurice Evans and Judith Anderson revival of 1942 and closed before its short season had been due to end. Flora had to be back in England by May to begin work as Queen Isabella in the film *Christopher Columbus* opposite Fredric March in the title role. March insisted that his wife, Florence Eldridge, would be perfect for the Queen. Sydney Box had a word with Flora and she agreed to play the secondary role of the Governess to the Infanta.

By the time production was under way Flora was involved in her next project and was released from the commitment. Although the film was without distinction, Flora would undoubtedly have benefited from a role of stature to follow her success as Countess von Platen.

During the time she had spent in America, Flora had made firm friends with Hector MacGregor, who told her of the little Theatre Royal at Windsor where he frequently worked. After returning from war service he had been given a job there at a time when his future had seemed uncertain. He suggested to Flora that if there were any play she particularly wanted to do she should write to John Counsell, the theatre's manager. First of all, Flora sent him a play which Counsell refused. He considered that the play was not good enough for her. He added, however, that were they to agree on a play he would be delighted to have her come to Windsor. Hector remembered someone in America suggesting that Flora should one day play Lady Cicely Wayneflete in Shaw's *Captain Brassbound's Conversion*. Her response had been that no one in England would offer her a comedy after playing Lady Macbeth. MacGregor told John Counsell of this suggestion and shortly afterwards he offered Flora the opportunity of playing the role Shaw had created for Ellen Terry. "Flora, as Lady Cicely, showed a side of herself that no one had ever seen before," John Counsell told me. "She was superb. She played it with great warmth and her own particular line of comedy, politely holding her own against impossible people with enormous sweetness and without any affectation. Exactly as she is. The part was really made for her." "Our next Ellen Terry . . ." "*The key for my interpretation was Lady Cicely's line in reply to Brassbound's proposal of marriage. 'But you don't love me,' she said, and he replied, 'What does that matter? Ever since I have known you, you've either made me laugh or feel friendly'. I based my interpretation on friendliness.*" Her years of experience as a social worker in the factory had given her the feeling for cheerful diplomacy which she employed in this role.

The production played at Windsor for two delightful weeks. The critics who made the journey from London all anticipated a transfer. Everything seemed set for Flora to appear in her first West End comedy since *Touch Wood*. Resistance came from an unexpected source. It seems that Shaw had promised Maurice Evans that his American production of *Man and Superman* would be the next Shaw play to go into the West End and that he could not afford to pay tax on more than one. He claimed to be paying £147 to the Exchequer for every £1 he got from the theatre. "Flora can get away with anything," he wrote to Kenneth Barnes, "and will until she is seventy. She can afford to wait." Afford to wait! How easy it was for him to say that and how difficult in reality it might be for an actor to return to a role at some unspecified time in the future when it would be more convenient for Shaw. He wrote to Flora to explain his position. "There is no question of your ability to get away with the part," he wrote. "You can get away with anything. Nobody else has had that gift since Gaumont, a charwoman whose voice was the croak of a gin sodden drunkard, fifty years ago. You are an angel in comparison."

The H. M. Tennent organization decided to put the play on with largely the same cast at the Lyric, Hammersmith, which was not included in Shaw's ban. Hector MacGregor, who had played Brassbound at Windsor, had another commitment and he was replaced by Richard Leech. Whilst playing at Windsor Flora was asked to make a personal appearance after the show at the local cinema where *Good Time Girl* was being shown. She walked in costume with some of the Brassbound crew to the cinema and was taken into the wings. Peeping into the auditorium she saw only a sprinkling of patrons. The manager of the cinema went out on the stage and asked the audience to welcome as their guest of honour 'That internationally famous film actress Miss Valerie Hobson!' Flora went on to a smattering of applause as pairs of lovers in the back row extricated themselves from passionate clinches.

Before the play opened at the Lyric, Flora joined with many other actors trained at RADA in a charity matinee at the Theatre Royal, Drury Lane, in aid of the rebuilding programme for the Malet Street Theatre which had been badly hit by enemy bombs. Queen Elizabeth was in the audience. Flora, who had been a member of the RADA Council since her return from America, played her old role of Mary Paterson in Act 2 Scene 1 of *The Anatomist* with Trevor Howard as Walter Anderson, Joan White recreating Janet, and Robert Beatty and Hugh Pryce as Burke and Hare. *The Times* wrote of "Miss Flora Robson drawing again tenderness from the depths of degradation no less movingly than when *The Anatomist* and her own reputation were new."

*Captain Brassbound's Conversion* opened to huge praise. "No actress of any quality can possibly fail with her ladyship," proclaimed the *Observer*, "Flora Robson does far more than not fail. Parted from the stark and doomstruck daughters of woe whom she usually has to enact, she saunters, piping songs of innocence, to a new and happy triumph in the fairy tale Morocco of Shaw's invention. To the light and frothy comedy Miss Robson brings a conquering simplicity and humanity. The acting side of the play is all here, a Floral dance without a false step." At the final curtain on the first night Flora was asked to make a speech. "This is Flora's holiday," she began. In character she politely asked the critics to persuade Shaw to let her take the company into the West End with the play. Eventually she visited Shaw to attempt to persuade him herself. He would not relent. During their conversation Flora spoke of her Lady Macbeth in New York. He later wrote, "I doubt if you are wise to confuse your new reputation as an ingénue by playing Lady Macbeth. It is all very well to have two lines, but you should take care not to let them get tangled. If you tour in the part you had better play it and Lady Cicely on alternate nights." This letter was followed by one of his famous postcards which advised her, "I have been thinking over it and am convinced that you should never play another murderess, much less a savage chieftainess, and that if you do a classic alongside Brassbound it should be *The Way of the World*. Millamant would intensify your triumph as a charmer. Lady M would almost cancel it." Flora went on tour with only Lady Cicely. Shaw had told her he would recommend her for the leading role in his next play but nothing came of it.

Some years later Flora was on holiday in Morocco with Uncle John. "*We were visiting Marrakesh, and had a look at the animal market on our first day. The market place was full of Moroccans, and handsome Berbers who arrived from the mountains on camels or donkeys; men with the deep look of distance in their eyes. They looked through me, polite but cold, and I felt ashamed that I wasn't veiled. A group of ragged musicians were playing strange music nearby. The leader of the group walked towards me with his hand outstretched for 'baksheesh'. It was a tense moment. Then I remembered what Lady Cicely would have done and took the outstretched hand, shook it and said 'How d'you do?' The laugh I got from the crowd in the market place was greater than any I ever had in the theatre. The musician laughed until the tears poured down his face and insisted on shaking hands with the whole party. The entire bazaar was helpless with laughter. Lady Cicely really was my part.*"

## 5

Henry Sherek asked Flora to star in *Charles and Mary Lamb*, which was due to open in July 1949. Flora agreed. Shortly afterwards, E. P. Clift approached her to play the leading role in a new play by Lesley Storm for a May opening. Flora read the play and saw in the character similar opportunites to those she had found in *Autumn*. Sherek agreed to allow her to open in the Storm play so long as she was available for his production when the time came.

Flora took a suite at the Savoy Hotel. She asked for a room without a view and shut herself in for two weeks to study the role. She had longed for a part as good as Lady Brooke had been. Her failure to bring the comedy into the West End would be less disappointing were she able to make a success of this. The play was *Black Chiffon*, in which she would play Alicia Christie. Mrs Christie is accused of shop-lifting. She has stolen a black chiffon night-gown similar to the one her future daughter-in-law wears, only a few days before the wedding. The play is concerned with the shock of embarrassment which affects the whole of her respectable family and with her decision whether to plead temporary insanity or to face prison. She chooses the latter and pleads guilty so as not to prejudice her son's marriage by exposing the private feelings of the family in a public court. Flora felt the play had a bad ending because it left inconclusive the relationship between Robert Christie and his son. Their feud was one of the strongest contributory factors to the situation. Flora spoke to Miss Storm and a new ending was written which greatly improved the play. Wyndham Goldie, whom Flora has called her favourite stage husband, was Robert Christie. Anthony Ireland played the psychiatrist who helps Mrs Christie to realize why she stole the night-gown and Janet Barrow played the Nanny. The younger generation was represented by Rachel Gurney, who played Flora's pregnant daughter (Miss Gurney was herself pregnant for part of the run), Dorothy Gordon was the future daughter-in-law and Owen Holder was the son. Flora had seen Holder in *The Winslow Boy* in New York and visited him in his dressing-room. "She complimented me on my performance," he remembered, "and said in parting that she would like to have me in a play with her. I treated it as a kind thought and forgot it. Yet within a few months of my returning to London E. P. Clift was on the telephone asking me to be in *Black Chiffon*, on Flora's orders! I was given the play to read. The management wanted my answer the same afternoon so I leafed through it in a taxi on my way home. I was appalled. It struck me as an inferior piece and quite unworthy of so great an actress. However, since Flora was prepared to do it, who was I to refuse? And how glad I am that I did not, for by watching her in rehearsal I saw with my own eyes how an immaculate talent could transform not only her own ill-written character, but the entire ill-written play into something resembling a work of art. She is one of the few who have realized the alchemist's dream of turning base metal into gold."

"It is the best thing Flora Robson has done," declared Beverley Baxter in the *Evening Standard*, "and she gives a performance which just must be seen." Darlington wrote that "her ability to play women at or near the end of their emotional tether is proverbial but can never be taken merely for granted. She makes Alicia a living woman." *The Times* found her wonderfully well-suited to the part: "In her embarrassed confession to the family, in her reconstruction for the psychiatrist of the mood in which she committed the theft and in her solution of the final dilemma Miss Robson never once loses her hold on the house." It was the play she had been looking for and when the time came for her to leave the cast to join the other play she pleaded with Henry Sherek to release her and allow her to stay. He agreed.

Flora had begun to miss her father more and more. Immediately after his death she had been busy and had tried not to brood on her loss, but as time went on he came more and more into her mind. *"There was one scene where I had to go on stage crying. Sometimes I would think of Father and the tears would come. I was standing at the side of the stage one night and they wouldn't come. I thought to myself, 'He's not here. Nobody cares for me any more.' But still I couldn't cry. I was completely dried up. Then I looked at the back of the stage and the curtains suddenly billowed out in a breeze. It was like a signal. I thought, 'He is here!' and the tears sprang into my eyes. Every night, after that, I looked at these curtains and they blew out. I knew perfectly well that it was caused by a draught when someone opened or closed a door in the wings but I couldn't get over the feeling that he was in the theatre and was watching me act as he had done of old.'*

The play ran for a year and closed to allow the cast to take a holiday before a national tour and a subsequent transfer to Broadway. Flora took Uncle John to Italy. She took him abroad as often as she could. It was wonderful to have him with her, especially when they visited old churches and cathedrals as he knew so much about their architecture. "Flora Robson adored her Uncle John," actress Ruth Kettlewell wrote to me. "He had a small and beautiful parish in Northumberland. She was most generous to him and the little country church at Bolam. For a time he was my Father Confessor, and in his 'advice' before giving me Absolution, he would say, 'Flora says you mustn't stay too long in Rep.' Flora would take him abroad for holidays, and she was good to her two aunts, the Misses Mackenzie who looked after him." Flora was good to all her family. Her niece Doreen Wade feels this is one of her most wonderful qualities. There was no member of Flora's family who did not receive some kindness from her. Flora had not forgotten how her family had stood by her in her years of struggle. During the holiday in Italy she collapsed with exhaustion in Alassio and Uncle John nursed her through a rest cure. They watched the pilgrims on the way to Rome and he compared them with Chaucer's pilgrims on the way to Canterbury. All the medieval pilgrims found their equivalents in the modern procession.

The tour of *Black Chiffon* visited twelve cities. At one performance in Sheffield the performance was interrupted by derisive laughter from a crowd of drunks in a box. Different actors have different ways of reacting to this. Those who do not know how to cope might blunder on. Others might turn to the audience and directly criticize the offender. A comic actor might find a line to turn against him. Flora simply paused, remaining quite still and waited for the noise to stop. The audience turned on the drunks and demanded that they be thrown out. This accomplished, Flora went on with the play.

When *Black Chiffon* crossed the Atlantic there were several changes in the cast. Raymond Huntley replaced Wyndham Goldie. Richard Gale was the son, Patricia Hicks his future wife and Patricia Marmont was Flora's daughter. The company rehearsed on the Atlantic crossing, which was a rough one. Only once was the weather calm enough for a proper run-through of the play and this was broken up when someone spotted a whale. They arrived a day late. "*There was a hurricane coming up and the Gulf Stream was lifeless, which slowed us down. We rushed to Boston and had to go on that night without a rehearsal on the stage. It was boiling hot. There was no ventilation in the dressing-rooms — air-conditioning at the front of the theatre, but nothing, as is so often the case, for the actors. I was burning in the heat. It came to the last scene where I had to go in tears. I was trying to get my mood. I looked at the curtain. It hung absolutely flat. I thought, 'Father doesn't know I've got here.' I had always got my mood from looking at those curtains. 'He doesn't know I'm here.' Just before I went on the stage, the tail of the hurricane hit Boston and the curtains shot out wildly. I thought, 'He had to bring a hurricane, but he's come, he's come, he's come!' Tears poured down my face.*" Gilbert Miller, all those years before, had been wrong. Rather than find her tears false, American audiences were deeply moved by her performance. "Superlative acting once more animates a straggling British import," reported the *New York Herald Tribune* after the Broadway opening, "Like Dame Edith Evans in *Daphne Laureola*, Flora Robson floods several scenes with a magical authority quite lacking in the writing."

The production was beset by bad luck. The 48th Street Theatre let in the rain and before long Anthony Ireland and Raymond Huntley both went down with pneumonia. Shortly afterwards there began a very worrying time for Flora. Her doctor diagnosed what he thought to be a cancer and she was advised to go into hospital for exploratory surgery. It would have been impossible for the play to run without its star and the management agreed to suspend it for two weeks as the demand would warrant a re-opening after a short break. In order to avoid the story being leaked to the Press, Flora kept the true nature of her visit to the hospital a secret from everyone except her closest friends. Certain members of the company thought she was trying to get out of her contract and treated her rather shabbily. She was deeply hurt by this. Only Janet Barrow from the company came to visit her in hospital. Fortunately David Kidd was able to look after her. The tumour proved to be benign. David took her to spend the rest of her two weeks out at the home of interior designer Robb-Johns Gribbing in Southampton, New York. They took long walks together. He cooked and they played parlour games. Flora was rested and relieved of her worry when she returned to the play, but she never again felt the same happiness in the part. Bookings were affected by the interruption and although one act of the play was televised in order to attract audiences, the cast were soon given notice of closure. The management intended taking the show on the road but Flora was advised by her doctors to withdraw. She had a run-of-the-play contract but was not held to it as the advance proved unsatisfactory. During the last performance the actors could hear workmen taking the signs down from the outside of the theatre. The firelight on the stage had not been lit. An essential spotlight had been removed. Not one member of the management came to wish them goodbye. That performance was Flora's last Broadway appearance.

She was ordered to rest when she returned home. The Broadway run had been a dispiriting ordeal. Whatever she did next should be something in which she felt safe and happy. "She came to see a play at Windsor," John Counsell recalled. "She was very unhappy about what had happened in America. She said to me, 'Wouldn't it be lovely to play in this theatre again?' I asked her when she wanted to come. 'Will you have me?' she said. 'Flora,' I cried, 'Name the date and I'll scrub anything else!' " They were able to arrange a revival of *Autumn*. Wyndham Goldie directed, as well as repeating his role as Sir Brian. Hector MacGregor was the lover with Janet Barrow also in the cast. There was a short five-week tour.

While in New York, Flora had lunched with John Gielgud, who had told her of his plans to mount a production of *The Winter's Tale*, as part of the 1951 Festival of Britain celebrations. Flora was offered Paulina, her first role in Shakespeare in London since she had left the Old Vic. Gielgud was cast as Leontes, Diana Wynyard as Hermione, Brewster Mason as Polixenes, Lewis Casson as Antigonus, George Rose as Autolycus and Virginia McKenna as Perdita. The production was directed by Peter Brook. *"At the first readings I saw Paulina almost entirely as a comedy part. Then when we began to play together I saw it differently. I began to see her as garrulous, but good; tactless but sincere; and finally as the vital character who really does believe in the wisdom of the Oracle. With all her blundering and forcing herself onto people at inappropriate moments, she is deeply concerned for the welfare of Leontes, although even more concerned that the Oracle should be revered. She is thus able to nurse and sustain Hermione through those sixteen long years in complete faith and strength. To me the key to Paulina's character lies in Leontes' words, 'O grave and good Paulina, the great comfort that I have had of thee' and in her reply, 'What, sovereign* sir, I did not well, I meant well.' My greatest problem in the play came at the very end. Suddenly Paulina is married off to someone with whom she has had no scenes. I felt that I should find some point earlier in the play which would justify the later change in events. Peter Brook saw I was worried and I explained my point of view. He completely understood. Paulina was only married off, he told me, so she would have a partner for the obligatory dance. He asked if it would help if he cut the line about the marriage altogether. What a difference that made! At the end of the play he left me alone on stage in a deep curtsey to the court, stressing Paulina's loyalty to Leontes and Hermione."

The *Sketch* said of her performance, "Here is a character created in the round, endowed with a richness and precision of observation, and with a wit and humanity that are irresistible. This was truly a great performance." Virginia McKenna recalled, "*The Winter's Tale* was only my second play in London. I was twenty and quite overawed by all the illustrious actors gathered together for this production. I think my strongest recollection of Flora was her reality, both on and off stage. She had great strength, great compassion, sincerity and emotion – yet all these were used with restraint and understanding, allowing the audience to identify strongly with her and totally believe in her." Hamish Bell claims that Flora's performance as Paulina was the first modern Shakespearian performance, in that it did away with all the trappings of performance, the voice beautiful, florid delivery and theatrical emphasis formerly associated with playing in Shakespeare. I put this to Peter Brook, who wrote to me, "The startling quality of Flora's work was in its directness. Certainly she appreciated the epic nature of a verse play, but at the same time everything in it made simple human sense to her. In a lesser actress, this could have resulted in the taming-down that happens when Shakespeare is made naturalistic. With Flora, the down-to-earth understanding was coupled with the extraordinary warmth and intensity of her personality. The result was indeed 'modern Shakespeare'."

In the New Year's Honours List of 1952, along with Eric Drake, her old friend from Pembroke College, Flora was awarded the C.B.E. She had known of the honour for several weeks as her acceptance had been sought in advance. She was deeply moved that all her hard work should be recognized in this way and that she was regarded as a leading member of the profession she loved so much. "When I got to the theatre on New Year's Eve I found reporters all round the stage-door. They wanted photographs and I asked what it was for. I was supposed not to know anything about it. Diana Wynyard was rather cool with me and told me she didn't believe in honours. There were telegrams of congratulations from all the London theatre managements with the single exception of Tennents who were presenting The Winter's Tale. *The news of the award filled the theatre for the last week and there was applause for me when I went on. On the last night when I came from my dressing-room for the last part of the play Binkie Beaumont of Tennents was standing by my side. He said, 'I was listening in to the radio on Tuesday morning and I heard your name. I couldn't believe it. I turned it on again at nine o'clock and it was there again. I couldn't believe it.' That was all he said to me."*

During the run of the play Flora had been called to the film studios for the first time in four years. She was cast as Mary Rackham in *Tall Headlines*, which dealt with the way a family was affected by the execution for murder of one of the sons. It was written into Flora's contract for the film that she would not be called for the first 'shot' each day, which meant that she did not have to rise too early. It was a poor film with very little to recommend it.

The Duke of Gloucester presented Flora with her award. King George VI had died and the Duke was deputizing for the new Queen. "Are you doing anything at present, Miss Robson?" the Duke whispered as he slipped the medal onto the pin which had been provided. "I am rehearsing a ghost story, sir," she whispered back. Later she and Uncle John and their friend Maud Bell were photographed by waiting newsmen in the courtyard of the palace.

The ghost story was an adaptation of the Henry James story *The Turn of the Screw* by William Archibald and re-titled *The Innocents*. *"I never really understood* The Turn of the Screw. *In every version I have seen it has been played differently. When I played it on the radio I was told that the governess was in love with the children's guardian and that there weren't any ghosts at all. I couldn't understand that. Why should there be all that eerie music when the ghosts were supposed to appear? I saw the Benjamin Britten opera where the governess was suddenly the heroine and the boy fell into her arms and died. I never understood why he died."* Flora was joined again by Barbara Everest and the children were played by Jeremy Spenser and Carol Wolveridge. *"The children stole the play of course. I did all the work and they came on and no one noticed me. But that was right. I didn't feel jealous. I knew that would happen when I read the script."* "For a child rather simply brought up in the country," remembered Carol Wolveridge, "to be flung into the theatre and sent on tour, I was very fortunate to have Flora's influence. Her very presence and manner were stabilizing and her voice with its great calm created the security I so badly needed. Childish pranks could go so far and no further. One knew where to toe the line. Flora taught me how to play patience and gave me a beautiful green leather box of patience cards which I still treasure and use. She taught me how to do needlepoint, presenting me with a canvas and silks. I can remember sitting on the floor by her feet for hours over the needlepoint feeling safe and secure." Dilys Hamlett, who had recently graduated from the Old Vic School, was cast in the uncredited role of the lady Ghost, Miss Jessel. She also understudied Barbara Everest as the housekeeper and, with a grey wig and padding, went on for her after a fortnight. "My haunting appearances were not arduous," Miss Hamlett recalled, "and as I was new and keen I had learned the housekeeper's lines. Flora came in to take me through my lines the afternoon prior to my appearance. She was so supportive and very kind. I played for a week. Once I forgot to give her essential letters and very gently and simply she asked me, 'Has the post arrived?' When the play closed, Flora recommended me to BBC radio and I was given work immediately because of her interest. Her kindness gave me real encouragement and I am very sorry we have not worked together since."

"Very few actresses can curdle the blood faster than can Miss Robson and her confrontation with 'Miss Jessel', her shrieks of 'There, there, there!' pointing to the shadow in the corner left us cold and agape with fright," wrote Philip Hope-Wallace in the *Manchester Guardian*. Darlington claimed that the Henry James story made a very good thriller and gave Flora "a splendid chance to send cold water coursing down our backs. Indeed, by her own personal integrity she does succeed in lifting Mr Archibald's slick stage contrivances to that higher plane on which James wrote, and shows not only a leading actress in a good strong part, but a courageous woman fighting the powers of evil for a boy's soul." The play had a good run and was taken off only at a time when many plays were failing owing to London smog.

"About this time I received a letter from a London schoolteacher enclosing an essay on Bonnie Prince Charlie written by a twelve-year-old boy. 'When the Prince found he couldn't get away with being King,' the essay ran, 'he decided to leave Britain. He was helped to escape by Flora Robson.' I was charmed by this! Actually, I had been named after Flora MacDonald."

She was offered the part of Melita in the film of *The Malta Story* whilst she was still in the play. She was able only to film the interiors as the exteriors would be shot on location in Malta. An actress of the same build was found in Malta to double for her and Flora filmed her scenes at Pinewood. Hers was the role of a mother who believed her son was a true patriot only to discover he was an Axis spy. "It wasn't her finest role," wrote Sidney Sterck in the *Newcastle Journal*, "but those who heard the bombs whistle and saw the yellow buildings disintegrate as I did and came to know the strength of Maltese character, would say that much of it was embodied in Melita." In the

th Ronald Lewis in *Ghosts*
(Angus McBean Photograph: Harvard Theatre Collection)

With Michael Redgrave in *The Aspern Papers*
(David Sim)

Dragon Empress and her director, holas Ray – *55 Days at Peking*
(P.C. Films Corporation)

As Miss Binns in John Ford's *Seven Women*
(M.G.M.)

Isabelle's Mother in *Ring Round the Moon*
(Angus McBean Photograph:
Harvard Theatre Collection)

*Young Cassidy* and his mother. With
Rod Taylor.                    (M.G.M.)

Her farewell to the West End. With Joan Miller and
Joyce Carey in *The Old Ladies*          (Ken Rimell)

Flora and Robert Eddison like 'pale-eyed, impassioned old sheep' as Miss Prism and Canon Chasuble in *The Importance of Being Earnest*, her last success in the theatre. With Pauline Collins.
(Angus McBean Photograph: Harvard Theatre Collection)

The last great role of her career as Miss Fothergill in the BBC-tv presentation of *The Shrimp and the Anemone*. With Grant Bardsley.
(Don Smith: Courtesy of *Radio Times*)

Flora, as she is today
(Geoff Shields)

Honoured at Oxford
(Press Association)

spring of 1953 she was invited to play the Nurse in a new film version of *Romeo and Juliet* to be shot in Italy. Laurence Harvey was Romeo and an unknown newcomer with no acting experience, Susan Shentall, was cast as Juliet. The film was shot in Italy by Renato Castellani. "I am old enough to play the Nurse and just about ready to play Juliet," Flora told a reporter. As it was, she had to help Miss Shentall as much as she could with her role. In the scene where Juliet learns that Romeo has killed Tybalt, Juliet was supposed to cry. Miss Shentall could not find tears to order. Flora took her to one side and told her a sad story. Before she had finished tears were streaming down both their faces. Flora signalled to the director and the scene was shot. Castellani suggested that the Nurse should be younger than she was normally played. After all she had borne her own child at the same time that Juliet was born. He also suggested that she had been Capulet's mistress. Despite this, he reduced the bawdiness in the part and as he also cut most of the poetry, there was little left for Flora to play. He kept urging her to speak her lines at high speed. When she protested, saying that Shakespeare should not be spoken that way, Castellani's reply was, "Shakespeare is dead."

Early in 1953 Flora played Sister Agatha in *Journey to Earth*, by Bridget Boland, on the radio, with Betty Hardy also in the cast. Later that year the play, which was re-titled *The Return*, was presented at the Duchess Theatre. Flora played a nun who returned to the world after thirty-six years in a convent. Philip Hope-Wallace, in the *Manchester Guardian*, claimed that Flora succeeded "in doing something rather rare on the English stage, in presenting an ageing woman as a figure of dignity and compassion. It is an infinitely tender and sensitive performance."

Flora's mother had been ill in hospital. *"I heard that she had been allowed home and I was relieved that she was not as ill as I had thought. I knew Lila would take good care of her. One night I dreamt I saw my father. I hadn't seen him in a dream since his death. It was a cold, clear night with bright stars in the sky and he was warming his hands at a fire. He wasn't looking at me but smiling at someone beyond me. It was only a few weeks away from Christmas, and I thought to myself, in the way of dreams, 'He's with the shepherds. He's waiting for Jesus.' When I woke up I remembered it all vividly and immediately something was clear to me. He wasn't waiting for Jesus, he was waiting for Mother. I put a few things together and went down to Hove and discovered that she was dying."*

On the day Mrs Robson died Flora had a performance to do. She asked the stage manager to inform the rest of the cast of the news but warn them not to mention anything of it to her. She went on and all the company watched with admiration as she played her deeply emotional role with the same gentle restraint as always. No one in the audience knew the desperate sadness inside her which longed for release.

## 6

I once introduced an acquaintance of mine to Flora. To my profound embarrassment he launched into conversation by saying, "Dame Flora, there's something I've always wanted to ask you. Why did you appear in such rubbish in the fifties?" Flora calmly, and politely, replied that it was important for her to keep her feet on the boards, that she was able to do only what she was offered and she was offered no work of quality. In a letter to me, John Fernald wrote of Flora as "the perfect instinctive actress. I don't think the reliability of her instinct always extended to the plays she chose," he continued. "Like a great many other leading performers she tended, as time went on, to accept only those roles which she felt suited her personality; she became less and less concerned with the quality of the play itself. In this, I believe, she showed a vulnerability, a frailty, which was part and parcel of her nature."

In *No Escape* Flora played Rachel Lloyd, a woman who has grown embittered after being deserted by her fiancé on the eve of their wedding for another woman. When, twelve years later, he reappears, and tries to get money from her, she murders him. The wife turns up and attempts to blackmail Rachel. In the end Rachel drives herself over a cliff. David Langton played the former fiancé and Miriam Karlin the wife. Also in the cast were Janet Barrow, Peter Williams, Francis Matthews and Noel Hood. John Fernald directed the play which opened at the Devonshire Park Theatre, Eastbourne, on 5 July 1954, subsequently touring for sixteen weeks through England, Scotland and Ireland. The favourite headline which cropped up in almost all the towns it played was NO ESCAPE FOR FLORA ROBSON. The *Manchester Guardian* reported, "This is really a solo played by Miss Robson – unavailingly as far as this critic is concerned – upon your nerves. Her talents in this sort of part are well known, but here she does not seem well served by her material. The writing has all the passion in the world but somehow fails to make contact; certainly not because it is bardic or obscure, with all those lines like 'The past is never done with'. It mutters and howls like a chained dog: alarming, impressive even, but with no bite."

Throughout the tour it was Flora's intention to take the play into the West End. As the weeks went by she began more and more to doubt the material. The entire build of her role was destroyed by the appearance of the comic wife in the last act. She informed the management that she would prefer not to continue with the play. Several people, the author particularly, were quite understandably incensed as Flora was well received in the play wherever she went. Flora then began to worry about the other members of the cast, several of whom had young families, who would be thrown out of work and told the management that she had changed her mind. By this time the management had decided that the play should not go in. Their original outlay had been covered and it seemed that the rest of the cast agreed with the decision.

"I could not believe my ears when Henry Sherek told me that Flora had agreed to do *A Kind of Folly*" recalled Owen Holder. Holder, who had been the original son in *Black Chiffon*, had written a comedy and Flora was enchanted by the leading role. "We opened in Brighton," he continued, "to the kind of reception an author dreams of but seldom knows. In fact the audience's laughter throughout the first and second acts was such that I feared the play must go down the drain in the third, that the last act couldn't sustain such applause, and that we should end, not with a bang, but a whimper. But we didn't. To my amazement we triumphed, and the Press confirmed our triumph. Our reception for the rest of the tour was the same; and on the last night in Edinburgh, we were left with the sound of stamping feet and shouts of acclaim echoing in our ears."

The reception of the play acted like a tonic on Flora. She had never had any confidence in her ability to play comedy. There is a kind of artifice in comedy which Flora does not have in her character. All the qualities which made her a great emotional actress, her reality and her depth, were intensified by an innate sincerity and honesty. It is useless playing a practical joke on Flora, she will always take it seriously, and even when the joke has been explained she will not understand the reason it was perpetrated. One weekend a celebrated theatrical couple invited her to their country house. She laughed along with them the whole time only to realize by a chance remark shortly before she left that her hosts had been making fun of her all weekend. Flora trusts people at face value, always accepting everything she is told without question, never feeling she need suspect anyone of perverse motives. In the playing of comedy it is the awareness of perversity beyond the apparent face of things which differentiates it from the playing of other kinds of drama.

*A Kind of Folly* was a comedy of manners set in 1910. The plot concerned one William Ashby who has both a wife and a mistress named Sarah. Flora was Sarah, the wife, Jean Kent was Sarah, the mistress, Wilfrid Hyde-White was Ashby, with Jack Gwillim and Owen Holder, himself, in support. "I very much enjoyed doing

*A Kind of Folly,*" Jean Kent wrote to me. "I remember it as a charming play, and one that would bear reviving. I remember best the pretend sword fight with parasols between Flora and myself and how I was always worried that I might catch her in the eye. Fortunately I never did."

In a small ingénue role was a young actress at the beginning of her career. "I had one rather funny little scene. It was a gift of a part really," recalled Sylvia Syms. "Flora was a very generous actress. Whenever I watched her on the stage I noticed that she paid tremendous attention to other people. She listened. We had a very triumphant tour. There were lots of laughs and Flora got her laughs too. When we got to London, we opened at the Duchess Theatre to a sort of silence all the way through. It was terrifying. They didn't laugh at any of her lines. They were waiting for something dramatic to happen and it was a very jolly, silly sort of play. It must have been a terrible experience because we weren't prepared for it. She looked rather frightened by the time the interval came." "When I got to the theatre on that sad second night," continued Owen Holder, "after Fleet Street's dreadful drubbing, I stopped at Flora's dressing-room door to apologize for having written her a bad play. 'No, my dear,' she said. 'I can only apologize to you. I made it bad.' Flora Robson shouldn't have been Damed, she should have been canonized."

Harold Conway wrote, "I'm sorry, but I nearly wept last night – not even her graciousness and flashes of humour could disguise the waste of a fine actress." Yvonne Mitchell claimed a woman said to her, "Oh she was funny enough, but if I go to see a play with Flora Robson in it, I want to see her murder someone." *The Times* added, "Miss Flora Robson, though her accomplishment is unfailing, seems out of place in this masquerade of emotional ideas until the time comes for her quietly to remove the masks and declare a sincere belief in reality."

Although Flora had twice appeared in plays on American television she had appeared only once in Britain in an excerpt, with Leslie Banks, from *Fire Over England*, in November 1936. Her first appearance in a full-length play was as the Nurse in *Romeo and Juliet*. Harold Clayton directed her in a traditional interpretation. This Nurse was an old lady and Flora bandaged her feet so she would remember she was old and hobbled from set to set. She told a reporter that she found it difficult to treat the television camera as an audience and said it was like staring at a man with a monocle. *The Stage* thought hers was "an interpretation that was nothing short of brilliant, had all the kindliness tempered by worldly willingness to compromise that the part demands, and the touches of ageing lechery were pointed to a nicety." David Horne was Capulet, Owen Holder was Paris, Tony Britton was Romeo and Virginia McKenna was Juliet. "She was the rock to which I clung," remembered Miss McKenna, "my anchor in the stormy passions of Shakespeare's love story – and although that is how it should be in the context of the play it does not necessarily follow, as it did on that occasion, that the play should spill over into real life. Acting with Flora Robson assumes an added dimension and it was an experience I shall always remember."

The disappointment of the failure of the comedy led Flora to seek security for her next stage appearance. As before, she returned to her friends at the Theatre Royal, Windsor, in the role which Reginald Denham and Edward Percy had written for her, Mrs Smith in *Suspect*. Flora directed the play herself. Peter Williams, who had been with her in *No Escape* was cast as Dr Rendle. "My strongest memories of both productions are of what a warm and friendly person Flora was to work with at all times. Knowing how often stars make sure that the spotlight remains the whole time on them only, it was so refreshing to work with one who encouraged and delighted in the younger members of the company." After the Windsor opening there was a tour of three weeks before it opened at the Royal Court. Once again the critics deplored Flora's choice of play whilst praising her handling of the material. Bernard Levin deplored "the waste of a national asset like Miss Flora Robson". The *Observer* noted, "Miss Flora Robson brings down the first curtain by twitching at the jaw, the second by swooning and the third by doing something quite undisclosable with an axe . . . but were it not for the last act, when Miss Robson soars above her script in a confessional aria of scorching intensity, I should dismiss this piece with considerable curtness. As it is, a superb actress is magnoperating for all of twenty minutes, and the sight is something not to be missed." The run did not last long. The days when such a play as *Suspect* would even open in the West End were numbered. Not many months later, at the same theatre, there would be seen the beginnings of a revolution in theatre style and tastes with the production of John Osborne's *Look Back in Anger*.

Her success as the Nurse on television led to an offer to play Miss Moffatt in Emlyn Williams's semi-autobiographical play *The Corn is Green* on the small screen. *The Stage* called it a part that might have been written for her. "Flora Robson's schoolmistress was really superb," declared the *Observer*, "one of her very best performances, deep and knobbly, reeking of sublimation." Morgan Evans was played by Hugh Evans and Billie Whitelaw was Bessie Watty. The play was televised from Cardiff and Flora paid a visit to the College of Music and Drama to choose students to appear in the classroom scene. One of those chosen was Anthony Hopkins. During rehearsals she heard that Uncle John was ill. Permission was given for her to travel to Bolam but he died before she arrived. Once again she faced a performance filled with deep personal grief and an audience of, this time many thousands, saw only her professionalism and integrity. First Johnnie had gone away; then her father had died; she had lost faith with Tony Guthrie; now Uncle John was gone too. She had depended on them all for their support in her work and in her private life. She would face the future alone.

## 7

*Black Chiffon* had given Flora her longest run until *The House by the Lake*, in which she chalked up an uninterrupted run of 736 performances. It got off to rather a shaky start. Again it was in itself not a particularly good play. It was lambasted by the critics who were getting rather tired of seeing Flora distinguishing inferior material. "If Miss Flora Robson wishes to appear in this sort of bilge," wrote Bernard Levin, "instead of the great plays which should be the normal complement of so great an actress, it is none of my business." The first murder in this piece was committed by Andrew Cruickshank. The second murder was the only interesting part of the play. Cruickshank hypnotized Flora to kill herself and the climax of the play hung on whether or not this was successfully accomplished. "When it comes to this kind of thing," asserted Philip Hope-Wallace in the *Manchester Guardian*, "Mr Cruickshank has no peer for suave villainy; he insinuates like the original serpent in Eden. As for Miss Robson, she wrings her hands, nay her feet too – not to mention our hearts. Earlier she can bang down the telephone (caught trying to get help) and make the whole house jump." *The Times* commented, "Miss Robson passes dazzlingly from the days of early and happily married love to neurotic despair; and the scene quite thrillingly culminates in the ticking out of the seconds that must elapse before she pulls the trigger of the pistol at her head. It may not be a first rate thriller, but it is acted by all concerned in first rate style". There was poor business even in the tiny Duke of York's Theatre. Peter Daubeny, who presented the play, was motoring to Oxford with his wife. He decided to telephone the theatre manager, without consulting the author or the director, John Fernald, to instruct him to post notice on all contracts, convinced that he had a flop on his hands. After three attempts he could not get through to the theatre and decided to delay the notice until after the weekend. Later he bumped into Hugh Mills, the author of the play, who told him that there had been almost a capacity house that night. Daubeny later wrote that the telephone call-box had turned into an alchemist's cell.

"*I arranged to watch a woman put under hypnosis and regressed in time, and noted many things which I worked into my performance. The process in real life was very slow and the patient's reactions were small and quiet. I needed to heighten what I saw to make sufficient impact. Truth, in a play such as this, heightens the suspense. The experience taught me something else. I realized from the hypnosis session that everything we have done or experienced remains coiled up inside us for the rest of time. The record of every sight and sound I have known is stored in my heart. When I have needed it for my work I have drawn from this record. And I realized that by releasing these old feelings in my work, I have freed my soul of many sorrows."*

"Flora's great gift was simplicity and immediacy of feeling," Andrew Cruickshank wrote to me. "I only had to mention the word 'Titanic' to her and her eyes would fill with tears. She had a powerful voice but without much tone. There was always a huskiness. But this added to the honesty of the statement. There was not much grace in her movement but this again she turned to enormous advantage because her movement was always truthful. She managed to extract the emotional pith of a scene and pitch it beautifully so that the audience could understand and sympathize with it. This is what she did with Bridie's Mary Paterson which I shall never forget." Sylvia Coleridge, who was also in the cast, wrote to me, "My opinion of what particular quality has made Flora's such an exceptional talent, is basically her total commitment to the Christian way of life and thought, which illumines her work and her relationships with her colleagues, and enables her audiences to relate to a human being, with the same pains, terrors and joys as themselves, not (as is so often the case with a star) a being from another planet far removed from the chores and humdrum routine of everyday life. She taught me by sheer example – not by preaching! – that 'being still' on the stage can result in being too still and not listening, therefore distracting the attention of an audience from the action of the scene. At the call one evening she told the assembled company, 'You have all known me on one of the greatest days of my life.' She had been to Buckingham Palace for lunch and sat next to Prince Philip."

Flora had met royalty on several occasions. In 1947 she had been a guest at a Buckingham Palace garden party. As she was making her curtsey to the King and Queen the band struck up a selection from *Iolanthe* with 'Bow, bow, ye lower middle classes'! The lunch at the palace resulted from the Queen's expressed wish to meet some 'ordinary people'. It was a delightful treat for Flora and she was pleased to discover that the royal couple had seen her on television a few days earlier. Television opened up new vistas for Flora and she was the first of the great classical actors to come to terms with the medium. Sylvia Coleridge told her how much she feared the television cameras. "In those days they advanced on you like brontosauruses!" Flora told her, "Take three deep breaths and feed them with nuts." Before the thriller opened, Flora played in a television presentation of *Message for Margaret* with Rosalie Crutchley as the other Margaret. Both were acclaimed for their playing and Flora was given the *News Chronicle* Award for the Best Television Actress of the Year. Another success was a presentation of *The Return* with her former teacher Helen Haye as the Prioress. A telecast of *Autumn* was less successful. The play was now dated and one critic found Flora hopelessly miscast. She was too old at fifty-five for the romance to seem credible. Four days after Christmas in 1957 she was the Mystery Guest on the television panel game 'What's My Line?' "*Before the programme Eamonn Andrews and I discussed my appearance. Lady (Isobel) Barnett had been phenomenally successful at guessing both people's professions and the identities of the mystery celebrities. I suggested to Eamonn that I should assume a kind of Edith Evans voice. It would become a frequent practice to use a false voice but I was the first. After we had spoken I was hidden in a dressing-room. Eamonn told me to lock the door and not open it to anyone. After a while there was a knock on the door. It was Lady Barnett who pretended to be lost. I didn't answer and eventually she went away. She first guessed me to be Edith Evans, but guessed my true identity before time was up. I don't think Edith Evans was too pleased about it!*"

Her contract with Rank was on the verge of expiry. Advantage was taken of her long run in casting her in four films in a row, all of which proved routine and largely unmemorable. The first was *High Tide at Noon*, the story of simple Canadian fisher-folk. Flora had no good scenes. She had to weep a little, look sympathetic and caring, say the right tender thing and pour coffee a couple of times. In *No Time for Tears* she played a dried-up night-sister in a children's hospital. Her one moment came when she spoke to a young nurse. "They're all our children while they are here. But don't try to put yourself in a mother's place. Don't give one child your heart to keep. He'll only break it." The young nurse in this scene was Sylvia Syms. During the short run of *A Kind of Folly* Sydney Box had spotted Sylvia and offered her a screen test. Flora took her to Mount Fort the night before so she could appear at the studio fresh and rested. She had her chauffeur drive her over. Sylvia had learned an acting piece but all she was expected to do was to act glamorous "got up like Mae West's grandmother" as she recalled. No contract was offered. Flora told her she felt they had made the wrong decision and they might regret it later. She could see that Sylvia had exactly the right kind of talent. Six months later Associated British gave her a long-term contract and the Rank Organisation had to hire her at great expense for the many films she subsequently made for them. Flora would not see Sylvia again until the summer of 1980 when she saw her give a brilliant performance as Mrs Christie in a revival of *Black Chiffon*. In her review of *No Time for Tears*, C. A. Lejeune wrote at length about the film industry's neglect of Flora, wishing someone would write parts of the stature given to Françoise Rosay by French directors. "Miss Robson is our Mme Rosay, hasn't anybody noticed? Actresses of her quality are few in England. She is a selfless worker with a plain, strong beauty, who commands, more than ever since her appearance in television plays a faithful, large and vastly varied public . . . An actress with the power to play Lady Macbeth and Thérèse Raquin has been cast as drab wives and maids of all sorts, women without continuity or character. I think the big boys of the film industry have slipped up here. Looking for a type they've missed the individual."

*Innocent Sinners* was Flora's second opportunity to work in an adaptation of a Rumer Godden novel. *An Episode of Sparrows* was the story of an unwanted child growing up on the bomb sites of the East End of London. She makes a garden in a bombed-out church and comes into contact with an elderly lady who has only a few months to live. June Archer was the child, and Flora was Olivia Chesney. She spends her life looking out of the window at the children in the street whom she calls her sparrows. "The street is so rich in all the things I've never had . . . Oh living, just living." "*I had to do a fall in the film. I fell into a relaxed heap. Immediately a crowd of alarmed assistants rushed forward to help me to my feet. They were most surprised to find I was perfectly unharmed. Rather apologetically the director, Philip Leacock, begged for a second 'take'. He wanted my hat to fall off as I fell. I loosened the hat and fell again and the hat rolled away at exactly the right moment. They didn't know of the excellent training I had received at RADA all those years before.*"

In *The Gypsy and the Gentleman* she was cast, as C. A. Lejeune put it, "in a part that has no particular bearing on the plot." Nevertheless it was a glamorous role as a noted Regency actress, Mrs Haggard. The film starred Melina Mercouri and Keith Michell and was directed by Joseph Losey. "*The Gypsy and the Gentleman* was one of the less happy experiences of my life," Joseph Losey wrote to me. "This remark in no way refers to Flora Robson. She was always patient, generous, very human and very easy to work with. These qualities plus exceptional discipline and concentration made and make her the actress she is. I may also say that she was always dedicated and avoided anything false. I remember her personally with gratitude and affection." Also cast in the film was Helen Haye. Miss Haye had the greatest role in her career, during the fifties, as the Dowager

# FLORA

Empress of Russia in the play *Anastasia*. Her natural dignity lent great authenticity to her portrayal. Although chosen to recreate the role in the film with Ingrid Bergman, a misunderstanding resulted in Helen Hayes being given the part. She had completed filming with Losey and spoken her last line to Keith Michell, "Goodnight Deverill, I shall not see you again." Less than two weeks later she died. Robert Donat died about a year later. His last line on film, spoken to Ingrid Bergman in *The Inn of the Sixth Happiness*, was uncannily similar. Looking old, tired and terribly ill, he walked away from the camera. Flora was at the premiere with many of his old friends. Tears poured down her cheeks. With Robert she said 'goodbye' to many of the golden moments of her early life.

Towards the end of the run of *The House by the Lake*, Alexander Solodovnikov, the director of the Moscow Arts Theatre on a visit to London, expressed a wish to see Flora's performance. Afterwards he declared her to be the finest English actress he had ever seen. "Our actors could not play the same roles for two years," he said. "I told her it was a real artistic deed." Flora's chief formative influence had been Michael Chekhov, Stanislavsky's disciple, consequently Solodovnikov's comments filled her with delight.

She was given the choice of continuing the London run of the play into a third year without a provincial tour, or of closing in London and taking the play on the road for three months. She had always loved taking theatre to people who would not normally see West End plays and chose the latter course. The cast was given two weeks off, the first rest for Flora and Andrew Cruickshank for two years. The provincial tour was immensely successful, though again there was much criticism of the play. In the early thirties she had fought to get away from the Flora Robson role of 'tortured spinster' but over the last few years she had been forced to accept a new kind of type-casting simply to remain in the public eye, hoping to redress the balance with better roles in films and television. But it had been a blank and barren patch. She resolved to do her best to restore herself to the position in which she had found herself after *The Winter's Tale*.

## 8

Television provided the first worthwhile role for several years. "Miss Flora Robson might have been born to play Nurse Cavell," declared *The Sunday Times*, "Had she done nothing else she should be remembered with gratitude." Flora had wanted to play Edith Cavell for many years. Plans for her to appear in the Cecil Forrester and Bechhofer Roberts play on Broadway were abandoned when war broke out. Flora had lunched one day with Hugh Beaumont, the drama adviser to Associated Television, who had given her carte blanche in choosing a play for television. Earlier still she had approached Tennents with the idea of doing a play in the theatre about Cavell and, as a result, a young former actor, Peter Draper, whose wife was distantly related to Nurse Cavell, had written a script. Flora chose to do this with A.T.V. It was entitled . . . *And Humanity*, from the words on the Cavell monument in Charing Cross Road. "Viewers may have been shocked last night," wrote Philip Phillips in the *Daily Herald*. "They saw a Nurse Edith Cavell far removed from Anna Neagle's famous portrayal of a young idealist . . . Miss Robson gave them a plain, naive, kindly, middle-aged, Victorian woman – who infringed the rules of war and was executed. She helped to get Allied soldiers back to their own lines because she was 'sorry for the boys'. Not from reasons of patriotism." Viewers were left with the moving image of Flora as Edith Cavell tidying up her cell before going to her death.

On 5 July 1958 she set off for a well-deserved holiday in Ravello on the Bay of Naples, the day after the Honorary Degree of Doctor of Letters had been conferred upon her at Durham University. Professor G. B. A. Fletcher, the public orator, described her as a well-graced actress dedicated to her art. Flora was moved to return a prophet with honour in her own land. There were offers of plays but Flora turned them down. Too many of them had specially written Flora Robson roles and she longed for something which would offer her a challenge. "I've always thought of Flora Robson as holding, in her fruitful Salad Days, a unique position in the theatre," Dame Wendy Hiller wrote to me. "Because of her very special quality one wouldn't liken her to anyone – she stood alone. A plain woman by conventional standards, with a singularly beautiful voice and a quality of integrity and goodness – yet I felt she was never fully stretched and had a far wider range than she was given the chance to use."

There was a little radio work. In all, she had over one hundred and twenty radio credits to her name by this time. As well as plays she had made numerous contributions to programmes of poetry, many for Patric Dickinson, in addition to several broadcasts for schools. She had been busy as President of the RADA Council, making it her business to see as many student productions as she was able and to talk to and encourage the students themselves. Knowing how discouraged the young actor could become, she has always made a point of encouraging anyone who wants to go on the stage. "There are too many who want to discourage," she says.

Almost a quarter of a century after her last appearance there, late in 1958 Flora was asked to return to the Old Vic. John Fernald, who was also at this time Principal of RADA, directed her as Mrs Alving in Norman Ginsbury's version of *Ghosts* with Michael Hordern as Pastor Manders and Ronald Lewis as Oswald. Flora opted for a slow build to the final scene as she had always done in the past. Many of the critics felt that she took too long to achieve her peak. "When Dame Sybil Thorndike played the part I seem to remember that she came near to eating the whole of her forearm off, trying to repress her screams," wrote Philip Hope-Wallace in the *Manchester Guardian*. "When Oswald said to this Mrs Alving, 'Don't scream mother, I can't bear it', Miss Robson had really contributed little more than a few puzzled gasps." However, J. W. Lambert wrote in *The Sunday Times*, "I shall be surprised if any of us have an opportunity to see [Mrs Alving] played with greater truth or beauty than Flora Robson is bringing to her now. In her presence she is all the lady of the big house; in her gestures gentle, yet determined – until the very bitter end – she is all the mother; in her voice which so surprisingly combines the richness of maturity with the golden lightness of youth, she is all woman. Tenderness and hardness alternate and blend, hope and despair by turns illuminate and quench her wild, unflinching eyes."

"I am criticized constantly because I take it quietly," Flora wrote to Rita Room, "but Mrs Alving doesn't know anything about the illness and soon after Oswald has *told* her of it, her mind strays to something she believes *much* worse – his incestuous infatuation for Regina. When at the end of the play, she is left alone with Oswald, she says, 'And now have I taken away all that remorse and that self-reproach'. By this I think she knows nothing of the nature of the illness, which is never mentioned by name. ('You'll soon be working again' and 'I'll nurse you and look after you'.) Her great sorrow is that he should think he brought it on himself, and she works hard to relieve him of guilt."

Ronald Lewis was greatly praised for his Oswald. Michael Hordern attempted an unusual approach to Pastor Manders, allowing the pompous aspects of the character to come to the fore. This met with derision from many of the critics. Later in the season he was scheduled to play Macbeth and Cassius so that when the production transferred to the Duchess Theatre he was replaced. The actor chosen was Donald Wolfit.

"I remember Flora most," John Fernald wrote to me, "and I think her colleagues will remember her most for the generosity of her professional relationships. She was never 'difficult', never 'grand' with those she acted with. She was completely lacking in all those vices so often associated with stars. It took such an excessively suspicious star as Donald Wolfit to suspect her, needless to say, without the slightest justification, of intending to destroy his chances of holding the attention of the audience in the long first act of *Ghosts* by clicking her knitting needles!" Wolfit treated her with animosity and scorn. Seldom in her career had Flora met with difficult actors. There had been Oscar Homolka in *Close Quarters*, Laughton and two actresses in America. Wolfit attempted by all means in his power to destroy Flora's performance. One of his methods was to throw her timing. He would pause on the penultimate word of a speech unexpectedly so that Flora would have to wait and take another breath, or so that she would stumble into her next speech. She was never able to say anything to him offstage as he would brush rudely past her. One night she heard him plotting quite openly with another member of the cast how they would steal moments from her. The run at the Duchess lasted only a month before the company set out on tour. Wolfit left the cast after the first week in Brighton to Flora's great relief, and was replaced for the rest of the tour by Eric Dodson.

Flora had attempted another great role on television in Brecht's *Mother Courage and Her Children*. She was not ideally cast in the role of the tough, garrulous camp-follower. Had she been given the length of a rehearsal period in the theatre she might have found a better level in a part in which there was much more than had met her eye. Timothy Bateson recalled for me, "One day after rehearsal Rudolph Cartier, the director, gave notes to the assembled cast. He gave some words of encouragement to Flora but said she needed to work to bring out the comedy. After he had gone, Flora turned to me and said, 'Bring out what comedy? It's well known that I'm useless in comedy. If I'd known there was any comedy in it I would never have agreed to play the part.'" OH MISS ROBSON YOU'RE TOO REFINED, headlined the *Daily Mirror*. "The gravest handicap was the miscasting of Flora Robson in the name part," wrote Maurice Richardson in the *Observer*. "Miss Robson is everybody's favourite actress. She is not only a very good woman herself, but she has played good, or at any rate repressed, women so often that the mould seems to have set, especially round the voice-box. Instead of the tough *vivandière* of the Thirty Years War . . . she instantly suggested the social worker, thinly disguised, the crypto hospital matron." *The Times* called her reading, "fatally well bred" but the *Manchester Guardian* added that she "made a fine moment of refusing to recognize her dead son, and for some time after this moment one was inclined to give her the benefit of the doubt whenever her acting misfired."

Flora's career had almost ground to a halt by 1959. She badly needed a role to stretch her, to extend her, or she might as well give up the theatre altogether. She had once written a letter to Basil Dean turning down an unsuitable role in a play the script of which had been mistakenly sent to her. "My only chance of success on the stage, as

I have so many handicaps," she wrote, "is to act in plays no other actress can do as well." But good fortune was once more smiling on her. She had survived the difficult years between. Waiting for her was a role as ideally suited to her own particular qualities as had been Pirandello's Stepdaughter, O'Neill's Abbie, Bridie's Mary Paterson and Lady Catherine Brooke. And it would bring in its wake an accolade greater than any she had ever known.

# 6

## Most Beautiful Evenings

### 1959–1970

#### 1

'IT'S STILL NO romance for Flora' revealed the *Manchester Daily Mail* after *The Aspern Papers* opened there. "Supremely well though she acts these painful parts, it's surely time she was given a holiday from them." Flora had not quite got the measure of Miss Tina. There had been a difficult rehearsal period. Basil Dean, the director, had spent most of the time working closely with Beatrix Lehmann, who had the role of a centenarian. As usual, he would continually stop the actors in rehearsal, so that none of them had a good run at their scenes. Michael Redgrave, who was responsible for the adaptation of the Henry James story and was also acting the leading role, had taken over the direction from Dean the day before the play opened in Newcastle. It was unsettling for all of them though Miss Lehmann won great praise from the Press and cheers from the audiences. Flora was still working painstakingly to come to terms with the most beautifully drawn character it had been her opportunity to play for many years.

Michael Redgrave had conceived of making an adaptation from the James story when filming in Hollwood in 1947. He acquired the rights to *The Aspern Papers* and shortly afterwards completed a first draft of the play. After two further drafts the play had remained unproduced. In 1958, Fred Sadoff suggested that Flora should play the role of Miss Tina. Flora had read the story some years earlier and when it was put to her that she might play in a stage version she replied that there was surely no part for her. She was told it had been hoped she would play Miss Tina, the niece. "But aren't I too old?"

Flora asked. "She is just a little girl." On the contrary, Miss Tina as described by James was "a piece of middle-aged female helplessness". Flora was impressed by Redgrave's adaptation and agreed to play the role when his and her commitments permitted.

Redgrave's role was that of 'H. J.' – Henry Jarvis, or Henry James even, – the character representing the 'first person' in the story who has come to Venice in search of a Miss Bordereau. It is believed that over eighty years earlier she had a romance with a poet, Jeffrey Aspern, of whom H. J. is a biographer. He takes rooms in Miss Bordereau's house in order to elicit from her what he can of the years with Aspern, which were his most inspired, and immediately prior to his early death. In order to gain access to the letters and papers which still exist in an old trunk under the old lady's bed, he attempts to woo her simple-minded niece. The old lady dies of a heart-attack on realizing H. J.'s purpose. Gauche Miss Tina suggests to H. J. that he might marry her. When he refuses, she reveals that she has burned all the letters. After he has left her to her life of loneliness she methodically burns the Aspern Papers which she had kept as a dowry for her intended husband.

Flora's mistaken memory of the story would remain the basis for her characterization. She had remembered the heart of the woman, not her external self. The strength of her eventual success was this individual approach which invested the character with a life which even Henry James may not have seen, allowing the audience greater insight into the piece as a whole. This ability was Flora's lasting genius.

*"In order to find how Miss Tina felt I looked into my own past. There is a scene where H. J. takes her out for the evening. She has not left the house for many years. The most compelling moment is when she realizes she will be able to go to Florian's and buy ice-cream. I was once appearing in a play at Blackpool. Walking along the promenade one day I turned and was confronted by a small and delicately beautiful little boy who was looking with saucer eyes at the golden sands stretched out before him. It was as though he were seeing paradise for the first time. He exclaimed, with glorious joy in his voice, 'I can see the sands,' That was my inspiration for the line when, with the same incredulous ecstasy I said, 'Oh, can I buy an ice?' H. J. commented on the charming dress I was wearing, flattering me for it was old-fashioned. My line in the script was, 'My aunt told me to wear it.' (She was hoping to marry off Miss Tina.) I obtained permission from Michael to add, 'It is my best one,' which is the kind of thing a little girl might say. At the end of the scene H. J. offers her his arm. He is dressed glamorously in an opera cloak. It is the most wonderful thing that has ever happened to Miss Tina. I remembered an incident in my adolescence. Hugh Rennie, Lila's lovely Scotsman, brought a handsome French-Canadian soldier friend to tea. I was fourteen, like*

*Juliet, and quite sexless, skinny and with pigtails. He sat next to me at table. 'Would you like some strawberries out of my garden?' I asked him. With his wonderful accent, half-French, half-American, he replied, 'Sure' and I handed them to him. I nearly died of joy! When we left the room, he was ahead of me at the door. He stood back to let me go through first. I floated through the door. When I was out of sight I raced upstairs, kicking all the brass stair rods in my speed, and flung myself on my bed and squealed with delight. When Michael offered me his arm I folded up in coy delight. I took his arm and walked out of the door with him in a flood of giggles. The audience clapped solidly through the break between the scenes and only stopped when the curtain rose for the next scene. It reminded everyone of the first time they fell in love."*

"It was left to Miss Flora Robson to give the performance of the evening, and perhaps of her distinguished career," observed A. Alvarez in the *New Statesman*, "as the dowdy middle-aged niece she moved unhesitatingly from awkwardness, shuffling and tongue-tied, through an uncertain, hesitant tenderness to a final desolation and calm. She presented a whole process of life. And it was a performance wholly without mannerisms; each move was thought out and restrained; over everything was the mark of intelligence. In this way the full profundity of the James character came through. Her intelligence and skill matched his as a writer. It is the only way." The Press was unanimous in its praise. The entire play was a success, the adaptation was welcomed and Beatrix Lehmann lauded. Bernard Levin wrote in the *Daily Express*, "Sir Michael has caught James's mood exactly – a mood that changes and shifts like the colours in an opal but, like an opal never reflects enough light to dazzle the onlooker." "Sir Michael," commented Harold Hobson in *The Sunday Times*, "is that model of unselfishness, an author who has written himself the third-best part in the play."

It is possible that, in writing the adaptation, Redgrave had imagined the part would afford him greater prominence. On paper the character of H. J. appears a most attractive role. Its rich and finely achieved variety is due entirely to the skill of the adaptor who has visualized a character not directly described by James. It must have proved a bitter disappointment to Redgrave, the actor, to discover that the attention of the audience was riveted on the two women and the mystery that lay behind the bedroom door. As Flora had found in *The Innocents*, the observer in adaptations of James' stories did all the work only to have the play stolen by the other characters.

The *Evening Standard*'s panel of judges selected Flora as Best Actress of the Year. "Goodness is not the easiest quality to portray on the stage," remarked Peggy Ashcroft as she presented Flora with her trophy. Flora was delighted. "I have won film awards and T.V.

# FLORA

awards," she said, "but never a theatre award. And the theatre is my love." She concluded her short speech with her line from the play after she and H. J. have returned from the ice-cream adventure, "This has been one of the most beautiful evenings of my life."

It seemed to Flora, at the time, that she had achieved the peak of her success, that nothing could delight her more. But in June 1960 her name appeared in the Queen's Birthday Honours List. There had been no advance warning this time. Flora was created a Dame of the British Empire. Immediately she learned of the honour her mind raced back into the past. A little girl in a white dress with lots of frills and a pale blue sash, with white satin slippers on her feet was slipping into her outdoor coat. She wound her muffler round her and went in search of her father. She could see him standing at the end of the passage talking to her teacher. He turned round, his face flushed with excitement, and saw her. "Flora," he cried, "you're going to be an actress. Our next Ellen Terry!" His words, as always had come true, for she had dedicated her life to proving him right. He had taught her always to strive for excellence, never to settle for anything less. From the many thousands of actresses who had pursued a life in the theatre, Flora joined Ellen Terry, Sybil Thorndike and the handful of others to be honoured in this way. Flora put her hands to her face as her eyes filled with tears. "If only they were alive to share it with me," she sobbed, "my mother and father. If only they could have lived to see this day."

There were letters and telegrams from all over the world, from actors, directors, fans and friends. One arrived from Buckingham Palace. "I was delighted to see your name in the Birthday Honours List." It was signed "Philip". A treasured letter came from Tony Guthrie. "You dear old thing, I'm so glad about your Dame," he wrote. "Loving congratulations. Never was greater talent 'recognised'," and, showing how well he understood Flora, he added, "I wish your dear parents had been there to share and enjoy the glory." Seldom has an honour met with such universal approval, for Flora was loved by intellectuals and scholars and by the ordinary man and woman in the street. It secured for her a lasting place in the history of her beloved theatre. She had arrived at the very top of her chosen profession as a result of her dedication and integrity without hurting anyone on the way. Hers was the triumph of a truly good woman.

2

"The day before the daily papers were to publish the Queen's Honours List, the word was out, through the management to the cast, that Flora was to receive the D.B.E.," recalled Robert Beatty, who had replaced Michael Redgrave as H. J. "Naturally we were all delighted and one by one, before the evening's performance, we stopped by her dressing-room to congratulate her. She was thrilled and bubbling over with excitement. Before I left her to go to my dressing-room to change and make-up for the show she stopped me and said, 'Bob, I hope you don't mind, but you know the scene where we come back from Florian's. Would you mind if tonight I say – This has been the most beautiful evening of my life?' Of course I didn't mind and quite understood. I'm not even sure I would have noticed the change but I might have. It is typical of Flora's consideration for her fellow actors that she would mention it to me."

The play continued to delight audiences. One night there was a visitor for Flora. The stage-door keeper had detained a suspicious looking character. There had been a regrettable incidence of theft backstage and he had been instructed only to allow bona fide visitors through to the dressing-rooms. This visitor demanded to see Flora but refused quite adamantly to give his name. He was dressed in a raincoat that had seen better days and had long hair and a long grey beard. In the end Flora went out to see who it was. There, in the rain, taking time off from his role as King Lear at Stratford upon Avon, stood her old friend Charles Laughton. He was soon inside, chatting gaily about her performance. Some months later he wrote to her hoping to see "your darling frolicking self. That's what you are, Flora, a frolicker." There was some talk of taking the play to Broadway where he would direct it. Flora wrote to George Freedley that she wasn't sure she could afford to work in America. "When I came last time I paid 60% in taxes, plus 10% extra to an agent. With the high cost of hotels, and 5% tax on the bills and a house to keep up in England I find it a strain to make things pay. I find it hard after long runs that I cannot afford a rest, or to lie fallow for a while." When the play eventually opened there, Wendy Hiller played Miss Tina, with Maurice Evans and Françoise Rosay.

Leonard Schach, from South Africa, was another visitor. "My first meeting with Flora was a very strange one," he told me. "George Freedley, who was the curator of the New York Public Libraries and the founder of the Theatre Collection, had introduced me to all the important people in American theatre. He told me that the one person I ought to know in England was Flora. When I arrived in England I spoke to Flora on the telephone and she invited me to spend the weekend at Mount Fort. It snowed on the way down and it was a cold, wet night when I arrived. I knocked on the door and a woman opened it and invited me in. I put down my bag and shook the snow off. I asked the woman if she would kindly tell Miss Robson I had arrived as I was very cold. 'I *am* Miss Robson,' she replied,

# FLORA

'I'm really very much prettier than films make me.' Well, after that inauspicious start we became great friends. Every year I asked her if she would come out to South Africa to do a play for me. When I saw her early in 1960, she said, 'You haven't asked me to come to South Africa this year.' I replied that I was tired of asking her, because she always said 'no'. Then she told me she would like to come out and play in *The Aspern Papers*."

Flora sailed to South Africa on the mail-ship. Robert Beatty would follow later by air and the rest of the cast would be South African actors with Leonard directing. His mother threw a cocktail party to honour Flora. "All the members of my company made a real effort. The boys had suits on and all the girls wore hats. I'd never seen any of them looking like that before. When the Stage Manager was introduced to Dame Flora she was so excited she dropped into a deep curtsey in front of her!" Schach recalled. "Flora felt very strongly about the racial situation. Unfortunately, in those days there was no way of playing to multi-racial audiences. We were able to arrange visits to coloured schools, and Flora gave poetry recitals. We had non-whites to rehearsals and every Monday night I got permission for performances to be given to non-white audiences. Flora went out of her way, almost to the point of exhaustion, to make as many visits as she could, and on some days would not finish in the schools until six thirty and then do an evening show. Her performance was exemplary, a great, great artistic achievement. She endeared herself to everyone."

During her stay in Cape Town, before setting out on tour, Flora saw Leonard Dixon, a young coloured teacher, give a brilliant performance as Macbeth. Some days later she was pleased to meet him at an Indian restaurant, one of the few pleasant places permitted to non-whites. Over dinner she casually suggested to him that he might consider training for the theatre at RADA. Flora took his address and promised she would get in touch with him after her return to England. He was thrilled by her interest but took the matter of RADA with a pinch of salt. He was certain she would soon have forgotten about him. Characteristically true to her word, she spoke to John Fernald on her return and wrote to Leonard suggesting he write to him. Leonard had been raised in an environment which led him to expect very little from life and failed to write. Instinctively Flora understood his doubts and wrote again. This time her faith communicated itself and he wrote the letter which was to change the course of his life. Flora's faith paid a handsome dividend for Leonard Dixon is now the Director of Drama Studies at Loughborough University.

"Flora was crazy to see as much as she could of the wild-life," continued Leonard Schach. "One of the South African firms presented her with a new movie camera. We visited eight or nine game reserves. One day Flora spotted an exquisite beetle and she raced around photographing it. Suddenly there was this crashing noise and a herd of elephants made straight for us. We were petrified. But Flora couldn't miss an opportunity and opened the roof of the car and photographed the herd as they came crashing through the undergrowth. When she eventually showed the film there was no sign of the elephants. The beetle came out marvellously. In the excitement she had forgotten to remove the tele-photo lens. She was heartbroken."

Shortly after her return from South Africa, Flora was the subject of 'This is Your Life' on BBC television. Eamonn Andrews, the presenter, was somewhat apprehensive. In those days the show was transmitted live and the previous week footballer Danny Blanchflower had refused to allow the invasion of his privacy, which meant that there had been no show. Flora, on the other hand, was delighted to take part. Among the surprise guests was a colleague from Welwyn; Charles Laughton was seen in a filmed message from New York; Tony Guthrie, James Mason and Henry Oscar contributed memories. The greatest surprise came when Paul Robeson's massive frame appeared in the door. Flora had led a campaign to have his passport restored by the American government and this was the first time she had seen him since then. Another delightful event occurred at a charity performance at the London Palladium, 'The Night of a Hundred Stars'. Sixteen well-known actors, including Tony Britton, John Neville and John Fraser, discarded their shirts and sang 'There is Nothing Like a Dame' from *South Pacific*. Flora, dressed in a slinky gown, entered in the middle of it! The last few months had been a dazzling celebration of all her years in the theatre.

## 3

"Basil Dean let me read a comedy he was hoping to produce," recalled Elspeth March. "It was very, very funny and I was mad about it. I said to Basil, 'Please, please let me try it out somewhere.' He replied that he had promised it to Flora. Flora was in *The Aspern Papers* and I went to see her and I told her I had read the play and was very keen to do it. She said, well, the fatal thing. She said, 'I'm contracted to do a Lesley Storm play, *Time and Yellow Roses*, after *The Aspern Papers*, and, you know, everything I do never runs less than two years.' I thought as she said it, 'Oh what a hostage to Fate'. The Lesley Storm play ran for only about three weeks. By the time I had sorted out about doing the comedy the author had withdrawn it. It disappeared into limbo and I wasn't able to do it anyway." Keith

Baxter recalled to me in a letter, "I met Dame Flora at a bumpy moment in my life. In 1960 Elizabeth Taylor was lying seriously ill in the London clinic and production of the film *Cleopatra* – then being made in England – came grinding to a halt. Shortly afterwards Peter Finch (Caesar), Stephen Boyd (Antony) and myself (Octavius) were sacked. ('Released from our contracts' was the euphemism used.) It was an awful blow for me and when my agent broke the news I could hardly speak. 'But pop over to the Piccadilly,' he said. 'They're very keen on you for a new play with Flora Robson.' I read with Dame Flora the next day. She was gentle and sympathetic. 'I know you're depressed about the film,' she said,' but do you think you could be happy with us? Of course, I'm not Elizabeth Taylor!' She drove me back to her new home in Islington for a drink, both of us puffing away at cigarettes as the Bentley purred up Rosebery Avenue. I liked her enormously at once. I remember her wonderful buoyancy, her sense of fun, her earthy, sexual awareness. She was delightful on train-calls – knitting furiously in amazing colours (once a pair of socks for the Mayor of Johannesburg) and terrific company back at the digs in Jesmond Dene in Newcastle, sitting in a cloud of cigarette smoke. On the opening night of *Time and Yellow Roses* at Her Majesty's Theatre in Aberdeen, when she took her curtain-call, she reached out and presented Patricia Healey and me to the audience, saying she was proud to introduce us. It was a warm and touching gesture and quite typical of Flora to have done it."

The play was a view of African politics as seen from a London penthouse flat; guilt over misapplied capitalism and atonement by death. Flora had an expensive wardrobe and a dull part with only one good scene, which was shared by Keith Baxter. "[They] play this last scene with such depth of true, unexaggerated feeling, such exactitude of timing and intonation, that I, at any rate for the moment, forgot the tedium which was welling up inside me," pronounced Harold Hobson in *The Sunday Times*. "She was wonderful to act with," continued Keith Baxter. "The play was not a success and there were the usual post-mortems afterwards, but it was always really splendid being on stage with her." "Our play is not a success," Flora wrote to George Freedley. "I am not surprised. Although it has a good idea it does not knit together and I don't like my part. But it had the most successful tour I have *ever* done."

Flora had kept contact with the Cardiff College of Music and Drama. Whenever she was in the area she would call in informally and spend time with the students. On 21 July 1961 there was an official invitation for her to visit a Congregation of the University of Wales in Cardiff. Presenting her with an honorary doctorate, the Principal of University College, Swansea, announced, "We pay our tribute not only to a great actress, not only to a personality of singular grace, but also to one who throughout a highly successful career has made it her care to further the well-being, the education, and the advancement of young and struggling members of her own profession." A further honour came her way when Julian Herington took over the Playhouse at Jesmond near Newcastle upon Tyne and asked Flora for her permission to name it the Flora Robson Playhouse. She promised she would perform the opening ceremony and appear there whenever she could.

Late in 1961 Flora was invited to play at the Connaught Theatre in Worthing as Miss Moffatt in *The Corn is Green*. Brook Williams played Morgan Evans, the role his father Emlyn had created some twenty-three years previously. The play was subsequently presented in Brighton and was then taken to South Africa on tour. Flora was intrigued to find how well the black people responded to the character of Morgan, whose face, black from the mine, allowed each of them to identify strongly with this most Welsh of plays. The tour was less successful than her previous one. Leonard Schach felt he had brought her out again too soon. Flora regretted that this might be the last opportunity she would have of playing in South Africa. Equity, the actor's union, was taking steps to forbid its members to play there because of the political situation. She had done her best when in South Africa to perform before all races at all levels of society, and had performed to an all-black audience in a theatre that had previously been exclusively white. She had read Shakespeare to African children and Walter Scott to Indian children. Towards the end of this visit she gave a poetry reading to a multi-racial audience at the University of Natal. One of the poems she read was 'The Little Black Boy' by Blake. "I am not subversive. I am not even politically minded," she said. "I just enjoy my work – whoever the audience." She believes to this day that banning the visits of actors is a mistake. Artists carry the example of our civilization to people who might never know there was a civilization other than the one in which they were raised.

She set sail for her return in a cargo ship. "*I always like to come back from Africa the exciting way, up through the Indian Ocean.*" In mid-ocean she received a wireless cable offering her the role of the Dragon Empress in the film *55 Days at Peking*. She was enjoying her voyage enormously but she had made no films for five years, there was little theatre work and the money offered was excellent. She disembarked rather hurriedly, to the chagrin of the captain who had made special arrangements for her trip, flew to Nairobi and caught a plane home before flying to Madrid where the film was to be shot.

She was met at Madrid airport by the film's director Nicholas Ray.

It was one of the last great film epics and dealt with the Boxer uprising. Flora's role had originally been intended for Garbo at a reported fee of half a million dollars, rather a lot more than Flora was paid. She wore robes actually worn by the Empress Tzu Hsi at the time. The studios were unbearably hot and Flora had to wear a thick latex make-up which created a Chinese look. Because of this mask it was impossible for her to wear a wig or she would have passed out. She was sent to have her hair dyed, supposedly, black. The result was a hideous green. Further dyeing produced a rich black colour but shortly after the completion of the film her hair began to fall out and Flora has had to wear wigs in public and private ever since. The other Chinese notables in the film were played by the remarkable dancer-actor Robert Helpmann and by Leo Genn. The Allies were represented by Charlton Heston and David Niven. Flora was delighted to be reunited with Niven. It was over twenty years since they last worked together, on *Wuthering Heights*.

Flora is almost unrecognizable as the Empress with her raven-black hair, dark brown eyes and a small red mouth painted on her own generous lips. She worked hard to interpolate Chinese-sounding upward inflections and musical notes into her voice. Generally seen from a great distance, the Empress seems remote and inaccessible. There was one scene where Flora, high on her throne with her back to the camera, was addressed by David Niven. "It was incredibly hot in Spain with no air-conditioning in the studios," he wrote to me. "Hacking my way through a long speech to the Empress of China, I, as British Ambassador, stopped in full spate and said, 'I can't go on because Flora has four eyes.' Nicholas Ray, the director, was very upset and several hundred extras were disconcerted. I continued, but then stopped again – she *had* got four eyes! What had happened was her periwinkle blue eyes had seemed strange for the Empress of China so she had been given brown contact lenses and in the heat they had slipped half way down her cheeks!"

When the film was released, almost two years later, Margaret Hinxman wrote in the *Daily Herald*, "The one unpredictable character is the Dowager Empress of China superbly played by Flora Robson. In her presence you feel the awe of a majesty that might never be understood by an Occidental mind." There is an interesting final scene as the broken Empress in sober clothes is seen for the first time from above, moving through the elaborate palace. "The water supports the ship," she says. "The water destroys the ship. The dynasty is finished. The dynasty is finished."

"I am going to Newcastle upon Tyne to reopen the repertory theatre which is to be called the Flora Robson Playhouse," Flora had written to George Freedley. "Then I stay on to rehearse and play

*The Corn is Green* for two weeks. I chose this because I have just been playing it in Africa. I didn't want too much study or work as I am tired out, and have a bit of heart strain. The heights and heat of Africa, and the far too numerous social engagements left me quite breathless. Then I did a film in Spain, one of the epics, *55 Days at Peking*. I am the Empress of China, all too glad to be on a throne again, and not at a kitchen sink."

The Miss Moffatt at Newcastle was surrounded by yet another cast of actors and her Morgan Evans this time was Trevor Bannister. "I look back on my engagement with Dame Flora as one of the happiest and most informative of my career," Bannister, now a television comedy star, wrote to me. "I was rather apprehensive of working with such a distinguished actress but I was soon placed at ease by her warmth. Playing with her I noticed more than once a rather wicked twinkle in her eye which made me feel she was sometimes not far from a 'corpse' or at least a giggle. Such warmth, truth and sincerity combined with professionalism is a rarity. Also stamina – I remember at one celebratory party we danced the 'twist' together till the small hours. Her most important quality as an actress was her generosity to her fellow actors on stage which could only extract the best from them. How I would love to work with her again."

4

In an effort to find a part worth playing Flora again looked to a past success. *Close Quarters* had proved an unhappy experience in the thirties only because of the difficulty of her relationship with Homolka. With a more sympathetic fellow actor it might have been different. It was the kind of play Flora liked doing, with a slow build to a good last scene. There was no specified age for either of the characters. Griffith Jones was engaged to play Gustav, and with John Fernald directing, the play went out on a sixteen-week tour. As with the revival of *Autumn* the play proved badly dated. "The cast . . . is distinguished; the performances are notable; but the play, first presented twenty-seven years ago with Dame Flora in the same part, is an embarrassing anachronism," admitted Campbell Page in the *Manchester Guardian*. "No modern playwright would now produce a work which relied on references to the Freedom Party and the Minister of the Interior to produce an atmosphere of menace, nor would he expect an audience to discover novelty in victimization and police arrests at night."

Griffith Jones had first worked with Flora in the film *Catherine the Great* thirty years earlier. In a letter to me he recalled those days when he drove Flora from the studios up to London in his 'ancient' Morris. "Working with her in the two-character play, a daunting experience for any two artistes of temperament, I realized that the fun-loving Flora of the bull-nosed Morris in the rain, pumping along the Watford by-pass to London, was still at the centre of Dame Flora. It was her radiant humanity (which is in her smile), dominating a dedicated artiste, which explained her success with critics and the public. No monstre sacré here. No ego embalmed in the nimbus of continued success. A human being, a woman much loved, who can convey with skilled artistry her own essential nature."

In the tenth week of the tour Flora was ordered home with an abscess in her left eye. It had begun with a bad cold and skin trouble near her eye which developed over a period of three weeks. She had asked the stage manager to have the lights dimmed because the strong light was agonizing, but eventually the pain was too much to bear. She returned to Brighton, where she now lived, and her understudy, Margaret Lang, took her place for that and the following week. Flora rejoined the cast and was able to play for the rest of the tour.

She made a film for MGM British as Miss Gilchrist in *Murder at the Gallop*, in which Margaret Rutherford appeared in her delightful impersonation of Miss Marple. The character was that of a gentle, shy ladies' companion who turned out, as in all Agatha Christie stories, to have rather more about her than had, perhaps, immediately met the eye.

Late in 1963 she was given the choice of the two leading female roles in Ibsen's *John Gabriel Borkmann*. In the forties, Sybil Thorndike and she had hoped to do a C.E.M.A. tour of the play. Flora would have played Ella to Sybil's Mrs Borkmann. Sadly the project had not come to fruition. The drawback to doing the play on this occasion was that Donald Wolfit would be playing Borkmann. Flora was naturally apprehensive about working with him again but there were increasingly fewer parts for women, and a return to the classics would perhaps stimulate her career as much as it would invigorate her art.

*"I chose to play Mrs Borkmann. I preferred not to be Ella as it would have meant I had to be in love with Borkmann. As it turned out a letter was discovered written by Ibsen in which he said just how Mrs Borkmann should be played and he never meant her to be a viper! She loved her husband and thought him a genius and longed for him to come downstairs to her. I followed Ibsen's intention but this was criticized by the Press who thought I had tried to make her too sympathetic."*

Margaret Rawlings was cast as Ella. I wrote to ask what she remembered of the production. Quite frankly she told me she was unable to remember very much, only the difficulty of learning "the rather Victorian translation, the very difficult relationship between Flora and Donald, and a crazy American director". "It may well be that Mr Ross [David Ross, the director] came to the conclusion that with three players of the stature of Flora Robson, Margaret Rawlings and Donald Wolfit at the head of his cast the less directorial interference there was the better it might be," wrote T. C. Worsley in the *Financial Times*. "This was a miscalculation. Certainly one didn't want them cluttered up with ingenious producer's notions. But there was no need to go to the other extreme." With no support from her director and a hostile leading man it is little wonder that Flora was unhappy and insecure on the first night. She and several of the rest of the cast were still struggling with their lines.

Flora had tried, on several occasions, to give up smoking. A New Year's resolution at the beginning of 1964 began a determined effort. In March she was called to work on the film *Guns at Batasi*, in which she was cast as Miss Barker-Wise, a tough Lancashire, Socialist MP The film was set in Africa and concerns a native revolt in a British army camp. Miss Barker-Wise thinks she has all the answers to the African problem only to take entirely the wrong course of action in a crisis. Richard Attenborough was finely cast as the RSM. Director John Guillermin suggested to Flora that in order to help her project the toughness of the woman she should chain-smoke throughout. Wasted was all her good work in ridding herself of the habit. It was adventurous casting and Flora rose to the occasion with a vigorous and somewhat uncharacteristic performance. The Cleveland (U.S.A.) Critics Circle voted her their award as the Best Supporting Actress of 1964 for this film.

Shortly afterwards she was given a marvellous role as Mrs Cassidy in the film of the early life of Sean O'Casey, *Young Cassidy*. There was an excellent script by John Whiting, and John Ford was due to direct with Sean Connery in the title role. In the event Rod Taylor played the part and Ford was taken ill after shooting only about twenty minutes of the film. Former cinematographer Jack Cardiff took over direction. Flora could not have been bettered by any other non-Irish actress, and even then it would have been difficult to find one with her special qualities of warmth. If anything, the Cassidy home is rather too clean and attractive to make the situation credible but the performances of Taylor and Flora create their own atmosphere. Other distinguished members of the cast included Michael Redgrave as the poet W. B. Yeats, Edith Evans as Lady Gregory, as well as Maggie Smith and Julie Christie as the women in O'Casey's life. "My final accolade, however, goes to Flora Robson, whose shining performance in a small role dominates even this galaxy of great players," wrote Michael Thornton in the *Sunday Express*. "It is, movingly, the apotheosis of careworn motherhood, wonderfully etched by Dame Flora with her inexpressibly beautiful voice. There is here an indefinable something which surely everyone would wish to see and remember in a mother."

A visit to the Flora Robson Playhouse in Newcastle where she did her third production of *The Importance of Being Earnest*, this time as Lady Bracknell, a part she didn't enjoy playing, was followed by her first return to Hollywood for over twenty years. John Ford had been impressed by her work in *Young Cassidy* and had invited her to join the cast of *Seven Women* which would prove the last film of his distinguished career. Patricia Neal was due to play the leading role but when she was taken ill her friend Anne Bancroft stepped into the part. When Flora arrived at the MGM studios in Culver City she noticed a huge billboard which proclaimed the stars of the film – Miss Neal, Sue Lyon, Margaret Leighton, Dame Flora Robson, Mildred Dunnock, Betty Field, Anna Lee and Eddie Albert. She politely explained that it was unwritten law amongst titled actors that their title should not be used professionally. The sign was immediately repainted which intrigued the Hollywood Press. Flora stayed with her old friend John Abbott in the hills above Hollywood. Stepping into his home is like entering an enchanted domain far from the tawdriness of that artificial town. There is an atmosphere of perfect tranquillity. Ornate wood-carvings adorn the walls, and the ceilings are rich with seemingly classical European plasterwork. Every inch of the décor is John's painstaking work and his own paintings hang in heavy frames which he made himself. It was a delight for Flora to return to such civilization after a long day at the studio and John, to this day impeccably English, enjoyed entertaining a friend from home. The gentility extended, on this occasion, to the studio floor, where John Ford regularly entertained his ladies to tea from a silver service.

Anyone who saw the official MGM poster for the film was grossly misinformed, as is so often the case in cinema advertising. **FOR EACH OF THE SEVEN SINS THERE IS ONE OF THE SEVEN WOMEN**, it trumpeted, adding, 'Seven who defied what no man dared, each for a reason that was hers alone.' It was the story of six women missionaries and a woman doctor trapped by bandits in north China near the Mongolian border. For a John Ford picture it is a rather lame affair, self-consciously studio-bound, but *The Times* claimed, "Margaret Leighton and Flora Robson are used to better effect than ever before on the screen." There is one scene which superbly illustrates Flora's greatest talent as a screen actress. The

Bancroft character is drunk. All the other characters sit round the supper table as she subjects them to a torrent of abuse. Each of them has suffered great hardship but it is as though the director has told them all to do nothing as they passively listen to the doctor's drunken outburst. The camera moves round and lights on Flora. Although, like the others, she is doing nothing, she is listening and thinking and feeling. Her eyes are full of the history of her character, and of all the pain and tragedy she recognizes in the doctor. It is an illuminating moment. Flora was impressed by Ford. "*In sequences with a large number of people he paid meticulous attention to every movement and gesture. It was almost as though he were directing a ballet. Very likely this went back to his training in the days of silent film when the picture alone told the story. Working with John Ford I was continually conscious of the fact that he was making a motion picture and that it must move, move, move. His scenes were never static or dominated by dialogue. He was unusual among directors in that he preferred to shoot strictly in sequence. Everything was so thoroughly rehearsed that even in the most difficult of scenes he seldom needed more than one 'take'.*"

Two mediocre film roles followed. *Eye of the Devil* reunited her with David Niven, Deborah Kerr and Emlyn Williams. Flora had the role of Countess Estelle, a member of an ancient family with a mysterious secret. One key scene was filmed at St Etheldreda's Roman Catholic Church in the City of London. "*The priest had given MGM permission to shoot the scene there without fully understanding what was going on. Filming is a long, slow process and often boring to an observer so the Father was not there for much of the time. He looked in at one point and watched a part of the scene where Donald Pleasance was conducting what, to all intents and purposes, appeared to be a celebration of Mass. The Father came over to me during a break in the filming and told me that Donald had not got it quite right. I felt it politic not to inform him that it was the celebration of a demonic form of Mass which he had witnessed!*" When the film was released, some three years later, Nina Hibbin, in the *Morning Star*, claimed, "There have been sillier films but few of them have taken themselves so seriously." There was a tragic postscript to this film when Sharon Tate, one of Flora's co-stars, was the victim of a brutal demonic murder. The second film, *The Shuttered Room*, was another horror story supposedly set in New England but filmed in Britain with a cast including Gig Young, Carol Lynley and Oliver Reed. Aunt Agatha, her role, was a kind of modern witch and wise-woman who turned out to be the only character in the film with any sense. Robert Robinson wrote in *The Observer*, "The film's attraction is Flora Robson's whole-hearted impersonation of the Charles Addams grandmother. She is foreboding personified." There were several plays for her on the radio, and a BBC television serialization of *David Copperfield* in which she played the redoubtable Betsey Trotwood, a character she had earlier played on the radio in America with Richard Burton as David. She was also to be seen briefly as a Mother Superior in the star-studded *Those Magnificent Men in their Flying Machines*.

It was at this time that Flora began seriously to prepare for her retirement. Many were sceptical that she would take such a step, as it is unusual for an actor to retire. Those who announce such an intention seem simply to be craving attention at a difficult patch in their careers. Flora was in earnest. She made financial arrangements which would provide her with a living income for the rest of her life, and told reporters she would retire when she reached the fiftieth anniversary of her theatrical debut. There had been no good work for her in the theatre since *The Aspern Papers* and the work she was offered in films was of a diminishing standard.

There was dismal news from Newcastle. Julian Herington, formerly director of the operating company of the Flora Robson Playhouse, wrote to me, "Support for the theatre came from many different business, social and political groups. It was a pioneer theatre in obtaining sponsorship and private patronage in addition to limited public subsidy. The Arts Council was a reluctant contributor. A 'private' theatre of this nature did not suit its master plan at the time. Newcastle Corporation had rejected the Playhouse building in 1958/9 as 'demolition property'. Now it was decided to municipalize this property with the active encouragement of the Arts Council.

"The Corporation eventually announced a Road Scheme which included the destruction of the entire theatre. Compulsory purchase was threatened. In order to resist any manoeuvre by the Corporation to make capital of the theatre, its existing grants and compensation, as a result of the owner's resignation, backed by the courageous and generous encouragement of some three hundred local creditors, the Company was put into voluntary liquidation. In June 1966 the Playhouse was closed. This forced the Corporation at least to pay minimal compensation to the Company, enabling them to pay just seven shillings in the pound to all creditors – all those private people and groups who had made the theatre possible in the first place. The Corporation now commenced to operate the theatre for a period during which considerable sums of money were lost. The entire building was then demolished. No road has been constructed. One concrete pier stands in a bed of stinging nettles where once there had been a live and successful theatre."

A young writer, Nicholas de Jongh, later a drama critic for *The Guardian*, interviewed Flora and wrote, in *Prompt* magazine, a scathing attack on the theatre critics of the day who were responsible for virtually killing her career. The actress who had numbered Agate and St John Ervine among her more ardent admirers was now dismissed by the likes of the arch-cynic Kenneth Tynan, whose antipathy to Flora had been obvious for several years. Tynan's talent seems to have been an ability to relish only what he could destroy or discover and record in glittering journalese. Flora's work permitted him few opportunities for praise, as warmth, subtle observation and depth of emotion were qualities to which he seldom responded. The power of a critic is limited to the credence placed in him by the reader, but a cumulative onslaught can do great damage to the image of a performer. And Tynan had more strings to his bow, holding a position of influence at the National Theatre. Flora was the only classically based actress Dame of the English theatre not to be asked to play there.

## 5

Flora told Nicholas de Jongh that she would enjoy the chance to play in Greek drama, especially under a Greek director, and spoke of her admiration of Katina Paxinou. "The Greeks understand the stylization of the drama," she said. "We imitate grief – they control it." As it transpired, 1966 became what Flora would later describe as her Greek year.

Although Leonard Schach had not made a film before, he was pressed into service by Anthony Heller on an Anglo-Greek project entitled *A Cry in the Wind*. Leonard recalled, "We flew off to Greece to finalize the locations and then we went to see Katina Paxinou, our star. She was quite enchanting and very feminine. We said we were starting in two weeks' time and she told us she was very much looking forward to it. We said we would all catch the island boat to travel out together. There was a pause. 'Island boat?' she said. 'Paxinou does not travel by island boat.' She expected to be flown out with a helicopter to take her to the island. She asked where we would stay. We all planned to stay in fishermen's cottages as there were no hotels on the island. 'Paxinou not stay in fisherman's cottage,' she said. She would expect to be flown by helicopter to a mainland hotel. Heller said, 'I'm sorry but we cannot afford all this.' And she said, 'Paxinou cannot play the film. Good afternoon.' There we were, weeks before we were to shoot, with no star, and the whole relentless machinery of the film grinding forwards. I don't know where it came from but I suddenly heard myself saying, 'You know, it's the kind of role Flora Robson would be marvellous in.'"

Heller thought Flora would never agree at such short notice but they telephoned her and to their delight she agreed immediately. A script was sent to her. The film would be shot entirely in the Greek language and Flora's voice would be dubbed. "She arrived a month later," Leonard continued, "very excited about doing the film. She got off the boat and greeted me in Greek. She had found a Greek professor who had taught her the correct pronunciation for all the Greek text in the script so that in the dubbing her mouth would be in the right position. She took the trouble to do all that! That's typical of her. We had the leading actor of the Greek National Theatre in the film. He was the only man to have played in every Greek play that had ever been written yet he could neither read nor write. His wife, a schoolteacher, taught him all his words. He turned up to meet Flora in an impeccable morning suit, goodness knows where he got it from. He went down on one knee and kissed Flora's hand."

Flora sent a postcard to George Freedley. "The peace here is wonderful – one bus, one taxi and lots of donkeys. No sounds but the sea, cicadas and frogs." When she arrived on the beach for her first day of shooting as Anasthasia, the village witch, she was charmed to find a sign on Anasthasia's little shack which read 'PHLORA'S PHOLLY'. Off the set she swam and played Scrabble and soaked up all the wonderful good will of the place and its people and the warmth of the sun. This warmth did not permeate the film, which Raymond Durgnat described as "cold and awkward". Nina Hibbin, in the *Morning Star*, felt Flora played her role with "ruggedness and conviction". The cumulative experience of these months was to be invaluable in her next venture. She was asked to play Hecuba in *The Trojan Women* "*I learned the whole part lying on the beach in the Greek sunshine. We performed it in the Assembly Hall in Edinburgh which has a round stage in the middle. It was a big success but the real success went to Andromache, the part Sybil Thorndike rehearsed me in at RADA. Cleo Laine was splendid in the part and fully deserved all her praise. Esmond Knight, who is partially blind, was superb as Menelaus. We all had to climb up steps onto the stage and it would have been so easy for him to fall over the side but he managed better than anyone. We looked down to see the steps. He felt with his feet and went up and down the steps with ease. He gave a wonderful performance.*" Moira Redmond, who was cast as Helen of Troy, wrote to me, "One day, watching Dame Flora rehearse, I was so moved that I burst into tears. I had to pretend I had a dreadful cold so that I could bury my face in a handkerchief. I, personally, don't think the English can act Greek tragedy – they have too much of a stiff upper lip to be able to release themselves – but Dame Flora must be the noblest exception of them all." Frank Cox wrote in *Plays and Players* of the "beautifully judged lead by Flora Robson. Jean-Paul Sartre's version of the play was cleverly decked out with images of the Vietnam war and the bitterness of the original came across." W. A. Darlington felt he must "bottle up my own feeling how much I would have preferred to see Dame Flora match herself against that performance of Dame Sybil's, which still glows in my mind as the greatest tragic performance I have seen a woman give. Yet even in this pale substitute for the magnificent original Dame Flora distinguishes herself very greatly. Denied the high tragic tone, compelled to describe Helen as a brazen hussy and refer to the Trojan horse as a cheap trick she still managed to generate a force of true emotion." Mamie Crichton, in the *Daily Express*, added, "Except for the introductory passage . . . Flora Robson, as Hecuba, the stricken queen of Troy, is on stage the whole time, desolate in sorrow, furious in hate, and magnificent in her final defiance of the gods. A tour de force of tremendous range." Cleo Laine wrote to me, "I felt her dignity and strength, which seems to glow from her both on stage and in film and is conveyed also in her beautiful speaking voice, so right for Hecuba. I had seen Dame Flora in Ibsen's *Ghosts* at the Old Vic, a performance that stunned me and always does when I think of it. I learned one important thing from her and that was the need to be heard when speaking softly or at any volume. This means diction, dotting the I's and crossing the T's, so to speak. I think my success in the part of Andromache was due to her example. I wanted to have that kind of strength, yet warmth at the same time."

In the autumn of 1966 Flora agreed to play the leading role of a woman barrister in a courtroom drama *Justice is a Woman*. Peter Saunders had orginally intended the part for Margaret Lockwood, who was unavailable. The play would have a four-week tour commencing in Brighton before going into the Vaudeville Theatre, where Sybil Thorndike and Athene Seyler were concluding a run of *Arsenic and Old Lace*. "*Because I had been in the film and then straight into* The Trojan Women *I didn't have time to learn the part before I started work on it. Lawyers are the most difficult parts to learn because they do all the talking, asking questions and getting replies which do not necessarily lead to the next question. Everyone was impatient with me. They thought I was very slow. I wasn't at all well. I'd got a poisoned tooth but I tried to struggle on because the leading man had been taken to hospital, and I felt it was unfair for both of us to be away. The poison spread and I was in pain in my shoulders, my arms and hands, everywhere. In addition my ankles began to swell and I developed a bad bronchial cough. Everyone had the cough. We were working in a place that was used as a bingo hall at night and they were sweeping up in the morning when we got there and we swallowed all the dust. I went to a doctor who told me I had no temperature but that I should rest if I felt I needed it. The following morning my pulse was racing at a rate of a hundred and fifty and I had a high temperature."* She was forced to stay home only a few days before the opening in Brighton. Saunders in his autobiography claimed to have spoken to his own specialist about Flora's ankle condition. His diagnosis, without examination, was that the condition had probably been brought on by nerves and, depending on the person, might last two days or two months. Flora's understudy was warned that she should stand by for the opening and Saunders visited Flora at home. He asked when she thought she would be able to begin rehearsals again and she replied that she might be fit in two weeks. He explained that the 'might' was worrying from his point of view. Flora asked him if he wanted her to give up the part. To her great relief he said that he did. Constance Cummings was rehearsed into the role taking over on the last week of the tour. The play opened to indifferent reviews and had only a short run. The two-month illness diagnosed by Saunders's doctor was to trouble Flora for more than fourteen years in varying degrees before she found a drug which would control it.

Robert Bolt had written a new version of his play *The Critic and the Heart*, his first to be professionally produced. *Brother and Sister* opened with the death off-stage of William Brazier, a painter of genius. Flora was offered the part of Winifred Brazier, his sister, who through her life had nourished her brother's creativity. Nigel Stock was in the cast. He had first met Flora at the Old Vic when he was eleven years old, playing Macduff's son. He recalled watching her from the wings with great awe, and her kindness to him at the time. The tour of *Brother and Sister* opened at the Royal Court, Liverpool. Whenever she worked in Liverpool she would stay with Mrs Dorothy Kelly, whom she thought the most wonderful landlady. Her home was very down-to-earth and like all actors who stayed there she knew Mrs Kelly as Dot. Mrs Kelly still called her Flo.

"Flora Robson is such a marvel at getting across hidden frustrations and wracked suffering that only she, with the exception of Peggy Ashcroft, could have got this character, and indeed the play itself, such hushed attention," the correspondent of the *Morning Telegraph* reported back to New York. "The curtain rises to find Flora Robson, alone on the stage, torn by hysterical tears. That we of the audience readily accept that she has been sobbing for hours is, in technique alone, a feat of acting. The weakness of Bolt's treatment of his story is that the other characters do not come alive. If the play finds favour it will be Flora Robson's personal triumph. A great actress to the rescue." It was not destined to be seen in the West End. "*Robert Bolt took the play off himself. It was misdirected. My character had had an awful life overshadowed by a dreadful brother. The way I was directed made her appear tedious. I believe I could have made it another* Aspern

Papers *but I was not allowed to play her sympathetically. I was sorry for I felt it was a good play which deserved to be seen. I wish I was the sort of person to have had the courage to walk out – but that is so much against my nature. I defended the other actors but never myself."*

Before working on the Bolt play Flora had accepted an invitation from George Rylands to appear in the inaugural recital in the Purcell Room on London's South Bank. "She read quite perfectly," Rylands recalled, "in all kinds – the noble, the witty, the rhetorical." During the tour Marjorie Westbury read on the radio a story called 'Eyes Down' which Flora had written. Towards the end of 1967 Flora was accorded a great honour by the BBC when an entire season of plays was transmitted on the radio under the banner of the Flora Robson Festival. Flora was able to choose seven plays which would be newly recorded. She chose to play Sister Agatha in *The Return, Mary Tudor*, Alicia Christie in *Black Chiffon*, Mrs Malaprop in *The Rivals*, Olwen Peel in *Dangerous Corner*, and Sister Bonaventure in *Bonaventure* by Charlotte Hastings. She said she would like to do a play about Queen Elizabeth I. Alison Plowden wrote *Sweet England's Pride*, a play about Elizabeth and Essex, especially for her. By the time she recorded this play, Flora was delighting audiences with the last great triumph of her theatrical career.

## 6

"Dame Flora instantly reminds us how much we've missed her by showing what a fine comedy actress she is," proclaimed Peter Lewis in the *Daily Mail*. "The lilt of her head movements, the pause of her ungainly body, speak volumes of anguished spinsterhood – the kind that wrote a three-volume novel in younger days." Eric Shorter in the *Daily Telegraph* added, "Those members of the company of *The Importance of Being Earnest* who take it seriously emerge with the best effect. Chief among these undoubtedly is the delicious Flora Robson, whose acting as Miss Prism is a model which will fix the role for future generations as Edith Evans once fixed Lady Bracknell."

"*Binkie Beaumont begged me to play the part. I wasn't too keen as it meant giving up star-billing. Miss Prism is one of the smallest parts in the play. He continued to try to persuade me and I asked him who was to play Canon Chasuble. He said they were trying to get Robert Eddison. I said, 'Right, if you get Robert I'll play it.' I knew that my only chance of success was to play her seriously, tragically even. I knew that Robert would want to do it this way too because we had played together all those years before at Cambridge. It was my fourth attempt at the play. Miss Prism suited me much better than had Gwendolen or Lady Bracknell, because she was unsophisticated. I'm not very good at grand parts – only Queen Elizabeth,* but she had such wonderful language. I got laughs as Miss Prism from the first reading, and it was the same in front of an audience. I took it very seriously. When I said, 'Do not speak slightingly of the three-volume novel?' I added, 'I wrote one myself in earlier days' very nostalgically, as though it had been a masterpiece, though really it had been dreadful. In the following line – 'The good ended happily, and the bad unhappily. That is what Fiction means,' I got three *laughs in the one line!"*

Her approach to the role was an unusual one. Philip Hope-Wallace wrote of "the extraordinary strength in Dame Flora Robson's gently feminine Miss Prism, twice as effective as the 'battle axe' stereotype". Hamish Bell told me he rushed home to read the text to find out what liberties she had taken with her interpretation. Instead he found the character there in Wilde's original exactly as she had played it. This approach had never been previously perceived. Flora did with Miss Prism what she did with every role she played. She found the real woman.

"Dame Flora Robson sees Prism, Miss Laetitia Prism, as no-one else has done. She is not a comic governess any more than her Canon is a comic parson. Once she was sentimentally sweet enough to write a three-volume novel, and a three-volume novel she remains," claimed the *Illustrated London News*. "When Cecily says, 'How wonderfully clever of you!' Dame Flora looks proud, regretful and shy – an expression seen for half a second, that flashes by like an eloquent shadow." "With brilliant inspiration [Flora Robson and Robert Eddison] play as an elderly Héloise and Abelard," claimed Ronald Bryden in the *Observer*. "Gleaming at each other like pale-eyed impassioned old sheep, they languish and swoon in panting, tragic infatuation, separated by the Early Church's commands about celibacy. Beside their lust, the leads indeed seem trivial." "Flora Robson almost makes it Miss Prism's play," declared Helen Dawson in *Plays and Players*. "Stumbling with embarrassed gestures, grabbing back words she accidentally lets out, greeting her Reverend's every phrase as though it were a revelation. Her joy in the last act at retrieving her handbag is a high-point of stage ecstasy." J. C. Trewin added, in *The Lady*, "I would listen in enamoured silence if Dame Flora read aloud every word of her three-volume novel."

"Flora was filled with child-like glee at her wonderful notices," recalled Robert Eddison, "quite like a little girl!" "I think Flora's talent for comedy has been too little recognized," Sir John Gielgud wrote to me. "Her acting in *Captain Brassbound's Conversion*, Dodie Smith's *Touch Wood*, and as Miss Prism in an otherwise unsatisfactory revival of *The Importance of Being Earnest* were all brilliant and somewhat unexpected in an actress usually associated with tragic or dramatic roles." Her success in the part led her to accept another small comedy role in the next production at the Theatre Royal, Haymarket, as Isabelle's mother in a revival of Christopher Fry's adaptation of Anouilh's *Ring Round the Moon*. Once the play was in rehearsal she wondered if, in fact, she had been mistaken in taking the part. She was at odds with the director who had also directed her in *Brother and Sister*. After one miserable rehearsal she was heard to say, "Pick, pick, pick! He'll pick it till it bleeds!" In the event she again made a success. Sheridan Morley in the *Tatler* recorded, "Into a somewhat fey setting bursts Flora Robson like a minor whirlwind, playing the girl's mother to the hilt of her newly found career as a slightly zany comedienne." The correspondent for the *Illustrated London News* remarked that she "turns a relatively minor role into a glorious comic creation. The whole character is in the coy laugh that follows, 'I'm quick with my little romances, a big child really!'" Maureen O'Brien who was an enchanting Isabelle, recalled for me in a letter, "I was rather young at the time and very much awed by working with Flora. I remember her once ticking me off for running down from my dressing-room at the last moment before I was due to go on. She always stood in the wings for ages before her entrance, preparing. I liked to prepare in my dressing-room and didn't change my ways. She ticked me off very nicely. She might like to know that, nowadays, I stand, like her, for as long as I can in the wings, drinking in the rest of the play and the atmosphere of the audience, before I go on. She once told me how, when she was playing Miss Prism, the audience had uttered an actual 'aah' of sympathy and affection at a certain moment. This had utterly taken her aback. 'I know I have always been respected by my public,' she said, 'but I have never been loved.' I was astounded. It seemed a curiously sad remark from one of the most loved actresses of the century."

In the summer of 1969 she was given a film role which allowed her an enjoyable holiday in the sun. Her role in *Fragment of Fear* was no more than a fragment in itself, however. She was cast as Lucy Dawson, a sweet English woman, "played firmly in sensible shoes" as Penelope Houston put it in *The Listener*, who, within minutes of the commencement of the film, is found strangled in the ruins of Pompeii. The film details the search for her murderer by her nephew, played by David Hemmings. The audience never discovers the identity of the murderer though why she was killed becomes clearer by the end. *Variety* claimed of her performance that Flora is "often at her most devious when she's playing an apparently innocent role".

The previous year she had been seen on television as May Beringer in the Play of the Month presentation of Rodney Ackland's adaptation of Walpole's novel *The Old Ladies*. With her were two old friends,

Athene Seyler as Lucy Amorest and Katina Paxinou as the sinister gypsy-like figure, Agatha Payne. Both Miss Beringer and Mrs Payne have bed-sitting rooms in Miss Amorest's house. Miss Beringer lives in her sad and empty past, treasuring one precious memento, a piece of amber, which is coveted, with tragic consequences, by the greedy Agatha Payne. "*Paxinou was a wonderful actress. Her Elektra was the most exciting performance I have ever seen. No more than half a dozen people in the audience would have understood the Greek. After the recognition scene with Orestes, she uttered a terrible howl and flung herself round his neck and hung onto him. The entire gallery stood up and cheered. I've never heard such an ovation. She was really magnificent in those big parts, as was Sybil Thorndike. I think she rather overplayed the part in* The Old Ladies, *she was too big for it.*" Sylvia Clayton remarked in *The Daily Telegraph*, "The play offered three bravura parts for elderly actresses. Flora Robson, who could, I felt, have played any one of them, caught the profound loneliness and irritating effusiveness of the spinster." Flora told the Press that she hoped to be able to play both the other roles on future occasions. Perhaps as a result of this, she was offered the role of Agatha Payne in a revival which would begin a short tour at the Yvonne Arnaud Theatre in Guildford before going into the West End. She had not liked the way the role had been played by Edith Evans in the original production, or by Paxinou on television, and accepted the challenge.

"*It's a very unhappy play to be in. The actors always seem to fall foul of each other. Somehow everyone ends up acting against each other. When we were out on tour it was reported back to the management, 'They are all fighting one another and the play isn't getting anywhere.' Miss Beringer always runs away with the play. I think I did in the television version and Joyce Carey did on the stage.*" "As the alarming Agatha, . . . is a somewhat subdued Flora Robson," wrote John Barber in *The Daily Telegraph*. "Dame Flora has silences that are sometimes glum rather than sinister and the savagery she is always threatening never quite comes to the boil. I did not quite catch from her the obscene, greasy slobbering creation in the Hugh Walpole novel on which the play is based." Many of the Press found her too subdued though Harold Hobson in *The Sunday Times* observed in her playing the characteristic of her art as an actress: "She convinces us that Agatha Payne is a real woman, a bit fonder than most of garish hats and cheap jewellery, but fundamentally human . . . she scared me more than any of her predecessors."

No praise that she received was any comfort to Flora. She knew she had failed and was giving a poor performance, far below the standard she had always tried to maintain. Ironically *The Old Ladies* was playing in the theatre which had been the scene of her first triumph. The ghost of Mary Paterson haunted her round every corner of the Westminster Theatre. The contrast between then and now was too painful to consider.

A new resolution occupied her mind. The time had come for her to retire. As soon as she had made the decision it was as though a great weight had dropped from her. She had more than fulfilled any promise she had made or responsibility she felt for her public as an actress. It was fifty years since she had begun her studies at the Academy. The struggle for suitable roles and the anxiety over keeping herself fit for strenuous runs had worn her down. She was tired. "*There had been one major precedent. Shakespeare retired from the theatre. I decided I should go too.*"

It was the end of an era in theatrical history. A whole generation of theatre-goers have never seen Flora on stage. Her name is part of history, and one with Sybil Thorndike, Edith Evans, Ellen Terry even, though Flora is still alive. To theatre-goers who can remember her performances her career is difficult to categorize. She had begun as the avant-garde actress of her generation. In the years when she should have been playing one classical role after another, following the pattern of other actresses of her stature, she was seen only in mediocre thrillers. As an actress in the commercial theatre she brought greater depth and presence to her portrayals than the writing warranted because of her background in experimental and classical theatre. Perhaps it is futile even to attempt to categorize her. In all she did, her work was highly individual and her career followed a unique course. Laurence Olivier wrote to me, "The whole festival of talents that has always been in Flora caught one in an always surprised, utterly real way. The combination of her voice, looks, personality and sheer acting genius, once seen, haunts one forever."

# 7

# Lady in Retirement
## 1970–1981

### 1

CAN YOU PICTURE Flora as she makes her way down the Brighton street? She is no longer as tall as she was. To her surprise she is quite two inches shorter. But she still walks erect, with brisk purpose. There was an occasion a few years ago, when she was a mere seventy-five, when she and I were to recite poetry for victims of rheumatoid arthritis, a task she faithfully performs three times a year. It was a lovely day and we decided to walk the mile or two to the church where we thought the recital was to be given. To our surprise, the church was deserted. There was no sign of the coaches and wheelchairs and the dozens of cheerful helpers. Flora suddenly remembered the venue had been changed to a hall we had passed a mile or so back, and there was only about five minutes to go before we were due to start! We began to run back along the way we had come, each of us overcome by the terror of the professional actor of not being at the theatre by curtain rise. I tried to thumb a lift as we hurried along. Eventually a car with two youths in the front drew up and Flora and I piled in the back. "I've never done this before," she said, "I'm so grateful to you. If ever you need anything – help of any kind, just write to me. My name is Flora Robson." We drew up in front of Hove Town Hall and Flora and I disembarked, she, all the time, profusely thanking both young men who were overawed by their surprise passenger. Moments later we were dashing down corridors and straight on to the platform amid loud and welcoming applause. I was short of breath but Flora with ease and assurance immediately stepped forward, her breath

## LADY IN RETIREMENT

perfectly controlled. Her voice calm and gentle and incredibly youthful, she began to read the first poem.

As she walks along, few people recognize her. Those who do may nudge a friend and smile but seldom will anyone disturb her. She is the unofficial first lady of Brighton and everyone respects her privacy. One day a little old lady reached out a hand to touch Flora, quite gently, as she passed. The woman drew away, overcome by a kind of religious ecstasy. Flora may stop and talk to a small child. Children will always talk to her for she is never patronizing and inspires their complete trust. Their faces take on a special quality. Children are so seldom treated as human beings. Years ago she stayed with her friend, the distinguished American actress, Helen Hayes. Miss Hayes and her husband Charles MacArthur had adopted a little boy. Jim, as James MacArthur is known to his family, was very shy when a child and hid from strangers. Flora didn't make the fuss of him that others had but waited until he was ready to come to her. She was the first stranger with whom he made contact, sharing with her a precious toy. She might pause and talk to a friendly dog and regret the fact that she no longer has a pet of her own. There had always been a dog in Flora's life, but the loss of Jackie, her dearest pet, some years ago, filled her with such sadness she decided it would be the last. Several times Jackie has come to her in a dream and sits up smiling as she always did. "I know she is trying to tell me how wonderful it is in heaven," Flora told me.

On her way perhaps she will stop and talk to the workmen in the road, or shopgirls, or anyone who looks lonely. One Christmas she saw a group of derelicts sitting by the roadside and asked them to join her for a drink. The landlord of the public house she took them to refused to serve them. Flora emerged with several flagons of cider and the party was held outside.

Her retirement from the stage has held good. "*I am no longer very interested in the theatre. I much prefer to listen to music than go to the theatre. I have a season ticket for the Brighton Philharmonic and I look forward to their concerts more than anything else. In church I am very easily distracted. Because I am an actress I am always watching people and storing things up in case they will be useful. But when the music starts I am drawn away and my thoughts are lifted up to God.*" Flora's interest in helping young people, together with her new interest in music, has led to a rewarding involvement with the Brighton Youth Orchestra. This began when she was approached by conductor David Gray to act as the narrator in a performance of *Peter and the Wolf* at the Brighton Festival. "She responded readily to the enthusiasm of the youngsters and the dedication of those who worked with them," Gray wrote to me. "She recognizes the value of regular work sessions, the value of the chance for them to play in big concerts, of their experience of visiting other countries on concert tours and perhaps, above all, the value of shared spiritual, musical experience for these youngsters who come from every conceivable kind of background. In spite of her modest demeanour she is quite one of the most charismatic personalities I have ever known. When you walk on a stage before an audience with her the applause has a different quality of sound from that which I have heard with any other international celebrity I have worked with. There is not the usual *sforzando* start, followed by a *decrescendo* – the applause is just a sustained *forte* throughout. I can only interpret this as a feeling audiences have for her of great respect and love. She seems to exude an almost saintly and mysterious aura when she is performing. This seems to intrigue audiences. I think they feel she has an understanding of life which she wants to share with them." Flora works with the orchestra whenever she is able and, in an effort to raise funds for a foreign tour, recorded *Peter and the Wolf* and *Carnival of the Animals* with them. In addition, privately, and with no publicity, she herself financed the cost of sending members of the orchestra abroad, who otherwise would have been unable to go.

She has supported the efforts of an organization to open a new Arts Centre in the Old Market in Brighton as well as helping with amateur dramatic companies. On one occasion the Brighton Theatre Group presented *Lady Audley's Secret* and Flora honoured them by directing it. She befriended Pauline Richardson, a former nurse, who had suffered injuries to her spine. Doctors had advised her to live with her disability. With Flora's help and encouragement she enrolled for an Open University course. Her success in this opened up a new world for her in her sixties. Miss Richardson has written many fine poems which Flora uses in her recitals. Flora was able to help her publish a book of her poetry.

There is always work to be done for the many charities which interest her. The Council for the Single Woman and her Dependants, Hamilton Lodge School for the Deaf, the King George's Pension Fund for Retired Actors, the Evelyn Norris Home for Retired Actors in Worthing, and the Chalfont Centre for Epilepsy are those she considers her special charities. Flora holds the record for the greatest amount of money to be achieved by an appeal on the radio. A cheque for two thousand pounds appeared in her mail one morning months after the relevant appeal. The donor had heard her in a radio play and the cheque was a tribute to her performance. She performs every duty with enthusiasm and interest, yet her energy isn't boundless. Illness after illness is worsened because she refuses to cut down on her engagements, and organizers over-exploit her good-heartedness.

## LADY IN RETIREMENT

She looks with despair at the pile of letters she receives every day, the majority of which call for a personal reply. Her calendar is an almost illegible mass of appointments. Sometimes she feels she is unable to cope with it all. But to anyone who suggests she give up her public life she counters, "The Queen made me a Dame. I must prove myself worthy of it."

### 2

Although *The Old Ladies* was her last West End appearance she worked once more in a play on the stage. "I had a serious illness when I was sixty-nine," recalled John Counsell. "My chairman suggested that perhaps I should think of retiring from the Theatre Royal at Windsor when I was seventy. It so happened that when I was coming up to my seventieth birthday we had had seventy-eight weeks without losing on a single production, our longest run. I thought then that I didn't really need to resign. Everything seemed to be going all right! I decided that it would be rather fun to be seen in action on my seventieth birthday and chose to play Chasuble in *The Importance of Being Earnest*. My wife (Mary Kerridge) would play Lady Bracknell and my daughter Elizabeth would play Gwendolen. I was talking to Peggy MacGregor, Hector's widow, who still works in the box-office. 'What's Flora doing?' They are great friends, you see. She said, 'She's retired now.' 'Could you sound her out?' I said, 'and see if she would play Prism.' To cut a long story short, she agreed. 'There are three love stories in the play,' she said, 'the two between the young ones and that between Chasuble and Prism. Can you conceive of being passionately in love with me?' I said, 'My dear Flora I have been passionately in love with you ever since I was a student and first saw you at Oxford in 1923!' Her conception of the role is totally idiosyncratic. Marvellous laughs coming in places you've never seen simply because Chasuble and Prism are played as two sincere people. This was supposed to be my swan-song. What prouder way could there be for me to retire than playing opposite the great Flora Robson?" The play was directed by Joan Riley, who had appeared in the children's plays Flora had directed at Welwyn in the early twenties. Although she enjoyed being back in Windsor with her old friends, Flora was unhappy about her performance. She was insecure in her dialogue and would check and re-check her words before the curtain rose. It had been five years since she had appeared in a play and she felt she was losing her nerve. She resolved that this would be her final appearance. It was not to be John Counsell's last. To this day the director of the Theatre Royal, he occasionally appears in plays as well.

# FLORA

There has been plenty of work for Flora in films, television and radio. Shortly after *The Old Ladies* she had gone on location to Cyprus to film *The Beloved*. It was never released in the cinema, perhaps because her co-star, Raquel Welch, gave an acting performance of a quality which might have jeopardized her career as a vacuous sex-symbol. Flora was distressed at the change she found in Jack Hawkins, who was also in the film, due to the throat operation which had robbed him of his voice. It was the last time they would work together. The film was eventually released as a video feature with a new title designed to exploit its star – Raquel Welch in *Sin*. Flora co-starred with Beryl Reid in the film which aimed to do for the British cinema what the *Whatever Happened to Baby Jane* cycle of films had done for Hollywood and its ageing stars. *The Beast in the Cellar* was a poor film which wasted the talents of both its leading players. Eric Braun, in *Films and Filming*, wrote of Flora's "splendidly tragic muse's face and perhaps the most beautiful speaking voice on the English acting scene". There was a better role for her in *Alice's Adventures in Wonderland* in which she was cast as the Queen of Hearts. This star-studded treatment of the story drew directly from the Tenniel drawings and was visually exciting. Flora had a song, 'Off with Their Heads', which surprised those in her audience who had never heard her sing before. She chose to play the role as an old ham actress and is consequently very funny, sweeping round the sets, her voice thundering down to a resonant *basso* as she orders execution after execution. She went to Italy to make *La Grande Scrofa Nera*, also known as *Comedy and Tragedy and All That*. Filmed with an international cast, it was intended to be dubbed in several languages. Flora found the filming extremely difficult. The sound quality was totally unimportant so the technicians would call out to one another whilst the action was being shot. She found it impossible to concentrate. The film vanished without trace before its release.

The seventies saw the advent of all-star cast movies made especially for television. Flora worked on five of these. In *The Canterville Ghost* she played Mrs Umney to David Niven's Ghost, with Maurice Evans as Lord Canterville also in the cast. Niven was also in the cast of *A Man Called Intrepid* based on the best-selling book. She played a nun, Sister Luke, who aided the heroine against the Nazis and distinguished a few otherwise bare moments in a tedious teleplay. She wore the same pair of shoes as the Prioress in *Les Misérables*, a well-made version of the classic Victor Hugo novel. Flora brought warmth and sweetness to the otherwise grim tale. She was asked to play the madame of a brothel in *Gauguin the Savage*. Although she had played prostitutes early in her career she wondered whether there was anything to be gained from playing such a role at this stage. A glance at the script made up her mind. There was nothing for her to act and she turned the part down. Shortly afterwards, the company came back with another offer. She was asked to play a nun yet again. She promptly agreed to do it when she heard it would be filmed on location in Tahiti. She enjoyed working with David Carradine, who was cast as Gauguin. For the first time she understood that so-called 'method' acting was little different from the 'giving and receiving' principle she had always practised. Carradine was wonderful to act with. She could see the thought in his eyes. Their scene together was one of the highlights of an otherwise patchy film. In 1980 she was cast as Miss Pross in *A Tale of Two Cities*. She relished the scene in which she had to fight Madame Defarge, who was played by Billie Whitelaw. "I am an Englishwoman," Miss Pross had to announce. It was a delightful film to make. As when she played Miss Prism for the first time, everyone laughed at virtually all her lines, though she was often unable to see the joke herself. I visited the set at Shepperton. "I would *pay* to work with Dame Flora," her dresser told me, "She is such a wonderful old trouper." Someone else on the set said, "Young actresses should be made to watch her. They would learn their craft that way." Handicapped by execrable dialogue, she played the housekeeper in *Dominique*, a thriller for the cinema, with Jean Simmons and Cliff Robertson. For her fiftieth film she played one of the three Stygian witches with one eye between them in the spectacular MGM film *Clash of the Titans* which also starred Laurence Olivier.

Comedian Ernie Wise wrote to me, "Eric Morecambe and I first met Dame Flora when she was touring (in *No Escape*). The landlady used to split the house in two, variety on one side and legitimate on the other. Although it was frowned on for one side to meet the other, Dame Flora used to come and talk to us about variety. One night after her show she came to see us at the theatre where we were appearing, and watched our act. We have been friends ever since. When we come to Brighton she always comes and sees us. Little did we realize, all those years ago, that one day she would be a guest on our show. I am very proud to know her." Flora appeared with Morecambe and Wise on one of their television shows, first of all in a sketch, as herself, and then in one of Ernie Wise's little playlets in which she played Queen Elizabeth I, with Eric as Shakespeare and Ernie as Walter Raleigh. She played the blind grandmother in a serialization of Johanna Spyri's *Heidi*, winning a new audience. To her delight, little children recognized her in the street. Maureen O'Brien, Diana Rigg and Billie Whitelaw were among her co-stars when she appeared in *The Serpent Son*, a television treatment of the *Oresteia* of Aeschylus. "Apart from being a very dear woman," Diana Rigg wrote to me, "she is also a marvellous actress in that she commits herself absolutely to whatever she is doing." "It was ten years since *Ring Round the Moon*," wrote Maureen O'Brien. "My best moments were watching her work, and, almost better, watching the younger actresses, to whom she was a sort of myth in herself, watching her. They couldn't believe how wonderful she was, how she made you cry and then laugh, moving so effortlessly from tragedy to pathos to comedy sometimes in the space of only one line, never losing the rhythm of the speech. She complained of difficulty in learning her lines and invented small actions for her character to make – such as clasping her hands together at certain moments – as a sort of mnemonic for reminding her of the next word. She was very funny about it, but it also distressed her not to be able to remember as she used."

She has continued to broadcast occasionally. Charlotte Hastings has written a series of radio plays especially for her. There are always many letters of appreciation from older listeners who have few pleasures other than their radios. In 1976 she finally played Mrs Danvers in a radio adaptation of *Rebecca*.

Perhaps the single great success of her retirement years was as Miss Fothergill in the television adaptation of L. P. Hartley's *The Shrimp and the Anemone*, which formed the first part of the *Eustace and Hilda* trilogy. John Whitehead has been a friend ever since *The Anatomist*, in which he had appeared as one of the students. He had left the stage to run a pharmacy. When he retired he came to live in Brighton and was able to help Flora with this role. As a boy he had known Hartley, and was able to tell her all about the characters that peopled his novels. Miss Fothergill had been a real person, known by a different name, and Flora found the background information most useful in creating her character. *Eustace and Hilda* opens with the two children, brother and sister, trying to save a half-eaten shrimp from a sea anemone. Their own relationship is symbolized – she the beautiful, possessive anemone, he the self-sacrificing shrimp. The boy Eustace meets an invalid lady in a thick, dark veil, being pushed in her wheelchair along the cliffs by her companion. She is a nightmare figure with half her face hideously disfigured. Eventually he befriends her. She dies and leaves him the fortune which starts him off in life. Many actors avoid working with children, notorious as they are for stealing scenes. Flora enjoys every opportunity of working with youngsters. Perhaps she recalls in them her own beginnings. She welcomes their straightforward approach to acting. Her approach has always been the same. The scenes between her and Grant Bardsley, who played Eustace, were deeply touching. "Grant Bardsley . . . not only looked as Hartley himself must have looked in childhood – well-scrubbed, anxious and faintly floppy – but was genuinely eccentric in his own right," claimed Michael Ratcliffe in *The Times*. "Indignant, stubborn, giggly, querulous, savage or adoring: one could never be quite sure what this old-fashioned child would say or do next, and watching to find out became one of the two chief pleasures of the production . . . Everyone was well cast but the other great delight was provided by Flora Robson as the boy's benefactress, Miss Fothergill. Why don't we see her more often? Few stage actresses have ever understood the needs of the small screen so serenely or so well." Director Desmond Davis won an award at the Monte Carlo International Television Festival for this episode. Flora was an official guest at the Festival, where she was entertained by Prince Rainier and Princess Grace. Her badge of identification gave her as being *Mme Flora Robson, Comédienne*. If there was one thing she had never considered herself to be it was a comedienne in the English sense! Her performance was voted to be the best by an actress in the Festival yet the International Jury was split on whether to give her the Best Acting Award. Several jurors felt the part was too small and she lost the award. All good actors know there is no such thing as a small part. When a performance is as rich as Flora's was, the character is alive in all the moments we don't see. Flora basked in the praise and attention she received and the decision of the jury was felt by many to be poorly justified.

Among several offers of work in the theatre she was asked to play the housekeeper in a West End revival of *Rosmersholm*. "They think because I played Miss Prism that I will play any small part," she said at the time. "But how could I steal the play as the housekeeper?" She has always said that there was only one part which might tempt her back. That would be a good play about the aged Elizabeth I. Bette Davis, making a personal-appearance tour of Britain, visited the Theatre Royal at Brighton. "I believe there is another Queen Elizabeth in the audience," she said, and Flora was given an ovation.

At the end of 1978 Flora was invited by the Society of West End Managers to present one of their annual awards. When she stepped onto the platform she was given a tremendous reception. For a moment she looked quite overcome, before delivering a short, prepared speech. She paused and then said quite simply, "I had forgotten how lovely it is to be applauded." The hearts of all present went out to her and she was applauded to the echo.

3

To publicize the amateur production of *Lady Audley's Secret*, Flora made an appearance on a television magazine programme which went out to the southern region. One person who saw the programme

# FLORA

was Ernie Broadwood, her former boyfriend, whom she had not seen for fifty years. He wrote to her reminding her of their friendship. He had been married but his wife had died. Some months later a policeman came to Flora's door. Ernie had been found dead. The letter Flora had written him in reply was found in his pocket. He carried it with him wherever he went. Flora found out the time of the funeral and went to it. Walking along the path ahead of her was Ernie's brother who turned and recognized her. Gone were the antipathies of former times. They talked and laughed about the past and what might have been a sad occasion blossomed with joyous recollection.

If there is one thing Flora dislikes about being old it is losing all her friends. She lost another link with the days at Welwyn Garden City when Kath Hill died. Naturally Flora went to her funeral and, at the final moments of the committal, read a poem by John Donne. Whenever she is able, she attends the memorial services for distinguished members of her profession. At the service for Peter Daubeny, she was so impressed by the Zulu choir which sang a lament that she promptly took steps to adopt and support a Zulu child in Peter's memory. At a memorial service for actor Dennis Price she was delighted to run into the former Muriel Box, now married to Lord Gardiner. *"After the service we decided to go together for a cocktail at the Ritz. The waiters recognized both of us and made an enormous fuss. I was bubbling with merriment inside at their attention – 'My lady this, and my lady that' – and I rather think Muriel felt the same. Here we were, two distinguished ladies – she Lady Gardiner and me a Dame. We both wanted to laugh because we remembered the humble origins from which we had come."*

There are many occasions for looking back. The day before the fiftieth anniversary of the opening of the Oxford Playhouse the company presented a Golden Gala in celebration. Flora had been the first person to set foot on the stage of the original Playhouse building. She and Richard Goolden were the only actor-members of the original company still alive and they and John Gielgud, who had joined the company in its second term, took a bow together at the end of the evening's proceedings. Earlier, Flora had appeared in a scene from Act Two of *The Importance of Being Earnest* with Marius Goring and Jane Asher. The following year Flora was invited back to Oxford to receive an honorary degree at Oxford University. It was a day of great pride for her. "Oxford, and the honour, was marvellous," she wrote to me. "Starting at 10.30 a.m. at Jesus, with champagne and strawberries. It *poured* with rain so the procession through the streets was cut. Harold Macmillan is Chancellor and sat high on a throne in black and gold at the top of the stairs. He is almost blind, and read his Latin script with the paper covering his face. I thought as I couldn't see him that I was listening to God. I was cheered mightily. Lunch at All Souls. I had the seat of honour on the right of Macmillan with the French Ambassador on the other side. Macmillan entertained me with great charm. A garden party at Magdalen in heavy rain, so we were all under a marquee. Then a grand dinner, Gaudy night, at All Souls. I was the only woman with four hundred men so I was well-fed and given all the honours, and did not have to speak, or speechify, just enjoy it." She had not expected anything so wonderful as this honour. Some time later she entertained Helen Hayes to lunch at her home. I was present and felt privileged to be sitting at table with Queen Elizabeth I, Mary of Scotland, Mary Tudor, Victoria Regina, the Dowager Empress of China, the Dowager Empress of Russia, and two of the most charming women I have ever met. Each in her lifetime had been honoured by having a theatre named after her, as well as numerous other honours. Flora spoke with great pride of her Oxford honour, adding, "It made me ambitious. If Cambridge were to honour me too, I would die a happy woman."

Marius Goring joined her again, this time with Anna Carteret, in a scene from *The Importance of Being Earnest* in a tribute to Lilian Baylis at the Old Vic. Backstage there was a dressing room marked 'Dames', for herself, Peggy Ashcroft, Edith Evans and Sybil Thorndike. Dame Peggy was repeating her notable impersonation of Lilian Baylis. Before the first act Dame Edith arrived with a crowd of admirers who took up most of the dressing-room space. Flora slipped out and joined Miss Carteret and some of the younger actresses in their dressing-room. Dame Edith went into the auditorium at the interval with her party and Flora returned. By now her beloved Sybil had arrived. She was stricken with arthritis and her daughter had to push her in her chair to the wings. Dame Sybil insisted on walking onto the stage with her walking stick. When she returned to the wings she was in agony. The applause was wonderful and the audience called for her to return. Flora admired the courage it took her to walk out on-stage again.

Shortly after her retirement Tony Guthrie and Judy were visiting Brighton. Flora joined them for lunch. *"We talked of this and that. It was good to see them both again. We talked about nothing special as I recall. After lunch we said goodbye in the open air. I walked away from them and for some reason I turned to look back. Tony was still standing there looking at me, watching me go. It was an oddly moving moment and it was the last time I saw him."* A month later Tony died at Annagh-ma-Kerrig on his mother's birthday. There was a tribute to him on television which Flora watched alone. Someone said that the only thing Tony had missed out of life was having a son. So many years before, Flora had wanted nothing more than to give him a family. This news nearly broke her heart.

## 4

Flora had moved from Mount Fort when the builders began encroaching on what had been a perfect view. She had lived for a short time in London but had moved to Brighton when she found a pleasant little house in Marine Gardens. It was a long, narrow house in a quiet lane. She was able to build a small room on the roof which became known as the Lighthouse. Originally this room was intended to house her piano, which she had been forced to leave behind in London. It proved impossible to haul the piano up there and so the Lighthouse became a welcome haven for visitors, myself included. There was a view of the sea and a little patio crowded with potted geraniums. Flora lived here alone until, upon the death of her husband, her sister Shela came to live with her. Badly affected by her bereavement, Shela had lost her memory and Flora was content to take her turn in caring for her family. *"All my life I have merely been the person to provide money. It had been up to the others to nurse the sick and watch as our elderly relatives died. I had been too busy with my career. Now I am able to be a proper member of the family."* Apart from taking care of Shela, Flora pays a small pension to her former dresser. Flora regards this as her personal responsibility. It is this kind of unique generosity that makes her as much loved for her private as she is for her public self.

The years at Marine Gardens were marred only by one unhappy incident when she was burgled of all her most treasured possessions. Among these was a Regency silver inkstand which had belonged to Ellen Terry. Apart from Dame Ellen's name, it was engraved with the names of all its subsequent owners. Margaret Irwin had presented it to Dame Irene Vanbrugh, and Sir Kenneth Barnes had presented it to Flora. She had planned to pass it on to Gemma Jones, an actress she very much admires. The theft of this piece was pointless as its easy identification means it was virtually impossible to sell and its melted-down value would be negligible.

Her two other surviving sisters, Lila and Margaret, shared a house together in Hove. After Lila's death, Margaret, Flora and Shela found a house where all of them could live together, part of a Victorian Gothic terrace near the centre of Brighton. The house had originally been built as a 'home for reformed prostitutes'. "An actress come full circle," Flora told the Press to the horror of some of her smart friends! The house is now a home-from-home, as Mount Fort had been, for all thirty-one Robson descendants. Flora delights in bringing together all the branches of the family so they can get to know one another and keep the Robson spirit alive.

Flora has never had perfect health and during the last few years she has had more than her fair share of illness. She was eventually successful in giving up smoking. Ironically it was shortly afterwards that she developed the bronchial condition which has tormented her ever since. Whenever she is able she gets to the sun. She goes to the Isles of Scilly, where she still has old friends. A feature of her stay is reading poetry in St Mary's Church. *"The Scilly Islanders work so hard to make sure people enjoy themselves. My poetry reading is my way of thanking them."* Not long ago she was taken to Montserrat in the West Indies. She listened with interest to everything she was told by the islanders. Their economic survival depends on their ability to export their goods. All the major shipping lines had abandoned the route which had included them. On her return Flora contacted a firm which she knew operated a line of smaller craft, hoping to arrange for a boat to make regular visits to the island. She was disturbed that poor parents leave their babies strapped under their houses with the pigs, when they go to work. She is making every effort to have a pre-school child care clinic opened on the island. There is much in her past which she loves and enjoys celebrating but her interest is still firmly fixed on the future and what projects she can give her attention to. She works far too hard but as long as she continues to move forward she will not grow old.

A long-held ambition was realized when she visited the Holy Land on a pilgrimage with several other Sussex people. Later, on the television programme 'Songs of Praise' she was asked to choose a hymn. She chose 'Dear Lord and Father of Mankind'. She had always loved the music. In explaining her choice she recalled the loveliest day of her visit to the Holy Land. *"It was so simple and so real. We had communion on the shores of Lake Galilee, just a plain table, and I was honoured by being asked to read a lesson. As we read and sang, all the trees, the big bamboos hung over and listened to us. I always think old trees listen. They're so old and wise. And a lovely white dove flew over Canon Hester's head, and the little fishes, St Peter's fishes, plop, plop, plop, plop, plop . . . everyone was listening to us there very quietly. When I looked at the hymn I found in the third verse, 'O Sabbath rest by Galilee, O calm of hills above, Where Jesus knelt to share with thee, The silence of eternity, Interpreted by love.' It's all there . . ."*

Once again she was able to visit Leonard Schach, who was now living and working in Tel Aviv. "She gave a recital for us," he recalled. "She felt she couldn't cope with a whole evening on her own and so I got a harpist friend to share the programme. I invited our great actress, Rovina. She was the only person alive who had actually worked with Stanislavsky. She was the equivalent of Flora, with a glorious voice, tall, straight as a die, impeccably dressed with a great, great personality and revered by everyone. She arrived looking magnificent in a white trouser-suit and I invited her to meet Flora backstage afterwards. The meeting was rather like the one between Livingstone and Stanley. I was holding a party for Flora at home afterwards but couldn't invite Rovina as there are eighty-one steps to my home and she was unable to cope with them. The British Ambassador was at the party to meet Flora. She was in her element and having a marvellous time. About twelve o'clock, Rovina appeared at the house. 'I went home,' she said, 'and I could not forget this wonderful performance.' She had got some people to carry her down to my house. This caused an absolute sensation, of course. In appreciation for what Flora had given her that evening, she presented her with a little book of psalms which Stanislavsky had given her in 1917."

How does Flora spend her days? She does her share of housework and takes her turn in looking after Shela. The mornings are set aside for tackling her mountain of correspondence. She dreads the pile of letters each morning, only enjoying the ones which specify that no reply is necessary. She very much enjoys cooking. When she lived in Hollywood she couldn't boil an egg and would ask David Kidd round to cook for her. Now she is a superb cook, always experimenting with new recipes. She specializes in delicious soups and sauces. She will look in on old friends. Perhaps an old people's home will ask her for tea. "They're all younger than me, you know," she told me once. There is a constant stream of visitors and she chats to them. Margaret does her jigsaw puzzles and Flora is still knitting socks.

One day I sorted out her collection of photographs. I sat in the kitchen and spread them all on the large refectory table, sorting them into different piles. There were photographs of her with Flynn and Muni, with Paul Robeson, Laurence Olivier and Tony Guthrie. There were old studio portraits of Flora trying to look beautiful, trying to look tempestuous, trying to look dramatic. There were Miss Tina and Miss Prism, Queen Elizabeth and Mary Paterson. There were bad memories of Oscar Homolka and cherished ones of Robert Donat; piles of photographs of Flora with children, Flora with dogs. There was the huge photograph of Gary Cooper, "I promised you a snap-shot and here it is," and one of a lovely young actress signed with affection from 'Bidsie'. There were shots of Flora standing in one of her kitchens, sitting in one of her houses playing the piano, sipping a cold drink through a straw at a rehearsal at the Sadler's Wells Theatre in 1933. There was one of a tiny girl with Flora's

## LADY IN RETIREMENT

unmistakable eyes, a picture of Uncle John, a portrait of her father. There was a photograph taken after she was awarded the C.B.E., one taken of her standing outside the Palace after she was made a Dame, and one of her at Oxford University in a rain-spotted gown. Whilst I was busily working my way through yet another envelope of such treasures, Flora wandered by the table intent on some other purpose. She stopped for a moment, her attention caught by a photograph on top of one of the piles. I think it was the pile I had designated, 'Flora addressing public meetings'. She picked up the photograph. "This was in America," she said. "it was an open-air rally in Providence, New Jersey, I think. I was speaking about the friendship of the United Nations. There were over five thousand people in the audience." She paused for a moment, still staring at the photograph, and added, in a voice somewhere between bewilderment and awe, more to herself than to me, "The things I've done in my life . . .".

# Awards and Honours

*Honours*

Awarded – The Finnish Order of the White Lion and the White Rose for Services to Humanity – 1949
Created – Commander of the British Empire – 1952
Created – Dame Commander of the British Empire – 1960
Hon. D. Litt. University of London
Hon. D. Litt. University of Wales
Hon. D. Litt. University of Durham
Hon. D. Litt. University of Oxford
Hon. Fellow St. Anne's College, Oxford
Hon. Fellow Sunderland Polytechnic

*Acting Awards*

Royal Academy of Music – Verse Speaking Competition (1912) – Bronze Medal
Royal Academy of Dramatic Art – Bronze Medal (1921)
Film Weekly – Best Actress in a British Film (1937) – for *Fire Over England*
Evening News – Third Best Actress in International Films (1938) – for *Farewell Again*
National Board of Review (US) – Best Acting Category (1939) – Voted into the Top Ten for *We are not Alone*
Nominated for an Academy of Motion Picture Arts and Sciences Award (The Oscar) 1946, for her performance in *Saratoga Trunk*
News Chronicle Award – Best Television Actress (1956) – for *The Corn is Green*
News Chronicle Award – Best Television Actress (1957) – for *Message for Margaret*
Evening Standard Award – Best Actress of the Year (1960) – for Miss Tina in *The Aspern Papers*
Cleveland (US) Critics' Circle Award (1964) – for *Guns at Batasi*
Voted Best Actress at the Monte Carlo Television Festival (1978) – for *The Shrimp and the Anemone*. No award was made.

# Index

The following abbreviations are used:

| | | | |
|---|---|---|---|
| BG | Ben Greet's Pastoral Players | TCF | Twentieth Century Fox |
| CFT | Cambridge Festival Theatre | TRH | Theatre Royal Haymarket |
| FRP | Flora Robson Playhouse | TRW | Theatre Royal Windsor |
| MGM | Metro-Goldwyn-Mayer | TV | Television |
| OVC | Old Vic Company | UA | United Artists |
| OXP | Oxford Playhouse | WB | Warner Brothers |
| RA | Radio | WMT | Westminster Theatre |
| RADA | Royal Academy of Dramatic Art | | |

Page numbers in italics indicate the use of a direct quote from interview, correspondence or writings.

The dates listed indicate first-nights in the case of plays, release dates in the case of films, and broadcast dates in the case of radio and television. Where possible the length of the run of each play is listed, with the exception of the following:

> Oxford Playhouse, one week's run for every play
> Cambridge Festival Theatre, one week's run for every play
> Old Vic Company, 1933–1934, four weeks' run divided between Old Vic Theatre and Sadler's Wells Theatre

Abbott, John, xi, 116, 146, 206
Academy of Dramatic Art (see Royal Academy of Dramatic Art)
Academy of Motion Picture Arts and Sciences Awards (Oscars), 82, 122, 125, 131, 145, 148, 149, 155, 160, 166, 232
Ackland, Rodney, 215–16
Adam, Ronald, 79–80, 99
Addinsell, Richard, 106
Aeschylus, 223

Agate, James, xiii, *2, 56–7, 63, 69, 74, 85–6, 86, 88, 89, 92, 95, 97, 100, 110–11, 113*, 129, *133, 153,* 209
Ainley, Henry, x, 1, 2, 6, 62, 63, 64, 67, 105
Albanesi, Meggie, 16, 25
Albert, Eddie, 206
*Alice's Adventures in Wonderland* (film, TCF, 1972), 222
Allen, Jack, xi, 101, *161*
Allen, John, xii, 65

# INDEX

Allen, Percy, xii, *87*
Allenby, Frank, 110
*All for Love* (Dryden) (CFT 2.11.29), 45
*All God's Chillun Got Wings* (O'Neill) (Embassy 13.3.33; Piccadilly 10.4.33 7 weeks) 76-7, 78-80
Allgood, Sara, 58-9
Alvarez, A, *195*
Ambassador's Theatre, 33, 57
*Anatomist, The* (Bridie) (WMT 7.10.31 127 perfs), 1-3, 61-7, 170, 185, 192, 217, 224, 230
Anderson, Jean, 52
Anderson, John, *143*
Anderson, Dame Judith, 138, 168
Anderson, Marion, 53
Anderson, Maxwell, 141
*. . . and Humanity* (Draper) (TV, ATV, 5.3.58), 189
Andrews, Eamonn, 186, 199
Andreyev, Leonid, 53, 55
Ankers, Evelyn, 135
*Anna Christie*, (O'Neill) (WMT 7.4.37 5 weeks), 110-11
*Anne of England* (Ginsbury, ad. Canfield/Borden) (St James, NY, 7.10.41 7 perfs), 138-9, 166
Anouilh, Jean, 215
Archer, June, 187
Archibald, William, 177, 178
Arkell, Reginald, 161
Armstrong, William, 16, 157
Arts Theatre, 77, 138, 153
Arundell, Dennis, xi, 78, 85, 94, 101
Arts Council of Great Britain (formerly C.E.M.A.), 149, 153, 204, 208
Ashcroft, Dame Peggy, xi, *68*, 195, 212, 227
Asher, Jane, 226
Ashton, Sir Frederick, 61
Ashwell, Lena, 27
*Aspern Papers, The* (James, ad. Redgrave) (Queens, 12.8.59, 370 perfs), 193-7, *232*; (Tour, South Africa from 29.9.60), 198; and 199, 208, 212, 230
Asquith, Anthony, 60-61
Associated British Pictures, 117, 123, 186
Associated Television (ATV), 188-9
*As You Like It* (Shakespeare) (BG 1922), 21; and 45
Atkins, Robert, 16
Attenborough, Sir Richard, 205
Austin, Jerry, 147
*Autumn* (Surguchev, ad. Kennedy) (St Martin's 12.10.37, 161 perfs & tour), 112-15; (Tour from April 1951), 175; (TV, ATV 21.4.57), 186; and 116, 124, 171, 192, 203
Ayliff, H. K., 76
Aynesworth, Allan, 89

*Bahama Passage* (film, Paramount, 1942) 136-7, 138, 139
Balcon, Sir Michael, 162
Balsam, Martin, 166
Bancroft, Anne, 206-7
Banks, Leslie, 105, 108, 182
Bannerman, Kay, 153
Bannister, Trevor, xi, *203*
Barber, John, *216*
Bardsley, Grant, 224-5
Baring, Maurice, 40
Barnes, Howard, *137*, *148*, *168*
Barnes, Sir Kenneth, 12, 13, 15, 25, 58, 64, 228
Barnett, Lady (Isobel), 186
Barnstormers, The (Welwyn Garden City), 25, 36, 37
Barrie, Sir James M, 110
Barrow, Janet, *172*, 174, 175, 180
Barrymore, Ethel, 148
Bateson, Timothy, xi, *191*
Bax, Clifford, xii, xiii, *2*, 57, *62*

Baxter, Anne, 148
Baxter, Beverley, *172*
Baxter, Keith, xi, *200*
Baylis, Lilian, 16, 18, 82, 84-5, 88, 89, 92-3, 227, 235
*Beast in the Cellar, The* (film, Tigon-British, 1971) 222
Beatty, Robert, xi, 170, *196-7*, 198
Beaumont, Binkie, 177, 213
Beaumont, Hugh, 188-9
Belasco Theatre (Los Angeles), 148-9
Bell, Hamish, xi, 176, 214
Bell, Maud, 177
Bellamy, Cecil, 32
*Beloved, The* (film, Filmex, made 1971), 222
Benavente, Jacinto, 53
Benchley, Robert, 129
Benson, Sir Frank, 12, 13, 26, 46
Bergman, Ingrid, 145, 146, 188
Bergner, Elizabeth, xi, 83, 84
Bernhardt, Sarah, 76, 100, 114
Bertrand, Felix, 11, 96
Best, Edna, 129
*Bertrayal* (Andreyev) (a.k.a. *The Thought*) (CFT 25.10.30), 53; (Little 7.1.31. 5 weeks) 55-7
Biddle, Esme, 21-2
Bird, Richard, 71
*Black Chiffon* (Storm) (WMT 3.4.49 409 perfs) 172-3 (48th Street Theatre, NYC, Sept 1950) 174-5 (RA, BBC 17.2.68) 213; and 181, 184, 187
*Black Narcissus* (film, The Archers, 1947) 159-60, 164
Blair, Mary, 79
Blanchflower, Danny, 199
Blake, William, 201
Bogart, Humphrey, 127, 136
Boland, Bridget, 179
Bolt, Robert, 212-13
Bolton, Guy, 32, 33
*Bonaventure* (Hastings) (RA, BBC, 21.9.68), 213
Booth, D. H., 60
Borden, Ethel, 138-9
Box, Muriel, (see Lady Gardiner)
Box, Sydney, 37, 157, 163, 168, 186
Braddon, Angela, 49
Bradley, A.C., 90
Braun, Eric, *222*
Brecht, Bertolt, 191
Bridie, James (O. H. Mavor) xii, xiii, 1, *2*, *54*, 62, 72, *91-2*, 93-4, 95, 185, 192
Briggs, Hedley, 60
Brighton Hippodrome, 110
Brighton Philharmonic Orchestra, 219
Brighton Theatre Group, 220
Brighton Theatre Royal, 181, 191, 201, 225
Brighton Youth Orchestra, 219-20
Bristol Theatre Royal, 19-21
British Broadcasting Corporation, 32, 34, 40, 41, 50, 101, 124, 178, 179, 199, 208, 213, 215-16, 223-225
British Empire Shakespeare Society, 7, 64-5
British Instructional Films, 60
Britten, Sir Benjamin, 177
Britton, Tony, 183, 199
Broadwood, Ernie, 38, 129, 225-6
Bromfield, Louis, 129
Bronowski, Jacob, 44
Brontë, Emily, 122
Bronson, Arthur, *141*
Brook, Peter, xi, 175, *176*
*Brother and Sister* (Bolt) (Tour from 10.4.67) 212-213, 215
Brown, Ivor, *58*, *91*, *92*, *94*, *100-101*, *102*, *113*, *159*
Browne, Maurice, 53, 55-7
Bruce, Henry. J, 66

234

# INDEX

Bryan, Jane, xi, *126*, 127, 128
Bryant, Arthur, 101
Bryden, Ronald, *214*
Bucks County Playhouse (Philadelphia), 141
Buckton, Florence, 26, 29
Burrell, J. L. A., 33
Burton, Richard, 208

Cadell, Jean, 110
*Caesar and Cleopatra* (film, Rank, 1945), xii, 154–5, 157, 158
Cagney, James, 127
Calvert, Phyllis, 152
Cambridge Festival Theatre, 39–55, 58, 66, 67, 74, 82, 85, 98, 110, 123, 166, 213
Cambridge (Massachusetts) Summer Theatre, 141
Cambridge University, 227
Cameron, Audrey, xi, *33*
Canfield, Mary Cass, 138–9
*Canterville Ghost, The* (film, Butricia, 1975), 222
*Captain Brassbound's Conversion* (Shaw) (TRW July 1948) 169–70 (Lyric Hammersmith October 1948) 170–71; and 29, 214
Cardiff College of Music, 183, 200–201
Cardiff, Jack, xi, 160, 205
Carey, Joyce, xi, 216
'Carnival of the Animals' (Saint-Saëns), 220
Carradine, David, *223*
Carroll, Leo G, 121, 138
Carroll, Madeleine, 136
Carter, Charles, 110
Carteret, Anna, 227
Cartier, Rudolph, 191
Casson, Ann, 60
Casson, Christopher, 59
Casson, Sir Lewis, 59, 60, 175
Castellani, Renato, 179
*Catherine the Great, The Rise of* (film, London Films–UA, 1934) 83–4, 86, 203
Cavell, Edith, 188–9
Celli, Faith, 28–9
Chalfont Centre for Epilepsy, 220
Chekhov, Anton, 45, 50, 51, 85
Chekhov, Michael, 188
*Cherry Orchard, The* (Chekhov) (CFT, 10.5.30), 50; (OVC, 9.10.33), 85–6; and 111
Chester, Elsie, 11, 12
Christie, Dame Agatha, 204
Christie, Julie, 205
Clare, Mary, 17, 133
Clark, Petula, 102
*Clash of the Titans* (film, MGM 1981), 223
Clayton, Harold, 182
Clayton, Sylvia, *216*
Clements, Sir John, 55, 60
Cleveland (US) Critics' Circle, 205, 232
Clift, E.P., 171, *172*
Clive, Colin, 13
*Close Quarters* (Somin, ad. Lennox) (Embassy 26.6.35, TRH 17.7.35), 99–101; (Tour from 25.2.63), 203–4; and 191 (RA, BBC, 16.1.60)
Coleridge, Sylvia, xi, *185*, 186
*Comedy and Tragedy and All That* (La Grande Scrofa Nera) (film, Nuova Linea Cinemato grafica, 1972, unreleased), 222
Compton, Fay, 112
Congreve, William, 30, 89
Connelly, Marc, 129
Connery, Sean, 205
*Constanza* (Benavente) (CFT, 18.10.30), 53
Conway, Harold, 86, *182*
Cooke, Alistair, 44, 59
Cooper, Gary, 145, 146, 149, 230
Cooper, Dame Gladys, 76, 114–15
Copeland, Elizabeth, *133*

*Corn is Green, The* (Williams) (TV, BBC, 22.1.56), 183–4, *232*; (Connaught, Worthing 27.11.61; Tour South Africa from 8.2.62), 201; (FRP 25.9.62), 203
Cotsworth, Staats, 141
Coulouris, George, xi, 52, *62*, 148
Council for the Encouragement of Music and the Arts (C.E.M.A.) (see Arts Council)
Council for the Single Woman and Her Dependants, 220
Counsell, Elizabeth, xi, 221
Counsell, John, xi, *169*, *175*, *221*
Couper, Barbara, 161–162
Court, Hazel, 163
Coward, Sir Noël, 95
Cox, Frank, 210
Craig, Edith, 8, 64–5
Crawford, Anne, 152
Creswell, Peter, 26, 29, 31, 41, 42, 101, 102
Crichton, Mamie, *211*
Crisp, Donald, 131
Croft, Grace, 4–5, 6–7, 9
Cruickshank, Andrew, xi, 184, *185*, 188
Crutchley, Rosalie, 186
*Cry in the Wind, A* (film, Contemporary Greek 1968) 209–10
Cukor, George, 148
Cummings, Constance, 212
Curie, Eve, 150–1
Curtiz, Michael, 131–2
Czinner, Paul, 83, 84

D'Albie, Julian, 23
*Damask Cheek, The* (van Druten, Morris) (Playhouse, NY, 20.10.42), 141–5, 146
*Dance Pretty Lady* (film, British Instructional 1931), 60–1
*Dancing Girl, The* (Jones) (RADA), 12
Dane, Clemence, xii, 17, 18, 103, 105
*Dangerous Corner* (Priestley) (Lyric 17.5.32), 70–3; (RA, BBC, 1.6.68), 213
Daniell, Henry, 131–2
Darch, Frank, 22
Darlington, W.A., xii, *68*, *85*, *90–1*, *97*, *113*, *161–2*, *172*, *178*, *211*
Daubeny, Sir Peter, 184, 226
*David Copperfield* (Dickens) (RA, US, 24.11.50; TV, BBC, from 16.1.66), 208
Davis, Bette, 126, 127, 129, 130, 140, 141, 146, 225
Davis, Desmond, 225
Dawson, Helen, *214*
Dean, Basil, xiii, 17, 94–5, 112–15, 191, 193, 199
de Bear, Archie, *122–123*
de Casalis, Jeanne, 33
d'Egville, Louis, 11
de Havilland, Olivia, 131
de Jongh, Nicholas, 208–209
de Musset, Alfred, 29
Denham, Reginald, xi, xiii, 26, 29, 30, *31–2*, *33*, 57, 129, *134*, 135, 140, 146, 183
Denis, Frank, 22
*Desire under the Elms* (O'Neill) (Gate, 24.2.31 7 weeks), 57–9, 61, 62, 154, *192*
de Valois, Dame Ninette, 49, 60
Devonshire Park Theatre, Eastbourne, 180
Dickinson, Patric, 44, 189
Dietrich, Marlene, 108, 165
*Divertissements*, (RA, BBC 26.1.27), 40
Dixon, Leonard, xi, 198
Dobujinsky, Mstislav, 138
Dodson, Eric, 191
*Dominique*, (film, Sword & Sorcery, 1978), 223
Donat, Robert, x, xii, xiii, 43, 44–52, 57, 58, 59, 65, 74, 82, 95, 96–8, 100, 127, 188, 230
Donne, John, 226

# INDEX

Dors, Diana, xi, *164*
Douglas, Tom, 33
Douglass, Margaret, 142
Downs, B.W., 110
Drake, Sir Eric, xi, 60, 176
Draper, Peter, 189
*Drawback, The* (Baring) (RA, BBC, 26.1.27), 40
Dryden, John, 45, 92
Duchess Theatre, 162, 179, 182, 190
Duke of York's Theatre, 184
du Maurier, Dame Daphne, 157
du Maurier, Sir Gerald, 14, 37
Dunning, Ruth, xi, 161
Dunnock, Mildred, 206
Durgnat, Raymond, *210*
Durham University, 189, 232
Duse, Eleonora, 76, 114

Eddison, Robert, xi, 44, 52–3, 56, *68*, *78*, 213, *214*
Edinburgh Assembly Hall, 210
Edward VII, 105
Edward VIII, 15, 108
Eldridge, Florence, 168
Elizabeth I, 3, 17, 93, 101, 102–7, 108, 111, 125, 129–33, 141, 161, 213, 223, 225, 227, 230
Elizabeth II, 102, 177, 185, 196, 221
Queen Elizabeth, the Queen Mother, 64, 102, 170, 185
*Elizabeth the Queen* (Anderson) (McCarter Theatre, Princeton, NJ, USA 15.7.42; Bucks County Playhouse Philadelphia 24.8.52), 141
Ellis, Jane, 25–6, 30
Elsom, Isobel, 134–5
Embassy Theatre, 57, 76–7, 79–81, 99–100
*Epic that Never Was, The* (TV, BBC, 24.12.65), 108
Equity, American Actors', 139, 141
Equity, British Actors', 201
Ervine, St John, *2*, 75, *75–6*, *101*, 209
Esmond, Jill, 110
*Ethel Fry* (Hamilton) (Tour from 19.2.45), 156
Euripides, 11, 14, 15, 33–4, 40, 45, 47, 210–11
*Eustace and Hilda* (Hartley) (TV, BBC, 30.11.77), 224–5, 232
Evans, Dame Edith, 59, 138, 174, 186, 205, 213, 216, 217, 227
Evans, Hugh, 183
Evans, Maurice, 137–8, 168, 169, 197, *222*
Evelyn Norris Home, 220
*Evening Standard*, Award, 195, 232
Everest, Barbara, 138–9, 148, 177–8
*Eye of the Devil* (film, MGM, 1968), 207
*Eyes Down* (Robson), 213

Fagan, J. B. 25–31, 39, 42, 45
Fairbanks, Douglas, Jnr., xi, *63*, 83–4, 114
Farebrother, Violet, 153
*Farewell Again*, (film, Pendennis-London, 1937) (a.k.a. *Troopship*), 108–9, 116, 117, 232
Farnell, L. R., 26, 27
Farquharson, Robert, 86, 87
Farrar, David, 162
*Fata Morgana*, (Vajda) (Ambassadors, 15.9.24, 243 perfs.), 33
Ferber, Edna, 146
Fernald, John, xi, *180*, 184, 189, *190–1*, 198, 203
Ffrangcon-Davies, Gwen, 59, 90, 101, 110
Field, Betty, 206
*55 Days at Peking* (film, Allied Artists, 1963) 201–3
*Film Weekly* Award, 116, 232
Finnemore, R.J., *112*
*Fire over England* (film, Pendennis, 1937) 3, 102–7, 114, 115, 116, 125, 130, 133, 135, 163, 164, 182, 232
*First and the Last, The* (Galsworthy) 25
Fitzgerald, Geraldine, xi, *119–20*, 121

Flemyng, Robert, 65
Fletcher, G. B. A., 189
Fletcher, Helen, *157*
Flora Robson Festival, (RA, BBC 1967–8), 213
Flora Robson Playhouse, 201, *202–3*, 206, 208
*Flowers are Not for You to Pick, The* (Guthrie) (RA, BBC, 10&11.4.30., 18&19.12.30), 50, 152
Flynn, Errol, x, 130–2, *133*, 141, 230
Fontanne, Lynn, 141
Forbes-Robertson, Johnson, 41
Ford, John, 107, 205–7
Forrester, Cecil, 188
*For Services Rendered* (Maugham) (Globe 1.11.32 Six weeks) 73–6, 77, 94
Forsyth, James, xii, xiii, *34*
48th Street Theatre, NY, 174–5
*Fragment of Fear* (film, Columbia, 1970), 215
Fraser, John, 199
Freedley, George, *139*, 197, 200, 203, 210
French, Leslie, xi, 22, *23–4*
French, Vera, 22, 23
*Frieda* (film, Rank, 1947), 161, 162
*Frightened Bride, The* (See *Tall Headlines*)
Frith, J. Leslie, 43
Fry, Charles, 7
Fry, Christopher, 215

Gainsborough Films, 152, 153
Gale, Richard, 174
Galsworthy, John, 13, 25
Garbo, Greta, 86, 110, 116, 127, 144, 202
Gardiner, Lady (formerly Muriel Box) xi, 37, 60, 157, 226
Gardiner, Lord, 226
Gate Theatre, 57–61, 62
*Gauguin the Savage* (film, 1980), 222–3
Gay, Helen (Nelly), (née Robson) (sister), 5, 6, 8
GBS Theatre (RADA), 64
Genn, Leo, 110, 202
*Gentleman Dancing Master, The* (Wycherley) (CFT 17.5.30), 50
George V, 102
George VI, 64, 102, 177, 185
Geyl, Professor, 49
*Ghosts* (Ibsen) (OVC 12.11.58; Duchess 6.4.59) 111, 190–1, 211
Gielgud, Sir John, xi, xiii, *30*, 34, 75, 175, *214*, 226
Gilliatt, Sidney, 152
Gilpin, John, xi, *157*
Ginsbury, Norman, 138–9, 190
Gish, Lillian, 110, 148
Glaspell, Susan, 45
Globe Theatre, 73
Duke of Gloucester, 177
Gobineau, Joseph-Arthur, comte de, 101
Godden, Rumer, 159, 187
Godfrey, Peter, 57–8, 60
Golden, Michael, 153
*Golden Hind, The* (Bryant/Creswell) (RA, BBC, 10.6.35), 101
Goldie, Grace Wyndham, xii, *101*,
Goldie, Wyndham, 112–15, 158, 172, 174, 175
Goldwyn, Samuel, 117, 118, 121, 122, 123
*Good Time Girl* (film, Rank, 1947), 163–4, 170
Goolden, Richard, xi, 26, 27, 29, 101, 226
Gordon, Dorothy, 172
Goring, Marius, xi, 44, 85, *88*, *89*, 102, 111, 226, 227
Goulding, Edmund, 126, 127
Princess Grace of Monaco, 225
Graham, Morland, 49, 85
Grainger, Percy, 132
*Grande Scrofa Nera, La* (See *Comedy and Tragedy and All That*)
Granger, Stewart, 115, 165, 167
Grantham, Wilfred, 102

236

# INDEX

Graves, Robert, 107
Gray, David, xi, *219–20*
Gray, Terence, 45, *52*
*Great Day* (film, RKO 1944) 153–4
Green, Dorothy, 26
Greene, Graham, 107
Greenwood, Joan, 165
Greenwood, Ormerod, 65
Greet, Sir Ben, x, 18–24, 26, 69, 86
Grey, Anne, *72*
Grey, Earle, 26, *27*, 29
Grey, Mary, *29*, 30
Guillermin, John, 205
*Guilty* (Zola, ad. Boutall) (Lyric, Hammersmith, 18.4.44), 152–3, 187
Guinness, Sir Alec, xi, *62*, *86*
*Guns at Batasi* (film, TCF 1964), 205, *232*
Gurney, Claud, 93–4
Gurney, Rachel, xi, *172*
Guthrie, Lady (*née* Bretherton) 47, 54, 61–2, 66, *227*
Guthrie, Sir Tyrone, x, xii, xiii, 1–*2*, 26, *27*, 29, 31, 32–4, 40–1, 43–4, *44*–55, 58, 61–2, 65–6, 67, 68, 69, 70, 71, *72*, 74, 81–*2*, 84–7, *87*, 88–9*3*, 94, 95, 110, 137, 138, 140, 149, 15*2*, 153, 167, 184, 196, 199, *227*–8, 230
Gwillim, Jack, 181
*Gypsy and the Gentleman, The* (film, Rank 1958), 187–8

Haas, Dolly, 125, *126*
Hale, Alan, 131
Hall, Anmer (A. B. Horne), 41, 42, 43–61, 65, 66, 67, 68, 69–70, 110–11
Hall, Ella (formerly Ella Voysey, Ella Donat), xi, xii, 43, *44*, 47, *48*, 49, *52*, 57, 65
Hall, Richard, 44
Hamilton Lodge School for the Deaf, 220
Hamilton, Patrick, 156
*Hamlet* (Shakespeare) (RADA), 13
Hamlett, Dilys, xi, *178*
Hankin, St John, 28
Hanley, Jenny, 163
Hanley, Jeremy, 163
Hanley, Jimmy, 163
Hannen, Nicholas, 110
Hardwicke, Sir Cedric, 74, 76–7, 78, 133
Hardy, Betty, xi, *65*, *91*, *92*, 95, *96*–8, 100, 10*2*, 179
Harris, Julie, 166
Harrison, Kathleen, 16*2*
Hartley, L. P., 224
Harvey, Laurence, 179
Hastings, Charlotte, 213, 224
Havoc, June, 148
Haw-Haw, Lord (William Joyce), 144
Hawkins, Jack, 34, 110, 115, 167, *222*
Haye, Helen, 13, 14, 17, 70, 186, 187–8
Hayes, Helen, xi, *86*, 188, *219*, 227
Hayes, Patricia, 110
*Head-On Crash* (Miller) (Queen's 1.2.33, 3 weeks) 76–8
Healy, Patricia, 200
*Heartbreak House* (Shaw) (OXP 22.10.23), 25–7, 154
Hecht, Ben, 119
*Heidi* (Spyri) (TV, BBC, from 20.10.74), *223*
Heifetz, Jascha, 11*2*
Heller, Anthony, *209*–10
Helpmann, Sir Robert, *202*
Hemmings, David, *215*
*Henry VIII* (Shakespeare) (OVC, 7.11.33), 86–7, 88, 111
Henry Miller Theatre, NY, 129, 134–5
Henson, Leslie, 161

Hepburn, Katharine, 107
Her Majesty's Theatre (formerly His Majesty's), 6, 8, 97–8
Her Majesty's Theatre, Aberdeen, 200
Herington, Julian, xi, *201*, *208*
Heston, Charlton, *202*
Hibbin, Nina, *207*, *210*
Hicks, Patricia, 174
*High Tide at Noon* (film, Rank 1957) 186
Hill, Kathleen, 38, 39, 41, *226*
Hill, Sinclair, 59–60
Hiller, Dame Wendy xi, *189*, 197
Hinxman, Margaret, *202*
Hilton, James, 125
His Majesty's Theatre (see Her Majesty's Theatre)
Hitchcock, Sir Alfred, 124, 125
Hobbs, Carleton, 66, 101
Hobson, Sir Harold, *90*, *195*, *200*, *216*
Hobson, Valerie, 157, 170
Holden, William, 128
Holder, Owen, xi, *172*, *181*, *182*
*Holiday Camp* (film, Gainsborough 1947) 161, 162–3
Holm, Celeste, xi, *142*, 143, 144, 149
Homolka, Oscar, 99–101, 191, *203*, 230
Hood, Noel, 180
Hope-Wallace, Philip, *178*, *179*, *184*, *190*, *214*
Hopkins, Anthony (actor), 183
Hopper, Victoria, 114
Hordern, Michael, 190
Horne, A. B. (see Anmer Hall)
Horne, David, 53, 55–6, 18*2*
*Horror Tonight* (see *The Thirsty Death*)
*House by the Lake, The* (Mills) (Duke of Yorks, 9.5.56 736 perfs) 184–5, 188
Houston, Penelope, *215*
Houston, Renee, 15*2*
Howard, Leslie, 133, 156
Howard, Trevor, 170
Howard, William K, 103–7
Howe, George, 110
Hugo, Victor, *222*
Hull, Henry, 148
Hunter, Ian, 94
Huntley, Raymond, 174
Huston, John, 121, 12*2*
Hutchinson, R. C. 115
Hyde-White, Wilfrid, 181
Hyson, Dorothy, 94

Ibsen, Henrik, 29, 45, 51, 110, 190, 211
*I Claudius* (film, London Films, unreleased, made 1937), 107–8
*Importance of Being Earnest, The* (Wilde) (OXP 29.10.23), 25, 28; (OVC 5.2.34), 88–9; (FRP 3.11.64), 206; (TRH 8.2.68), 213–14; (TRW 15.4.75), *221*; and *226*, 227
*Innocents, The* (Archibald) (Her Majesty's July 1952), ix, 177–8, 195
*Innocent Sinners* (film, Rank 1958), 187
*Invisible Stripes* (film, WB 1939), 128, 136
*Iphigenia in Tauris* (Euripides) (RA, BBC 14.5.25) 33–4, (CFT 19.11.29), 45–7
Ireland, Anthony, *172*, 174
Irving, Sir Henry, 69, 105
Irwin, Margaret, *228*

Jackson, Barry, 73, 76, 77, 78
Jackson, Glenda, 164
James, Henry, 163, 177, *178*, 193–5
Jeans, Ursula, 85, 93
John, Evan, 45, 48, 49, 50, 51, 5*2*
*John Gabriel Borkmann* (Ibsen) (Duchess, 4.12.63) 204–5
Johnson, Amy, 107
Johnson, Moffatt (Johnnie), 12–15, 65, 83, 184

# INDEX

Jones, Barry, 95
Jones, Gemma, 228
Jones, Griffith, xi, 203, *204*
Jones, Henry Arthur, 12
Johnson, Ben, 50
*Journey to Earth* (Boland) (See *The Return*)
Judson, Stanley, 49
Junge, Alfred, 160
*Justice is a Woman* (Roffey, Kinnoch), 211

Karlin, Miriam, 180
Karsavina, Tamara, 66
Kauffer, McKnight, 69
Keen, Malcolm, 33
Kelly, Captain, 34, 35, 36, 96
Kelly, Dorothy, 212
Kelsall, Moultrie, 50
Kennedy, Margaret, 112
Kent, Jean, xi, 152, *164*, 181, *182*,
Kerr, Deborah, xi, 159, *160*, 207
Kerridge, Mary, 221
Kettlewell, Ruth, xi, *173*,
Kidd, David, xi, 129, *167*, 174–5, 230
*Kind of Folly, A* (Holder) (Duchess 15.2.55), 181–2, 186
*Kingdom of God, The* (Martinez-Sierra) (CFT 24.5.80), 51, 69
King George's Pension Fund, 220
Knight, Esmond, xi, 60, 163, 210
Korda, Sir Alexander, 83, 84, 93, 94, 95, 98, 99, 101, 102, 103–9, 116, 117, 132–3, 163

Lacey, Catherine, 55, 123
*Ladies in Retirement* (Denham/Percy) Henry Miller Theatre, NY, 26.3.40 5 months), 129, 140; (and RA, BBC 0.0.6.45)
*Lady Audley's Secret* (Braddon ad. Hazelwood) (CFT 1.2.30), 48–49, 52, 54; (Arts January 1933), 77, 78; (Brighton Theatre Group) 220, 225
*Lady from the Sea* (Ibsen) (Playhouse 24.2.36 1 perf), 110, 137
*Lady Vanishes, The* (RA, US.), 132
Laine, Cleo, xi, 210, *211*
Lambert, J. W., *190*
*Lancelot of Denmark* (Geyl) (CFT 15.2.30), 49
Lanchester, Elsa, 82, 85, *92*, 93, 129
Landi, Elissa, 31
*Land of Heart's Desire, The* (Yeats) (OXP 3.3.24), 25, 31
Lang, Fritz, 123
Lang, Margaret, 204
Langton, David, 180
Lansbury, Angela, xi, 146, *147–8*, *149*, 230
*Last Train South* (Hutchinson) (St Martin's 11.8.38), 115–16, 117, 130
Laughton, Charles, 82, 84, 85–8, 90–3, 103, 105, 107–8, 129, 133, 191, *197*, 199
Launder, Frank, 152
Lawrence, David, xi, *160*
Lawson, Wilfred, 133
Leacock, Philip, 187
Lee, Anna, 206
Lee, Auriol, 142
Leech, Richard, 170
Lehmann, Beatrix, 193, 195
Leigh, Vivien, 103, 104, 106, 155
Leighton, Margaret, 206
Le Jeune, Caroline, *84*, *162*, *187*
Lennox, Gilbert, 99
Leontovitch, Eugenie, 112
Leslie, Paul, 111
Levin, Bernard, *183*, *184*, *195*
Lewis, Peter, *213*
Lewis, Ronald, 190
*Life in the Theatre, A* (Guthrie), xii, xiii, *43–4*

*Lion has Wings, The* (film, London Films 1939), 133
Little Theatre, 55–7
Liverpool Repertory Theatre, 16
Liverpool Royal Court Theatre, 212
Livesey, Roger, 33, 85
Llewellyn, Richard, 123
Lockwood, Margaret, 211
Loder, Sir Giles, 160
Loder, John, 129
London Films, xiii, 83, 93, 98, 99
London Palladium, 199
Lord, Pauline, 110–11
Losey, Joseph, xi, *187*
*Love for Love* (Congreve) (OXP 28.1.24), 30; (OVC 6.3.34), 89
Lynley, Carol, 207
Lyon, Sue, 206
Lyric Theatre, 70–1, 73
Lyric Theatre, Hammersmith, 153, 170
Lunt, Alfred, 141
Lupino, Ida, 136

MacArthur, Charles, 119, 219
MacArthur, James, 219
MacArthur, Molly, 30
*Macbeth* (Shakespeare) (BG 1922), 19, 22; (OVC 2.4.34) 90–3, 97; (RA, BBC 13.10.35), 101; (National Theatre, NY, 31.3.48), 166–8; and 101–2, 111, 137–8, 161, 171, 187, 198, 212; (and RA, BBC 6.3.49)
McCormick, Myron, 142
MacDaniel, Hattie, 146
MacDonald, Flora, 178
MacGill, Moyna, 17, 146, 148, 149
MacGregor, Hector, 166, 169, 170, 175, 221
MacGregor, Peggy, 221
McKee, Douglas, 144
McKenna, Virginia, xi, 175, *176*, *183*
Mackenzie, Sir Compton, 60
MacKenzie, Alec, 38
MacKenzie, Captain John (Flora's grandfather), 5, 96
MacKenzie, Grandmother, 38, 96
MacKenzie, Revd John (Uncle John), 38–9, 41, 42, 64, 114, 158, 171, 173, 177, 183–4, 231
McKern, Mrs, 11
McLaglen, Victor, 38
Macmillan, Harold, 226–7
McPherson, Colvin, *133*
MacPherson, Margaret (Aunt Margaret), 5, *173*
Maeterlinck, Maurice, 14, 31
*Malade Imaginaire, Le*, (Molière) (CFT 8.3.30), 50, 52
Malet Street Theatre (rebuilt as Vanbrugh Theatre), 12, 14–15, 170
Malleson, Miles, 13, 16, 72
*Malta Story, The* (film, British Film Makers 1953), 178
*Man About the House, A* (Young, ad. Perry) (Piccadilly, 27.2.46), 157–9
*Man Called Intrepid, A* (film, Lorimar 1979), 222
Mander, Raymond, xi, 106
March, Elspeth, xi, 114, *199*
March, Fredric, 168
Marmont, Patricia, 174
Marsden, Betty, 114
Marshall, Arthur, xi, 44, *49*
Marshall, Brenda, 131
Marshall, Herbert, 95, 133
Martinez-Sierra, Gregorio, 51
Queen Mary, 105, 114
*Mary Read*, (Bridie/Gurney) (His Majesty's 21.11.34; Phoenix 28.1.35, total 108 perfs), 95–8; and 72, 93–4, 107; (and RA, BBC, 22.4.50)

238

# INDEX

Mary Tudor (Grantham) (Playhouse, 12.12.35 142 perfs), 102; (RA, BBC, 15.12.51) (RA, BBC, 13.1.68), 213
Mason, A. E. W., 103
Mason, Brewster, 175
Mason, Elliot, 50, 94
Mason, Haddon, 163
Mason, James, 44, 85, 101, 105, 199
Massey, Raymond, 29, 59, 104, 107, 108
Master Builder, The (Ibsen) (OXP 19.11.23), 25, 29
Matthews, A. E., 111
Matthews, Francis, 180
Matthews, Lester, 148
Mattingley, Garrett, 168
Matrimonial News (Guthrie) (RA, BBC, 21.1.44), 152
Maugham, W. Somerset, 73, 75, 77
Measure for Measure (Shakespeare) (CFT 25.1.30), 48; (OVC 4.12.33), 87–8
Medium, The (Mille/deVylar/Levy) (CFT 1.3.30), 49
Merchant of Venice, The (Shakespeare) (BG 1922), 22
Mercouri, Melina, 187
Merivale, Philip, 17, 18, 114
Merry Wives of Windsor, The (Shakespeare) (CFT 29.11.30), 54, 85
Message for Margaret (Parish) (WMT, 28.8.46; Duchess 21.10.46), 161–2; (TV, 5.5.56), 186, 232
Metro-Goldwyn-Mayer (MGM), xii, xiii, 107, 125, 144, 147–8, 149, 204, 206, 207, 223
Meyer, Rudolph, 59
Michell, Keith, 187–8
Midsummer Night's Dream, A (Shakespeare), 8, 51; (BG 1922), 22
Miller, Gilbert, 129, 133–4, 138–9, 174
Miller, Lawrence, 76–8
Millington, Rodney, xi, 60, 80
Mills, Hugh, 184
Milne, A. A., 30
Milton, Ernest, 69, 110
Miserables, Les, (film, Norman Rosemont 1978), 222
Miss Elizabeth's Prisoner (RADA), 11
Mr Pim Passes By (Milne) (OXP 4.2.24), 30
Mitchell, Yvonne, 182
Moeller, Philip, 33
Molière, (Jean Baptiste Poquelin), 50, 52
Monte Carlo Television Festival, 225, 232
'Morecambe and Wise Show' (TV, BBC, 26.8.70), 223
Morecambe, Eric, 223
Morley, Robert, 161
Morley, Sheridan, 215
Morris, Lloyd, 141–2
Moscow Arts Theatre, 112, 188
Mother Courage and her Children (Brecht) (TV, BBC 30.6.59), 191
Murray, Gilbert, 12, 31, 46
Muni, Bella, 126–8
Muni, Paul, 107, 125–8, 147, 230
Murder at the Gallop (film, MGM, 1963), 204

Naked (Pirandello) (CFT 3.5.30), 50
Nares, Owen, 64, 72
National Board of Review (US), 127, 232
National Film Archive, xii, 108
National Theatre of Great Britain, 101–2, 209
Neagle, Dame Anna, 116, 189
Neal, Patricia, 206
Neale, J. E., 101
Neilson-Terry, Phyllis, 58
Neville, John, 199
Newcombe, Jessamine, 134
News Chronicle Award, 186, 232

Newton, Robert, 123
New York Film Critics' Award, 122
Ney, Marie, xi, 57, 71, 94, 110
Night of a Hundred Stars, 199
Niven, David, xi, 120, 202, 203, 207, 222
No Escape (Davies) (Tour from 5.7.54), 180–1, 183, 223
Norfolk, Edgar, 161
No Time for Tears (film, Associated British-Pathé, 1957), 186–7
No Trifling with Love (de Musset) (OXP 26.11.23), 29
Nugent, Frank S, 127

Oberon, Merle, 107, 108, 119–21, 123, 133
O'Brien, Maureen, xi, 215, 223, 224
O'Casey, Sean, 205
Old Ladies, The (Walpole, ad. Ackland), x; (TV, BBC 9.6.68), 215–16; (WMT 4.11.69, Duchess), 216, 221, 222
Old Vic, 16, 18, 26, 57, 65, 82, 84–93, 108, 137, 144, 153, 167, 178, 211, 212
Olivier, Lord (Laurence), xi, 95, 103–7, 119, 121, 123, 217, 223
O'Neill, Eugene, 57–8, 76, 78–9, 110–11, 192
One Precious Year (film, Paramount 1932), 72
One Way of Living (Bridie), xiii, 2, 54
Oresteia (Aeschylus) (See The Serpent Son)
Osborne, Canon, 38–9
Osborne, John, 183
Oscar, Henry, 67, 69, 104, 164, 199
Othello (Shakespeare) (BG 1922), 21, 23–4; (St James 4.4.32) 69; and 78, 80–1
Oxford, Lady (Margot Asquith) 60
Oxford Playhouse, xii, 25–32, 39, 41, 42, 46, 89, 104, 221, 226
Oxford University, 9, 26, 28, 29, 161, 226–7, 231, 232
Oxford University Dramatic Society (O.U.D.S.), 26, 29, 45

Page, Campbell, 203
Palace Theatre, 160–1
Paramount Pictures, 72, 136–7
Parish, James, 161
Parker, Jack, 61
Parker, Ralph, 52
Pascal, Gabriel, 154–6
Paull, Helen, (née Gay) (Flora's niece), 117–19
Paxinou, Katina, 45, 209, 216
Pearce, Guy, 103
Peck, Gregory, 140
Pembroke College, (Cambridge) Rowing Club, 48, 49, 50, 60, 176
Percy, Edward, 129, 141, 183
Perry, John, 157
Peter and the Wolf (Prokofiev), 219, 220
Pettingell, Frank, 94
Prince Philip, Duke of Edinburgh, 185, 196
Philip Morris Playhouse, 132
Phillips, Philip, 189
Phipps-Walker, Margery, 45, 50, 51, 52, 68, 98–9
Piccadilly Theatre, 80, 158, 200
Piccoli, Raffaelo, 44
Pihodna, Joe, 162
Pilgrim Trust, 84, 92
Pinero, Sir Arthur, 14
Pirandello, Luigi, 41, 43–4, 50, 51, 67–8, 192
Pittsburgh Playhouse, 141
Playfair, Nigel, 76
Playhouse, The, 102
Playhouse, The (NY), 142
Pleasance, Donald, 207
Plowden, Alison, 213
Poe, Edgar Allan, 40

# INDEX

*Poison Pen* (film, Associated British, 1939) 123–4
Pommer, Erich, 105, 106
Portman, Eric, 58, 154
Power, Tyrone, 47
Price, Dennis, 162, 164, 226
Priestley, J. B., xi, xii, 69, 70, *71*, *72*, *74*, *75*
Prudential Assurance Company, 41, 66
Pryce, Hugh, 170
Purcell Room, 213
Purdom, C. B., *25*, 88
Purdom, Edmund, 25

Quartermaine, Leon, 85

Rachel (Elisa Felix), 76, 111
Raft, George, 128
Rainer, Luise, 116
Prince Rainier, 225
Rains, Claude, 13, 17, 18, 131, 155
Rambert, Dame Marie, 61
Rank, Lord, 164
Rank Organisation, xiii, 156–7, 163–4, 186
Ratcliffe, Michael, *225*
Rathbone, Basil, *72*, 133
Ratoff, Gregory, 112
Rawlings, Margaret, xi, 55, 57, 60–1, 110, 204, *205*
Rawlings, Marjorie Kinnan, 139
Ray, Nicholas, 201–2
*Rebecca* (film, Selznick 1940), 124–5, 138; (RA, BBC 25.12.76), 224
Redgrave, Sir Michael, xi, 44, *48*, *49*, 157, 161, 167–8, 193–5, 197, 205
Redmond, Moira, xi, *210*
Reed, Oliver, 207
Réjane, Gabrielle-Charlotte, 76
Reid, Beryl, 222
Reinhardt, Max, 99
Rennie, Hugh, 73, 194
*Restless* (see *The Beloved*)
*Return, The* (Boland) (formerly *Journey to Earth*) (RA, BBC 14.1.53), 179; (Duchess 9.11.53 10 weeks), 179; (TV, BBC 25.3.56), 186; (RA, BBC 4.11.67), 213
*Return of the Prodigal* (Hankin) (OXP 12.11.23), 28–9
Revere, Anne, 140
Richardson, Maurice, *191*
Richardson, Pauline, 220
Richardson, Sir Ralph, xi, 73–4, *75*, 76, 77, 78, 133
Rigg, Diana, xi, 223–4
Riley, Joan, 221
*Ring Round the Moon* (Anouilh ad. Fry) (TRH 30.10.68), 215, 224
Ritter, Eric (Flora's brother-in-law), 71, 228
Ritter, Shela (*née* Robson) (sister), x, 6, 71, 228, 230
*Rivals, The* (Sheridan) (OXP 3.12.23), 29; (RA, BBC 15.4.68), 213; and 47, 89
R.K.O. Radio Films, 153–4
Roberts, Bechhofer, 188
Robertson, Cliff, 223
Robeson, Essie, 76, 80
Robeson, Paul, xii, xiii, 76, 78–81, 199, 230
Robinson, Robert, *207*
Robson, David (Flora's father), 5–10, 17, 24, 33, 44–5, 47, 64, 102, 109, 114, 139, 151, 158, 173, 174, 179, 184, 196, 230
Robson, David (brother), 5, 6, 15–16
Robson, Eliza (*née* MacKenzie) (mother), 5, 8, 9, 109, 139, 151, 158, 179, 196
Robson, Dame Flora
  Direct quotes: 5, 6, 12, 14, 15, 18, 19–20, 23, 29, 32, 37, 38, 38–9, 40, 41–2, 42, 43, 46, 47, 48, 51–2, 56, 58, 59, 60, 62–3, 63, 64, 66, 71, 79, 90, 94–5, 103, 106, 106–7, 108, 113, 115, 120, 121, 125, 127, 128, 129, 130–1, 147, 150, 154, 155–6, 158, 164, 166, 167, 173, 174, 175–6, 176–7, 177, 178, 179, 184–5, 186, 187, 201, 204, 207, 210, 211–12, 212–13, 213–14, 216, 217, 219, 226, 227, 228, 229
  *Quotes from letters*: 42, 100, 102, 143–4, 145, 152, 190, 197, 200, 203, 210, 226–7
  *as Adviser*: ix–x, 120–1, 131,
  *her Ambition*: 6, 7, 9, 110, 133, 227
  *her Awards*: 7, 14, 116, 127, 148, 165, 176, 189, 195–6, 200–1, 205, 221, 225, 226–7, 231, 232
  *on Broadway*: 133–5, 137–9, 141–5, 166–8, 174–5
  *with Children*: 95, 109, 163, 177–8, 212, 219, 220, 223, 224, 230
  *and Colour Prejudice*: 144, 146, 198, 201
  *and Comedy*: 28, 30, 48–9, 78, 88–9, 141–5, 169–171, 175, 181–2, 191, 213–15, 221, 222, 223, 225
  *her Difficulties with fellow actors*: 20–1, 74, 78, 100, 137, 190–1, 204–5, 216
  *her Dramatic Technique*: 13, 14, 43, 46, 58, 70, 80, 100, 102, 119, 122, 126, 141, 161, 167, 173–4, 176, 182, 185, 212, 214, 224
  *her Faith*: 113, 179, 185, 219, 229
  *her Family Ties*: 6, 71, 95–6, 109, 124, 138–9, 156, 173, 179, 196, 228, 229, 230
  *in Hollywood*: 117–23, 125–33, 136–7, 146–9, 206–7
  *her Humanity*: 139, 144, 198, 226, 229
  *Illnesses*: 8, 14, 27, 38, 65, 101, 104, 114, 151, 174–5, 203, 204, 211–12, 220, 229
  *Inspiration*: 5, 43, 50, 62–3, 79, 90, 96, 102, 158, 172, 194–5
  *Knitting*: 140, 147, 200, 230
  *her Longing for Children of her own*: 54, 102, 109, 228
  *her Looks*: 2, 9, 10, 15–16, 31, 33, 44, 55, 56, 59, 63, 76, 109, 113, 116, 134, 142, 143, 165–6, 167, 189, 218
  *her Naïveté*: 12, 17, 20, 82–3, 94, 118, 181
  *Negativism*: 10, 17–18, 19, 26, 34–5, 48, 55, 56, 66, 101, 104, 116
  *Nerves*: 8, 10, 16, 17, 205, 221
  *Optimism*: 40–2, 66, 67, 134
  *Personal Philosophy*: 15, 83, 113, 114,
  *her Pets*: 158, 219, 230
  *her Power to move an audience*: 7, 63, 87, 113, 114, 115, 134, 174, 224
  *Professional aid to other actors*: 52–3, 65, 80–1, 119–20, 132, 145, 146, 147–8, 172, 178, 186, 198, 200, 201
  *Professionalism*: 22–3, 126, 179–80, 184, 197, 210, 218–19
  *her Public Image*: 115, 135, 165, 215, 219, 220
  *her Pursuit of Excellence*: 6, 8, 9, 24, 28, 33, 42, 64, 196
  *on Radio*: 50, 101, 132, 152, 163, 220, 224
  *her Relationship with her father*: 5, 9–10, 15, 42, 44–5, 173, 178, 184, 196
  *and Retirement*: 208, 217, 218–31
  *her Sense of Adventure*: 98–9, 171, 199, 201
  *her Shyness*: 79, 83–4
  *Singing*: 6, 25, 52, 54, 62–3, 88, 89, 142, 222
  *her Single-Mindedness*: 9, 24, 39, 124–5, 208
  *her Skills (Fencing, Falls, Riding etc)*: 11, 34, 36, 53, 96, 161, 166, 182, 187
  *in South Africa*: 198–9, 201
  *on Television*: 124, 140, 175, 182–3, 183–4, 185–6, 188–9, 191, 199, 215–16, 222–3
  *her Thrift*: 6, 22, 83, 118, 208
  *and Type-casting*: 29, 72, 73, 75–6, 95, 109, 124, 136–7, 182, 188, 189
  *her Unconventional Behaviour*: 51–2, 80, 128, 132, 136, 142, 199, 203, 218, 219, 228
  *her Voice*: 7, 8, 10, 11, 14, 24, 27, 31, 63, 86, 87, 97, 123, 167, 168, 177, 185, 189, 206, 211, 217, 218, 222

# INDEX

*her Work for Charity*: 164–5, 218, 220, 229
*her work with Amateur Actors*: 25, 37, 141, 220
*as a Writer*: xiii, 122, 213
Robson, Hilda (*née* Sedgeman) (sister-in-law), 95, 156, 163
Robson, Hugh (nephew), xi, *95*, *109*, 156, 163
Robson, John (brother), 5, 47, 95, 156, 158, 163
Robson, Lila (sister), 5, 6, 8–9, 25, 73, 151, 179, 194, 228
Robson, Margaret (sister), xi, 5, 6, 8, 228, 230
Roc, Patricia, 152
Rolfe, Alan, xi, *65*, *68*
*Romeo and Juliet* (Shakespeare) (RADA), 12; (BG 1922), 21, 22–3; (film Rank 1954), 179; (TV, BBC 22.5.55), 182–3
Room, Rita, xi, 100, 102, 190
Roosevelt, Eleanor, 154
Rosay, Françoise, 165, 187, 197
Rose, George, 175
Rosenbloom, 'Slapsie' Maxie, 129
*Rosmersholm* (Ibsen) (CFT 31.5.30) 51–2, 225
Ross, David, 205
Ross, Oriel, xi, 94
Rosson, Hal, 101
Rovina, Hanna, 230
Royal Academy of Dramatic Art (RADA) (formerly Academy of Dramatic Art), x, 6, 7, 9–15, 16, 25, 59, 64, 96, 110, 170, 187, 189, 198, 210, 217, 232,
Royal Academy of Music, 7, 232
Royal Court Theatre, 26, 27, 183
Rutherford, Dame Margaret, 204
Rylands, George, xi, *45*, *213*

Sabatini, Rafael, 125
Sadler's Wells Theatre, 92, 230
Sadoff, Fred, 193
St James Theatre, NY 138–9
St Martin's Theatre, 72
*Salomé* (Wilde) (Gate, 27.5.31), 60–1
Saltmarshe, Christopher, 50
Sanders, George, 101
*Saraband for Dead Lovers* (film, Ealing 1948), 165–6
*Saratoga Trunk* (film, WB 1945), 145–8, 149, 232
Sargeant, Frank, 22
Sartre, Jean-Paul, 210
*Satyr* (Leslie) (Shaftesbury 16.6.37 4 weeks), 111
Saunders, Peter, 211–12
Savoy Theatre, 100
Scaife, Christopher, 29, 32–3
Scaife, Gillian, 32, 41, 52, 53, 54, 69
Scala Theatre, 41
Schach, Leonard, xi, *197–8*, *198*, 198–9, 201, *209*, *210*, 229–30
Scott, Bertie, 86, 97
Scott, Harold, 50
Scott, Margaretta, 110
Scott, Sir Walter, 201
Scott, Zachary, 142, 144
Scottish National Players, 40, 49–50, 53
*Sea Hawk, The* (film, WB 1940), 125, 128, 129–33, 154
Selten, Morton, 105
Selznick, David O, 124
*Serpent Son, The* (*Oresteia* of Aeschylus, ad. Raphael) (TV, BBC, 14.3.79), 223
Seton, Marie, xii, xiii, 80
*Seven Women* (film MGM 1966), 206–7
Severn, Raymond, 126
Seyler, Athene, xi, 16, 69, 85, *89*, 93, 211, 216
Shaftesbury Theatre, 17, 111
Shakespeare, William, x, 7, 12, 13, 17, 18, 19, 24, 48, 54, 69, 84, 85, 86–8, 89–93, 101–2, 128, 142, 166–8, 175–7, 179, 182–3, 201, 217, 223

*Shall We Join the Ladies?* (Barrie) (Brighton Hippodrome 7.3.37 1 perf), 110
Shaw, George Bernard, xii, 25–8, 30, 34, 64, 122, 133, 154–6, 158, *169*, *170*, *171*
Shelley, Norman, 60–1
Shentall, Susan, 179
Sherek, Henry, 161, 171, 173, 181
Sheridan, Dinah, xi, *163*,
Sheridan, R.B., 29, 47, 89
Sherwood, Lydia, 69
*See Stoops to Conquer* (Goldsmith) (OXP 18.2.24), 31
Shorter, Eric, *213*
*Shrimp and the Anemone, The* (See *Eustace and Hilda*)
*Shuttered Room, The* (film, WB 1967), 207
Siddons, Sarah, 90
Sills, Milton, 125
Sim, Alistair, 55, 62
Simmons, Jean, 160, 223
Simpson, Vera, 37
*Sin* (see *The Beloved*)
*Sister Beatrice* (Maeterlinck) (RADA), 14
*Six Characters in Search of an Author* (Pirandello) (CFT 10.10.29), 41, 42–3, 45, 46, 53; (WMT 18.2.32 2 weeks) 67–8; and 192
*Skin Game, The* (Galsworthy) (RADA), 13
Smith, Dodie (C. L. Anthony), 94, *214*
Smith, Maggie, 205
Smith, Reginald, 26
Smith, Stevie, 164
Society of West End Managers, 225
Solodovnikov, Alexander, 188
Somin, W. O., 99
Sondergaard, Gale, 148
Speaight, Robert, 32, 60–1
Spenser, Jeremy, 177
Spyri, Johanna, 223
Stanislavsky, Konstantin, 122, 188, 230
*Stars in my Hair* (Denham), xiii, *31–2*, *33*
Stein, Paul, 123
Steinbeck, John, 129
Sterck, Sidney, *178*
Stewart, William, 7, 8
Stock, Nigel, 212
Storm, Lesley, 171–2, 199–200
*Storm Fighter, The* (de Bruyne/Hill) (St Martin's 12.6.32 3 Sunday perfs), 72
Strachey, Lytton, 101
Straight, Beatrice, xi, 166, *167*
Sullivan, Frances, 110
Sunday Players, 72
Surguchev, Ilya, 112
*Suspect* (Denham/Percy) (TV, NY 1942), 140; (Pittsburgh Playhouse 21.3.42; Cambridge, Mass, Summer Theatre 27.7.42), 140–1; (TRW 26.9.55; Royal Court 10.11.55), 183
Swansea, University College of, 200–1
*Sweet England's Pride* (Plowden) (RA, BBC 19.8.68), *213*
Swinley, Ion, 16, 33
Swinstead, Joan, xi, 14, *14–15*, 94
Sydney, Basil, 158
*Syler's Green* (Smith) (RA, BBC 5.8.47.), 164
Syms, Sylvia, xi, *182*, 186–7

*Tale of Two Cities, A* (film, Norman Rosemont 1980), 223
*Tall Headlines* (film, a.k.a. *The Frightened Bride*, Grand National 1952), 177
Tandy, Jessica, 78, 110, 138
Tannehill, Frances, xi, xii, 135–6, 138, 139
Tate, Reginald, 55
Tate, Sharon, 207
Taylor, Elizabeth, 200
Taylor, Rod, 205

# INDEX

Tearle, Godfrey, 101
*Tell-Tale Heart, The* (Poe) (RA, BBC 26.1.27), 40
*Tempest, The* (Shakespeare) (OVC 8.1.34), 88
*Temptation* (Townsend) (CFT 1.11.30), 54
Tennent, H. M., 170, 177, 189
Tenniel, Sir John, 222
*1066 and All That* (Arkell) (Palace 7.5.46), 161
Terry, Arthur, 50
Terry, Dame Ellen, 5, 8, 9, 10, 33, 42, 69, 76, 90, 105, 169, 196, 217, 228
Tetzel, Joan, 142
Thatcher, Torin, 110
Theatre Royal, Drury Lane, 92, 102, 170
Theatre Royal, Haymarket, 7, 94, 100, 213–15
*Thérèse Raquin* (Zola) (See *Guilty*)
*Thirsty Death, The* (Savior/Marchand) (Belasco, Los Angeles 28.6.43), 148–9
'This is Your Life' (TV, BBC 13.2.61), 199
Thorndike, Dame Sybil, 14, 16, 18, 34, 46, 49, *59*, 60, 70, 74, 152, 190, 196, 204, 210, 211, 216, 217, 227
Thornton, Michael, *206*
*Those Magnificent Men in Their Flying Machines* (film, TCF 1965), 208
*Thought, The* (See *Betrayal*)
*Thro' Train* (Guthrie) (RA, BBC 26.1.27), 40
*Time and Yellow Roses* (Storm) (St Martin's 11.5.61, 2 months) 199–200
*Tobias and the Angel* (Bridie) (CFT 15.11.30), 54, 67
Todd, Ann, 123
Toland, Gregg, 122
Tolstoy, Leo, 114
Toone, Geoffrey, xi, 44, *48–9*, *65*, 66, 123, 130, 166, *167*
*Touch Wood* (Smith) (TRH 16.5.34), 94–5, 169, 214
Townsend, W Thompson, 54
Tracy, Spencer, 140
Tree, Sir Herbert, 6, 7, 8, 18
Tree, Lady (Maud), 12, 64
Tree's Academy (see Royal Academy of Dramatic Art)
Trewin, J. C., xii, xiii, *214*, 235
*Triumph of Death, The* (Scaife) (Oxted 1924), 32, 41
*Trojan Women, The* (Euripides), 11, 14, 15; (ad. Sarte, Assembly Hall Edinburgh 22.8.64), 210–11
*Troopship* (see *Farewell Again*)
Tucker, Forrest, 129
*Turn of the Screw, The* (James) (RA, BBC 5.12.46), 163; (see also *The Innocents*), 177
Twentieth Century Fox, 112
*Two Gentlemen of Verona, The* (Shakespeare), 7
*2,000 Women* (film, Gainsborough 1944) 152, 153
Tynan, Kenneth, 209

*Undercurrents* (Barnes) (RADA 17.7.21), 16, 33, 72, 157
United Artists, xiii, 83, 117, 118
United Nations Organisation, 231
Urquhart, Molly, 62

Vajda, Ernest, 33
Vanbrugh, Dame Irene, 12, 16, 58, 89, 138, 228
Vanbrugh, Violet, 12, 58
Van Druten, John, 141–5, 148, 152
Van Gyseghem, André, 79, *80*
Van Valkenberg, Ellen, 56
*Varsity Coach, The* (Gray) (CFT 7.6.30), 52
*Vessels Departing* (Williams) (Embassy 3.7.33, 2 weeks), 80
*Viceroy Sarah* (See *Anne of England*)
*Volpone* (Jonson) (CFT 26.4.30), 50

Von Sternberg, Josef, 107–8
Voysey, Ella, (See Ella Hall)

Wade, Doreen (née Robson) (niece), xi, 173
Wales, University of, 200–1, 232
Wallis, Hal, 146
Wallis-Mills, Laura, 14
Walpole, Hugh, 215–16
Warner Brothers, 125–7, 128, 129–33, 136, 140, 144, 145, 146–8
Warner, Jack (actor), 162
Warner, Jack L. (Executive Producer Warner Bros), 127
*Warren Hastings* (Feuchtwanger) (CFT 10.10.30), 53
Watts Jnr, Richard, *134*
*We are Not Alone* (film, WB 1939), 125–7, 232
Webb, Gillian, 166
Webster, Margaret, 110, 137
Welch, Raquel, 222
Welwyn, Garden City, 24–5, 35–42, 61, 226
Welgar Shredded Wheat Company, 35–42, 61, 169, 199
Westbury, Marjorie, 213
Westminster Theatre, 1–2, 61–9, 110, 161, 216–17
Whale, James, 85
'What's my Line?' (TV, BBC, 29.12.57), 186
Whelan, Tim, 109
White, Joan, 64, 170
Whitehall Theatre, 138
Whitehead, John, 65, 224
Whitelaw, Billie, 183, 223
Whiteman, Madge, 20–1
Whiting, John, 205
Wilde, Oscar, 28, 60, 87, 88–9, 206, 213–14
Williams, Brook, 201
Williams, Emlyn, xi, *31*, *62*, 81, 107, 183, 201, 203
Williams, Peter, xi, 180, *183*
Williams, Stephen, *113*
*Will Shakespeare* (Dane) (Shaftesbury 17.11.21 62 perfs), x, 17–18, 62–4, 94, 131, 146
Wilson, A. E., *113*
Winchell, Walter, *134*, *139*
Windsor, Theatre Royal, 169–70, 175, 183, 221
Winwood, Estelle, 134
*Winter's Tale, The* (BG Theatre Royal, Bristol 27.3.22 1 perf. and in repertoire), 19–21; (Phoenix 27.6.51, 6 months), 175–7, 188
Wise, Ernie, xi, *223*
Wolfit, Sir Donald, 190–1, 204–5
Wolveridge, Carol, xi, 177–8
*Woman's Honour, A* (Glaspell) (CFT 19.10.29), 45
Wong Howe, James, 103, 109
Wood, Sam, 145–7
Worsley, T. C., *205*
Worthing, Connaught Theatre, 201
Wright, Haidee, 17, 34
*Wuthering Heights* (film, Goldwyn-UA 1939), ix, 117–23, 138, 202
Wycherley, William, 50
Wyler, William, 119–21
Wyman, Jane, 140
Wynyard, Diana, 112, 175, 176

*Years Between, The* (film, Rank 1946), 156–7, 166
Yeats, W. B., 25, 31, 205
*Young Cassidy* (film, MGM 1964), 205
Young, Francis Brett, 157–9
Young, Gig, 207
Yvonne Arnaud Theatre, Guildford, 216

Zetterling, Mai, 162
Zola, Emile, 152, 153